Maternal Perinatal Mental Health

Maternal Perinatal Mental Health

Editor

M. Carmen Míguez Varela

MDPI • Basel • Beijing • Wuhan • Barcelona • Belgrade • Manchester • Tokyo • Cluj • Tianjin

Editor
M. Carmen Míguez Varela
Department of Clinical
Psychology and Psychobiology
University of Santiago
de Compostela
Santiago de Compostela
Spain

Editorial Office
MDPI
St. Alban-Anlage 66
4052 Basel, Switzerland

This is a reprint of articles from the Special Issue published online in the open access journal *International Journal of Environmental Research and Public Health* (ISSN 1660-4601) (available at: www.mdpi.com/journal/ijerph/special_issues/perinatal_mental_health).

For citation purposes, cite each article independently as indicated on the article page online and as indicated below:

LastName, A.A.; LastName, B.B.; LastName, C.C. Article Title. *Journal Name* **Year**, *Volume Number*, Page Range.

ISBN 978-3-0365-2132-9 (Hbk)
ISBN 978-3-0365-2131-2 (PDF)

Contents

About the Editor

M. Carmen Míguez Varela

M. Carmen Míguez is a Doctor of Psychology with honors from the University of Santiago de Compostela (Spain). She is accredited as a European Specialist in Psychotherapy by the European Federation of Psychologists' Associations (EFPA). She is a professor of Clinical Psychology in the Department of Clinical Psychology and Psychobiology at the University of Santiago de Compostela in Spain. Her lines of research have focused on the study of addictive behaviors, mainly smoking, and mental health, as well as specifically in perinatal mental health. She has received various awards related to her research contributions.

Preface to "Maternal Perinatal Mental Health"

The present Special Issue focuses on women's mental health at two important points in their lives: pregnancy and postpartum periods. The aim of this Special Issue is to provide information that is useful and of interest to researchers and practitioners in mental health, maternal and child health, women's health, obstetrics/gynecology, and pediatrics. Fifteen articles are included in this Special Issue from different international research teams from seven countries (Spain, Mexico, China, Russia, Israel, Finland, and the United States), from both academia and the applied field. Many thanks to the 65 professionals who have participated in this book by providing high-quality contributions on various topics relating to perinatal mental health. Studies have been provided on prevalence, associated and/or risk factors, screening instruments, comorbidity, effects or consequences, and interventions. Their contributions show how much and how well work is being done in this growing field of perinatal mental health. My hope is that this Special Issue will encourage health care professionals to be more aware of the importance of this issue, to screen for prenatal and postpartum depression or anxiety, and to learn about mental health resources available in their communities.

M. Carmen Míguez Varela
Editor

International Journal of
Environmental Research and Public Health

MDPI

Article

Prevalence of Depression during Pregnancy in Spanish Women: Trajectory and Risk Factors in Each Trimester

M. Carmen Míguez * and M. Belén Vázquez

Department of Clinical Psychology and Psychobiology, Faculty of Psychology, University of Santiago de Compostela, 15782 Santiago de Compostela, Spain; mariabelen.vazquez.gomez1@rai.usc.es

* Correspondence: mcarmen.miguez@usc.es; Tel.: +34-881-81-3740

Abstract: The aims of this research were to determine the trajectories of probable depression and major depression during pregnancy and to identify the associated and predictor variables (sociodemographic, pregnancy-related, and psychological) for both conditions in each trimester of pregnancy. A longitudinal study was carried out with 569 pregnant Spanish women who were assessed in the first, second, and third trimesters of pregnancy. Depression was assessed using the Edinburgh Postnatal Depression Scale and a clinical interview. Measures of anxiety and stress were also included. The prevalence of probable depression in the first, second, and third trimesters was 23.4%, 17.0%, and 21.4%, respectively, and that of major depression was 5.1%, 4.0%, and 4.7%. Thus, the prevalence of both conditions was the highest in the first and third trimesters. The trajectories of probable depression and major depression followed the same pattern throughout pregnancy. All of the psychological variables studied were associated with both conditions in all three trimesters, with perceived stress being a predictor at all times. The association between the other variables and both conditions of depression was similar. Two exceptions stand out: having had previous miscarriages, which was only associated with probable depression and was also a predictor, in the first trimester; and complications during pregnancy, which was only associated with probable and major depression in the third trimester. These findings should be taken into account in routine pregnancy follow-ups, and necessary interventions should be started in the first trimester.

Keywords: pregnancy; antenatal depression; prevalence; trajectory; risk factors

Citation: Míguez, M.C.; Vázquez, M.B. Prevalence of Depression during Pregnancy in Spanish Women: Trajectory and Risk Factors in Each Trimester. *Int. J. Environ. Res. Public Health* **2021**, *18*, 6789. https://doi.org/10.3390/ijerph18136789

Academic Editor: Paul B. Tchounwou

Received: 20 May 2021
Accepted: 21 June 2021
Published: 24 June 2021

1. Introduction

Depression is one of the most prevalent psychological disorders, affecting women at twice the rate of men [1]. In women, vulnerability to depression is particularly high during pregnancy and in the postpartum period [2], as the birth of a child is a life event associated with numerous biological, hormonal, psychological, familial, and social changes.

Antenatal depression has received less attention than postpartum depression [3], as pregnancy was traditionally thought to protect women against the onset or relapse of depressive disorders. Depression during pregnancy has important consequences, both for mothers and their children. In particular, the main consequence of antenatal depression for mothers is a continuation of the state into the postpartum period, as depression in pregnancy is the main risk factor for postpartum depression [4–6]. Children of mothers with antenatal depression have been found to be more likely to have intrauterine growth retardation [7], be born preterm [7–10], and be small for gestational age [9,10], all of which are major causes of neonatal and infant morbidity and mortality.

On the other hand, there is a lack of longitudinal research addressing the prevalence of antenatal depression in each trimester of pregnancy, as most studies are cross-sectional, which makes it impossible to determine the trajectory of depression throughout pregnancy. This can lead to an inaccurate picture of the actual situation, as the prevalence of depression often varies throughout pregnancy [11–13]. The analysis of the trajectory of depression in the same sample of pregnant women is important because it enables the identification of the times of the greatest vulnerability since cross-sectional studies provide very different results, as they use different assessment instruments.

The few existing longitudinal studies have provided mixed results regarding the trajectory of depression. In particular, some studies found that the first and third trimesters of pregnancy are the times of the highest prevalence of probable depression [13–16] and major depression [13], although the values in the third trimester did not reach those observed in the first trimester. However, in a study conducted in China [17], although probable depression was also the most prevalent in the first and third trimesters, the prevalence rate was higher in the latter than in the former. The same pattern was observed in Italy for major depression [18]. In all cases, the trajectory of depression is V-shaped. By contrast, a study in India [19] reported the opposite trajectory (/\), with the highest prevalence occurring in the second trimester and the lowest prevalence in the third trimester. On the other hand, a study conducted in Korea [20] found that the presence of probable depression followed an ascending path (/) between the first and the third trimester.

As longitudinal studies on the prevalence of antenatal depression by trimester are scarce, there is also a lack of knowledge regarding the associated variables at each point. Specifically, we did not find any studies in the existing literature that have analysed the variables associated with antenatal depression in each trimester. Thus, it is not possible to know whether there are variables associated with depression that remain stable throughout the pregnancy, or whether there are others that are specific to a particular trimester and then disappear in the rest of the pregnancy. Identifying such associations would enable the implementation of prevention and intervention measures adjusted to each phase. In this respect, the variables that are the most frequently associated with depression in pregnancy are sociodemographic, obstetric, and psychological variables [21]. In particular, antenatal depression has been associated with low educational level [15,22–25] and low socio-economic level [17,22,24,26–29], being unemployed [22,30,31], and not having planned the pregnancy [15,17,19,25,27,29–34]. Regarding psychological variables, having a history of depression [17,23,26,31], as well as anxiety [26,33–36] or stress [33,34,36] are the variables that are the most frequently associated with antenatal depression. On the other hand, in regard to variables such as age and parity, the studies' findings are contradictory. Specifically, different studies have reported a relationship with younger age [18,37], while in others, it is related to older age [23,29]. Likewise, with respect to parity, both primiparity [36] and multiparity [19,23,26,31,32] have been associated with the presence of antenatal depression.

Monitoring women for depression throughout pregnancy will enable the identification of the most vulnerable phases and the variables associated with the presence of depression in each trimester. This would lead to more efficient help being offered in accordance with the real needs of future mothers and will prevent the depressive state and its associated consequences from extending to the postpartum period.

Therefore, the aims of the present research were first, to assess the trajectory of probable depression, assessed with a self-report instrument (EPDS), and of major depression, assessed with a clinical interview (SCID), during pregnancy; and second, to identify the associated and predictor variables (sociodemographic, pregnancy-related, and psychological) of both probable depression and major depression in each trimester of pregnancy. The study aimed to answer the following specific questions:

1. Is the trajectory of depression throughout pregnancy the same regardless of its severity?
2. Do the same variables predict the presence of probable depression and of major depression?
3. Which variables are the most closely associated with depression in each trimester? Are they the same, or are there trimester-specific predictors?

2. Materials and Methods

2.1. Procedure and Participants

The present research was conducted in accordance with the Helsinki Declaration and received previous approval from the ethics committees of all of the institutions involved.

It was a longitudinal study with three assessment waves: the 1st trimester of pregnancy (M = 10.87 weeks; SD = 2.36), the 2nd trimester of pregnancy (M = 20.69 weeks; SD = 1.21) and the 3rd trimester of pregnancy (M = 33.28 weeks; SD = 2.05). Pregnant women attending the primary public healthcare service in northwest Spain were recruited in the 1st trimester of pregnancy (*n* = 620). Women were eligible to participate if they were at least 18 years of age, were in the first trimester of pregnancy, spoke Spanish, and were willing to participate in subsequent assessments throughout the pregnancy. The exclusion criteria were: being under 18 years of age, having a gestational age equal to or greater than 15 weeks, not reading or speaking Spanish, and not having participated in any of the evaluations. The aims and procedures were explained, and the pregnant women who were willing to participate provided written informed consent. The final sample consisted of 569 women. The procedure and sample tracking characteristics are shown in Figure 1.

All women participated voluntarily in the study. The assessments were carried out personally and individually at the hospital prior to the women entering the protocolised pregnancy follow-up consultation. In each pregnancy trimester, all of the questionnaires and SCID interviews were administered personally by one psychologist who received SCID training and who was blind to the EPDS scores. The average duration of each interview was about 40 min.

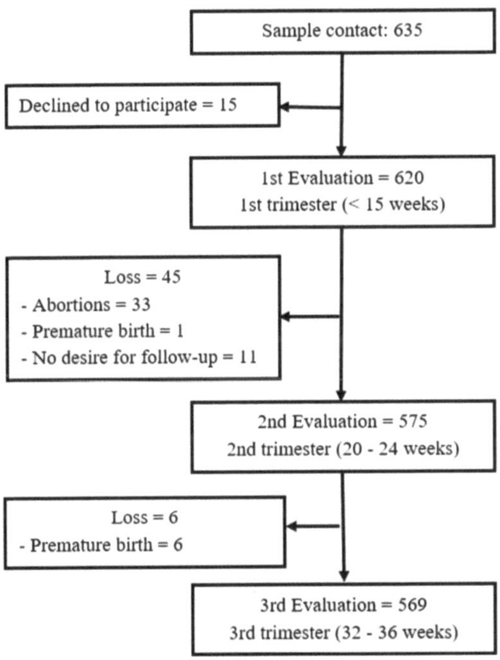

Figure 1. Flow diagram of recruitment and progress through the study.

2.2. Measures

2.2.1. Socio-Demographic and Pregnancy Information

Three ad hoc questionnaires including questions on socio-demographic (e.g., age, marital status, educational level, occupational status, and personal monthly income), pregnancy-related (e.g., parity, previous abortions, planned pregnancy, pregnancy reaction, complications, attendance at maternal classes), and psychological variables were elaborated on specifically for the study.

2.2.2. Depression

The Edinburgh Postnatal Depression Scale (EPDS) [38] is a self-reported questionnaire consisting of 10 items with 4 response options. The scores range between 0 and 30, with higher scores indicating a greater severity of depression. The Spanish validation of the EPDS for use in pregnancy was used [13], which determined that the most appropriate cut-off point for screening for probable antenatal depression was ≥ 10. The reliability of the EPDS during pregnancy was 0.81 in the first trimester, 0.82 in the second trimester, and 0.85 in the third trimester in the present study.

The Structured Clinical Interview for DSM-IV (SCID) [39] is a semi-structured interview that determines a formal diagnosis according to the Diagnostic and Statistical Manual of Mental Disorders (DSM-IV). The use of such interviews improves diagnostic reliability by standardising the assessment process and increases the diagnostic validity by facilitating the application of DSM diagnostic criteria and the systematic enquiry of symptoms that might otherwise go unnoticed.

2.2.3. Stress

The Spanish validation [40] of the Perceived Stress Scale (PSS) [41] was used. The PSS is a self-administered scale that measures the degree to which life situations in the previous month are rated as stressful. It consists of 14 items, with 5 response options. The scale ranges from 0 to 56, with higher scores indicating a higher level of perceived stress. With this sample, the reliability of the PSS during pregnancy was 0.86 in the first trimester, 0.88 in the second trimester, and 0.87 in the third trimester.

2.2.4. Anxiety

The State-Trait Anxiety Inventory (STAI) [42] assesses both the current level of anxiety and the individual's predisposition to suffering from anxiety. It consists of 40 items, 20 of which refer to the state subscale (STAI-E), with other 20 referring to the trait subscale (STAI-R). The score for each subscale ranges from 0 to 60, with higher scores indicating higher levels of anxiety. For the state subscale, the recommended cut-off point for women is greater than 31, and for trait anxiety, the cut-off point for woman is greater than 32 (75th percentile). In our sample, the reliability of the trait anxiety subscale in the first trimester of pregnancy was 0.88, and the reliability of the state subscale, 0.91. In the second and third trimesters, the reliability of the state anxiety subscale was 0.92.

2.3. Data Analysis

Data were analyzed using SPSS Statistics, version 22 (PASW Statistics for Windows, SPSS Inc., Chicago, IL, USA), and a significance level of $p < 0.05$ was applied. To test the differences between the presence or absence of depression, a chi-square test for discrete variables and Student's t-tests for continuous variables were performed. Cramers's V coefficients and Cohen's d were calculated in order to estimate the size of the effect.

Binary forward stepwise logistic regression analysis was also used to determine the variables predicting depression in pregnancy, according to the EPDS, and/or major depression, according to the SCID, in each trimester of pregnancy. The dependent variable was probable depression status (EPDS ≥ 10, yes/EPDS < 10, no) or major depression status (yes depression/no depression), and the independent variables were those variables for which significant differences were found in the two-by-two analyses. Likewise, Cronbach's alpha (α) was calculated in order to estimate the reliability of the scales.

3. Results

3.1. Characteristics of the Sample

The study sample was composed of 569 women ranging in age from 18 to 45 years, with a mean age of 32.80 years (SD = 4.75). Most of the women were married or cohabiting (94.9%); 46.4% (n = 264) had university education, and 35.3% (n = 201) had secondary education. Regarding employment status, 75.2% (n = 428) were working. Regarding personal monthly income, 44.6% (n = 254) stated that they earned less than 1000 euros per month. Pregnancy was planned in 85.9% (n = 489) of cases, 59.4% (n = 338) of the women were primiparous, and 93.0% (n = 529) reported having reacted positively to confirmation of the pregnancy. Likewise, 63.3% (n = 360) reported attending maternal education classes, with the mean attendance being 4.45 classes (SD = 4.33) out of the 10 classes offered on a regular basis.

3.2. Trajectory of Depression throughout Pregnancy

The prevalence of depression varied according to the time of the assessment and the assessment instrument used (Figure 2). The first trimester was the period during which the highest percentage of women had probable depression (23.4%) or major depression (5.1%). The prevalence of both probable depression (17.0%) and major depression (4.0%) was the lowest in the second trimester. In the third trimester, the prevalence of both probable depression (21.4%) and major depression (4.7%) was higher than in the second trimester but did not reach the values observed in the first trimester. Thus, the trajectories of probable depression and major depression followed the same pattern throughout pregnancy.

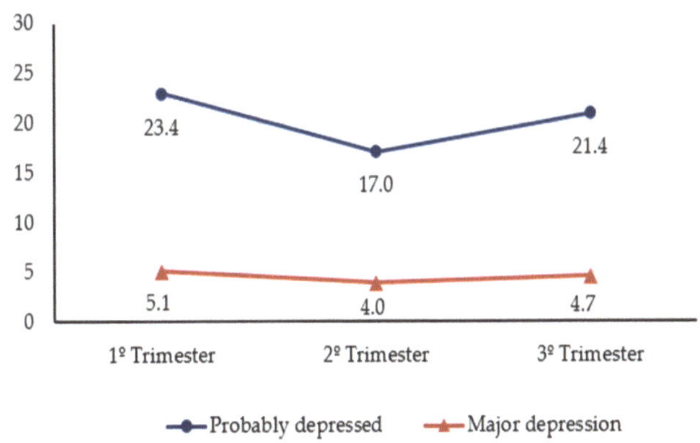

Figure 2. Trajectory of the prevalence of probable depression and major depression during pregnancy.

3.3. Variables Associated with the Presence of Depression

3.3.1. Sociodemographic Variables

Regarding the sociodemographic variables, the characteristics of the pregnant women experiencing probable depression or major depression in each trimester of pregnancy as well as the variables associated with both types of depression are shown in Table 1. Regarding the mean age, significant differences were found in the prevalence of probable depression in the first (31.99 vs. 33.05; t(569) = 2.254, p = 0.025, d Cohen = 0.25) and second trimesters (31.63 vs. 33.04; t(569) = 2.686, p = 0.007, d Cohen = 0.28), as these women were younger than the women who did not experience probable depression. For women experiencing major depression, the mean age was statistically significantly lower in the second (t(569) = 4.158, p < 0.001, d Cohen = 0.82; 28.83 vs. 32.97) and third trimesters (t(569) = 4.768, p < 0.001, d Cohen = 0.86; 28.63 vs. 33.01).

Having a lower level of education was associated with both depression conditions in all three trimesters of pregnancy, while a lower level of income was only associated with probable depression in the 1st and 2nd trimesters. On the other hand, not having a partner, not cohabiting, or not being married was not associated with either condition at any time.

3.3.2. Pregnancy-Related Variables

In terms of pregnancy-related variables, the characteristics of pregnant women with probable depression and major depression in each trimester of pregnancy as well as the variables associated with both conditions are shown in Table 2.

Having reacted negatively to the confirmation of pregnancy was associated with both probable and major depression at all time points. On the other hand, having had previous miscarriages was only associated with probable depression in the first trimester, while having had complications at some time during pregnancy was only associated with the presence of major depression in the third trimester.

3.3.3. Psychological Variables

Regarding the psychological variables, the characteristics of pregnant women with probable depression and major depression in each trimester of pregnancy as well as the variables associated with both types of depression are shown in Table 3.

Regarding perceived stress, significantly higher mean scores were found among women experiencing probable depression and women experiencing major depression. Specifically, women with probable depression had higher mean scores for perceived stress in the first (t(569) = −14.332, p <0.001, d Cohen = −1.63; 25.44 vs. 16.17), second (t(569) = −15.11, $p < 0.001$, d Cohen = −1.81; 25.69 vs. 14.55) and third trimesters (t(569) = −14.946, $p < 0.001$, d Cohen = −1.59; 25.33 vs. 15.08). In addition, the mean scores were significantly higher among women with major depression in the first (t(569) = −6.234, $p < 0.001$, d Cohen = −1.30; 26.66 vs. 17.89), second (t(569) = −7.953, $p < 0.001$, d Cohen = −1.82; 28.52 vs. 15.94) and third trimesters (t(569) = −8.343, $p < 0.001$, d Cohen = −1.74; 29.00 vs. 16.69).

All of the psychological variables studied were associated with both probable and major depression at all times. Thus, having a prior history of depression, having experienced a worsening of mood in previous pregnancies, having elevated state and trait anxiety as well as a higher level of stress were significantly associated with both probable depression and major depression.

Table 1. Characteristics of women with probable depression and major depression as a function of sociodemographic variables.

	Probable Depression						Major Depression					
First Trimester	No (n = 436)		Yes (n = 133)				No (n = 540)		Yes (n = 29)			
	n	%	n	%	χ^2	V	n	%	n	%	χ^2	V
Age												
≤30	121	27.8	55	41.4	8.825 **	0.13	166	30.7	10	34.5	0.180	
>30	315	72.2	78	58.6			374	69.3	19	65.5		
Marital Status												
Unmarried	20	4.6	9	6.8	1.001		25	4.6	4	13.8	4.778	
Married/Cohabiting	416	95.4	124	93.2			515	95.4	25	86.2		
Level of Education												
Primary/Secondary	215	49.3	90	67.7	13.809 ***	0.16	284	52.6	21	72.4	4.348 *	0.09
University	221	50.7	43	32.3			256	47.4	8	27.6		
Employment Status												
Working	339	77.8	89	66.9	6.419 *	0.11	410	75.9	18	62.1	2.835	
Not Working	97	22.2	44	33.1			130	24.1	11	37.9		
Pregnancy Influenced Employment					14.979 ***	0.16					8.892 **	0.13
No	365	83.7	91	68.4			439	81.3	17	58.6		
Yes	71	16.3	42	31.6			101	18.7	12	41.4		
Monthly Income (Euros)												
≤1000	183	48.2	71	65.1	9.783 **	0.14	240	51.6	14	58.3	0.413	
>1000	197	51.8	38	34.9			225	48.4	10	41.7		
Second Trimester	No (n = 472)		Yes (n = 97)				No (n = 546)		Yes (n = 23)			
Age												
≤30	134	28.4	42	43.3	8.372 **	0.12	159	29.1	17	73.9	20.727 ***	0.19
>30	338	71.6	55	56.7			387	70.9	6	26.1		

Table 1. *Cont.*

Marital Status												
Unmarried	23	4.9	6	6.2	0.287		27	4.9	2	8.7	0.642	
Married/Cohabiting	449	95.1	91	93.8			519	95.1	21	91.3		
Level of Education												
Primary/Secondary	235	49.8	70	72.2	16.200 ***	0.17	286	52.4	19	82.6	8.108 **	0.12
University	237	50.2	27	27.8			260	47.6	4	17.4		
Employment Status												
Working	360	76.3	68	70.1	1.642		418	76.6	10	43.5	12.956 ***	0.15
Not Working	112	23.7	29	29.9			128	23.4	13	56.5		
Pregnancy Influenced Employment												
No	367	77.8	52	53.6	24.166 ***	0.21	409	74.9	10	43.5	11.231 **	0.14
Yes	105	22.2	45	46.4			137	25.1	13	56.5		
Monthly Income (euros)												
≤1000	199	49.1	55	65.5	7.442 **	0.12	243	51.4	11	68.8	1.872	
>1000	206	50.9	29	34.5			230	48.6	5	31.3		
Third trimester	**No** (n = 447)		**Yes** (n = 122)				**No** (n = 542)		**Yes** (n = 27)			
Age												
≤30	130	29.1	46	37.7	3.335		157	29.0	19	70.4	20.637 ***	0.19
>30	317	70.9	76	62.3			385	71.0	8	29.6		
Marital Status												
Unmarried	22	4.9	7	5.7	0.132		27	5.0	2	7.4	0.313	
Married/Cohabiting	425	95.1	115	94.3			515	95.0	25	92.6		
Level of Education												
Primary/Secondary	225	50.3	80	65.6	8.948 **	0.13	284	52.4	21	77.8	6.661 *	0.11
University	222	49.7	42	34.4			258	47.6	6	22.2		
Employment Status												
Working	344	77.0	84	68.9	3.378		415	76.6	13	48.1	11.145 **	0.14
Not Working	103	23.0	38	31.1			127	23.4	14	51.9		
Pregnancy Influenced Employment												
No	290	64.9	67	54.9	4.066 *	0.09	342	63.1	15	55.6	0.626	
Yes	157	35.1	55	45.1			200	36.9	12	44.4		
Monthly Income (euros)					1.798							
≤1000	195	50.4	59	57.8			242	51.5	12	63.2	0.996	
>1000	192	49.6	43	42.2			228	48.5	7	36.8		

* $p < 0.05$, ** $p < 0.01$, *** $p < 0.001$.

Table 2. Characteristics of women with probable depression and major depression as a function of pregnancy-related variables.

	Probable Depression						Major Depression					
First Trimester	**No** (n = 436)		**Yes** (n = 133)				**No** (n = 540)		**Yes** (n = 29)			
	n	%	n	%	χ^2	V	n	%	n	%	χ^2	V
Parity												
Primiparous	270	61.9	68	51.1	4.928 *	0.09	329	60.9	9	31.0	10.197 **	0.13
Multiparous	166	38.1	65	48.9			211	39.1	20	69.0		
Previous Abortions												
No	336	77.1	83	62.4	11.280 **	0.14	398	73.7	21	72.4	0.024	
Yes	100	22.9	50	37.6			142	26.3	8	27.6		
Pregnancy Planning												
No	56	12.8	24	18.0	2.282		73	13.5	7	24.1	2.569	
Yes	380	87.2	109	82.0			467	83.5	22	75.9		
Pregnancy Reaction												
Positive	418	95.9	111	83.5	24.026 ***	0.21	507	93.9	22	75.9	13.684 ***	0.16

Table 2. *Cont.*

Negative	18	4.1	22	16.5			33	6.1	7	24.1		
Pregnancy Complication												
No	406	93.1	117	88.0	3.637		496	91.9	27	93.1	0.058	
Yes	30	6.9	16	12.0			44	8.1	2	6.9		
Second Trimester	**No** (n = 472)		**Yes** (n = 97)				**No** (n = 546)		**Yes** (n = 23)			
Parity												
Primiparous	292	61.9	46	47.4	6.959 **	0.11	327	59.9	11	47.8	1.332	
Multiparous	180	38.1	51	52.6			219	40.1	12	52.2		
Previous Abortions												
No	348	73.7	71	73.2	0.012		402	73.6	17	73.9	0.001	
Yes	124	26.3	26	26.8			144	26.4	6	26.1		
Pregnancy Planning												
No	59	12.5	21	21.6	5.575 *	0.10	72	13.2	8	34.8	8.519 **	0.12
Yes	413	87.5	76	78.4			474	86.8	15	65.2		
Pregnancy Reaction												
Positive	445	94.3	84	86.6	7.265 **	0.11	511	93.6	18	78.3	7.935 **	0.12
Negative	27	5.7	13	13.4			35	6.4	5	21.7		
Pregnancy Complication												
No	400	84.7	76	78.4	2.407		460	84.2	16	69.6	3.480	
Yes	72	15.3	21	21.6			86	15.8	7	30.4		
Third Trimester	**No** (n = 447)		**Yes** (n = 122)				**No** (n = 542)		**Yes** (n = 27)			
Parity												
Primiparous	271	60.6	67	54.9	1.295		322	59.4	16	59.3	0.001	
Multiparous	176	39.4	55	45.1			220	40.6	11	40.7		
Previous Abortions												
No	327	73.2	92	75.4	0.251		399	73.6	20	74.1	0.003	
Yes	120	26.8	30	24.6			146	26.4	7	25.9		
Pregnancy Planning												
No	56	12.5	24	19.7	4.048 *	0.08	72	13.3	8	29.6	5.687 *	0.10
Yes	391	87.5	98	80.3			470	86.7	19	70.4		
Pregnancy Reaction												
Positive	424	94.9	105	86.1	11.328 **	0.14	508	93.7	21	77.8	10.010 **	0.13
Negative	23	5.1	17	13.9			34	6.3	6	22.2		
Pregnancy Complication												
No	355	79.4	86	70.5	4.380 *	0.09	427	78.8	14	51.9	10.698 **	0.14
Yes	92	20.6	36	29.5			115	21.2	13	48.1		
Attendance at Maternal Classes												
No	149	33.3	60	49.2	10.357 **	0.14	193	35.6	16	59.3	6.190 *	0.10
Yes	298	66.7	62	50.8			349	64.4	11	40.7		

* $p < 0.05$, ** $p < 0.01$, *** $p < 0.001$.

Table 3. Characteristics of women with probable depression and major depression regarding psychological variables.

	Probable Depression						**Major Depression**					
First Trimester	**No** (n = 436)		**Yes** (n = 133)				**No** (n = 540)		**Yes** (n = 29)			
	n	%	n	%	χ^2	V	n	%	n	%	χ^2	V
History of Depression												
No	412	94.5	115	86.5	9.610 **	0.13	506	93.7	21	72.4	18.247 ***	0.19
Yes	24	5.5	18	13.5			34	6.3	8	27.6		
Worsening Mood in Previous Pregnancies (n = 234)												
No	147	87.5	50	75.8	4.908 *	0.15	184	86.0	13	65.0	6.049 *	0.16
Yes	21	12.5	16	24.4			30	14.0	7	35.0		

Table 3. *Cont.*

Trait Anxiety												
No	428	98.2	109	82.0	50.455 ***	0.30	491	90.9	21	72.4	10.463 ***	0.14
Yes	8	1.8	24	18.0			49	9.1	8	27.6		
State Anxiety												
No	419	96.1	93	69.9	77.467 ***	0.37	513	95.0	24	82.8	7.770 **	0.12
Yes	17	3.9	40	30.1			27	5.0	5	17.2		
Second Trimester	**No** (n = 472)		**Yes** (n = 97)				**No** (n = 546)		**Yes** (n = 23)			
History of Depression												
No	446	94.5	81	83.5	14.206 ***	0.16	510	93.4	17	73.9	12.267 ***	0.15
Yes	26	5.5	16	16.5			36	6.6	6	26.1		
Worsening Mood in Previous Pregnancies (n = 234)					15.040 ***	0.25					11.106 **	0.22
No	163	89.1	34	66.7			191	86.0	6	50.0		
Yes	20	10.9	17	33.3			31	14.0	6	50.0		
Trait Anxiety												
No	459	97.2	78	80.4	42.958 ***	0.28	522	95.6	15	65.2	38.396 ***	0.26
Yes	13	2.8	19	19.6			24	4.4	8	34.8		
State Anxiety												
No	464	98.3	75	77.3	70.950 ***	0.35	523	95.8	16	69.6	30.385 ***	0.23
Yes	8	1.7	22	22.7			23	4.2	7	30.4		
Third Trimester	**No** (n = 447)		**Yes** (n = 122)				**No** (n = 542)		**Yes** (n = 27)			
History of Depression												
No	423	94.6	104	85.2	12.348 ***	0.15	507	93.5	20	74.1	14.259 ***	0.16
Yes	24	5.4	18	14.8			35	6.5	7	25.9		
Worsening Mood in Previous Pregnancies (n = 234)					5.246 *	0.16					7.619 *	0.18
No	155	87.6	42	73.7			191	85.7	6	54.5		
Yes	22	12.4	15	26.3			32	14.3	5	45.5		
Trait Anxiety												
No	436	97.5	101	82.8	39.298 ***	0.26	519	95.8	18	66.7	41.005 ***	0.27
Yes	11	2.5	21	17.2			23	4.2	9	33.3		
State Anxiety												
No	438	98.0	90	73.8	84.056 ***	0.38	510	94.1	18	66.7	28.939 ***	0.23
Yes	9	2.0	32	26.2			32	5.9	9	33.3		

* $p < 0.05$, ** $p < 0.01$, *** $p < 0.001$.

3.4. Predictors of Depression in Each Trimester

Predictors of the presence of probable depression and major depression in each of the trimesters are shown in Tables 4 and 5.

Age, previous miscarriages, state anxiety, and perceived stress were predictors of probable depression in the first trimester. Specifically, being aged 30 years old or younger (OR = 2.55), having had previous miscarriages (OR = 3.28), having a high state of anxiety (OR = 3.97) as well as higher perceived stress (OR = 1.24) increased the likelihood of probable depression in the first trimester.

In the second trimester, having had probable depression in the first trimester (OR = 13.61) as well as higher perceived stress in the first (OR = 1.14) and second trimesters (OR = 1.35) increased the likelihood of having probable depression.

In the third trimester, the predictors of probable depression were having had major depression in the first trimester (OR = 5.43), probable depression in the second trimester (OR = 6.19), and an elevated state of anxiety (OR = 4.88) and higher perceived stress (OR = 1.16) in the third trimester.

In the first trimester, the predictors of major depression were having perceived that pregnancy had a negative influence on employment (OR = 3.20) and having higher perceived stress (OR = 1.13). In the second trimester, the predictors were being aged 30 years old or younger (OR = 1.26) and experiencing higher perceived stress (OR = 1.27). In the third trimester, the predictors were being aged 30 years old or younger (OR = 7.23) and experiencing higher perceived stress in the second (OR = 1.16) and in the third trimesters (OR = 1.18).

Table 4. Predictors of probable depression in each trimester.

Predictors in the First Trimester	B	WALD	*p*	OR [95% IC]
Age ≤ 30 years	0.94	4,04	0.045	2.55 [1.02–6.37]
Previous Miscarriages	1.19	7.13	0.008	3.28 [1.37–7.85]
High State Anxiety	1.38	4.70	0.03	3.97 [1.14–13,81]
High Perceived Stress	0.22	24.70	<0.001	1.24 [1.14–1.35]
Constant	−6.49	38.88	<0.001	0.002
Cox and Snell R2			0.343	
Nagelkerke's R2			0.501	
Predictors in the Second Trimester				
Probable Depression in the 1st Trimester	2.61	21.41	<0.001	13.61 [4.51–41.14]
Higher Perceived Stress in 1st Trimester	0.12	6.53	0.011	1.14 [1.03–1.24]
Higher Perceived Stress in 2nd Trimester	0.30	26.46	<0.001	1.35 [1.21–1.52]
Constant	−5.90	29.98	<0.001	0.003
Cox and Snell R2			0.402	
Nagelkerke's R2			0.611	
Predictors in the Third Trimester				
Major Depression in the 1st Trimester	1.69	6.49	0.011	5.43 [1.48–19.95]
Probable Depression in the 2nd Trimester	1.82	16.47	<0.001	6.19 [2.47–14.91]
High State Anxiety in 3rd Trimester	1.59	4.49	0.034	4.88 [1.13–21.13]
Higher Perceived Stress in 3rd Trimester	0.15	15.57	<0.001	1.16 [1.08–1.25]
Constant	−5.22	36.82	<0.001	0.005
Cox and Snell R2			0.368	
Nagelkerke's R2			0.555	

Table 5. Predictors of major depression in each trimester.

Predictors in the First Trimester	B	WALD	*p*	OR [95% IC]
Negative influence of Pregnancy on Work Situation	1.16	5.31	0.021	3.20 [1.19–8.63]
High Perceived Stress	0.12	12.21	<0.001	1.13 [1.05–1.21]
Constant	−5.45	37.28	<0.001	0.004
Cox and Snell R2			0.094	
Nagelkerke's R2			0.210	
Predictors in the Second Trimester				
Age ≤ 30 years	1.71	5.33	<0.001	1.26 [1.13–23.42]
High Perceived Stress in the 2nd Trimester	0.24	15.66	<0.001	1.27 [1.13–1.42]
Constant	−9.13	27.10	<0.001	0.000
Cox and Snell R2			0.127	
Nagelkerke's R2			0.398	
Predictors in the Third Trimester				
Age ≤ 30 years	1.98	4.98	0.026	7.23 [1.27–41.08]
High Perceived Stress in the 2nd Trimester	0.15	4.22	0.04	1.16 [1.01–1.34]
High Perceived Stress in 3rd Trimester	0.16	4.20	0.04	1.18 [1.01–1.37]
Constant	−11.51	20.60	<0.001	0.000
Cox and Snell R2			0.147	
Nagelkerke's R2			0.485	

4. Discussion

4.1. Trajectory of Depression during Pregnancy

The aim of the present longitudinal study was to analyse the trajectory of both probable depression and major depression during pregnancy. The prevalence of probable depression ranged from 17.0% to 23.4%, and the prevalence of major depression ranged from 4.0% to 5.1%. During pregnancy, the variation in probable depression and major depression followed the same pattern or trajectory. In both cases, the prevalence was the highest in the first trimester, decreased in the second trimester, and increased again in the third trimester, although not reaching the rates observed in the first trimester. It is possible that, as stated by Rallis et al. [14], this trajectory of depression may occur because the beginning of a pregnancy can be a time of strong psychological vulnerability involving multiple factors, such as hormonal, physical, psychological, and emotional adjustment to the new situation of pregnancy, which can increase vulnerability to the development of depressive symptoms. On the other hand, the third trimester is another critical time, as it also involves major physical and emotional changes in view of the approaching birth.

The findings of the few studies that have assessed the presence of depressive symptomatology in all three trimesters of pregnancy are variable. The same pattern as the one observed in the present study was also observed in studies conducted in China [16], Turkey [15], and Australia [14]. However, in the study by Weng et al. [17] conducted in China, although the two most prevalent times of depressive symptomatology were also the first and third trimester, the prevalence was higher in the latter than in the former. On the other hand, the prevalence observed in a study in Korea [20] follows a rising pattern from the first to the third trimester, and Ajinkya et al. [19] found to have the highest prevalence of depressive symptomatology in the second trimester and the lowest values in the third trimester. However, it should be noted that these studies use different scales and cut-off points to assess probable depression, such as the EPDS [17], the BDI [15,19], and the SDS [16]. On the other hand, some studies have identified different latent trajectory groups based on the total scores of depressive symptoms [43,44].

Regarding the trajectory of major depression, we can only compare our data with those reported by Marchesi et al. [18] in Italy, as this is the only study including a longitudinal follow-up in the three trimesters of gestation. The trajectory reported is similar to that observed in the present study, following a V-shaped pattern, with the prevalence of depression being the highest in the first and third trimesters, although in this case, the prevalence was the highest in the third trimester.

The differences between the trajectory observed in the present study and those observed in other studies may be due to cultural differences, the quality of prenatal care received and the levels of satisfaction with this prenatal care, the professionals carrying out prenatal care (midwives and/or obstetricians), health conditions, and the type and accessibility of healthcare (public/private) in each country.

4.2. Variables Associated with Probable Depression and Major Depression in Pregnancy

The second objective of this study was to identify the sociodemographic, pregnancy-related, and psychological variables associated with both probable depression and major depression in each trimester. This will enable us to determine whether any variables are specifically associated with a particular trimester of pregnancy, with one condition of depression or the other, or with both equally.

Regarding the sociodemographic variables, both probable depression and major depression were associated with younger age. In addition, an age less than or equal to 30 years old was found to be a predictor of major depression in the second and third trimester. This relationship was also found in other research in which being younger than 25 [31], younger than 20 [22], or aged 15–20 [25] was associated with an increased risk of antenatal depression. This relationship can be explained by the fact that younger women tend to have a more unfavourable and unstable economic position and lower-paid jobs, leading to lower income level [25].

On the other hand, in all trimesters of pregnancy, both probable depression and major depression were associated with lower educational level. These findings are consistent with those of previous studies [15,22,23,25]. This relationship can be explained by the fact that a low level of education is often related to socio-economic disadvantage [23], which is one of the most worrying aspects for women when facing motherhood, as they may fear that they will not be able to meet their children's needs [45]. Low socio-economic status is also often accompanied by increased stress, which is, in turn, considered a risk factor for depression. In the present study, lower income was associated with the presence of probable depression in the first and second trimesters. This finding is consistent with the findings of other authors, who observed associations with low socioeconomic status [22,24] and family income below the minimum wage [27]. Employment status is one of the factors related to both educational and economic status. Being unemployed was associated with the presence of probable depression in the first trimester and with major depression in the second and third trimesters, as was also found in other studies [22,30,31]. Giardinelli et al. [30] suggested that this relationship may be due to the fact that not working implies having a smaller social support network and some degree of isolation. Likewise, not being in paid work is associated with lower educational attainment and lower economic resources. Another possible factor explaining this association is the frustration that the women had after observing that being pregnant prevented them from having equal access to the labour market, as some women reported being dismissed from work, not being able to apply for positions of responsibility, or being obliged to request reduced working hours or job adaptations that often did not correspond to their professional category. This hypothesis would explain the observed association between the perception of the women that pregnancy had had a negative influence on their work situation and the presence of probable depression at all stages of pregnancy and with major depression in the first and second trimesters. It was also a predictor of major depression in the first trimester. Of note is a sociodemographic variable with which no association was found at any time during pregnancy with either probable or major depression. Not having a partner has been associated in some studies with antenatal depression [17,23,29], but not in this research. However, only 29 women claimed to not have a partner in the present study, and this could influence the results. On the other hand, the explanation for this finding could be that what is associated with depression is not so much with having or not having a partner, but with the quality of the relationship and how it is perceived by the woman as satisfactory or unsatisfactory.

Regarding pregnancy-related variables, parity, specifically being multiparous, was associated with probable depression in the first and second trimesters as well as with having major depression in the first trimester, and in this case, it was a predictor variable. This finding may be explained by the fact that women with more children bear a greater physical and emotional burden due to the demands of caring for a larger number of family members. While some studies corroborate this association [19,23,26,32], Redinger et al. [36] found the opposite, i.e., being nulliparous was associated with gestational depression.

Having had previous miscarriages was a predictor of probable depression in the first trimester, and no relationship was found at any other time or with the presence of major depression. One possible explanation is that miscarriages often occur in the first trimester and, therefore, those women with a history of miscarriage may experience greater distress at this time because of the fear of a repeat of the situation and because, in turn, they are reminded of the previous experience. This situation could make them vulnerable to developing depressive symptoms. Once this trimester is over, these symptoms disappear. Although other authors have also found an association between previous miscarriages and antenatal depression [19,29,32], in another study [31], this relationship was not significant.

Unplanned pregnancy was associated in the second and third trimesters with both probable depression and major depression. This association has been widely documented [19,29,30,32,46]. There are several possible explanations for this. First, unplanned or unwanted pregnancies carry an enormous emotional burden [47]. Another explanation involves the socio-demographic characteristics of women who find themselves in a situation of unwanted pregnancy. As such, women may not be financially or socially prepared to cope with the demands of pregnancy [48]. These women also tend to have more unstable social environments and may feel a lack of security and support from their partner (if any) and have more marital conflict [49,50]. All of these circumstances increase the risk of antenatal depression. On the other hand, having had a negative reaction to the confirmation of pregnancy was associated with both probable depression and major depression in all three trimesters. Although this variable may be related to the previous variable (unplanned/wanted pregnancy), negative reactions do not always occur in this context. However, the explanation for this relationship may be similar, as negative reactions such as resignation and anger, among others, are an added emotional burden. Moreover, the woman may feel guilty for having such reactions, even if the pregnancy was wanted, as the idealisation of motherhood and social pressure impose that it is politically incorrect to say (or think) something negative at this time.

With regard to the presence of pregnancy complications, an association was found with both probable depression and major depression in the third trimester. Other authors [19,25] have also found this relationship. The presence of complications is a stressful life event and a psychological burden for women that favours the appearance of depressive symptomatology. It should be borne in mind that what women consider to be a complication may not be a complication from a clinical point of view. For example, some women perceive back pain or nausea as a complication, whereas for a health professional, both entities would be considered physiological or normal. Therefore, the important point in psychological terms is not what is reflected in the medical history, but the woman's perception of the process.

Not attending maternal education classes was associated with both probable depression and major depression in the third trimester, the time of pregnancy when the women were assessed, as this is when these classes begin. Maternal education sessions aim to equip the mother and her partner with knowledge and skills to prepare them to cope with physical, emotional, and lifestyle changes in those areas of which they feel the most insecure. The mere fact of being in contact with other women in the same situation and with the same needs as well as having a healthcare professional who listens empathetically and resolves doubts can minimize the impact of the possible worries that most women have in pregnancy.

In terms of psychological variables, in all three trimesters, probable depression and major depression were both associated with a history of depression, the perceived worsening of mood in previous pregnancies, and with the presence of trait anxiety, state anxiety, and higher perceived stress.

The relationship with the presence of a history of depression has also been found by other authors in cohorts of pregnant women [23,31] as well as at specific times during pregnancy [17,26,46]. The explanation for this relationship is the existence of a vulnerability to depression that may be intensified by changes brought about by pregnancy and motherhood (e.g., sleep, rest, altered body image). Another explanation is that many women who are undergoing pharmacological treatment for a depressive episode may choose to interrupt it when they become aware of the pregnancy for fear of possible teratogenic effects on the foetus [51] and, therefore, the symptoms will possibly worsen and be prolonged throughout the perinatal period. In relation to this, in the present study, multiparous women who perceived a worsening of mood in previous pregnancies were more likely to have probable depression and major depression.

State anxiety was associated with both probable and major depression in all three trimesters of pregnancy and was also a predictor of probable depression in the first and third trimesters. This relationship is widely documented [26,33,35,36]. The main explanation is the frequent comorbidity of both disorders [35,52]. Ross et al. [53] concluded that more than 50.0% of pregnant women with depression had also been diagnosed with anxiety.

In terms of perceived stress, our data indicate that a high level of perceived stress is a predictor of both entities of depression at all points in pregnancy. This association is frequently found with other measures of stress such as the presence of stressful life events [33,36,46], and it must be borne in mind that pregnancy is considered stressful for many women because of the changes it brings about in their lives [54].

Thus, the study findings indicate that all of the psychological variables considered were associated with both probable depression and major depression at all stages of pregnancy. Therefore, it is crucial to take these variables into account in routine follow-up examinations.

Interpretation of the results obtained in the present research should take into consideration the limitation that no pre-pregnancy baseline measurements of psychological variables are available. Therefore, it is not possible to determine if there were any changes in pregnancy relative to the usual condition of the participants. The strengths of the study are mainly methodological. In particular, it is a longitudinal study (the first in Spain), which enabled us to identify both the associations between the variables and the predictors of depression status. In addition, the data were collected prospectively and individually by administering the questionnaires face-to-face to a large sample at all assessment times in order to minimize recall bias. This, in turn, resulted in low sample attrition. This is also the only study in which the prevalence and variables associated with both depressive symptomatology (assessed with a screening instrument) and major depression (assessed by clinical interview) have been analyzed together, providing a more complete view of the subject. This enabled us to understand the trajectory of two very different situations in terms of the severity of depression and to examine the similarities between the associated variables. In general, although the results do not indicate any notable differences, as the variables associated with both probable depression and major depression are similar, there are some exceptions. Specifically, previously having had a miscarriage was only associated with probable depression in the first trimester of pregnancy, while suffering pregnancy complications was only associated with major depression in the third trimester. Likewise, the level of income was only associated with probable depression in the first and second trimesters. However, lower educational level, having had a negative reaction to the confirmation of pregnancy, and all of the psychological variables were associated with both types of depression in all three trimesters. This finding reinforces the fact that the EPDS is a valid instrument for detecting women at risk of clinical depression if it is routinely implemented in pregnancy monitoring.

Regarding the clinical implications, this study enabled us to identify the variables associated with the presence of depression at different times. While some of these variables (i.e., sociodemographic variables) are unalterable, others (i.e., psychological variables) are potentially modifiable. Influencing these variables at an early stage could lead to a reduction in the prevalence and adverse consequences of depression. The study findings also enabled us to determine which variables should be assessed routinely in order to enable the necessary help to be offered at each stage, to predict which women are at the greatest risk of developing depression in pregnancy, and to develop specific interventions at the most appropriate time to prevent depression from extending to the postpartum period. The findings could thus help to improve care during the perinatal stage and prevent or reduce the likelihood of the women experiencing depression.

5. Conclusions

In the present study, the prevalence of probable depression in pregnancy was 23.4% in the first trimester, 17.0% in the second trimester, and 21.4% in the third trimester. The prevalence of major depression was 5.1% in the first trimester, 4.0% in the second, and 4.7% in the third trimester. The trajectories of both probable depression and major depression throughout pregnancy are therefore the same, being more prevalent in the first (in particular) and third trimesters. Regarding the variables associated with both probable depression and major depression, with the exception of variables such as having suffered previous miscarriages and pregnancy complications and/or having a lower level of income, no significant differences were found between probable and major depression. Regarding socio-demographic variables, a younger age, lower level of education, being unemployed, and the perception that pregnancy had a negative influence on employment stands out. Regarding the pregnancy-related variables, not having planned the pregnancy, negative reaction to the confirmation of the pregnancy, and not attending maternal education classes stands out. It should be noted that psychological variables were associated with probable depression and major depression in all three trimesters. In fact, the predictor variables are also mainly psychological, with perceived stress being a predictor for both conditions in all trimesters. The data indicate the importance of integrating mental health care as a part of routine pregnancy follow-up protocols. This would involve conducting assessments throughout pregnancy as early as the first trimester to detect women at risk of suffering depression.

Author Contributions: Conceptualization, M.C.M.; formal analysis, M.B.V.; investigation, M.B.V.; methodology, M.C.M. and M.B.V.; supervision, M.C.M.; data curation, M.C.M. and M.B.V.; writing—original draft, M.B.V.; writing—review and editing, M.C.M. and M.B.V. All authors have read and agreed to the published version of the manuscript.

Funding: This research received no external funding.

Institutional Review Board Statement: The study was conducted according to the guidelines of the Declaration of Helsinki, and approved by the Clinical Research Ethics Committee of Galicia (protocol code 2015/437 and date of approval 22 July 2015).

Informed Consent Statement: Informed consent was obtained from all subjects involved in the study.

Data Availability Statement: The data presented in the current study are available from the authors upon request.

Acknowledgments: We would like to especially show our gratitude to the pregnant women who participated for their patience and generous collaboration in this study.

Conflicts of Interest: The authors declare no conflict of interest.

References

1. WHO. Depresión. Datos y cifras [Depression. Data and numbers]. Available online: https://www.who.int/es/news-room/fact-sheets/detail/depression (accessed on 5 April 2019).
2. Kamysheva, E.; Skouteris, H.; Wertheim, E.H.; Paxton, S.J.; Milgrom, J. A prospective investigation of the relationships among sleep quality, physical symptoms, and depressive symptoms during pregnancy. *J. Affect. Disord.* **2010**, *123*, 317–320. [CrossRef]
3. Bowen, A.; Muhajarine, N. Antenatal depression. *Can. Nurse* **2006**, *102*, 26–30.
4. Lee, A.M.; Lam, S.K.; Sze Mun Lau, S.M.; Chong, C.S.; Chui, H.W.; Fong, D.Y. Prevalence, course, and risk factors for antenatal anxiety and depression. *Obstet. Gynecol.* **2007**, *110*, 1102–1112. [CrossRef]
5. Míguez, M.C.; Fernández, V.; Pereira, B. Depresión postparto y factores asociados en mujeres con embarazos de riesgo [Postpartum depression and associated factors in women with at-risk pregnancies]. *Behav. Psychol.* **2017**, *25*, 47–64.
6. Yonkers, K.A.; Smith, M.V.; Gotman, N.; Belanger, K. Typical somatic symptoms of pregnancy and their impact on a diagnosis of major depressive disorder. *Gen. Hosp. Psychiatry* **2009**, *31*, 327–333. [CrossRef] [PubMed]
7. Saeed, A.; Raana, T.; Saeed, A.M.; Humayun, A. Effect of antenatal depression on maternal dietary intake and neonatal outcome: A prospective cohort. *Nutr. J.* **2016**, *15*, 64–93. [CrossRef] [PubMed]
8. Eastwood, J.; Ogbo, F.A.; Hendry, A.; Noble, J.; Page, A. The impact of antenatal depression on perinatal outcomes in australian women. *PLoS ONE* **2017**, *12*, e0169907. [CrossRef] [PubMed]
9. Goedhart, G.; Snijders, A.C.; Hesselink, A.E.; Van Poppel, N.; Bonsel, G.J.; Vrijkotte, T.G.M. Maternal depressive symptoms in relation to perinatal mortality and morbidity: Results from a large multiethnic cohort study. *Psychosom. Med.* **2010**, *72*, 769–776. [CrossRef]
10. Herrero, T.; Driebe, A.; Fratto, V.; Hamlin, A.; Lacoursiere, D.Y.; Ramos, G.A. Positive antenatal Edinburgh Depression Scale: Examining behavioral and pharmacological therapy on maternal and neonatal outcomes. *J. Matern. Fetal Neonatal Med.* **2018**, 1–5. [CrossRef] [PubMed]
11. Felice, E.; Saliba, J.; Grech, V.; Cox, J. Validation of the Maltese version of the Edinburgh Postnatal Depression Scale. *Arch. Womens Ment. Health* **2006**, *9*, 75–80. [CrossRef]
12. Matthey, S.; Ross-Hamid, C. Repeat testing on the Edinburgh Depression Scale and the HADS-A in pregnancy: Differentiating between transient and enduring distress. *J. Affect. Disord.* **2012**, *141*, 213–221. [CrossRef]

13. Vázquez, M.B.; Míguez, M.C. Validation of the Edinburgh postnatal depression scale as a screening tool for depression in Spanish pregnant women. *J. Affect. Disord.* **2019**, *246*, 515–521. [CrossRef]
14. Rallis, S.; Skouteris, H.; McCabe, M.; Milgrom, J. A prospective examination of depression, anxiety and stress throughout pregnancy. *Women Birth* **2014**, *27*, e36–e42. [CrossRef]
15. Yanikkerem, E.; Ay, S.; Mutlu, S.; Goker, A. Antenatal depression: Prevalence and risk factors in a hospital based Turkish sample. *J. Pak. Med. Assoc.* **2013**, *63*, 472–477. [PubMed]
16. Yu, Y.; Li, M.; Pu, L.; Wang, S.; Wu, J.; Ruan, L.; Jiang, S.; Wang, Z.; Jiang, W. Sleep was associated with depression and anxiety status during pregnancy: A prospective longitudinal study. *Arch. Womens Ment. Health* **2017**, *20*, 695–701. [CrossRef] [PubMed]
17. Weng, S.C.; Huang, J.P.; Huang, Y.L.; Lee, T.S.; Chen, Y.H. Effects of tobacco exposure on perinatal suicidal ideation, depression, and anxiety. *BMC Public Health* **2016**, *16*, 623. [CrossRef] [PubMed]
18. Marchesi, C.; Bertoni, S.; Maggini, C. Major and minor depression in pregnancy. *Obstet. Gynecol.* **2009**, *113*, 1292–1298. [CrossRef]
19. Ajinkya, S.; Jadhav, P.R.; Srivastava, N.N. Depression during pregnancy: Prevalence and obstetric risk factors among pregnant women attending a tertiary care hospital in Navi Mumbai. *Ind. Psychiatry J.* **2013**, *22*, 37–40. [CrossRef]
20. Park, J.H.; Karmaus, W.; Zhang, H. Prevalence of and risk factors for depressive symptoms in Korean women throughout pregnancy and in postpartum period. *Asian Nurs. Res.* **2015**, *9*, 219–225. [CrossRef]
21. Míguez, M.C.; Vázquez, M.B. Risk factors for antenatal depression: A review. *World J. Psychiatr.* **2021**, in press.
22. Bödecs, T.; Szilagyi, E.; Cholnoky, P.; Sándor, J.; Gonda, X.; Rihmer, Z.; Horváth, B. Prevalence and psychosocial background of anxiety and depression emerging during the first trimester of pregnancy: Data from a Hungarian population-based sample. *Psychiatr. Danub.* **2013**, *25*, 352–358.
23. De Vargas, C.; Coll, N.; Da Silveira, M.; Garcia-Bassani, D.; Netsi, E.; César Wehrmeister, F.; ... Stein, A. Antenatal depressive symptoms among pregnant women: Evidence from a Southern Brazilian population-based cohort study. *J. Affect. Disord.* **2017**, *209*, 140–146. [CrossRef]
24. Husain, N.; Parveen, A.; Husain, M.; Saeed, Q.; Jafri, F.; Rahman, R.; Tomenson, B.; Chaudhry, I.B. Prevalence and psychosocial correlates of perinatal depression: A cohort study from urban Pakistan. *Arch. Womens Ment. Health* **2011**, *14*, 395–403. [CrossRef]
25. Thompson, O.; Ajayi, I. Prevalence of antenatal depression and associated risk factors among pregnant women attending antenatal clinics in Abeokuta north local government area, Nigeria. *Depress. Res. Treat.* **2016**, *16*, 1–15. [CrossRef]
26. Banti, S.; Mauri, M.; Oppo, A.; Borri, C.; Rambelli, C.; Ramacciotti, D.; Montagnani, M.S.; Camilleri, V.; Cortopassi, S.; Rucci, P.; et al. From the third month of pregnancy to 1 year postpartum. Prevalence, incidence, recurrence, and new onset of depression. Results from the perinatal depression-research & screening unit study. *Compr. Psychiatry* **2011**, *52*, 343–351. [CrossRef] [PubMed]
27. Benute, G.R.G.; Nomura, R.M.Y.; Reis, J.S.; Fraguas-Junior, R.; Lucia, M.C.S.; Zugaib, M. Depression during pregnancy in women with a medical disorder: Risk factors and perinatal outcomes. *Clinics* **2011**, *65*, 1127–1131. [CrossRef] [PubMed]
28. Ogbo, F.A.; Eastwood, J.; Hendry, A.; Jalaludin, B.; Agho, K.E.; Barnett, B.; Page, A. Determinants of antenatal depression and postnatal depression in Australia. *BMC Psychiatry* **2018**, *18*, 49. [CrossRef] [PubMed]
29. Weobong, B.; Asbroek, A.H.A.; Soremekun, S.; Manu, A.A.; Owusu-Agyei, S.; Prince, M.; Kirkwood, B.R. Association of antenatal depression with adverse consequences for the mother and newborn in rural Ghana: Findings from the DON population-based cohort study. *PLoS ONE* **2014**, *9*, e116333. [CrossRef]
30. Giardinelli, L.; Innocenti, A.; Benni, L.; Stefanini, M.C.; Lino, G.; Lunardi, C.; Svelto, V.; Afshar, S.; Bovani, R.; Castellini, G.; et al. Depression and anxiety in perinatal period: Prevalence and risk factors in an Italian sample. *Arch. Womens Ment. Health* **2012**, *15*, 21–30. [CrossRef]
31. Kheirabadi, G.R.; Maracy, M.R. Perinatal depression in a cohort study on Iranian women. *J. Res. Med. Sci.* **2010**, *15*, 41–49.
32. González-Mesa, E.; Kabukcuoglu, K.; Körükcü, O.; Blasco, M.; Ibrahim, N.; Kavas, T. Cultural factors influencing antenatal depression: A cross-sectional study in a cohort of Turkish and Spanish women at the beginning of the pregnancy. *J. Affect. Disord.* **2018**, *238*, 256–260. [CrossRef]
33. Mohammad, K.I.; Gamble, J.; Creedy, D.K. Prevalence and factors associated with the development of antenatal and postnatal depression among Jordanian women. *Midwifery* **2011**, *27*, 238–245. [CrossRef]
34. Waldie, K.E.; Peterson, E.R.; D'Souza, S.; Underwood, L.; Pryor, J.E.; Carr, P.A.; Grant, C.; Morton, S.M.B. Depression symptoms during pregnancy: Evidence from Growing Up in New Zealand. *J. Affect. Disord.* **2015**, *186*, 66–73. [CrossRef] [PubMed]
35. Fadzil, A.; Balakrishnan, K.; Razali, R.; Sidi, H.; Malapan, T.; Japaraj, R.P.; Midin, M.; Jaafar, N.R.N.; Das, S.; Manaf, M.R.A. Risk factors for depression and anxiety among pregnant women in Hospital Tuanku Bainun, Ipoh, Malaysia. *Asia Pac. Psychiatry* **2013**, *5*, 7–13. [CrossRef] [PubMed]
36. Redinger, S.; Norris, S.A.; Pearson, R.M.; Richter, L.; Rochat, T. First trimester antenatal depression and anxiety: Prevalence and associated factors in an urban population in Soweto, South Africa. *J. Dev. Orig. Health Dis.* **2018**, *9*, 30–40. [CrossRef]
37. Rich-Edwards, J.; Kleinman, K.; Abrams, A.; Harlow, B.L.; McLaughlin, T.J.; Joffe, H.; Gillman, M.W. Sociodemographic predictors of antenatal and postpartum depressive symptoms among women in a medical group practice. *J. Epidemiol. Community Health* **2006**, *60*, 221–227. [CrossRef]
38. Cox, J.; Holden, J.M.; Sagovsky, R. Detection of postnatal depression. Development of the 10-item Edinburgh Postnatal Depression Scale. *Br. J. Psychiatry* **1987**, *150*, 782–786. [CrossRef] [PubMed]

39. First, M.B.; Spitzer, R.L.; Gibbon, M.; Williams, J.B.W. Entrevista clínica estructurada para los trastornos del eje I del DSM-IV-versión clínica (SCID-CV) [Structured Clinical Interview for DSM-IV Axis I Disorders, Clinician Version (SCID-CV)]. 1997. Versión Clínica Ed. Masson. Barcelona. Available online: https://libreriaolejnik.cl/fichas/90090.pdf (accessed on 17 November 2015).
40. Remor, E. Psychometric properties of a European Spanish version of the Perceived Stress Scale (PSS). *Span. J. Psychol.* **2006**, *9*, 86–93. [CrossRef] [PubMed]
41. Cohen, S.; Kamarck, T.; Mermelstein, R. A global measure of perceived stress. *J. Health Soc. Behav.* **1983**, *24*, 385–396. [CrossRef]
42. Spielberg, C.D.; Gorsuch, R.L.; Lushene, R.E. *Manual of State-Trait Anxiety Inventory*; Consulting Psichologists Press: Palo Alto, CA, USA, 1970.
43. Ahmed, A.; Bowen, A.; Feng, C.X.; Muhajarine, N. Trajectories of maternal depressive and anxiety symptoms from pregnancy to five years postpartum and their prenatal predictors. *BMC Pregnancy Childbirth* **2019**, *19*, 26. [CrossRef]
44. Lee, H.; Kim, K.E.; Kim, M.Y.; Park, C.G.; Han, J.Y.; Choi, E.J. Trajectories of depressive symptoms and anxiety during pregnancy and associations with pregnancy stress. *Int. J. Environ. Res. Public Health* **2021**, *18*, 2733. [CrossRef] [PubMed]
45. Segre, L.S.; O'Hara, M.W.; Arndt, S.; Stuart, S. The prevalence of postpartum depression: The relative significance of three social status indices. *Soc. Psychiatry Psychiatr. Epidemiol.* **2007**, *42*, 316–321. [CrossRef] [PubMed]
46. Marcos-Nájera, R.; Rodríguez-Muñoz, M.F.; Lara, M.A.; Navarrete, L.; Le, H.N. A cross-cultural analysis of the prevalence and risk factors for prenatal depression in Spain and Mexico. *Cult. Med. Psychiatry* **2020**, 1–14. [CrossRef]
47. Koutra, K.; Vassilaki, M.; Georgiou, V.; Koutis, A.; Bitsios, P.; Chatzi, L.; Kogevinas, M. Antenatal maternal mental health as determinant of postpartum depression in a population based mother-child cohort (Rhea Study) in Crete, Greece. *Soc. Psychiatry Psychiatr. Epidemiol.* **2014**, *49*, 711–721. [CrossRef] [PubMed]
48. Sedgh, G.; Bankole, A.; Oye-Adeniran, B.; Adewole, I.F.; Singh, S.; Hussain, R. Unwanted pregnancy and associated factors among Nigerian women. *Int. Fam. Plan Perspect.* **2006**, *32*, 175–184. [CrossRef]
49. Bouchard, G. Adult couples facing a planned or an unplanned pregnancy. *J. Fam. Issues* **2005**, *26*, 619–637. [CrossRef]
50. Bouchard, G.; Boudreau, J.; Hébert, R. Transition to parenthood and conjugal life: Comparisons between planned and unplanned pregnancies. *J. Fam. Issues* **2006**, *27*, 1512–1531. [CrossRef]
51. Vesga-López, O.; Blanco, C.; Keyes, K.; Olfson, M.; Grant, B.F.; Hasin, D.S. Psychiatric disorders in pregnant and postpartum women in the United States. *Arch. Gen. Psychiatry* **2008**, *65*, 805. [CrossRef]
52. Falah-Hassani, K.; Shiri, R.; Dennis, C.L. Prevalence and risk factors for comorbid postpartum depressive symptomatology and anxiety. *J. Affect. Disord.* **2016**, *198*, 142–147. [CrossRef]
53. Ross, L.E.; Gilbert Evans, S.E.; Sellers, E.M.; Romach, M.K. Measurement issues in postpartum depression part 1: Anxiety as a feature of postpartum depression. *Arch. Womens Ment. Health* **2003**, *6*, 51–57. [CrossRef]
54. Van den Bergh, B.R.H.; Mulder, E.J.H.; Mennes, M.; Glover, V. Antenatal maternal anxiety and stress and the neurobehavioural development of the fetus and child: Links and possible mechanisms. A review. *Neurosci. Biobehav. Rev.* **2005**, *29*, 237–258. [CrossRef] [PubMed]

International Journal of
Environmental Research and Public Health

Article

Women's Depressive Symptoms during the COVID-19 Pandemic: The Role of Pregnancy

Karen Yirmiya [1,2], Noa Yakirevich-Amir [3], Heidi Preis [4], Amit Lotan [3,5], Shir Atzil [6,†] and Inbal Reuveni [3,5,*,†]

1 Department of Psychology, Bar-Ilan University, Ramat Gan 5290002, Israel; Karen.Yirmiya1@post.idc.ac.il
2 Interdisciplinary Center, Baruch Ivcher School of Psychology, Herzlia 4610101, Israel
3 Department of Psychiatry, Hadassah Medical Center, Jerusalem 9103401, Israel; noa269@gmail.com (N.Y.-A.); amit.lotan1@mail.huji.ac.il (A.L.)
4 Department of Psychology, Stony Brook University, Stony Brook, NY 11794, USA; heidi.preis@stonybrook.edu
5 Faculty of Medicine, The Hebrew University of Jerusalem, Jerusalem 9112102, Israel
6 Department of Psychology, The Hebrew University of Jerusalem, Jerusalem 9190401, Israel; Shir.Atzil@mail.huji.ac.il
* Correspondence: reuveni@hadassah.org.il
† Shir Atzil and Inbal Reuveni should be considered joint senior author.

Abstract: The Coronavirus Disease 2019 (COVID-19) pandemic has multiple ramifications for pregnant women. Untreated depression during pregnancy may have long-term effects on the mother and offspring. Therefore, delineating the effects of pregnancy on the mental health of reproductive-age women is crucial. This study aims to determine the risk for depressive symptoms in pregnant and non-pregnant women during COVID-19, and to identify its bio-psycho-social contributors. A total of 1114 pregnant and 256 non-pregnant women were recruited via social media in May 2020 to complete an online survey that included depression and anxiety questionnaires, as well as demographic, obstetric and COVID-19-related questionnaires. Pregnant women also completed the Pandemic-Related Pregnancy Stress Scale (PREPS). Pregnant women reported fewer depressive symptoms and were less concerned that they had COVID-19 than non-pregnant women. Among pregnant women, risk factors for depression included lower income, fewer children, unemployment, thinking that one has COVID-19, high-risk pregnancy, earlier gestational age, and increased pregnancy-related stress. Protective factors included increased partner support, healthy behaviors, and positive appraisal of the pregnancy. Thus, being pregnant is associated with reduced risk for depressive symptoms during the pandemic. Increased social support, engaging in health behaviors and positive appraisal may enhance resilience. Future studies of pregnant versus non-pregnant women could clarify the role of pregnancy during stressful events, and clarify aspects of susceptibility and resilience during pregnancy.

Keywords: COVID-19; pregnancy; depression; resilience; experiment

Citation: Yirmiya, K.; Yakirevich-Amir, N.; Preis, H.; Lotan, A.; Atzil, S.; Reuveni, I. Women's Depressive Symptoms during the COVID-19 Pandemic: The Role of Pregnancy. *Int. J. Environ. Res. Public Health* **2021**, *18*, 4298. https://doi.org/10.3390/ijerph18084298

Academic Editor: M. Carmen Míguez Varela

Received: 12 March 2021
Accepted: 13 April 2021
Published: 18 April 2021

1. Introduction

The Coronavirus Disease 2019 (COVID-19) pandemic created a global health crisis, and its mental health implications are only now beginning to unravel. Studies have reported increased levels of psychological distress, anxiety, depression, and post-traumatic stress disorder (PTSD) in the general population, and specifically in reproductive aged women [1–3]. The COVID-19 pandemic has multiple ramifications for pregnant women, including stress surrounding the uncertainty related to prenatal care and the risk of prenatal exposure to the virus [4].

The psychological impact of major stressful events on pregnant and postpartum women has been previously studied with conflicting results [5]. Some studies suggest that peripartum women are at high risk for developing mental health problems in the wake of major stressors, with high rates of depression and other perinatal mental health problems [6–9]. Contrarily, other studies demonstrate resilience among pregnant and postpartum women during natural disasters [10], as well as lower distress levels in the long term compared to women who were not pregnant when the disaster occurred [11]. During the COVID-19 pandemic, several studies revealed that pregnant women have higher rates of anxiety and depressive symptoms when compared to women who were pregnant before the pandemic emerged [12–16]. These studies mostly compared women who were pregnant during the COVID-19 pandemic to women who were pregnant before the pandemic. Interestingly, a study from China, in which pregnant and non-pregnant women were compared during the COVID-19 pandemic, yielded reduced risk for depression, anxiety, insomnia and PTSD among women who were pregnant [17]. A more recent study that compared postpartum women to women who were never pregnant did not show any significant differences in general anxiety and depressive symptoms [18]. There is no doubt that the pandemic affected women's lives intensely; however, there may also be unexpected positive aspects [19]. Hardships experienced during the perinatal period have been previously shown to yield positive outcomes, such as post-traumatic growth [20]. Further studies are warranted to delineate the role of pregnancy on the susceptibility to stress among reproductive-age women.

It is unclear whether pregnancy is a time of increased vulnerability for the onset or worsening of a mental illness, as some research suggests [21], or rather it is more specific for the postpartum period or for a subgroup of vulnerable women [22]. Research suggests that for some women pregnancy serves as a protective developmental stage, as suggested by the low suicide rate during pregnancy and during the two years after giving birth [23,24]. Moreover, attenuated emotional and physiological responses to stress during pregnancy may also contribute to enhanced resilience in pregnant women [25,26]. This may be related to the effect of estrogen on cortisol, as evidenced by blunted cortisol responses to stress in postmenopausal women receiving estrogen treatment [27,28]. During pregnancy, women cope with stress in various ways. Dispositional optimism, social support, and physical activity are related to better psychological and physical well-being during pregnancy [29,30]. A longitudinal study from China revealed that education levels and resilience were associated with both adaptive and maladaptive coping, and that women with maladaptive coping styles experienced more postpartum depression [31]. Among a Spanish cohort of pregnant women, lower resilience was related to obsessive and catastrophic thoughts about the pandemic, while adaptive coping strategies, such as physical exercise or relaxation, were effective in coping with pandemic-related restrictions [32]. Partner support, emotional support and being outdoors have been found to increase resilience and positive coping during the pandemic for women in the perinatal period [33,34]. Determining pregnancy-specific traits, resources, and behaviors that improve pregnant women's mental health during crises could promote resilience during pregnancy.

Untreated depression during pregnancy is associated with detrimental long-term effects on the mother and the infant [35–38]. Women who experience stress during pregnancy, even without depression, are less likely to maintain optimal health behaviors, including healthy eating, vitamin use, and exercise [39,40]. Therefore, examining the potential effects of the pandemic on the mental health of pregnant women is crucial for early identification of depressive symptoms during pregnancy, and the prevention of the long-term outcomes on both the mother and her offspring.

The present study is part of an ongoing international collaboration aiming to investigate the psychological implications of the COVID-19 pandemic among pregnant women [4,34,41]. The results from the United States (US) sample revealed that pregnant women experienced substantial anxiety during the COVID-19 pandemic [4,34]. Increased stress related to the pandemic, as measured by the Pandemic-Related Pregnancy Stress Scale (PREPS), was associated with an increased risk for anxiety above and beyond sociodemographic and obstetric variables [4,42]. The aim of the current study was to determine the risk for depressive symptoms in pregnant and non-pregnant women in Israel during the COVID-19 pandemic, and to identify bio-psycho-social contributors that increase the risk of experiencing depressive symptoms. The results of this study could contribute to the understanding of the role of pregnancy on the vulnerability for depression during times of global crisis.

2. Materials and Methods

2.1. Participants and Study Design

During the second week of May 2020, we recruited a sample of 1380 women through women-related and pregnancy-related social media groups and public pages on Facebook. The advertisements invited non-pregnant women to share their experiences during the COVID-19 pandemic and pregnant women to share their pregnancy experiences during the COVID-19 pandemic. Our inclusion criteria were age 18 years or older and being able to read and write in Hebrew. There were no other exclusion criteria. Women who wished to participate in the study signed an electronic informed consent, and completed the questionnaires online through Qualtrics, a secure online survey system. After identifying 13 duplicate responses, the final sample included 1114 pregnant women: 81 in the first trimester; 430 in the second trimester; 570 in the third trimester; and 33 women who did not report their gestational age but were identified as being pregnant, and 256 non-pregnant women. The majority of women were born in Israel (N = 1187, 86.6%). Participants who completed the questionnaire were enrolled in a raffle to win a ILS 600 gift card (equivalent to approximately USD 150). The study was approved by the Hebrew University of Jerusalem Institutional Review Board on 11 May 2020 (approval number 114120).

2.2. Instruments

Sociodemographic variables included age, years of education, economic status (below average/average or above average), relationship status (married or cohabiting/some or no relationship), current employment status (working or studying/homemaker, unemployed or receiving disability benefits), and number of children under 18.

COVID-19-related variables included having direct contact with an individual medically diagnosed with COVID-19 (no/yes), thinking that one had COVID-19 even if one was not tested (no/unsure/yes), and having access to outdoor space (yes, whenever I want/sometimes/rarely).

Depressive symptoms were assessed using the Patient Health Questionnaire-2 (PHQ-2) [43], which includes the first two items of the PHQ-9 [44]. The two questions inquire about the frequency of depressed mood and anhedonia over the past 2 weeks, on a scale of 0 (not at all) to 3 (nearly every day). The final scores range from 0 to 6 with a higher score indicating a greater risk for depressive disorder. In addition, a cut-off of $\geq$3 was used. The PHQ-2 has been shown to be efficient to rule out depression in 60–80% of pregnant women [45]. In pregnancy, the sensitivity of the PHQ-2 was 69–84% and the specificity was 79–84% [45].

Stress related to pregnancy during the COVID-19 pandemic was assessed using the PREPS questionnaire, a novel instrument created by Preis, Brittain, and Lobel [42], a multidisciplinary research and clinical team with expertise in developing validated instruments to assess prenatal maternal stress and coping. Item themes were based on news articles and media interviews regarding women's experiences during the COVID-19 pandemic, as there was limited research available at the time [42]. Item wording was tested for face validity by pregnant and non-pregnant women before the Stony Brook COVID-19 Pregnancy Experiences (SB-COPE) Study launch. The PREPS questionnaire was translated to several languages, and was found to have good psychometric properties in different populations [46,47]. For the current study, the scale was translated to Hebrew using the forward-and-back translation technique by bilingual researchers (see Supplementary Materials Figure S1). The instrument includes 15 items describing thoughts and concerns that pregnant women might have owing to the COVID-19 pandemic, rated on a scale from 1 (very little) to 5 (very much). The PREPS includes three independent, internally consistent, factors: stress associated with preparations for birth and the postpartum period (7 items; PREPS-Preparedness), stress associated with worries about perinatal COVID-19 infection (5 items; PREPS-Infection), and positive aspects of the pandemic in the context of pregnancy (3 items; PREPS-Positive Appraisal) [42,48]. Confirmatory factor analysis (CFA) was conducted on the Hebrew version to replicate the three-factor structure of the PREPS previously identified, which yielded a good model fit (CFI = 0.929, TLI = 0.910, RMSEA = 0.078). The internal consistency of the subscales PREPS-Infection and PREPS-Preparedness was relatively high ($\alpha > 0.8$). Although the internal consistency of the PREPS-Positive Appraisal subscale was lower than the $\alpha = 0.70$ criterion, inter-item correlation coefficients of all items were > 0.32. Scale scores were calculated as the mean response to items on the corresponding factor.

General stress was assessed using a single general question: "How much stress do you currently have in your life?". Participants were asked to score their answer on a 5-point scale ranging from 1 (very little) to 5 (very much).

Anxiety symptoms were assessed using the Generalized Anxiety Disorder-7 (GAD-7) scale [49], a 7-item self-report instrument to assess anxiety symptoms. Respondents report the frequency of symptoms over the last 2 weeks on a scale ranging from 0 (not at all) to 3 (nearly every day). Individual scores were calculated as a sum of item responses ranging from 0 to 21. The GAD-7 was found to have good reliability and validity for screening anxiety among pregnant women [50,51].

Social support included two single-item questions on perceived support from family or friends and perceived support from a partner (1 = very little to 5 = very much).

Health behaviors were assessed by a single-item question assessing the extent to which women were practicing health behaviors, such as taking vitamins, exercising, and sleeping enough (1 = very little to 5 = very much).

Obstetric factors included gestational age (in weeks), self-reported high-risk pregnancy status (no/yes/unsure), and whether participants had a prenatal care appointment canceled or rescheduled owing to the COVID-19 pandemic (no/yes).

2.3. Statistical Analysis

Statistical analysis was conducted using SPSS for Windows, version 23 [52] and AMOS 21 [53]. We used χ^2 and t tests to examine differences between pregnant and non-pregnant women, with $p < 0.05$ considered statistically significant. Propensity-score matching was performed using Stata version 16.1 [54], KMATCH module [55] with the default parameters, which matches treated and untreated observations with respect to covariates based on propensity-scores, including estimation of treatment effects based on the matched/balanced observations, while including post-matching regression adjustment. For post-estimation evaluation of data balancing, kernel density estimates before and after matching were generated using the "kmatch density" command. Pearson's correlation coefficients were used to assess associations among all study variables. A hierarchical linear regression analysis was conducted among the pregnant women's cohort to predict the risk for depressive symptoms from all the sociodemographic, psychological, and medical factors. A second hierarchical linear regression analysis was conducted among the pregnant and non-pregnant cohorts with the same predictors as the first regression, to examine the contribution of these variables above and beyond the factor of pregnancy in predicting depressive symptoms.

3. Results

3.1. Group Differences between Pregnant and Non-Pregnant Women

Pregnant women reported significantly fewer depressive symptoms than non-pregnant women (see Figure 1a, Table 1). The difference in the depressive symptoms score remained significant even after controlling for age, education, relationship status, income, number of children and employment status ($F_{(1)} = 8.48$, $p < 0.005$). Our data demonstrate that 15.6% of pregnant women were depressed, as defined by a clinical cut-off of 3 or higher [56], whereas 21.9% of non-pregnant women reached this criteria ($X^2_{(1)} = 5.83$, $p = 0.02$). No significant differences were observed between pregnant and non-pregnant women in levels of stress and anxiety (Table 1). Pregnant women were less likely to think that they had COVID-19 than non-pregnant women (Figure 1b, Table 1). Pregnant women also reported having more social support and engaging in more health behaviors than non-pregnant women (Table 1). All differences remained significant following the Bonferroni correction for multiple comparisons, except for education level.

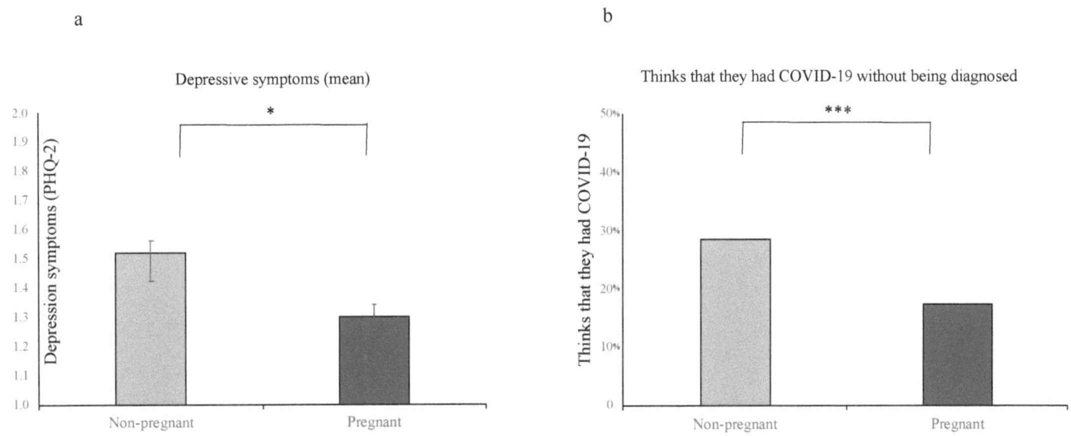

Figure 1. Mental health resiliency in pregnant women. (**a**) Pregnant women show fewer depressive symptoms than non-pregnant women. Depression symptoms were measured using the Patient Health Questionnaire-2 (PHQ-2), which inquires about the frequency of depressed mood and anhedonia over the past two weeks. (**b**) Pregnant women are less concerned that they have COVID-19, even without being diagnosed, compared to non-pregnant women. Note: PHQ-2 = Patient Health Questionnaire-2. * $p < 0.05$, *** $p < 0.001$.

Table 1. Means and standard errors for main study factors among pregnant and non-pregnant women.

Study Variables	Pregnant N = 1114		Non-Pregnant N = 256		χ^2/*t*-Test (df), *p*	Effect Size
	M/%	S.D.	M/%	S.D.		
Sociodemographic variables						
Age	31.88	4.22	35.71	5.42	$t_{(1366)} = 12.38, p < 0.001$	0.79
Years of Education	16.10	2.62	16.59	3.42	$t_{(1368)} = 2.15, p = 0.03$	0.16
Income (Below average)	13.2%		15.6%		$X^2_{(1)} = 1.03, p = 0.31$	−0.93
Relationship status (Married or cohabiting)	96.5%		85.9%		$X^2_{(1)} = 44.87, p < 0.001$	0.18
Current employment status (working)	85.7%		85%		$X^2_{(1)} = 0.07, p = 0.80$	−0.01
Number of children under 18	1.00	1.15	1.93	1.16	$t_{(1368)} = 11.60, p < 0.001$	0.80
COVID-19 related variables						
Contact with someone diagnosed COVID-19	8.5%		9.4%		$X^2_{(1)} = 0.18, p = 0.67$	−0.01
Think they had COVID-19 without being diagnosed	17.4%		28.5%		$X^2_{(1)} = 16.23, p < 0.001$	−0.11
Access to outdoor spaces (whenever)	84.9%		85.2%		$X^2_{(1)} = 0.01, p = 0.91$	0.003
Psychological variables						
Family/friends support (1–5)	3.93	1.09	3.67	1.15	$t_{(1368)} = -3.30, p = 0.001$	0.23
Partner support (1–5)	4.48	0.78	4.21	0.89	$t_{(1329)} = -4.19, p < 0.001$	0.32
Health behaviors (1–5)	3.27	0.99	2.92	1.10	$t_{(1368)} = -5.09, p < 0.001$	0.33
Stress (1–5)	2.91	1.01	2.86	1.05	$t_{(1368)} = -0.64, p = 0.52$	0.05
Anxiety (GAD-7)	5.96	4.76	5.66	5.65	$t_{(1368)} = -0.91, p = 0.36$	0.06
Depression (PHQ-2)	1.30	1.41	1.52	1.56	$t_{(1368)} = 2.06, p = 0.04$	0.15

To account for potential sample selection bias, we applied regression-adjusted propensity-score matching using a combination of age and education (Supplementary Figure S2 and Supplementary Table S3) or age, education, income and employment status (Supplementary Figure S3 and Supplementary Table S4) as covariates. The models showed that while providing the expected superior propensity-score matching, significant effects of pregnancy on PHQ2 scores were consistent with the non-matched results.

3.2. Multivariate Correlates of Depressive Symptoms among Pregnant and Non-Pregnant Women

Being pregnant significantly predicted lower levels of depressive symptoms. Furthermore, women who had lower income, fewer children, women who were unemployed, and those who thought that they had COVID-19 were found to be at higher risk for depressive symptoms. Women with higher perceived partner support and women engaged in more health behaviors had fewer depressive symptoms. The current model explained 9% of the variance in depressive symptoms. The results of the hierarchical linear regression among pregnant and non-pregnant women, with the depressive symptoms score as the dependent variable, are shown in Table 2. The associations between all predicting variables are detailed in Supplementary Table S1.

Table 2. Multiple hierarchical linear regression analyses—prediction of depression (PHQ-2) score among non-pregnant and pregnant women.

Variables	Step 1 (β)	Step 2 (β)	Step 3 (β)
Step 1: Sociodemographic variables			
Being pregnant	−0.08 *	−0.07 *	−0.06 *
Age	−0.03	−0.02	−0.03
Years of Education	−0.05	−0.05	−0.04
Income (Below average)	0.16 ***	0.13 ***	0.11 **
Relationship status (Married or cohabiting)	0.06	0.06	0.05
Current employment status (working)	0.11 **	0.11 **	0.10 **
Number of children under 18	−0.02	−0.02	−0.09 *
Step 2: COVID-19 related variables			
Contact with someone diagnosed COVID-19		−0.02	−0.01
Think they had COVID-19 without being diagnosed		0.10 **	0.10 **
Access to outdoor space (whenever)		0.06	0.05
Step 3: Social support and health behaviors			
Family/friends support (1–5)			−0.04
Partner support (1–5)			−0.10 **
Health behaviors (1–5)			−0.11 ***
F	7.95 ***	7.16 ***	8.17 ***
R^2	0.05	0.06	0.09
ΔR^2	0.05 ***	0.01 **	0.03 ***

* $p < 0.05$, ** $p < 0.01$, *** $p < 0.001$.

3.3. Multivariate Correlates of Depressive Symptoms among Pregnant Women

Among the sociodemographic variables tested, pregnant women who had lower income, fewer children, and women who were unemployed reported elevated depressive symptoms. Women who believed that they had COVID-19 (even if not tested) also reported higher depressive symptoms scores. Women with higher perceived partner support and women who engaged in more healthy behaviors reported fewer depressive symptoms. Among the obstetric variables, having a high-risk pregnancy and earlier gestational age significantly predicted higher depressive symptoms scores. The above-mentioned variables together explained 12.5% of the variance in depressive symptoms among pregnant women. Finally, the PREPS-Preparedness stress scale predicted higher depressive symptoms scores, the PREPS-Positive Appraisal scale predicted lower depressive symptoms scores, while the PREPS Infection stress scale did not predict depressive symptoms. The final model explained 18.5% of the variance in depressive symptoms. The results of the hierarchical linear regression among pregnant women, with the depressive symptoms score as the dependent variable, are shown in Table 3. Pearson's correlation coefficients among all predictive variables are presented in Table S2 in the Supplementary Material.

Table 3. Multiple hierarchical linear regression analyses—prediction of depression (PHQ-2) score among pregnant women.

Variables	Step 1 (β)	Step 2 (β)	Step 3 (β)	Step 4 (β)	Step 5 (β)
Step 1: Sociodemographic variables					
Age	−0.02	−0.02	−0.03	−0.04	−0.005
Years of Education	−0.05	−0.06	−0.04	−0.03	−0.03
Income (Below average)	0.14 ***	0.13 ***	0.11 **	0.09 *	0.08 *
Relationship status (Married or cohabiting)	0.06	0.06	0.05	0.04	0.03
Current employment status (working)	0.11 **	0.11 **	0.10 **	0.09 *	0.09 **
Number of children under 18	−0.02	−0.01	−0.10 **	−0.10 **	−0.08 *
Step 2: COVID-19 related variables					
Contact with someone diagnosed COVID-19		−0.02	−0.01	−0.01	−0.02
Think they had COVID-19 without being diagnosed		0.09 **	0.08 *	0.08 *	0.06 *
Access to outdoor space (whenever)		0.06	0.04	0.03	0.02
Step 3: Social support and health behaviors					
Family/friends support (1–5)			−0.07	−0.06	−0.05
Partner support (1–5)			−0.09 *	−0.07 *	−0.08 *
Health behaviors (1–5)			−0.14 ***	−0.13 ***	−0.09 *
Step 4: Obstetric factors					
Gestational age (weeks)				−0.06	−0.09 *
Prenatal appointment altered/canceled				0.08 *	0.02
High-risk Pregnancy				0.10 **	0.07 *
Step 5: Pandemic-Related Pregnancy Stress (PREPS)					
Preparedness					0.25 ***
Infection					0.03
Positive Appraisal					−0.07 *
F	7.39 ***	6.26 ***	7.85 ***	7.68 ***	10.11 ***
R^2	0.05	0.06	0.10	0.12	0.18
ΔR^2	0.05 ***	0.01 **	0.04 ***	0.03 ***	0.06 ***

* $p < 0.05$, ** $p < 0.01$, *** $p < 0.001$.

4. Discussion

The outbreak of COVID-19 in Israel began at the end of February 2020 and reached the first peak during March and April 2020. During this time, an almost complete lockdown took place for 8 weeks, with substantial social and economic restrictions continuing for months. Furthermore, information on the effects of the virus on pregnancy outcomes and fetal development was scarce. Fear from being infected with the virus, social isolation and the economic turmoil caused by the pandemic had a notable impact on the mental health and wellbeing of the general population, with increased risk for depression and anxiety among women [1,57]. The results of the present study indicate that during the first wave of the COVID-19 pandemic, pregnant women had fewer depressive symptoms than non-pregnant women. Moreover, pregnant women were less likely to think that they have COVID-19 than non-pregnant women. Our results are in line with previous studies that compared pregnant to non-pregnant women's responses to the COVID-19 pandemic [17,58]; however, these studies were with relatively smaller samples. Our results may indicate that being pregnant contributes to enhanced resilience in times of crisis and severe stress, and warrant further research on the underlying mechanisms.

Psychosocial determinants are well-known factors that affect vulnerability to experience depression throughout life, and specifically in the perinatal period. In the present study, pregnant women reported experiencing more perceived partner support than non-pregnant women, and partner support significantly predicted lower levels of depressive symptoms among pregnant and non-pregnant women during the pandemic. Partner support is a well-known protective factor against depression during the perinatal period [59–62], especially in times of crisis and stress [63]. These results are consistent with reports of pregnant women during the COVID-19 pandemic that demonstrate higher perceived social support was associated with less depressive symptoms [21], whereas a lack of social support was related to increased risk for perinatal depressive symptoms [64]. In a mixed-methods pilot study from the US, pregnant women who reported feelings of isolation and loneliness also reported that partner support was the most important protective factor which helped them to cope with the pandemic [33]. Moreover, we found that health-related behaviors were significantly more frequent among pregnant women than among non-pregnant women, and that these behaviors also significantly predicted fewer depressive symptoms. The relationship between health behaviors and depression is well-established in the literature [65–67], and specifically during pregnancy [68]. This relationship has been reported both at non-challenging times and during the pandemic [21,69]. In a parallel study in the US, pregnant women who were engaged in more positive health behaviors were also found to have less anxiety symptoms [34]. A Finnish study monitoring pregnant women's daily patterns of heart rate variability, physical activity and sleep data showed that these variables were associated with coping better with pandemic-related restrictions [70]. Therefore, improving women's social support networks and encouraging socially distant healthy activities, such as online fitness classes suitable for pregnant women, may be targets for enhancing resilience to depression among pregnant women during the pandemic.

We found that vulnerability for depression is also associated with financial and employment problems. In Israel, pregnant women are protected by law from layoffs during pregnancy and the postpartum period [71], and women receive paid maternal leave for the first fourteen weeks after birth [72]. These factors may protect against experiencing depressive symptoms and enhance resilience among pregnant women, especially in light of the detrimental economic and psychosocial effects of the COVID-19 pandemic. This is supported by recent findings from Canada, which showed that pregnant women with high income compared to low income were less likely to experience distress and psychiatric symptoms during the COVID-19 pandemic [12]. Another recent study from the US revealed that COVID-19-related financial stress was associated with a significantly increased likelihood of depression during pregnancy [73]. Implementing policies related to job security and stable income for pregnant women may serve as protective factors and improve their mental health.

Among the obstetric variables measured in the study, depressive symptoms were inversely correlated with gestational age and were positively correlated with a high-risk pregnancy. Pregnancy complications are well-known risk factors for postpartum and antenatal depression [74,75]. Women who have a high-risk pregnancy should be considered at risk for depression, especially during the COVID-19 pandemic. Our findings, which show increased levels of depression earlier in pregnancy, are not in line with research reporting higher levels of depression towards the end of the pregnancy [76]. Interestingly, a recent longitudinal study of 135 pregnant women showed an increase in depressive symptoms after COVID-19 compared to measurements before the pandemic started. However, the levels of depressive symptoms after COVID-19 were as high as those during early pregnancy [77]. It is unclear whether depression levels earlier in pregnancy in our cohort were related to the unique circumstances of the initial stages of the pandemic, or rather reflect a possible rise in depression symptoms during the beginning of pregnancy. Further research is needed to confirm and understand the results regarding the relation between gestational age and depressive symptoms.

Depression scores among pregnant women were predicted by several factors related to the pandemic. First, women believing they have COVID-19 (even without being diagnosed) was associated with a higher depressive symptoms score. Second, the Preparedness Stress score predicted a greater likelihood of depressive symptoms, indicating that women who were worried about being unprepared for the birth due to the pandemic were more likely to experience depressive symptoms. In line with these results, a recent study of women who were pregnant during the COVID-19 pandemic found that higher depressive symptoms were associated with more concerns about not getting the necessary prenatal care [21]. We also found that the pandemic-related positive appraisal score reflected resilience, as it was inversely associated with the depressive symptoms score. The transition to motherhood is an opportunity for personal growth and finding meaning in life and gratitude [78]. Positive appraisal, in other words, focusing on the "positive aspects of a stressful situation when one possesses the intrapersonal and tangible resources that help to ensure a favorable outcome" [79], has been shown to be predictive of lower distress levels in pregnant women [79,80]. Having a positive attitude towards the effects of the pandemic on a woman's pregnancy and expected birth may represent a coping mechanism, which allows women to cope and adjust to the major life change they are about to undergo. Implementing psychotherapeutic interventions that enhance the use of positive appraisal and changes in maladaptive cognitive processes may contribute to reducing perinatal depressive symptoms during the pandemic.

There are several limitations to this study. First, the study was conducted online with self-report questionnaires. However, this enabled the recruitment of a large number of women during a short period of time, which was crucial in light of the rapidly progressing situation worldwide. Second, it should be noted that this is a cross-sectional study, which provides a snapshot of the mental health of women in May 2020. During that time, there was a relatively small number of COVID-19-related infections and death cases (an average of 2.188 new infections and 0.233 new death cases per million people per day [81]). However, the lockdown and movement restrictions applied, as well as the uncertainty regarding the influence of the COVID-19 pandemic worldwide, created an atmosphere of stress and anxiety. The results may not necessarily signify a direct causal association between pregnancy and resilience, but rather suggest that other factors that are related to pregnancy, such as social connection and support, may mediate the relationship between pregnancy and resilience. Future stages of the current study and other studies will be able to evaluate the course of mental health symptoms and their sequela throughout the pandemic. Third, this type of self-selected sampling could be biased because most participants were born in Israel, married, and secular, limiting the generalizability of our results. The pandemic has disproportionately impacted racial minorities and lower-income families [82], which are underrepresented in our cohort. Moreover, more severely depressed women are probably less likely to go online and be willing to participate in a study. Lastly, PHQ-2 may not be ideal for the assessment of depression during pregnancy, as there are different instruments that specifically address anxiety and depression during the perinatal period. However, this instrument was chosen as it is a concise and internationally validated screening tool for depression [43,56,83,84]. The psychometric properties are good and show that a negative response to the PHQ-2 rules out depression efficaciously [45]. The major strength of this study is the relatively large cohort that was recruited over a short period of time, facilitating the investigation of the specific effects of COVID-19-pandemic-related variables.

5. Conclusions

Being pregnant may operate as a protective factor against depressive symptoms during a time of crisis, such as the COVID-19 pandemic. Increased social support, engaging in more health behaviors and applying positive appraisal are related to enhanced resilience from depression during pregnancy. Future studies that compare pregnant versus non-pregnant women could clarify the role of pregnancy on women's mental health during times of hardship. Furthermore, studies would benefit from distinguishing between experiences of depression and anxiety that call for professional help, as opposed to cases in which some degree of sadness, anxiety, fear, anger, and short-term adjustment issues are reasonable and even expected responses [85]. As the pandemic continues, prospective follow-up of women through the perinatal period may yield more information regarding the differential effects of stress during pregnancy and postpartum and should identify the mechanisms of mental health effects of COVID-19. Promoting economic policies and psychosocial interventions to protect pregnant women during the COVID-19 pandemic is essential to ensure positive long-term outcomes and minimize societal and gender gaps.

Supplementary Materials: The following are available online at https://www.mdpi.com/article/10.3390/ijerph18084298/s1, Table S1: Pearson correlations of study variables among pregnant and non-pregnant women, Table S2: Pearson correlations of study variables among pregnant women. Table S3: Propensity-score matching using a combination of age and education—Stata output, Table S4: Propensity-score matching using a combination of age, education, income and employment status—Stata output. Figure S1: COVID-19 Related Thoughts in Pregnancy (Preis, Mahaffey, and Lobel, 2020), Figure S2: Propensity-score matching using a combination of age and education—evaluating balancing of the data, Figure S3: Propensity-score matching using a combination of age, education, income and employment status—evaluating balancing of the data.

Author Contributions: K.Y., H.P., S.A. and I.R. designed the study. K.Y. and N.Y.-A. conducted the data collection. K.Y., A.L. carried out statistical analysis. All authors have read and agreed to the published version of the manuscript.

Funding: No funds: grants, or other support was received.

Institutional Review Board Statement: This study was performed in line with the principles of the Declaration of Helsinki. Approval was granted by the Ethics Committee of the Hebrew University of Jerusalem Institutional Review Board (approval number 114120).

Informed Consent Statement: Informed consent was obtained from all subjects involved in the study.

Data Availability Statement: The datasets used and/or analyzed during the current study are available from the corresponding author upon request.

Acknowledgments: We are grateful to H.P., Brittain Mahaffey and Marci Lobel for initiating this international research collaboration. K.Y. would like to thank the Azrieli Foundation for the award of an Azrieli Fellowship.

Conflicts of Interest: The authors declare no conflict of interest.

References

1. Xiong, J.; Lipsitz, O.; Nasri, F.; Lui, L.M.W.; Gill, H.; Phan, L.; Chen-Li, D.; Iacobucci, M.; Ho, R.; Majeed, A.; et al. Impact of COVID-19 pandemic on mental health in the general population: A systematic review. *J. Affect. Disord.* **2020**, *277*, 55–64. [CrossRef]
2. Salari, N.; Hosseinian-Far, A.; Jalali, R.; Vaisi-Raygani, A.; Rasoulpoor, S.; Mohammadi, M.; Rasoulpoor, S.; Khaledi-Paveh, B. Prevalence of stress, anxiety, depression among the general population during the COVID-19 pandemic: A systematic review and meta-analysis. *Glob. Health* **2020**. [CrossRef] [PubMed]
3. Pierce, M.; Hope, H.; Ford, T.; Hatch, S.; Hotopf, M.; John, A.; Kontopantelis, E.; Webb, R.; Wessely, S.; McManus, S.; et al. Mental health before and during the COVID-19 pandemic: A longitudinal probability sample survey of the UK population. *Lancet Psychiatry* **2020**, *7*, 883–892. [CrossRef]
4. Preis, H.; Mahaffey, B.; Heiselman, C.; Lobel, M. Vulnerability and resilience to pandemic-related stress among U.S. women pregnant at the start of the COVID-19 pandemic. *Soc. Sci. Med.* **2020**. [CrossRef] [PubMed]
5. Harville, E.; Xiong, X.; Buekens, P. Disasters and Perinatal Health: A Systematic Review. *Obstet. Gynecol. Surv.* **2010**, *65*, 713–728. [CrossRef] [PubMed]
6. Truijens, S.E.M.; Boerekamp, C.A.M.; Spek, V.; Van Son, M.J.M.; Oei, S.G.; Pop, V.J.M. Increased Levels of Depressive Symptoms among Pregnant Women in The Netherlands After the Crash of Flight MH17. *Am. J. Epidemiol.* **2015**. [CrossRef] [PubMed]
7. Goto, A.; Bromet, E.J.; Ota, M.; Ohtsuru, A.; Yasumura, S.; Fujimori, K. The Fukushima Nuclear Accident Affected Mothers' Depression but Not Maternal Confidence. *Asia Pac. J. Public Health* **2017**. [CrossRef]
8. Brock, R.L.; O'Hara, M.W.; Hart, K.J.; McCabe-Beane, J.E.; Williamson, J.A.; Brunet, A.; Laplante, D.P.; Yu, C.; King, S. Peritraumatic Distress Mediates the Effect of Severity of Disaster Exposure on Perinatal Depression: The Iowa Flood Study. *J. Trauma Stress* **2015**. [CrossRef]
9. Nishigori, H.; Sugawara, J.; Obara, T.; Nishigori, T.; Sato, K.; Sugiyama, T.; Okamura, K.; Yaegashi, N. Surveys of postpartum depression in Miyagi, Japan, after the Great East Japan Earthquake. *Arch. Womens Ment. Health* **2014**. [CrossRef]

10. Harville, E.W.; Xiong, X.; Buekens, P.; Pridjian, G.; Elkind-Hirsch, K. Resilience after Hurricane Katrina among pregnant and postpartum women. *Womens Health Issues* **2011**, *20*, 1–5. [CrossRef]
11. Pomer, A.; Buffa, G.; Ayoub, M.-B.; Taleo, F.; Sizemore, J.H.; Tokon, A.; Chan, C.W.; Kaneko, A.; Obed, J.; Iaruel, J.; et al. Psychosocial distress among women following a natural disaster in a low- to middle-income country: "healthy mothers, healthy communities" study in Vanuatu. *Arch. Womens Ment. Health* **2019**. [CrossRef] [PubMed]
12. Berthelot, N.; Lemieux, R.; Garon-Bissonnette, J.; Drouin-Maziade, C.; Martel, É.; Maziade, M. Uptrend in distress and psychiatric symptomatology in pregnant women during the coronavirus disease 2019 pandemic. *Acta Obstet. Gynecol. Scand.* **2020**, *99*, 848–855. [CrossRef]
13. Wu, Y.; Zhang, C.; Liu, H.; Duan, C.; Li, C.; Fan, J.; Li, H.; Chen, L.; Xu, H.; Li, X.; et al. Perinatal depressive and anxiety symptoms of pregnant women during the coronavirus disease 2019 outbreak in China. *Am. J. Obstet. Gynecol.* **2020**, *21*, 1–9. [CrossRef]
14. Zanardo, V.; Manghina, V.; Giliberti, L.; Vettore, M.; Severino, L.; Straface, G. Psychological impact of COVID-19 quarantine measures in northeastern Italy on mothers in the immediate postpartum period. *Int. J. Gynecol. Obstet.* **2020**. [CrossRef]
15. Hessami, K.; Romanelli, C.; Chiurazzi, M.; Cozzolino, M. COVID-19 pandemic and maternal mental health: A systematic review and meta-analysis. *J. Matern. Neonatal. Med.* **2020**, 1–8. [CrossRef]
16. Racine, N.; Hetherington, E.; McArthur, B.A.; McDonald, S.; Edwards, S.; Tough, S.; Madigan, S. Maternal depressive and anxiety symptoms before and during the COVID-19 pandemic in Canada: A longitudinal analysis. *Lancet Psychiatry* **2021**. [CrossRef]
17. Zhou, Y.; Shi, H.; Liu, Z.; Peng, S.; Wang, R.; Qi, L.; Li, Z.; Yang, J.; Ren, Y.; Song, X.; et al. The prevalence of psychiatric symptoms of pregnant and non-pregnant women during the COVID-19 epidemic. *Transl. Psychiatry* **2020**. [CrossRef]
18. Hompson, K.A.; Bardone-Cone, A.M. 2019-nCOV distress and depressive, anxiety and OCD-type, and eating disorder symptoms among postpartum and control women. *Arch. Women's Ment. Health* **2021**, 1–10.
19. Nelson, B. The positive effects of covid-19. *BMJ* **2020**. [CrossRef] [PubMed]
20. Denckla, C.A.; Mancini, A.D.; Consedine, N.S.; Milanovic, S.M.; Basu, A.; Seedat, S.; Spies, G.; Henderson, D.C.; Bonanno, G.A.; Koenen, K.C. Distinguishing postpartum and antepartum depressive trajectories in a large population-based cohort: The impact of exposure to adversity and offspring gender. *Psychol. Med.* **2018**. [CrossRef]
21. Lebel, C.; MacKinnon, A.; Bagshawe, M.; Tomfohr-Madsen, L.; Giesbrecht, G. Elevated depression and anxiety symptoms among pregnant individuals during the COVID-19 pandemic. *J. Affect. Disord.* **2020**. [CrossRef] [PubMed]
22. Bloch, M.; Schmidt, P.J.; Danaceau, M.; Murphy, J.; Nieman, L.; Rubinow, D.R. Effects of Gonadal Steroids in Women with a History of Postpartum Depression. *Am. J. Psychiatry* **2000**, *157*, 924–930. [CrossRef] [PubMed]
23. Oates, M. Suicide: The leading cause of maternal death. *Br. J. Psychiatry* **2003**, *183*, 279–281. [CrossRef] [PubMed]
24. Payne, J.L. Depression: Is pregnancy protective? *J. Women's Health* **2012**, *21*, 809–810. [CrossRef]
25. De Weerth, C.; Buitelaar, J.K. Physiological stress reactivity in human pregnancy—A review. *Neurosci. Biobehav. Rev.* **2005**. [CrossRef] [PubMed]
26. Christian, L.M. Physiological reactivity to psychological stress in human pregnancy: Current knowledge and future directions. *Prog. Neurobiol.* **2012**. [CrossRef]
27. Komesaroff, P.A.; Esler, M.D.; Sudhir, K. Estrogen Supplementation Attenuates Glucocorticoid and Catecholamine Responses to Mental Stress in Perimenopausal Women1. *J. Clin. Endocrinol. Metab.* **1999**. [CrossRef]
28. Herrera, A.Y.; Hodis, H.N.; Mack, W.J.; Mather, M. Estradiol Therapy After Menopause Mitigates Effects of Stress on Cortisol and Working Memory. *J. Clin. Endocrinol. Metab.* **2017**. [CrossRef]
29. Lobel, M.; Hamilton, J.G.; Cannella, D.T. Psychosocial Perspectives on Pregnancy: Prenatal Maternal Stress and Coping. *Soc. Pers. Psychol. Compass* **2008**. [CrossRef]
30. Ng, Q.X.; Venkatanarayanan, N.; Loke, W.; Yeo, W.-S.; Lim, D.Y.; Chan, H.W.; Sim, W.-S. A meta-analysis of the effectiveness of yoga-based interventions for maternal depression during pregnancy. *Complement. Ther. Clin. Pr.* **2019**, *34*, 8–12. [CrossRef]
31. Yu, M.; Gong, W.; Taylor, B.; Cai, Y.; Xu, D.R. Coping Styles in Pregnancy, Their Demographic and Psychological Influences, and Their Association with Postpartum Depression: A Longitudinal Study of Women in China. *Int. J. Environ. Res. Public Health* **2020**, *17*, 3654. [CrossRef] [PubMed]
32. López, D.M.L.; Hinojo, C.A.B.; Bernal, J.E.A.; Laiz, M.F.; Santiago, J.A.; Vilches, V.G.; Fernández, M.C.; Moral, A.B.; Perdigones, A.O.; Rodríguez, B.R.; et al. Resilience and psychological distress in pregnant women during quarantine due to the COVID-19 outbreak in Spain: A multicentre cross-sectional online survey. *J. Psychosom. Obstet. Gynecol.* **2021**, 1–8. [CrossRef]
33. Farewell, C.V.; Jewell, J.; Walls, J.; Leiferman, J.A. A Mixed-Methods Pilot Study of Perinatal Risk and Resilience During COVID-19. *J. Prim. Care Community Health* **2020**. [CrossRef]
34. Preis, H.; Mahaffey, B.; Heiselman, C.; Lobel, M. Pandemic-related pregnancy stress and anxiety among women pregnant during the COVID-19 pandemic. *Am. J. Obstet. Gynecol.* **2020**, *2*, 100155.
35. Grigoriadis, S.; VonderPorten, E.H.; Mamisashvili, L.; Tomlinson, G.; Dennis, C.-L.; Koren, G.; Steiner, M.; Mousmanis, P.; Cheung, A.; Radford, K.; et al. The Impact of Maternal Depression during Pregnancy on Perinatal Outcomes. *J. Clin. Psychiatry* **2013**. [CrossRef]
36. Jarde, A.; Morais, M.; Kingston, D.; Giallo, R.; MacQueen, G.M.; Giglia, L.; Beyene, J.; Wang, Y.; McDonald, S.D. Neonatal Outcomes in Women with Untreated Antenatal Depression Compared With Women Without Depression. *JAMA Psychiatry* **2016**. [CrossRef]

37. Gentile, S. Untreated depression during pregnancy: Short- and long-term effects in offspring. A systematic review. *Neuroscience* **2017**, *342*, 154–166. [CrossRef] [PubMed]
38. Talge, N.M.; Neal, C.; Glover, V. Antenatal maternal stress and long-term effects on child neurodevelopment: How and why? *J. Child Psychol. Psychiatry* **2007**, *48*, 245–261. [CrossRef] [PubMed]
39. Lobel, M.; Cannella, D.L.; Graham, J.E.; DeVincent, C.; Schneider, J.; Meyer, B.A. Pregnancy-specific stress, prenatal health behaviors, and birth outcomes. *Health Psychol.* **2008**, *27*, 604–615. [CrossRef]
40. Ibrahim, S.M.; Lobel, M. Conceptualization, measurement, and effects of pregnancy-specific stress: Review of research using the original and revised Prenatal Distress Questionnaire. *J. Behav. Med.* **2020**, *43*, 16–33. [CrossRef] [PubMed]
41. Preis, H.; Mahaffey, B.; Pati, S.; Heiselman, C.; Lobel, M. Adverse Perinatal Outcomes Predicted by Prenatal Maternal Stress among U.S. Women at the COVID-19 Pandemic Onset. *Ann. Behav. Med.* **2021**, *55*, 179–191. [PubMed]
42. Preis, H.; Mahaffey, B.; Lobel, M. Psychometric properties of the Pandemic-Related Pregnancy Stress Scale (PREPS). *J. Psychosom. Obstet. Gynecol.* **2020**, *41*, 191–197. [CrossRef] [PubMed]
43. Kroenke, K.; Spitzer, R.L.; Williams, J.B.W. The Patient Health Questionnaire-2: Validity of a two-item depression screener. *Med. Care* **2003**, *41*, 1284–1292. [CrossRef]
44. Spitzer, R.L.; Kroenke, K.; Williams, J.B.W. Validation and utility of a self-report version of PRIME-MD: The PHQ Primary Care Study. *J. Am. Med. Assoc.* **1999**. [CrossRef] [PubMed]
45. Vlenterie, R.; Van Ras, H.W.; Roeleveld, N.; Pop-Purceleanu, M.; Van Gelder, M.M. Epidemiological evaluation of the Patient Health Questionnaire-2 in a pregnant population. *J. Psychosom. Res.* **2017**. [CrossRef]
46. Weitkamp, K.; Romer, G.; Rosenthal, S.; Wiegand-Grefe, S.; Daniels, J. German Screen for Child Anxiety Related Emotional Disorders (SCARED): Reliability, validity, and cross-informant agreement in a clinical sample. *Child. Adolesc. Psychiatry Ment. Health* **2010**. [CrossRef] [PubMed]
47. Ilska, M.; Kołodziej-Zaleska, A.; Brandt-Salmeri, A.; Preis, H.; Lobel, M. Pandemic-related pregnancy stress assessment–Psychometric properties of the Polish PREPS and its relationship with childbirth fear. *Midwifery* **2021**, *96*, 102940. [CrossRef]
48. Schaal, N.K.; La Marca-Ghaemmaghami, P.; Preis, H.; Mahaffey, B.; Lobel, M.; Castro, R.A. The German version of the pandemic-related pregnancy stress scale: A validation study. *Eur. J. Obstet. Gynecol. Reprod. Biol.* **2021**. [CrossRef]
49. Spitzer, R.L.; Kroenke, K.; Williams, J.B.W.; Löwe, B. A Brief Measure for Assessing Generalized Anxiety Disorder. *Arch. Intern. Med.* **2006**. [CrossRef]
50. Zhong, Q.-Y.; Gelaye, B.; Zaslavsky, A.M.; Fann, J.R.; Rondon, M.B.; Sanchez, S.E.; Williams, M.A. Diagnostic Validity of the Generalized Anxiety Disorder—7 (GAD-7) among Pregnant Women. *PLoS ONE* **2015**. [CrossRef]
51. Gong, Y.; Zhou, H.; Zhang, Y.; Zhu, X.; Wang, X.; Shen, B.; Xian, J.; Ding, Y. Validation of the 7-item Generalized Anxiety Disorder scale (GAD-7) as a screening tool for anxiety among pregnant Chinese women. *J. Affect. Disord.* **2021**, *282*, 98–103. [CrossRef] [PubMed]
52. IBM. IBM SPSS Statistics 23. *Release Notes* **2016**. [CrossRef]
53. Arbuckle, J.L. *Amos*; IBM SPSS.: Chicago, IL, USA, 2012.
54. STATA. *Stata: Software for Statistics and Data Science*; STATA: College Station, TX, USA, 2020.
55. Jann, B. KMATCH: Stata module for multivariate-distance and propensity-score matching, including entropy balancing, inverse probability weighting, (coarsened) exact matching, and regression adjustment. In *Statistical Software Components*; IDEAS: Nashville, TN, USA, 2017.
56. Arrieta, J.; Aguerrebere, M.; Raviola, G.; Flores, H.; Elliott, P.; Espinosa, A.; Reyes, A.; Ortiz-Panozo, E.; Rodriguez-Gutierrez, E.G.; Mukherjee, J.; et al. Validity and Utility of the Patient Health Questionnaire (PHQ)-2 and PHQ-9 for Screening and Diagnosis of Depression in Rural Chiapas, Mexico: A Cross-Sectional Study. *J. Clin. Psychol.* **2017**. [CrossRef] [PubMed]
57. Wang, C.; Pan, R.; Wan, X.; Tan, Y.; Xu, L.; Ho, C.S.; Ho, R.C. Immediate Psychological Responses and Associated Factors during the Initial Stage of the 2019 Coronavirus Disease (COVID-19) Epidemic among the General Population in China. *Int. J. Environ. Res. Public Health* **2020**, *17*, 1729. [CrossRef] [PubMed]
58. Sade, S.; Sheiner, E.; Wainstock, T.; Hermon, N.; Salem, S.Y.; Kosef, T.; Battat, T.L.; Oron, S.; Pariente, G. Risk for Depressive Symptoms among Hospitalized Women in High-Risk Pregnancy Units during the COVID-19 Pandemic. *J. Clin. Med.* **2020**, *9*, 2449. [CrossRef]
59. O'Hara, M.W.; Swain, A.M. Rates and risk of postpartum depression—A meta-analysis. *Int. Rev. Psychiatry* **1996**. [CrossRef]
60. Milgrom, J.; Hirshler, Y.; Reece, J.; Holt, C.; Gemmill, A.W. Social Support-A Protective Factor for Depressed Perinatal Women? *Int. J. Environ. Res. Public Health* **2019**, *16*, 1426. [CrossRef]
61. Stapleton, L.R.T.; Schetter, C.D.; Westling, E.; Rini, C.; Glynn, L.M.; Hobel, C.J.; Sandman, C.A. Perceived partner support in pregnancy predicts lower maternal and infant distress. *J. Fam. Psychol.* **2012**. [CrossRef]
62. Seguin, L.; Potvin, L.; St-Denis, M.; Loiselle, J. Chronic stressors, social support, and depression during pregnancy. *Obstet. Gynecol.* **1995**. [CrossRef]
63. Lee, D.T.; Sahota, D.; Leung, T.N.; Yip, A.S.; Lee, F.F.; Chung, T.K. Psychological responses of pregnant women to an infectious outbreak: A case-control study of the 2003 SARS outbreak in Hong Kong. *J. Psychosom. Res.* **2006**. [CrossRef]
64. Brik, M.; Sandonis, M.A.; Fernández, S.; Suy, A.; Parramon-Puig, G.; Maiz, N.; Dip, M.E.; Ramos-Quiroga, J.A.; Carreras, E. Psychological impact and social support in pregnant women during lockdown due to SARS-CoV2 pandemic: A cohort study. *Acta Obstet. Gynecol. Scand.* **2021**. [CrossRef]

65. Cooney, G.M.; Dwan, K.; Greig, C.A.; Lawlor, D.A.; Rimer, J.; Waugh, F.R.; McMurdo, M.; Mead, G.E. Exercise for depression (Review). *Cochrane Libr.* **2013**. [CrossRef]
66. Rebar, A.L.; Stanton, R.; Geard, D.; Short, C.; Duncan, M.J.; Vandelanotte, C. A meta-meta-analysis of the effect of physical activity on depression and anxiety in non-clinical adult populations. *Health Psychol. Rev.* **2015**. [CrossRef] [PubMed]
67. Ashdown-Franks, G.; Sabiston, C.M.; Stubbs, B. The evidence for physical activity in the management of major mental illnesses. *Curr. Opin. Psychiatry* **2019**. [CrossRef]
68. Davenport, M.H.; McCurdy, A.P.; Mottola, M.F.; Skow, R.J.; Meah, V.L.; Poitras, V.J.; Garcia, A.J.; Gray, E.C.; Barrowman, N.; Riske, L.; et al. Impact of prenatal exercise on both prenatal and postnatal anxiety and depressive symptoms: A systematic review and meta-analysis. *Br. J. Sports Med.* **2018**. [CrossRef]
69. Davenport, M.H.; Meyer, S.; Meah, V.L.; Strynadka, M.C.; Khurana, R. Moms Are Not OK: COVID-19 and Maternal Mental Health. *Front. Glob. Womens Health* **2020**. [CrossRef]
70. Niela-Vilén, H.; Auxier, J.; Ekholm, E.; Sarhaddi, F.; Mehrabadi, M.A.; Mahmoudzadeh, A.; Azimi, I.; Liljeberg, P.; Rahmani, A.M.; Axelin, A. Pregnant women's daily patterns of well-being before and during the COVID-19 pandemic in Finland: Longitudinal monitoring through smartwatch technology. *PLoS ONE* **2021**, *16*, e0246494. [CrossRef] [PubMed]
71. Labor branch—Ministry of Labor, Welfare and Social Services. Maternity Rights in Workplace. Available online: https://www.gov.il/he/Departments/Guides/workers-rights-during-maternity-leave (accessed on 17 August 2020).
72. Labor branch—Ministry of Labor, Welfare and Social Services. Workplace Rights of Pregnant Women and Their Spouses. Available online: https://www.gov.il/he/departments/guides/labor-rights-during-pregnancy-and-birthwork (accessed on 17 August 2020).
73. Thayer, Z.M.; Gildner, T.E. COVID-19-related financial stress associated with higher likelihood of depression among pregnant women living in the United States. *Am. J. Hum. Biol.* **2020**. [CrossRef] [PubMed]
74. Biaggi, A.; Conroy, S.; Pawlby, S.; Pariante, C.M. Identifying the women at risk of antenatal anxiety and depression: A systematic review. *J. Affect. Disord.* **2016**. [CrossRef] [PubMed]
75. Rodrigues, P.B.; Zambaldi, C.F.; Cantilino, A.; Sougey, E.B. Special features of high-risk pregnancies as factors in development of mental distress: A review. *Trends Psychiatry Psychother.* **2016**, *38*, 136–140. [CrossRef]
76. Okagbue, H.I.; Adamu, P.I.; Bishop, S.A.; Oguntunde, P.E.; Opanuga, A.A.; Akhmetshin, E.M. Systematic Review of Prevalence of Antepartum Depression during the Trimesters of Pregnancy. *Open Access Maced. J. Med Sci.* **2019**. [CrossRef]
77. Perzow, S.E.; Hennessey, E.-M.P.; Hoffman, M.C.; Grote, N.K.; Davis, E.P.; Hankin, B.L. Mental health of pregnant and postpartum women in response to the COVID-19 pandemic. *J. Affect. Disord. Rep.* **2021**, *4*, 100123. [CrossRef]
78. Prinds, C.; Hvidt, N.C.; Mogensen, O.; Buus, N. Making existential meaning in transition to motherhood—A scoping review. *Midwifery* **2014**. [CrossRef]
79. Ibrahim, S.M.; Nicoloro-SantaBarbara, J.; Auerbach, M.V.; Rosenthal, L.; Kocis, C.; Busso, C.E.; Lobel, M. Pregnancy-specific coping and changes in emotional distress from mid- to late pregnancy. *J. Reprod. Infant Psychol.* **2019**. [CrossRef]
80. Giurgescu, C.; Penckofer, S.; Maurer, M.C.; Bryant, F.B. Impact of Uncertainty, Social Support, and Prenatal Coping on the Psychological Well-being of High-risk Pregnant Women. *Nurs. Res.* **2006**. [CrossRef]
81. Ministry of Health. Israeli Ministry of Health Basket. 2021. Available online: https://www.health.gov.il/hozer/mk03_2018.pdf (accessed on 12 April 2021).
82. Hooper, M.W.; Nápoles, A.M.; Pérez-Stable, E.J. COVID-19 and Racial/Ethnic Disparities. *JAMA* **2020**, *323*, 2466–2467. [CrossRef]
83. Matthey, S.; Bilbao, F. A comparison of the PHQ-2 and MGMQ for screening for emotional health difficulties during pregnancy. *J. Affect. Disord.* **2018**. [CrossRef]
84. Löwe, B.; Kroenke, K.; Gräfe, K. Detecting and monitoring depression with a two-item questionnaire (PHQ-2). *J. Psychosom. Res.* **2005**. [CrossRef]
85. Ng, Q.X.; Lim, D.Y.; Chee, K.T. Not all trauma is the same. *Proc. Natl. Acad. Sci. USA* **2020**, *117*, 25200. [CrossRef]

International Journal of
Environmental Research and Public Health

MDPI

Article

Perinatal Anxiety Symptoms: Rates and Risk Factors in Mexican Women

Janeth Juarez Padilla [1], Sandraluz Lara-Cinisomo [1], Laura Navarrete [2] and Ma. Asunción Lara [2,*]

[1] Department of Kinesiology and Community Health, College of Applied Health Sciences, University of Illinois at Urbana-Champaign, Champaign, IL 61820, USA; janethj2@illinois.edu (J.J.P.); laracini@illinois.edu (S.L.-C.)
[2] Innovation and Global Health Department, Ramon de la Fuente Muñiz National Institute of Psychiatry, Tlalpan, Mexico City 14370, Mexico; laurae@imp.edu.mx
* Correspondence: laracan@imp.edu.mx; Tel.: +52-55-4160-5170

Abstract: Anxiety during pregnancy and after childbirth can have negative consequences for a woman and her baby. Despite growing interest in the perinatal mental health of Mexican women living in the U.S., perinatal anxiety symptom (PAS) rates and risk factors have yet to be established for women in Mexico. We sought to determine PAS rates and identify risk factors, including the traditional female role (TFR) in a sample of Mexican women. This secondary data analysis is based on 234 Mexican women who participated in a longitudinal study on perinatal depression in Mexico. Anxiety symptoms were assessed in pregnancy and at six weeks postpartum. Rates were determined through frequencies, and multiple logistics regressions were conducted to identify risk factors in the sample. The PAS rate was 21% in pregnancy and 18% postpartum. Stressful life events and depressive symptoms were associated with a higher probability of PAS. Adherence to TFR increased the probability of prenatal anxiety; lower educational attainment and low social support during pregnancy increased the probability of postpartum anxiety. The PAS rates were within the range reported in the literature. The TFR was only associated with anxiety in gestation, highlighting the role of this culturally relevant risk factor. Culturally responsive early interventions are therefore required.

Keywords: perinatal anxiety symptoms; traditional female role; risk factors

Citation: Juarez Padilla, J.; Lara-Cinisomo, S.; Navarrete, L.; Lara, M.A. Perinatal Anxiety Symptoms: Rates and Risk Factors in Mexican Women. *Int. J. Environ. Res. Public Health* **2021**, *18*, 82. https://dx.doi.org/10.3390/ijerph18010082

Received: 14 December 2020
Accepted: 18 December 2020
Published: 24 December 2020

1. Introduction

Anxiety during the perinatal period (pregnancy and first postpartum year) is a global health issue because of its negative consequences for the mother and her baby [1–4]. However, perinatal anxiety symptoms (PAS) are not always diagnosed or treated, increasing the risks for both. Previous data show that women in low- and middle-income countries have a high prevalence of anxiety compared to those in more affluent countries [5]. Although anxiety has been assessed in individuals of Mexican descent living in the U.S. and Mexican women [6–8], the prevalence of PAS in Mexico has not been fully studied. To our knowledge, only one study has explored anxiety symptoms in Mexican women. Navarrete et al. (2012) found a 14.8% prevalence of anxiety in pregnancy and 10.6% at six weeks postpartum in Mexican women with depressive symptoms [9]. However, the study did not explore risk factors to explain observed rates because its focus was depressive symptoms.

While risk factors, such as not having a partner [10,11], lower social support [12–14], lower partner satisfaction [15–17], and multiparity [18] for perinatal depression have been identified, their associations with PAS have yet to be determined among perinatal women living in Mexico. Cesarean delivery and stressful life events [18–21] are risk factors for PAS in Colombia, Australia, and Rwanda, while resilience has been identified as a protective factor for PAS [22]. Nevertheless, these factors have not been tested in women living in Mexico.

During the perinatal period, Mexican women may experience culturally relevant stressors that may increase their risk of PAS such as traditional female role (TFR) expectations. Adherence to the TFR, defined as being submissive, conforming, indecisive, and passive, attributed to socialization within a structure that undervalues women, is particularly relevant here [23,24]. Although the TFR has been associated with depression in Mexican women at six weeks postpartum [25], its links with anxiety have not been tested. It is important to understand the role of the TFR as a risk factor for PAS to develop interventions and improve women's mental health during pregnancy and the postpartum period.

The purpose of this study was to determine PAS rates in a sample of women receiving prenatal care who were followed postpartum to identify demographic, psychosocial, and culturally relevant risk factors to inform interventions and treatment options. We hypothesized that (a) women would have higher rates of anxiety during pregnancy than in the postpartum period; (b) cesarean delivery, psychosocial stressors (i.e., high levels of stressful life events, low social support, low educational attainment, not having a partner, and low partner satisfaction) would increase the likelihood of PAS; and (c) high depressive symptoms, low resilience levels, and high adherence to the TFR would increase the likelihood of anxiety during the perinatal period.

2. Materials and Methods

2.1. Participants

A non-probabilistic sample of 280 pregnant women receiving prenatal care agreed to participate in the parent study. Of these women, 234 (83.6%) were assessed during pregnancy and followed up at six weeks postpartum and were included in this study (Figure 1). Women were approached in the waiting rooms of a hospital that provides comprehensive medical care to state employees and a primary health center that provides prenatal and other medical care to the local community. To be eligible, women had to be at least 20 years of age, ≥26 weeks pregnant, and living in the Mexico City metropolitan area; women with bipolar disorder were excluded. Eligible participants who agreed to be interviewed provided written consent.

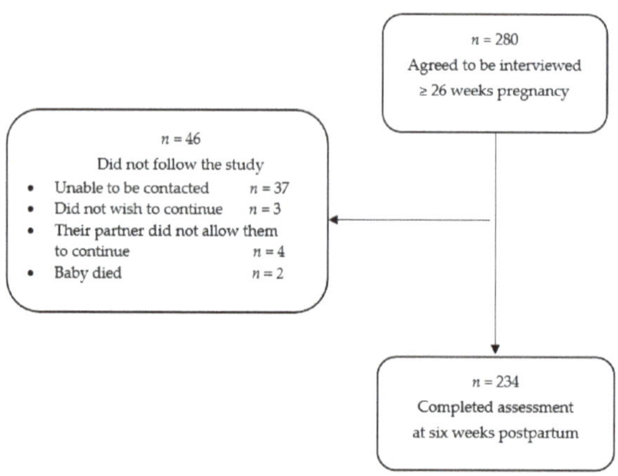

Figure 1. Participant flow diagram.

2.2. Procedures

Data were collected by trained final year psychology students and graduate psychology research assistants affiliated to the lead research institution. Interviews were conducted at ≥26 weeks of pregnancy and six weeks postpartum. The study was approved by the Institutional Review Board (IRB) of Ramon de la Fuente Muñiz National Institute of Psychiatry.

2.3. Measures

Sociodemographic information, including age, monthly family income, marital status, and educational attainment, were collected during the enrollment interview (≥26 weeks pregnant). Obstetric data included the number of children (collected at ≥26 weeks pregnant) and type of delivery in this pregnancy (collected at six weeks postpartum). Anxiety symptoms were assessed using the 10-item anxiety subscale from the Symptoms Checklist-90 or SCL-90 [26]. Participants reported the degree of distress they had experienced during the previous fortnight using a five-point Likert scale (none = 0; extreme = 4). The scale was validated in Mexico [27,28]. A score of ≥18 was considered an indicator of high anxiety symptomatology [26]. This instrument showed an internal consistency of $\alpha = 0.80$ in Mexican women and has been used with perinatal women [9,29].

Because depression is treated as a risk factor here, the Patient Health Questionnaire (PHQ-9) was used to assess depressive symptoms [30]. This is a nine-item depression module from the full PHQ, specifically developed for use in primary care. The PHQ-9 has proven its usefulness as an assessment tool for the diagnosis of depression with acceptable reliability, validity, sensitivity, and specificity; a score of ≥10 indicates a risk of depression [31]. The PHQ-9 was validated in Mexican women, showing an internal consistency of 0.89 [32] and estimated for this sample showing adequate validity: pregnancy: $\alpha = 0.78$ and six weeks postpartum: $\alpha = 0.80$.

Resilience was measured with the Resilience Inventory (RESI; [33]), designed to measure resilience in Mexican mothers. The RESI comprises seven dimensions: positive attitude, sense of humor, perseverance, religiosity, self-efficacy, optimism and goal orientation. Response options range from 1 (not at all) to 5 (completely), while the total score indicates the degree of resilience. The RESI was validated in this sample demonstrating good internal consistency ($\alpha = 0.88$) in pregnant women and adequate concurrent validity for prenatal depressive symptoms ($r = 0.27$; $p = 0.00$) and stressful life events ($r = -0.19$; $p = 0.00$) [34]. In the absence of a pre-established cut-off point, the median minus one standard deviation [34] was used to determine high vs. low resilience.

Stressful life events were measured using the Life Events Scale, a brief, 12 item-form including potential stressors (such as illness, financial problems, accident, job loss or intimate partner violence) selected from the 23 original items [35], developed from Holmes and Rahe's instrument [36], among other scales. These twelve items were considered more pertinent in the perinatal period [37]. The scale evaluates the occurrence of each event over the past six months as well as the perceived degree of stress it produced (0 = event was not present; 1 = present but produced no stress, 2 = produced little stress, 3 = produced moderate stress, 4 = produced great stress). A cut-off point of 13 was calculated as the 75th percentile to determine high vs. low-stress life events.

The Spanish version [38] of the English Postpartum Depression Predictors Inventory -Revised (PDPI-R) social support subscale [39] was used during pregnancy and postpartum. The 12-item scale quantifies the presence of instrumental and emotional support from the woman's partner, mother, and other family members and friends. Each item is scored using dichotomous responses with a 0 (absent) or 1 (present), creating a possible summed range of scores from 0 to 12, where higher scores indicate greater support. This instrument has been validated in a sample of pregnant women and has shown adequate concurrent validity in postpartum samples [40]. The scale showed adequate reliability ($\alpha = 0.84$) [40]. In the absence of a pre-established cut-off point, the median minus one standard deviation [40] was used to determine high vs. low social support.

The marital satisfaction subscale was also taken from the Spanish version [38] of the PDPI-R [39]. The three-item scale measures how satisfied women feel about the relationship with their partner or the father of their child. Each item is scored using dichotomous responses with a 0 (absent) or 1 (present), creating a possible summed range of scores from 0 to 3. This scale showed adequate concurrent validity compared with the Edinburgh Postnatal Depression Scale ($r = 0.39$; $p = 0.001$) in a sample of pregnant Mexican women [40].

A cut-off point was determined using the median minus one standard deviation (1) for high vs. low relationship satisfaction.

The TFR was measured in pregnancy through eight questions from the submissive subscale of the Inventario de Masculinidad y Femineidad (IMAFE; [24]). The scale measures the personality traits expected in many cultures, particularly those of Mexican women [24]. Using a 0 ("I'm never or almost never like this") to 7 ("I'm always or almost always like this") scale, participants indicated the extent to which each trait describes them, such that higher scores represented higher levels of TFR. The items included were being conformist, submissive, indecisive, having a weak personality, being resigned, cowardly, withdrawn, and shy. This short version demonstrated adequate reliability in this sample ($\alpha = 0.83$) [25]. The submissive subscale has also shown adequate reliability in other Latin American countries, such as Colombia [41,42]. A cut-off point was determined using the median plus one standard deviation [25], indicating high vs. low adherence to a TFR.

2.4. Data Analyses

Frequencies/percentages were calculated for categorical data. The point prevalence of anxiety symptoms was calculated as the percentage of women with anxiety symptoms at each point of assessment (≥26 weeks pregnant; sixth week postpartum). The McNemar test was performed to determine whether there is a difference in the prevalence of anxiety between the two times. To identify risk factors for anxiety symptoms, a bivariate logistic regression analysis was conducted to estimate odds ratios (ORs) with 95% confidence intervals. To identify the PAS risk factors, multivariate logistic regressions were performed. All analyses were performed using the SPSS version 21 (IBM Corp, Armonk, NY, USA).

3. Results

3.1. Participants

Participants had an average age of 29 (SD = 6.2), with an average monthly income of $498.70 U.S. dollars (SD = 502.3), an average of 12 years of schooling (equivalent to middle school), and had at least one child. Most had a partner and had given birth by cesarean section. Table 1 shows the distributions of perceived social support, experienced stressful life events, and adherence to the TRF. During pregnancy, 20.4% met the criteria for depressive symptoms, and 17.1% met the cutoff at six weeks postpartum.

3.2. PAS Prevalence Rates and Risk Factors

PAS rates (SCL-90 ≥ 18) were 22.1% and 17.5% at six weeks postpartum (shown as Table 2). Results from the McNemar analysis showed that there was no significant difference between perinatal periods (McNemar $\chi^2 = 1.30$; $p = 0.25$).

3.3. Regressions to Determine the Effects of Risk and Protective Factors on PAS

The bivariate logistic regressions to determine associations between psychosocial and culturally relevant factors and anxiety symptoms during pregnancy indicated that prenatal women who were single were at more than twice the risk of reporting prenatal anxiety symptoms than women who were in a relationship (OR = 2.59); prenatal women with low resilience were nearly three times more likely to report prenatal anxiety symptoms than women with high resilience (OR = 2.87); prenatal women with high adherence to the TFR were four times as likely to report prenatal anxiety symptoms than women with low adherence to the TFR (OR = 4.07); prenatal women with low relationship satisfaction had a four times higher risk of reporting prenatal anxiety symptoms than women with high marital satisfaction (OR = 4.03); women with low social support had a greater likelihood of prenatal anxiety symptoms than those with high social support (OR = 6.17); women who experienced stressful events were eight times as likely to report prenatal anxiety symptoms than women who did not (OR = 8.40); having depressive symptoms increased the risk nearly sevenfold (OR = 6.63).

Table 1. Demographic, obstetric, and psychosocial risk factor characteristics.

		$\bar{x}$	SD
Age		28.9	6.2
Monthly family income		498.7	502.3
Educational attainment (years)		12.7	3.8
Number of children		0.81	0.89
		n	%
Marital status	Partnered	223	79.6
	Single	57	20.4
Delivery	Vaginal	85	36.3
	Cesarean	149	63.7
Resilience during pregnancy	Low	57	20.4
	High	223	79.6
Traditional female role during pregnancy	Low	206	73.6
	High	74	26.4
Marital satisfaction during pregnancy	Low	68	24.3
	High	212	75.7
Social support during pregnancy	Low	42	15.0
	High	238	85.0
Stressful life events during pregnancy	With events	59	21.1
	Without events	221	78.9
Depressive symptoms during pregnancy	With symptoms	57	20.4
	Without symptoms	223	79.6
Social support during the postpartum period	Low	40	17.1
	High	194	82.9
Stressful life events during the postpartum period	With events	45	16.1
	Without events	189	67.5
Depressive symptoms during the postpartum period	With symptoms	40	20.1
	Without symptoms	194	79.9

Note: n = 234 women; $\bar{x}$ = Mean; SD = Standard Deviation.

The bivariate logistic regressions (Table 3) to determine the association between psychosocial and culturally relevant factors and anxiety symptoms during the sixth week postpartum showed that prenatal women who were single were over twice as likely to report postpartum anxiety symptoms than married women (OR = 2.25); higher educational attainment is associated with a reduction in the probability of reporting postpartum anxiety (OR = 0.89); prenatal women with low resilience had twice the odds of reporting postpartum anxiety symptoms than women with high resilience (OR = 2.24); prenatal women with low marital satisfaction had more than twice the odds of reporting postpartum anxiety symptoms than women with high marital satisfaction (OR = 2.43); prenatal women with low social support had six times the odds of reporting postpartum anxiety symptoms than women with high social support (OR = 6.63); postpartum women with low social support had twice the odds of reporting postpartum anxiety symptoms than women with high social support (OR = 2.85); prenatal women who experienced stressful events had three times the odds of reporting postpartum anxiety symptoms than women who did not (OR = 3.47); postpartum women who experienced stressful events had seven times the odds of reporting postpartum anxiety symptoms than women who did not (OR = 7.39); prenatal women with depressive symptoms had four times the odds of reporting postpartum anxiety symptoms than women who did not (OR = 4.55); and postpartum women with depressive symptoms had eleven times the odds of reporting postpartum anxiety symptoms than women who did not (OR = 11.25).

In the multivariate model of anxiety in pregnancy, the following variables were included as risk factors: age, monthly family income, educational attainment, number of children, marital status, resilience, TFR, marital satisfaction, social support, stressful life events, and depressive symptoms during pregnancy. The model showed that prenatal women with high adherence to the TFR were at twice the risk of experiencing prenatal anxiety symptoms as women with low adherence to the TFR (OR = 2.28). Stressful events increased the risk of PAS fourfold (OR = 4.35), while prenatal women with depressive symptoms were at four times the risk of reporting prenatal anxiety symptoms as women without them (OR = 3.82) (Table 4).

Table 2. Perinatal anxiety symptom rates.

	Pregnancy (*n* = 280)	**Sixth Week Postpartum** (*n* = 234)
	n (%)	*n* (%)
With anxiety symptoms	62 (22.1)	41 (17.5)
Without anxiety symptoms	218 (77.9)	193 (82.5)

McNemar $\chi^2 = 1.30$, $p = 0.25$.

Table 3. Bivariate odds ratios (ORs) with 95% confidence intervals (CIs) for demographic, obstetric and psychosocial variables associated withanxiety symptoms in pregnancy and sixth postpartum week.

Variables	**Time 1. Pregnancy** (*n* = 280)	**Time 2. Sixth Week Postpartum** (*n* = 234)
	OR (95% CI)	OR (95% CI)
Age	0.99 (0.95–1.04)	0.97 (0.92–1.03)
Monthly family income	0.99 (0.89–1.03)	0.99 (0.84–1.49)
Single	2.59 (1.37–4.90) *	2.25 (1.05–4.80) *
Educational attainment	0.95 (0.89–1.03)	0.89 (0.81–0.97) *
Number of children	1.10 (0.81–1.50)	1.31 (0.78–1.63)
Cesarean delivery	–	1.15 (0.57–2.29)
Low resilience during pregnancy	2.87 (1.52–5.41) **	2.24 (1.03–4.89) *
Traditional female role during pregnancy	4.07 (2.23–7.41) **	1.95 (0.95–4.01)
Low marital satisfaction during pregnancy	4.03 (2.19–7.40) **	2.43 (1.17–2.42) *
Low social support during pregnancy	6.17 (3.07–12.41) **	6.63 (2.85–15.42) **
Stressful life events during pregnancy	8.40 (4.40–16.02) **	3.47 (1.66–7.27) **
Depressive symptoms during pregnancy	6.63 (3.49–12.58) **	4.55 (2.15–9.59) **
Low social support during the postpartum period	–	2.85 (1.31–6.18) *
Stressful life events during the postpartum period	–	7.39 (3.50–15.60) **
Depressive symptoms during the postpartum period	–	11.25 (5.14–24.61) **

** $p \leq 0.01$, * $p \leq 0.05$.

In the multivariate model of anxiety at six weeks postpartum, the following variables were included as risk factors: age, monthly family income, educational attainment, number of children, marital status, cesarean-delivery, resilience, TFR, marital satisfaction, social support, stressful life events, and depressive symptoms during pregnancy, and social support, stressful life events, and depressive symptoms during the postpartum period. The analysis showed that higher educational attainment was associated with a reduction in the probability of reporting postpartum anxiety symptoms (OR = 0.84), while women with low social support during pregnancy had almost five times the risk of reporting postpartum anxiety symptoms as women with high social support (OR = 5.60). Additionally, the risk of reporting postpartum anxiety symptoms was more than five times higher in those who experienced stressful events post-childbirth than in those who did not (OR = 5.42), while the risk of reporting postpartum anxiety symptoms was nine times higher in those with postpartum depressive symptoms than in those without them (OR = 9.03) (Table 5).

Table 4. Multivariate logistic regression model of anxiety symptoms during pregnancy.

Pregnancy (n = 280)		
	OR	95% CI
Age	1.01	0.95–1.08
Monthly family income	0.99	0.93–1.10
Educational attainment	1.06	0.94–1.20
Number of children	0.85	1.50–6.68
Single	1.72	0.70–4.25
Low resilience during pregnancy	1.16	0.48–2.78
Traditional female role during pregnancy	2.28 *	1.06–4.88
Low marital satisfaction during pregnancy	1.32	0.54–3.25
Low social support during pregnancy	2.25	0.92–5.50
Stressful life events during pregnancy	4.35 **	2.02–9.37
Depressive symptoms during pregnancy	3.82 **	1.72–8.48

$\chi^2 = 77.11$ $p = 0.00$ ** $p \leq 0.01$, * $p \leq 0.05$.

Table 5. Multivariate logistic regression model of six weeks postpartum anxiety symptoms.

Six Weeks Postpartum (n = 234)		
	OR	95% CI
Age	0.94	0.86–1.03
Monthly family income	0.99	0.96–1.22
Educational attainment	0.84 *	0.72–0.99
Number of children	0.82	0.32–2.11
Single	3.03	0.92–9.80
Cesarean delivery section	1.01	0.37–2.68
Low resilience during pregnancy	2.00	0.65–6.11
Traditional female role during pregnancy	0.90	0.31–3.08
Low marital satisfaction during pregnancy	5.06	1.50–20.84
Low social support during pregnancy	2.25 *	0.92–5.50
Stressful life events during pregnancy	0.98	0.31–3.08
Depressive symptoms during pregnancy	1.89	0.66–5.37
Low social support during the postpartum period	0.30	0.07–1.19
Stressful life events during the postpartum period	5.42 **	1.84–15.89
Depressive symptoms during the postpartum period	9.03 **	3.24–15.12

$\chi^2 = 72.11$ $p = 0.00$ ** $p \leq 0.01$, * $p \leq 0.05$.

4. Discussion

As hypothesized, low levels of social support, stressful life events, and depressive symptoms significantly increased the odds of PAS. The TFR increased the odds of anxiety symptoms during pregnancy. We found that women who reported low levels of social support during pregnancy had five times the odds of PAS. These findings support the growing body of research showing that low social support is associated with increased anxiety during the perinatal period [43–45]. However, previous studies did not include women living in Mexico, where there are 34.9 million women of reproductive age [46], with much of the research focusing on English-speaking countries (such as the United States, Europe, and Australia). To our knowledge, this is the first study to assess the role of social support in PAS in Mexico. Given that anxiety might be more culturally acceptable than depression [47], these findings can help pave the way to increasing discussions about perinatal mental health in Mexico, which continues to be severely understudied and inadequately addressed. These findings can also help inform intervention in Mexico and other Latin American countries, where the role of social support during the perinatal period may change as a result of family migration and women's increased workforce participation [48].

The results also showed that women who experienced stressful life events had nearly four times the odds of experiencing anxiety in pregnancy and nearly five times the odds of experiencing it postpartum. Although the assessment of stressful life events is based on retrospective data, the degree to which they caused stress is informative because stressful life events can have lasting, potentially detrimental effects particularly during a vulnerable period such as pregnancy and first-time motherhood [44,49,50]. Practitioners should therefore assess women living in Mexico for stressful life events to identify women at risk of developing PAS. Researchers are encouraged to develop early interventions to reduce the effects of stressful life events on the development of anxiety in these women.

As predicted, experiencing depressive symptoms at the time of assessment significantly increased the odds of PAS by a factor of 3.82 in pregnancy and of 9.03 postpartum. The growing body of research on depression shows that depression and anxiety are often comorbid [51,52]. However, the extent to which depression or depressive symptoms impact the likelihood of anxiety is less clear. This study helps clarify these associations and underlines the need to assess the presence of both throughout the perinatal period. While directionality was not established here, the results suggest that depressive symptoms might exacerbate feelings of anxiety, particularly in women where depression is stigmatized and not properly addressed. Results from a previous study show that prenatal anxiety symptoms were predictive of postpartum depressive symptoms in Mexican women [10]. As can be seen in Table 1, 20 percent of prenatal and postpartum women had depressive symptoms, which is at the top end of the range among women in the general U.S. population [53] and other countries [54], yet within the range of Latinas in the U.S. at 20–43% [15,18,55–57]. This highlights the importance of early prevention and detection.

Unlike the previously discussed risk factors, adherence to the TFR was significantly associated with PAS in pregnancy. A recent systematic review showed that the TFR was inconsistently associated with prenatal depression, but significantly and indirectly associated with postpartum depression [58]. Although this is the first study to examine the associations between TFR and PAS, we can draw on previous literature, which suggests that the limitations and gender-related biases women experience, particularly in a male-dominated culture, induce anxious symptoms and increase the risk of other mental health issues [59]. Because of the male-dominated culture in Mexico and the submissive role women and mothers are expected to assume, it will be important to determine how and why adherence to the TFR increases the risk of anxiety in women in Mexico to inform interventions and target specific policies that perpetuate those practices [60]. An additional necessary step is to determine why the TFR increased the odds of anxiety in pregnancy in this sample of Mexican women. One possible explanation is the social pressures pregnant women in Mexico experience. As previously mentioned, motherhood is revered in Mexico, but so are behaviors that may dictate what a woman can or cannot do, such as only seeking mental health treatment or participating in a study interview or experiment after receiving approval from her partner [37] and prioritizing bearing children even though they are working women [61–63]. The TFR might also conflict with the growing independence observed in Mexican women. For instance, although women in Mexico are engaged in the labor force and pursue higher education, they continue to experience gender-role expectations, such as serving as the primary caregiver and being submissive to a male partner [62,63]. These gender-role restrictions and expectations may be heightened in pregnancy when motherhood is added to the mix. Given the potentially complex factors that contribute to the TFR, future studies should determine whether the effects of this risk factor differ from pre-conception to pregnancy to help advance theory and inform intervention.

Though this study addresses significant gaps in the literature, several limitations exist. Preconception data on the risk factors involved could help explain whether the effect of stressful life events and low social support on anxiety symptoms is a function of motherhood or a consequence of those events. Previous literature has shown that stressful life events are indirectly associated with anxiety in adolescence and adulthood because of the rumination that ensues in the wake of these events [64]. It is possible that the onset of motherhood may trigger feelings associated with these stressful life events, which in turn could increase the risk of anxiety in women. However, this is speculation that should be tested by including those who have not conceived or given birth. A second limitation is the expectations and effectiveness of social support. Studies on depression in the perinatal period have shown that women in the perinatal period have specific expectations of and needs for social support during this life transition [65–67]. However, less is known about expectations of social support and their effects on anxiety. Future studies should therefore explore this area of inquiry to inform interventions. Moreover, because effective support is important, subsequent studies should also inquire as to how women define the support, they deem efficacious and help them identify sources of support that can provide this. A third limitation is the lack of information regarding the TFR before gestation. As suggested above, motherhood may increase specific gender-role expectations in the woman and those around her. It will therefore be important to assess levels of adherence to the TFR before gestation. On a related note, future studies should inquire as to whether adherence to the TFR is self-imposed or influenced by those around a woman, which can help inform interventions and psychoeducation before gestation and throughout the perinatal period. Furthermore, women in this study were predominantly Mexican women living in Mexico. Thus, the findings may be limited to Mexican women and it is unclear whether the findings would be the same for women from other Latin American countries or Latinas in the U.S.

Despite these limitations, the findings from this study can help inform clinical practice and increase early diagnoses by health care providers, particularly in Mexico, which can increase early intervention and decrease the long-term effects of PAS. For example, health providers working with perinatal women should assess anxiety levels as well as the presence of the risk factors identified here. Given the multigenerational implications of PAS, women and children will benefit from early prevention and appropriate treatment in the short- and long-term.

5. Conclusions

This study is the first to investigate PAS rates among women living in Mexico. PAS risk factors such as stressful life events, low social support, and depression support the findings in the literature. However, our study also found that the traditional female role was a risk factor for anxiety in pregnancy. This finding shows that the traditional female role is a temporary and culturally relevant risk factor among these women. Early culturally appropriate interventions are therefore needed. Although there is a dearth of interventions designed to address gender-role risk factors among Mexican mothers [10,68], researchers and clinical practitioners can draw on culturally-relevant interventions designed to improve poor maternal mental health outcomes among women of Mexican descent [69–71] and other Latina women. Recent studies using complementary and integrative health interventions, such as music therapy [72,73], have yielded encouraging results. The use of complementary and integrative health approaches is particularly important given potential fears of stigma and barriers to traditional psychotherapeutic and pharmacological interventions among Latina women [74]. While our study sampled perinatal women living in Mexico, the findings suggest that future studies on women of Mexican descent should consider evaluating culturally relevant factors such as the traditional female role.

Author Contributions: Conceptualization, J.J.P.; methodology, L.N. and M.A.L.; formal analysis, L.N. and M.A.L.; resources, M.A.L.; writing—original draft preparation, J.J.P., S.L.-C., L.N., and M.A.L.; writing—review and editing, J.J.P., S.L.-C., L.N., and M.A.L.; visualization, L.N. and M.A.L.; supervision, M.A.L. and S.L.-C. All authors have read and agreed to the published version of the manuscript.

Funding: The overall research project was supported by the Consejo Nacional de Ciencia y Tecnología (CONACyT, Mexico. CB-2009-01 133923) and the present study by the Minority Health and Health Disparities Research Training by National Institute on Minority Health and Health disparities (T37MD003405) Latino Mental Health Research Training Program at the University of Southern California.

Institutional Review Board Statement: Ethical review and approval were waived for this study, due to an Institutional Review Board error where the parent study approval document was not given a protocol code.

Informed Consent Statement: Informed consent was obtained from all subjects involved in the parent study.

Data Availability Statement: The data presented in this study are available on requested from the corresponding author. The data can be available from the repository of the Ramon de la Fuente Muñiz National Institute of Psychiatry.

Acknowledgments: We are grateful to the staff and patients at the Centro de Salud Ángel Brioso Vasconcelos and the Hospital Regional del ISSSTE. Adolfo López Mateos.

Conflicts of Interest: The authors declare they have no conflict of interest.

References

1. O'Hara, M.W.; Wisner, K.L. Perinatal mental illness: Definition, description and aetiology. *Best Pract. Res. Clin. Obstet. Gynaecol.* **2014**, *28*, 3–12. [CrossRef] [PubMed]
2. Harrison, V.; Moore, D.; Lazard, L. Supporting perinatal anxiety in the digital age; a qualitative exploration of stressors and support strategies. *BMC Pregnancy Childbirth* **2020**, *20*, 363. [CrossRef] [PubMed]
3. Field, T. Prenatal anxiety effects: A review. *Infant Behav. Dev.* **2017**, *49*, 120–128. [CrossRef] [PubMed]
4. Field, T. Postnatal anxiety prevalence, predictors and effects on development: A narrative review. *Infant Behav. Dev.* **2018**, *51*, 24–32. [CrossRef] [PubMed]
5. Dennis, C.L.; Falah-Hassani, K.; Shiri, R. Prevalence of antenatal and postnatal anxiety: Systematic review and meta-analysis. *Br. J. Psychiatry* **2017**, *210*, 315–323. [CrossRef]
6. Becerra, D.; Hernandez, G.; Porchas, F.; Castillo, J.; Nguyen, V.; Perez González, R. Immigration policies and mental health: Examining the relationship between immigration enforcement and depression, anxiety, and stress among Latino immigrants. *J. Ethn. Cult. Divers. Soc. Work* **2020**, *29*, 43–59. [CrossRef]
7. Donato, K.M.; Caron, L.; Hamilton, E. Migration and mental health in Mexico: Domestic migrants, return U.S. migrants, and non-migrants. *Front. Psychiatry* **2019**, *10*, 970. [CrossRef]
8. Farina, A.S.J.; Kremer, K.P.; Caldera Wimmer, S.; Villarreal-Otalera, T.; Paredes, T.; Stuart, E. Anxiety, depression, and trauma among immigrant Mexican women up to two-years post-partum. *J. Immigr. Minority Health* **2020**. [CrossRef]
9. Navarrete, L.E.; Lara, M.A.; Navarro, C.; Gomez, M.E.; Morales, F. Psychosocial factors predicting postnatal anxiety symptoms and their relation to symptoms of postpartum depression. *Rev. Investig. Clin.* **2012**, *64*, 625–633.
10. Lara, M.A.; Navarrete, L.; Nieto, L. Prenatal predictors of postpartum depression and postpartum depressive symptoms in Mexican mothers: A longitudinal study. *Arch. Women's Ment. Health* **2016**, *19*, 825–834. [CrossRef]
11. Weiss-Laxer, N.S.; Johnson, S.B.; Ghazarian, S.R.; Osborne, L.M.; Riley, A.W. Maternal behavioral health symptom profiles in early family life: Complexity and context. *Arch. Women's Ment. Health* **2020**, *23*, 429–439. [CrossRef] [PubMed]
12. De Castro, F.; Place, J.M.; Billings, D.L.; Rivera, L.; Frongillo, E.A. Risk profiles associated with postnatal depressive symptoms among women in a publicsector hospital in Mexico: The role of sociodemographic and psychosocial factors. *Arch. Women's Ment. Health* **2015**, *18*, 463–471. [CrossRef]
13. Chen, H.H.; Chien, L.Y. A comparative study of domestic decision-making power and social support as predictors of postpartum depressive and physical symptoms between immigrant and native-born women. *PLoS ONE* **2020**, *15*, e0231340. [CrossRef] [PubMed]
14. Gao, L.; Qu, J.; Wang, A.Y. Anxiety, depression and social support in pregnant women with a history of recurrent miscarriage: A cross-sectional study. *J. Reprod. Infant Psychol.* **2020**, *38*, 497–508. [CrossRef]
15. Marcos-Najera, R.; Rodriguez-Munoz, M.F.; Lara, M.A.; Navarrete, L.; Le, H.N. A cross-cultural analysis of the prevalence and risk factors for prenatal depression in Spain and Mexico. *Cult. Med. Psychiatry* **2020**. [CrossRef] [PubMed]
16. Mukherjee, S.; Fennie, K.; Coxe, S.; Madhivanan, P.; Trepka, M.J. Racial and ethnic differences in the relationship between antenatal stressful life events and postpartum depression among women in the United States: Does provider communication on perinatal depression minimize the risk? *Ethn. Health* **2018**, *23*, 542–565. [CrossRef] [PubMed]
17. Recto, P.; Champion, J.D. Social support and perinatal depression: The perspectives of Mexican-American adolescent mothers. *Issues Ment. Health Nurs.* **2020**, *41*, 932–939. [CrossRef] [PubMed]
18. Lara, M.A.; Le, H.N.; Letechipia, G.; Hochhausen, L. Prenatal depression in Latinas in the U.S. and Mexico. *Matern. Child Health J.* **2009**, *13*, 567–576. [CrossRef]
19. Clout, D.; Brown, R. Sociodemographic, pregnancy, obstetric, and postnatal predictors of postpartum stress, anxiety and depression in new mothers. *J. Affect. Disord.* **2015**, *188*, 60–67. [CrossRef]
20. Ricardo-Ramírez, C.; Álvarez-Gómez, M.; Ocampo-Saldarriaga, M.V.; Tirado-Otálvaro, A.F. Prevalencia de tamizaje positivo para depresión y ansiedad en gestantes de alto riesgo obstétrico en una clínica de Medellín, entre enero y agosto de 2013. Factores de riesgo asociados. *Rev. Colomb. Obstet. Ginecol.* **2015**, *66*, 94–102. [CrossRef]
21. Umuziga, M.P.; Adejumo, O.; Hynie, M. A cross-sectional study of the prevalence and factors associated with symptoms of perinatal depression and anxiety in Rwanda. *BMC Pregnancy Childbirth* **2020**, *20*, 68. [CrossRef] [PubMed]

22. Ma, X.; Wang, Y.; Hu, H.; Tao, X.G.; Zhang, Y.; Shi, H. The impact of resilience on prenatal anxiety and depression among pregnant women in Shanghai. *J. Affect. Disord.* **2019**, *250*, 57–64. [CrossRef] [PubMed]
23. Johannesen-Schmidt, M.C.; Eagly, A.H. Another look at sex differences in preferred mate characteristics: The effects of endorsing the traditional female gender role. *Psychol. Women Q.* **2002**, *26*, 322–328. [CrossRef]
24. Lara, M.A. *Inventario de Masculinidad-Femineidad: IMAFE*; El Manual Moderno: Mexico City, Mexico, 1993.
25. Albuja, A.F.; Lara, M.A.; Navarrete, L.; Nieto, L. Social support and postpartum depression revisited: The traditional female role as moderator among Mexican women. *Sex Roles* **2017**, *77*, 209–220. [CrossRef]
26. Derogatis, L.R. *Administration, Scoring and Procedures Manual-I for the Revised Version SCL-90R*; Johns Hopkins University School of Medicine: Baltimore, MD, USA, 1977.
27. Cruz-Fuentes, C.; López, L.; Blas-Gracia, C.; González, L.; Chávez, R. Datos sobre la validez y la confiabilidad de la Symptom Check List (SCL-90) en una muestra de sujetos mexicanos. *Salud Ment.* **2005**, *28*, 72–81.
28. Lara, C.; Espinosa, I.; Cárdenas, M.L.; Fócil, M.; Cavazos, J. Confiabilidad y validez de la SCL-90 en la evaluación de psicopatología en mujeres. *Salud Ment.* **2005**, *28*, 42–50.
29. Meades, R.; Ayers, S. Anxiety measures validated in perinatal populations: A systematic review. *J. Affect. Disord.* **2011**, *133*, 1–15. [CrossRef]
30. Spitzer, R.L.; Kroenke, K.; Williams, J.B. Validation and utility of a self-report version of PRIME-MD: The PHQ primary care study. Primary care evaluation of mental disorders. Patient Health Questionnaire. *JAMA* **1999**, *282*, 1737–1744. [CrossRef]
31. Kroenke, K.; Spitzer, R.L.; Williams, J.B. The PHQ-9: Validity of a brief depression severity measure. *J. Gen. Intern. Med.* **2001**, *16*, 606–613. [CrossRef]
32. Familiar, I.; Ortiz-Panozo, E.; Hall, B.; Vieitez, I.; Romieu, I.; Lopez-Ridaura, R.; Lajous, M. Factor structure of the Spanish version of the Patient Health Questionnaire-9 in Mexican women. *Int. J. Methods Psychiatr. Res.* **2015**, *24*, 74–82. [CrossRef]
33. Gaxiola Romero, J.C.; Frías Armenta, M.; Hurtado Abril, M.F.; Salcido Noriega, L.C.; Figueroa Franco, M. Validación del inventario de resiliencia (IRES) en una muestra del noroeste de México. *Enseñanza Investig. Psicol.* **2011**, *16*, 73–83.
34. Nieto, L.; Lara, M.A.; Navarrete, L.; Duenas, K.; Rodriguez, K. Psychometric properties of the resilience inventory for pregnant Mexican women. *Summa Psicol.* **2018**, *15*, 35–42. [CrossRef]
35. Lara, M.A.; Navarro, C.; Navarrete, L. The influence of life events and social support in a psycho-educational intervention for women with depression. *Salud Pública Mex.* **2004**, *46*, 378–387. [CrossRef]
36. Holmes, T.H.; Rahe, R.H. The social readjustment rating scale. *J. Psychosom. Res.* **1967**, *11*, 213–218. [CrossRef]
37. Lara, M.A.; Navarro, C.; Navarrete, L. Outcome results of a psycho-educational intervention in pregnancy to prevent PPD: A randomized control trial. *J. Affect. Disord.* **2010**, *122*, 109–117. [CrossRef] [PubMed]
38. Genovez, M.; Le, H. Identification of Salvadoran pregnant women at risk for postpartum depression. In Proceedings of the Poster Presentation, 25th Annual Conference Postpartum Support International, Seattle, WA, USA, 16 September 2011; pp. 14–18.
39. Records, K.; Rice, M.; Beck, C.T. Psychometric assessment of the postpartum depression predictors inventory-revised. *J. Nurs. Meas.* **2007**, *15*, 189–202. [CrossRef] [PubMed]
40. Ibarra-Yruegas, B.; Lara, M.A.; Navarrete, L.; Nieto, L.; Kawas Valle, O. Psychometric properties of the Postpartum Depression Predictors Inventory-revised for pregnant women in Mexico. *J. Health Psychol.* **2018**, *23*, 1415–1423. [CrossRef]
41. Martínez-Gómez, J.A.; Guerrero-Rodríguez, S.I.; Rey-Anacona, C.A. Assessment of construct validity and reliability of the inventory of masculinity and femininity in adolescents and young Colombian adults. *Av. Psicol. Latinoam.* **2012**, *30*, 170–181.
42. Rey, C.A. Pro-social skills, gender personality traits and acceptance of violence toward women in adolescents who have witnessed violence in their parents/Habilidades prosociales, rasgos de personalidad de género y aceptación de la violencia hacia la mujer, en adolescentes que han presenciado violencia entre sus padres. *Acta Colomb. Psicol.* **2008**, *11*, 107–119.
43. Feligreras-Alcala, D.; Frias-Osuna, A.; Del-Pino-Casado, R. Personal and family resources related to depressive and anxiety symptoms in women during puerperium. *Int. J. Environ. Res. Public Health* **2020**, *17*, 5230. [CrossRef]
44. Aktan, N.M. Social support and anxiety in pregnant and postpartum women: A secondary analysis. *Clin. Nurs. Res.* **2012**, *21*, 183–194. [CrossRef] [PubMed]
45. Razurel, C.; Kaiser, B.; Antonietti, J.P.; Epiney, M.; Sellenet, C. Relationship between perceived perinatal stress and depressive symptoms, anxiety, and parental self-efficacy in primiparous mothers and the role of social support. *Women Health* **2017**, *57*, 154–172. [CrossRef] [PubMed]
46. United Nations International Children's Emergency Fund. *Progress for Every Child in the SDG Era Country Profile*; UNICEF: Mexico City, Mexico, 2016.
47. Lara-Cinisomo, S.; Clark, C.T.; Wood, J. Increasing diagnosis and treatment of perinatal depression in Latinas and African American women: Addressing stigma is not enough. *Women's Health Issues* **2018**, *28*, 201–204. [CrossRef] [PubMed]
48. Caballero, M.; Leyva-Flores, R.; Ochoa-Marin, S.C.; Zarco, A.; Guerrero, C. Women who are left behind: The impact of international migration on the process of seeking health care. *Salud Pública Mex.* **2008**, *50*, 241–250. [CrossRef] [PubMed]
49. Lancaster, C.A.; Gold, K.J.; Flynn, H.A.; Yoo, H.; Marcus, S.M.; Davis, M.M. Risk factors for depressive symptoms during pregnancy: A systematic review. *Am. J. Obstet. Gynecol.* **2010**, *202*, 5–14. [CrossRef] [PubMed]
50. Leahy-Warren, P.; McCarthy, G.; Corcoran, P. First-time mothers: Social support, maternal parental self-efficacy and postnatal depression. *J. Clin. Nurs.* **2012**, *21*, 388–397. [CrossRef] [PubMed]

51. Ramakrishna, S.; Cooklin, A.R.; Leach, L.S. Comorbid anxiety and depression: A community-based study examining symptomology and correlates during the postpartum period. *J. Reprod. Infant Psychol.* **2019**, *37*, 468–479. [CrossRef]
52. Choi, K.W.; Kim, Y.K.; Jeon, H.J. Comorbid anxiety and depression: Clinical and conceptual consideration and transdiagnostic treatment. *Adv. Exp. Med. Biol.* **2020**, *1191*, 219–235. [CrossRef]
53. Dagher, R.K.; Bruckheim, H.E.; Colpe, L.J.; Edwards, E.; White, D.B. Perinatal depression: Challenges and opportunities. *J. Women's Health* **2020**. [CrossRef]
54. Woody, C.A.; Ferrari, A.J.; Siskind, D.J.; Whiteford, H.A.; Harris, M.G. A systematic review and meta-regression of the prevalence and incidence of perinatal depression. *J. Affect. Disord.* **2017**, *219*, 86–92. [CrossRef]
55. Lara-Cinisomo, S.; Grewen, K.M.; Girdler, S.S.; Wood, J.; Meltzer-Brody, S. Perinatal depression, adverse life events, and hypothalamic-adrenal-pituitary axis response to cold pressor stress in Latinas: An exploratory study. *Women's Health Issues* **2017**, *27*, 673–682. [CrossRef] [PubMed]
56. Lara-Cinisomo, S.; McKenney, K.; Di Florio, A.; Meltzer-Brody, S. Associations between postpartum depression, breastfeeding, and oxytocin levels in Latina mothers. *Breastfeed. Med.* **2017**, *12*, 436–442. [CrossRef] [PubMed]
57. Mukherjee, S.; Trepka, M.J.; Pierre-Victor, D.; Bahelah, R.; Avent, T. Racial/ethnic disparities in antenatal depression in the United States: A systematic review. *Matern. Child Health J.* **2016**, *20*, 1780–1797. [CrossRef] [PubMed]
58. Lara-Cinisomo, S.; Wood, J.; Fujimoto, E. A systematic review of cultural orientation and perinatal depression in Latina women: Are acculturation, Marianismo, and religiosity risks or protective factors? *Arch. Women's Ment. Health* **2019**, *22*, 557–567. [CrossRef] [PubMed]
59. Hackett, R.A.; Steptoe, A.; Jackson, S.E. Sex discrimination and mental health in women: A prospective analysis. *Health Psychol.* **2019**, *38*, 1014–1024. [CrossRef]
60. Navarro, D.M.; Robles, J.N.; Hernández, L.O. La mujer en México: Inequidad, pobreza y violencia. *Rev. Mex. Cienc. Políticas Soc.* **2014**, *59*, 117–146. [CrossRef]
61. Rafful, C.; Medina-Mora, M.E.; Borges, G.; Benjet, C.; Orozco, R. Depression, gender, and the treatment gap in Mexico. *J. Affect. Disord.* **2012**, *138*, 165–169. [CrossRef]
62. Diaz-Loving, R.; Aragon, S.R.; Aragóon, R.S. Rasgos instrumentales (masculinos) y expresivos (femeninos). *Rev. Latinoam. Psicol.* **2001**, *33*, 131–139.
63. DiGirolamo, A.M.; de Snyder, N.S. Women as primary caregivers in Mexico: Challenges to well-being. *Salud Pública Mex.* **2008**, *50*, 516–522. [CrossRef]
64. Michl, L.C.; McLaughlin, K.A.; Shepherd, K.; Nolen-Hoeksema, S. Rumination as a mechanism linking stressful life events to symptoms of depression and anxiety: Longitudinal evidence in early adolescents and adults. *J. Abnorm. Psychol.* **2013**, *122*, 339–352. [CrossRef]
65. Gress-Smith, J.L.; Roubinov, D.S.; Tanaka, R.; Cmic, K.; Gonzales, N.; Enders, C.; Luecken, L.J. Prenatal expectations in Mexican American women: Development of a culturally sensitive measure. *Arch. Womens Ment. Health* **2013**, *16*, 303–314. [CrossRef] [PubMed]
66. Negron, R.; Martin, A.; Almog, M.; Balbierz, A.; Howell, E.A. Social support during the postpartum period: Mothers' views on needs, expectations, and mobilization of support. *Matern. Child Health J.* **2013**, *17*, 616–623. [CrossRef]
67. Razurel, C.; Kaiser, B. The role of satisfaction with social support on the psychological health of primiparous mothers in the perinatal period. *Women Health* **2015**, *55*, 167–186. [CrossRef] [PubMed]
68. Stein, G.L.; Guzman, L.E. Prevention and intervention research with Latino families: A translational approach. *Fam. Process* **2015**, *54*, 280–292. [CrossRef] [PubMed]
69. Le, H.N.; Zmuda, J.; Perry, D.F.; Muñoz, R.F. Transforming an evidence-based intervention to prevent perinatal depression for low-income Latina immigrants. *Am. J. Orthopsychiatry* **2010**, *80*, 34–45. [CrossRef] [PubMed]
70. Baker-Ericzén, M.J.; Connelly, C.D.; Hazen, A.L.; Dueñas, C.; Landsverk, J.A.; Horwitz, S.M. A collaborative care telemedicine intervention to overcome treatment barriers for Latina women with depression during the perinatal period. *Fam. Syst. Health* **2012**, *30*, 224–240. [CrossRef]
71. Marsiglia, F.F.; Kulis, S.; Garcia Perez, H.; Bermudez-Parsai, M. Hopelessness, family stress, and depression among Mexican-heritage mothers in the southwest. *Health Soc. Work* **2011**, *36*, 7–18. [CrossRef]
72. Garcia-Gonzalez, J.; Ventura-Miranda, M.I.; Requena-Mullor, M.; Parron-Carreño, T.; Alarcon-Rodriguez, R. State-trait anxiety levels during pregnancy and foetal parameters following intervention with music therapy. *J. Affect. Disord.* **2018**, *232*, 17–22. [CrossRef]
73. Hepp, P.; Hagenbeck, C.; Gilles, J.; Wolf, O.T.; Goertz, W.; Janni, W.; Balan, P.; Fleisch, M.; Fehm, T.; Schaal, N.K. Effects of music intervention during caesarean delivery on anxiety and stress of the mother a controlled, randomised study. *BMC Pregnancy Childbirth* **2018**, *18*, 435. [CrossRef]
74. Lara-Cinisomo, S.; Wisner, K.L. (Eds.) *Perinatal Depression Among Spanish-Speaking Women: A global Perspective on Prevalence, Treatment, and Outcomes*; Springer: New York, NY, USA, 2014. [CrossRef]

International Journal of
Environmental Research and Public Health

Article

Predicting Postpartum Depressive Symptoms from Pregnancy Biopsychosocial Factors: A Longitudinal Investigation Using Structural Equation Modeling

Verónica Martínez-Borba [1,2], Carlos Suso-Ribera [1], Jorge Osma [2,3,*] and Laura Andreu-Pejó [2,4]

1 Department of Basic and Clinical Psychology and Psychobiology, Jaume I University, Avda, Vicent Sos Baynat s/n, 12071 Castellon de la Plana, Spain; borba@uji.es (V.M.-B.); susor@uji.es (C.S.-R.)
2 Instituto de Investigación Sanitaria de Aragón, C/ San Juan Bosco, 13, 50009 Zaragoza, Spain; pejo@uji.es
3 Department of Psychology and Sociology, Universidad de Zaragoza, C/ Atarazanas, 4, 44003 Teruel, Spain
4 Nursing Department, Jaume I University, Avda, Vicent Sos Baynat s/n, 12071 Castellon de la Plana, Spain
* Correspondence: osma@unizar.es; Tel.: +34-97-8645-390 (ext. 861390)

Received: 23 September 2020; Accepted: 12 November 2020; Published: 14 November 2020

Abstract: The prediction of postpartum depression (PPD) should be conceptualized from a biopsychosocial perspective. This study aims at exploring the longitudinal contribution of a set of biopsychosocial factors for PPD in perinatal women. A longitudinal study was conducted, assessment was made with a website and included biopsychosocial factors that were measured during pregnancy (n = 266, weeks 16–36), including age, affective ambivalence, personality characteristics, social support and depression. Depression was measured again at postpartum (n = 101, weeks 2–4). The analyses included bivariate associations and structural equation modeling (SEM). Age, affective ambivalence, neuroticism, positive, and negative affect at pregnancy were associated with concurrent depression during pregnancy (all $p < 0.01$). Age, affective ambivalence, positive affect, and depression at pregnancy correlated with PPD (all $p < 0.05$). Affective ambivalence ($\beta = 1.97$; $p = 0.003$) and positive ($\beta = -0.29$; $p < 0.001$) and negative affect ($\beta = 0.22$; $p = 0.024$) at pregnancy remained significant predictors of concurrent depression in the SEM, whereas only age ($\beta = 0.27$; $p = 0.010$) and depression ($\beta = 0.37$; $p = 0.002$) at pregnancy predicted PPD. Biopsychosocial factors are clearly associated with concurrent depression at pregnancy, but the stability of depression across time limits the prospective contribution of biopsychosocial factors. Depression should be screened early during pregnancy, as this is likely to persist after birth. The use of technology, as in the present investigation, might be a cost-effective option for this purpose.

Keywords: pregnancy; postpartum; depressive symptoms; risk factors; biopsychosocial; longitudinal studies; information and communication technologies

1. Introduction

Postpartum depression (PPD) is one of the most prevalent emotional disorders worldwide, with global estimates ranging from between 5% to 25% [1]. PPD is associated with both personal and economic burden [2]. First, negative health consequences for the women and the baby have been reported, such as inadequate gestational weight gain, low birth weight, preterm birth, inadequate weight gain in the baby, under-utilization of prenatal care services, increased substance use in the women, and increased maternal mortality [3,4]. Second, the economic costs of PPD include loss of productivity and health care expenses [5]. Not surprisingly, the American Psychiatric Association has indicated that all perinatal women should be assessed for both the presence of and risk for psychiatric disorders during pregnancy (twice), and during the first six months postpartum [6].

The biopsychosocial model of PPD is an attempt to comprehensively understand the risk for the onset of depressive symptoms, but also the protective factors associated with this disorder, so that prevention and treatment efforts can be developed in a more effective manner [7]. Several meta-analyses and systematic reviews have supported this biopsychosocial approach to PPD [8,9]. As a result of this, factors such as low educational and income level, ambivalence toward pregnancy, personal and family history of depression, perceived social support, and personality characteristics, among others, are now frequently investigated in the PPD literature [8,9]. Specifically, variables related to the increased risk of PPD are pregnancy ambivalence, neuroticism, negative affect and prenatal depressive symptoms [10–12]. On the contrary, positive affect and extraversion seem to be protective factors for PPD development [11,12]. There is sufficient evidence, however, that the best predictor of PPD is depressive symptomatology during pregnancy [8,9,13].

The research to date has clearly contributed to the development of the biopsychosocial approach to PPD. Nevertheless, there are a number of shortcomings in the literature on PPD that are yet to be addressed. For instance, most studies tend to investigate the contribution of only one or two risk factors altogether (e.g., Hetherington, McDonald, Williamson, Patten and Tough, 2018 [14]), so the communalities between biopsychosocial factors are not controlled and the unique contribution of each variable remains unclear [15]. This is important as it might help reduce the number of therapeutic targets to a more manageable set. Additionally, studies exploring the relationship between biopsychosocial factors and perinatal depressive symptoms are generally cross-sectional (e.g., Adamu and Adinew, 2018 [16]), so the predictive value of these variables in the evolution of depressive symptoms across the perinatal period is unclear. Research has shown that both the spontaneous remission and intensification of depressive symptoms exist [17], so longitudinal studies are fundamental if prevention and treatment programs are to be effectively developed.

In addition to the aforementioned shortcomings, previous research has revealed the important barriers to face-to-face evaluation in the perinatal period, including insufficient time for care providers, availability of mental health services, lack of time for the women, difficulties in combining child care with onsite appointments, geographical distance, and the high economic costs of traveling to academic or health care institutions [18]. The use of information and communication technologies (ICT) in the field of health (e-health) has emerged as an alternative to traditional face-to-face methods in response to these barriers. To the best of our knowledge, there is only one longitudinal study that used ICTs (e-mail) to explore emotional disorders in perinatal women [19]. However, a biopsychosocial approach to PPD was not adopted in this investigation, and complex associations between variables, for example via structural equation modeling (SEM), were not investigated.

With the aim of providing more robust evidence for the development of screening, prevention, and treatment programs for PPD, we have conducted a study exploring the unique contribution of a set of risk and protective biopsychosocial factors for PPD in perinatal women using SEM. A longitudinal design was implemented, and prenatal and postpartum assessments were conducted using ICT (i.e., a website). After a thorough literature research, the biopsychosocial factors included in the prediction of PPD were psychosocial factors with robust support in the literature (ambivalence toward pregnancy, neuroticism, extraversion, positive and negative affect, social support, and prenatal depressive symptoms) and a biological variable, namely age, with limited but promising evidence [8].

On the basis of previous research, we hypothesize that the perinatal risk factors for concurrent and prospective PPD will include age (i.e., being younger), affective ambivalence, neuroticism, and negative affect. On the contrary, we expect that extraversion, positive affect and social support will be protective factors for depressive symptoms. We anticipate that prenatal depressive symptoms will be the best predictors of PPD. We also expect that psychosocial factors will be intercorrelated, so that only a small subset of them will uniquely contribute to PPD in the SEM. The unique contribution of these variables is difficult to anticipate from the existing literature, and will be investigated in an exploratory manner. By testing these hypotheses, we expect to achieve our study goal, that is, explore the unique prospective contribution of a set of biopsychosocial factors in the mother in the prediction of PDD. To make the text more readable, we will interchangeably use the terms pregnancy and prenatal when referring to the assessments made before delivery.

2. Materials and Methods

2.1. Participants

The study was conducted between 2012 and 2015. The sample included 266 women who voluntarily registered on the MamáFeliz (HappyMom, hereafter MMF) website for assessment and completed the first evaluation (during pregnancy). These women were asked to respond to two assessments: one during pregnancy (between week 16 and week 36) and one at postpartum (between weeks 2 and 4 after delivery, according to the women's availability). During pregnancy, depression has been shown to be more prevalent during the second and the third trimesters [20]. At postpartum, the highest prevalence rates of depression were found between weeks 2 and 7 after delivery [21,22]. As observed in Figure 1, from the initial sample, 101 women also provided information in the postpartum (completers' sample). Sociodemographic characteristics of the sample, divided by group (completers vs. non-completers), will be described in the results section. Several guidelines have been proposed in the multiple regression literature for deciding the sample size required for analyses. For example, Harrell (2001) proposed a minimum of 10 participants for each predictor in the model. Our SEM included 8 predictors, and therefore we would require 80 participants according to this rule of thumb. Harris (2001) proposed at least n = 50 + p, where n is sample size and p is number of predictors. According to this, the minimum n would be 58 participants. Based on previous recommendations on required sample sizes when conducting multiple regressions [23,24], the current sample size was sufficient for the analyses conducted.

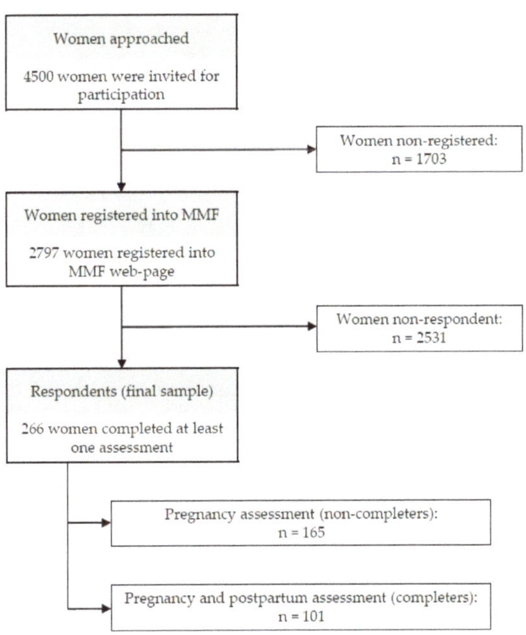

Figure 1. Flow diagram of participants.

2.2. Procedure

All the procedures described in the present study were approved by the ethical committees of the Hospital Universitario La Plana de Villareal (Castellón) and the Gobierno de Aragón (CP12/2012). The health professionals at the specialized public gynecology centers collaborating in the study disseminated the investigation with all consecutive potential participants meeting the eligibility criteria (see Table 1) and gave women a document with a unique code and the link to the MMF website. Once on the website, the women that voluntarily agreed to participate in the study had to accept the data protection and confidentiality policies and had to sign the online informed consent form before completing the online assessments. Health professionals participating in the study gave the information on how to participate to pregnant women meeting the inclusion criteria. However, the number of women not meeting the criteria or not willing to participate was not reliably collected by the health care providers due to time restrictions during consultations.

Table 1. Inclusion and exclusion criteria to participate in the study.

Inclusion	Exclusion
Being pregnant (weeks 16 to 36) Over 18 years of age Having internet access	Not being able to read and answer questions in Spanish
Signing the informed consent form	

The assessments were carried out entirely via the MMF website, which evaluated the most important biopsychosocial factors associated with perinatal depressive symptoms. E-mail reminders were used for the prospective assessments. At the end of each assessment, women received feedback about their present mental well-being as a result of their evaluation. If depressive symptoms were detected after the assessments, they received an e-mail recommending a consultation with their doctor for a more in-depth evaluation of their emotional state.

2.3. Measures

All sociodemographic and biopsychosocial data were assessed online via the MMF website. All the questionnaires mentioned below were administered in their full length.

2.3.1. Demographic and Biologic

We asked for nationality, educational level, relationship status and age; ad hoc questions were developed. To report on their nationality, women had to indicate the country (Spain only) or the region (i.e., South America or Central America, North America, Western Europe, Eastern Europe, North Africa, South Africa, Middle East countries, Far East countries, Southeast Asia, and Oceania) they were born in. Regarding educational level, women responded as to whether they had no studies, basic studies, secondary studies, bachelor studies, technical studies, university studies, a master's degree or doctorate studies. Women also indicated their marital status as follows: single, unmarried (with a stable partner), married, divorced, or widowed.

2.3.2. Psychological

Ambivalence toward pregnancy: This ad hoc item evaluated mixed feelings about pregnancy; "How often have you experienced feelings of ambivalence and/or contradiction about your pregnancy (for example, I have sometimes experienced joy, but also sadness or hope, but also worry)". This item has 4 response options ranging from 0 = "never" to 3 = "very often". Higher scores represent more ambivalence toward pregnancy.

The Beck Depression Inventory (BDI-II) [25,26]: This comprises 21 items and evaluates depressive symptoms and cognitions experienced during the last two weeks. Each item has 4 response options

(0 = "not at all" and 3 = "severely"), so the total score can range from 0 to 63. Higher scores indicate more severe depressive symptomatology. The recommended BDI–II cutoffs for women in Spain are 0–13 for minimal depressive symptoms, 14–19 for mild depressive symptoms, 20–28 for moderate depressive symptoms, and 29–63 for severe depressive symptoms [25,27]. In our sample, the reliability was good during both pregnancy ($\alpha = 0.81$) and postpartum ($\alpha = 0.85$).

The Positive and Negative Affect Schedule (PANAS) [28,29]: This evaluates positive and negative emotional experiences. It consists of 20 adjectives, 10 for each affect scale (i.e., Positive and Negative). Each item is divided into 5 grades (1 = "very slightly/not at all" and 5 = "extremely") and total scores for each scale can range from 10 to 50. In our sample, Cronbach alphas were very good (0.89 and 0.86 for positive and negative affect, respectively).

The Eysenck Personality Questionnaire revised (EPQ-R) [30,31]: This assesses patterns of behaviors, thoughts, and feelings (i.e., personality). The questionnaire is composed of 48 dichotomous (Yes/No) items (12 for extraversion, 12 for neuroticism, 12 for psychoticism, and 12 for lie). For this study we only used the neuroticism ($\alpha = 0.79$) and extraversion ($\alpha = 0.77$) scales.

2.3.3. Social

The Multidimensional Scale of Perceived Social Support (MSPSS) [32,33]: This is composed of 12 items that evaluate perceived social support in three domains (family, friends, and others). Each item has 7 response options (1 = "completely disagree" and 7 = "completely agree"). Total scores have a 12–84 range. Higher scores represent a higher perception of social support. In our sample, the psychometric properties of the three subscales were very good ($0.91 \leq \alpha \leq 0.94$), but the total MSPSS score was preferred to reduce the number of statistical comparisons between biopsychosocial variables included in this study and to reduce the risk of type I errors.

2.4. Data Analysis

First, we conducted a descriptive analysis comparing completers and non-completers using a Chi-squared test for categorical variables and a Mann–Whitney U test for continuous factors (a non-parametric test was selected due to the distribution of scores). This comparison between completers and non-completers was made to evaluate whether there were baseline differences between both samples that would help us understand dropouts and therefore would compromise the generalizability of the findings. This comparison, however, is not related to the main goal of the present work (i.e., to predict postpartum depressive symptoms from a biopsychosocial perspective). For the same reason, we calculated Spearman and not Pearson correlations to explore the relationship between prenatal psychosocial factors (age, affective ambivalence, personality, affect, and social support) and prenatal and PPD, considering the completers' sample only. Finally, SEM analyses were conducted to test a model that accounts for PPD from prenatal characteristics in the sample of completers. SEM has become a technique of choice when exploring complex associations between variables because of its advantages [34]. To name some examples, SEM allows the exploration of several relationships at the same time and facilitates the simultaneous use of a construct both as a dependent (i.e., prenatal depressive symptoms predicted by prenatal psychosocial factors) and as an independent variable (i.e., prenatal depressive symptoms predicting PPD) [35]. The fit for the proposed model was assessed with the Chi-square test, the root mean square error of approximation (RMSEA), the standardized root mean square residual (SRMR), the Tucker–Lewis index (TLI), and the comparative fit index (CFI). RMSEA and SRMR values smaller than 0.05 and TLI and CFI values greater than 0.95 reflect an excellent fit [36]. As recommended in the literature [37], maximum likelihood parameter estimation with standard errors and a mean-adjusted Chi-square test that is robust to non-normality (Satorra–Bentler MLM estimation) was used in the SEM.

Past research has indicated that adjustment to the alpha level is not necessary when exploratory studies include simple rather than intricate sets of hypotheses [38]. The present study's hypothesis is simple in the sense that we only anticipate that a reduced number of predictors will emerge from the SEM, while the exact unique contributions and their directions are not hypothesized (this would be a more intricate and confirmatory analysis). As a consequence, an uncorrected alpha level of 0.050 was used in the analyses.

3. Results

3.1. Demographic and Biopsychosocial Characteristics of the Participants: Comparison between Completers and Non-Completers

The demographic and biopsychosocial characteristics of the whole sample are presented in Tables 2 and 3. There were no significant differences in demographic and biopsychosocial characteristics between completers and non-completers, which supports the generalizability of the study results. Our sample (completers; n = 101) was composed of primiparous Spanish perinatal women between 16 and 36 weeks of gestation (mean = 24.42; SD = 8.62) of approximately 33 years of age, who were in a stable relationship and were well-educated. Most women had some degree of ambivalence toward pregnancy. Three out of four had minimal depressive symptoms, 24% had mild depressive symptoms, 4% had moderate depressive symptoms, and no participants had severe depressive symptoms.

Table 2. Biopsychosocial variables during pregnancy and postpartum.

Variable	Non-Completers		Completers		Comparison	
	Mean (SD; Range)	N	Mean (SD; Range)	N	U	p
Age	32.59 (4.39; 18–42)	165	33.54 (3.88; 23–42)	101	7474.00	0.157
Affective Ambivalence	0.93 (0.73; 0–3)	165	0.86 (0.74; 0–3)	101		
No	26.1%	43	30.7%	31	7869.00	0.390
Yes	73.9%	122	69.3%	70		
Neuroticism	3.77(3.43; 0–12)	165	3.69 (2.99; 0–12)	101	8191.00	0.815
Extraversion	8.10 (2.93; 0–12)	165	8.54 (2.67; 1–12)	101	7678.00	0.279
Positive Affect	29.70 (9.78; 0–50)	139	29.68 (8.92; 0–50)	101	6735.00	0.592
Negative Affect	16.50 (7.00; 0–40)	139	15.88 (5.82; 0–32)	101	6754.40	0.617
Social Support	75.13 (10.92; 12–84)	123	76.97 (7.84; 42–82)	101	5927.00	0.551
Pregnancy Depressive Symptoms	11.37 (7.40; 2–33)	134	10.21 (5.49; 1–26)	101	6499.50	0.603
Minimal	73.9%	99	72.3%	73	3446.00	0.602
Mild	11.2%	15	23.7%	24	169.50	0.765
Moderate	9.7%	13	4%	4	21.00	0.563
Severe	5.2%	7		0		
Postpartum Depressive Symptoms			8.54 (5.53; 0–25)	101		
Minimal			82.2%	83		
Mild			14.8%	15		
Moderate			3%	3		
Severe				0		

In the postpartum period, 82.2%, 14.8% and 3% of completers presented minimal, mild, and moderate depressive symptoms, respectively. No participant presented severe depressive symptoms in the postpartum.

3.2. Cross-Sectional and Longitudinal Bivariate Associations between Pregnancy Biopsychosocial Factors and Pregnancy and Postpartum Depressive Symptoms in the Sample of Completers

Table 4 shows Spearman correlations between prenatal psychosocial factors and prenatal and PPD symptoms in the sample of completers (n = 101). Prenatal depressive symptoms were positively associated with concurrent age (r = 0.21; p = 0.032), affective ambivalence (r = 0.38; p < 0.001), neuroticism (r = 0.34; p < 0.001), and negative affect (r = 0.36; p = 0.004). Conversely, prenatal depressive symptoms were negatively linked to positive affect (r = −0.49; p < 0.001). PPD symptoms were related to prenatal age (r = 0.27; p = 0.006), affective ambivalence (r = 0.20; p = 0.042), positive affect (r = −0.21; p = 0.033) and depressive symptoms (r = 0.47; p < 0.001). Being older, experimenting with more affective ambivalence, reporting less positive affect, and presenting depressive symptoms during pregnancy were associated with increased postpartum depressive symptoms. These correlations were between weak and moderate in strength. Social support and extraversion were not associated with concurrent and prospective depressive symptoms.

Table 3. Sociodemographic variables of the sample.

Variable	Non-Completers	Completers	Comparison	
	Frequency (%)	Frequency (%)	χ^2	p
Nationality				
Spanish Other	154 (93.3) 11 (6.7)	94 (93.1) 7 (6.9)	0.07	0.934
Educational Level				
<12 years >12 years	23 (13.9) 142 (86.1)	15 (14.9) 86 (85.1)	0.04	0.837
Parity				
Primiparous Multiparous	122 (73.9) 43 (26.1)	79 (78.2) 22 (21.8)	0.62	0.429
Relationship Status				
Not in a Relationship In a Relationship	42 (25.5) 123 (74.5)	17 (16.8) 84 (83.2)	2.70	0.100

Note: sample size was 165 for non-completers and 101 for completers.

Table 4. Bivariate correlations between psychosocial variables and depressive symptoms in the sample of completers.

Variable	Age	AM	N	E	PA	NA	SS	PRE Dep	POST Dep
Age	-	0.14	0.17	−0.8	−0.15	0.13	−0.18	0.21 *	0.27 **
AM		-	0.26 **	−0.01	−0.13	0.29 **	−0.17	0.38 ***	0.20 *
N			-	−0.21 *	−0.38 ***	0.49 ***	−0.26 **	0.34 ***	0.16
E				-	0.28 **	−0.05	0.23 *	−0.15	−0.18
PA					-	−0.17	0.34 ***	−0.49 ***	−0.21 *
NA						-	−0.03	0.36 ***	0.10
SS							-	−0.16	−0.10
PRE Dep								-	0.47 ***
POST Dep									-

Note: AM, affective ambivalence; N, neuroticism; E, extraversion; PA, positive affect; NA, negative affect; SS, social support; PRE dep, pregnancy depressive symptoms; POST dep, postpartum depressive symptoms. *** $p < 0.001$; ** $p < 0.010$; * $p < 0.050$. Sample size is 101.

As observed in Table 4, there were some significant associations between the biopsychosocial variables included in the study. Neuroticism was positively related to affective ambivalence ($r = 0.26$; $p = 0.009$) and negative affect ($r = 0.49$; $p < 0.001$), as well as negatively linked to extraversion ($r = -0.21$; $p = 0.038$), social support ($r = -0.26$; $p = 0.010$), and positive affect ($r = -0.38$; $p < 0.001$). Positive affect was positively associated to extraversion ($r = 0.28$; $p = 0.004$) and social support ($r = 0.23$; $p < 0.001$). Extraversion correlated positively with social support ($r = 0.23$; $p = 0.022$). Finally, affective ambivalence had a positive relationship with negative affect ($r = 0.29$; $p = 0.003$).

3.3. Structural Equation Model Predicting Postpartum Depressive Symptoms from Prenatal Biopsychosocial Factors in the Sample of Completers

In the model, psychosocial variables were placed according to their expected proximity with PPD (Figure 2). For instance, personality is, theoretically, the most distal factor related to PPD, while pregnancy depressive symptoms would be the most proximal factor to it.

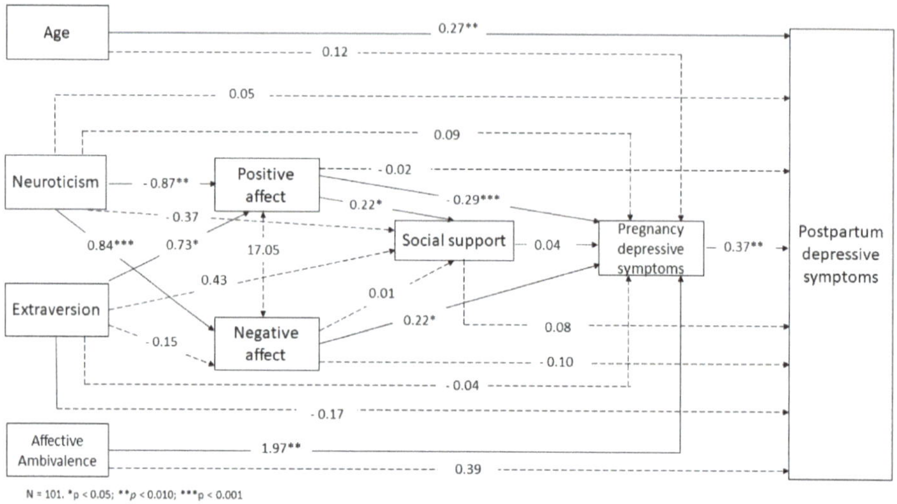

Figure 2. Structural Equation Model predicting depressive symptoms in the sample of completers.

As shown in Figure 2, distal psychological factors (i.e., neuroticism) were associated with more proximal psychological constructs (i.e., positive and negative affect). Specifically, neuroticism positively contributed to negative affect ($\beta = 0.84$; $p < 0.001$) and was negatively associated with positive affect ($\beta = -0.87$; $p = 0.003$). Contrary to neuroticism, extraversion contributed to more positive affect ($\beta = 0.73$; $p = 0.018$). In an intermediate level, positive affect was associated with more social support at pregnancy ($\beta = 0.22$; $p = 0.041$).

A number of cross-sectional associations with prenatal depressive symptoms also emerged. Specifically, positive associations were revealed for affective ambivalence ($\beta = 1.97$; $p = 0.003$) and negative affect ($\beta = 0.22$; $p = 0.024$), while positive affect was inversely linked to depressive symptoms ($\beta = -0.29$; $p < 0.001$). When exploring the longitudinal, prospective associations between study variables and PPD, only age ($\beta = 0.27$; $p = 0.010$) and prenatal depressive symptoms ($\beta = 0.37$; $p = 0.002$) predicted PPD. The proposed model showed an excellent fit ($\chi^2 = 5.072$, $p = 0.535$; degrees of freedom = 6; RMSEA < 0.001; 90% RMSEA CI < 0.001–0.118; CFI = 1.000; TLI = 1.045).

4. Discussion

The present study aimed at investigating a relatively comprehensive set of biopsychosocial factors associated with perinatal depressive symptoms. Similar to previous research, the biopsychosocial factors included in the study (i.e., age, ambivalence and personality) were cross-sectionally linked to depressive symptoms during pregnancy [8,9,39], and prenatal depressive symptoms were the best predictors of PPD [9,13]. New to this investigation, we observed that the predictive ability of prenatal biopsychosocial factors when predicting PPD becomes negligible, with the exception of age, when prenatal depressive symptoms were accounted for.

4.1. Factors Cross-Sectionally Associated with Prenatal Depressive Symptoms

As hypothesized, age, affective ambivalence, neuroticism and negative affect appear to be risk factors for concurrent depressive symptoms, while positive affect is likely to be a protective factor for concurrent prenatal depressive symptoms. A surprising finding was that extraversion and social support did not correlate with concurrent and PPD.

The relationship between age and perinatal depressive symptoms is not well established in the literature [8]. Our results are consistent with studies suggesting that older women are at higher risk of pregnancy depressive symptoms [40]. However, the strength of the cross-sectional associations found in the present investigation was weak, so the results should be interpreted with caution and replication should be encouraged.

Previous research has supported the association between neuroticism, which is defined as a tendency to experience negative affect when facing a stressor [41], and depressive symptoms [11]. These findings are important because pregnancy is a period in which important challenges are likely to occur due to the changes in the body and the environment [42], so women scoring high in neuroticism are likely to be at higher risk for presenting perinatal depressive symptoms. A similar finding was obtained with negative affect, a personality characteristic closely related to neuroticism. These results are consistent with past research in the perinatal literature [12], and again suggest that there are personality profiles associated with an increased risk of emotional distress in this population that should be taken into consideration in prevention and treatment programs.

In addition to these two risk psychological factors for depressive symptoms, this study investigated the role of two arguably protective factors for depressive symptoms, namely, extraversion and positive affect. Consistent with our expectations, positive affect was inversely associated with the severity of depressive symptoms, which is consistent with the idea that this personality characteristic is a protective factor against depressive symptoms in perinatal women [12]. Surprisingly, though, extraversion, which has been linked to decreased emotional distress in past research [11], and social support [43,44] were not significantly associated with depressive symptoms in our study. It is possible that the role of social support is more evident in disadvantaged populations. Our sample is not likely to be representative of such populations, as participants were generally well-educated adults that reported being in a stable relationship. In the light of the present investigation's findings, intrapersonal processes (i.e., experienced emotions) appear to be more important for prenatal depressive symptoms than interpersonal elements (i.e., social interactions and support). Another explanation could be that structural social support as measured in the present study (i.e., family support, friends support, and support from others) is negligible compared with functional social support (i.e., instrumental, emotional, informational, etc.). Because the literature in this regard is still scarce, the study results will require replication in similar (i.e., well-educated and maritally stable women) and different populations (i.e., less educated or single women for whom social support can play a more important role). Additionally, it would also be advisable to include different domains of social support (e.g., instrumental and emotional support). As recently suggested, social support to perinatal women should be provided by the right person, delivered at the right time, and should be of the right kind [45].

Overall, the aforementioned cross-sectional findings revealed in the bivariate analyses were supported by SEM, with the exceptions of age and neuroticism. As we predicted, when all biopsychosocial factors were included in a single model, a number of them ceased to significantly contribute to concurrent depressive symptoms, arguably due to shared variance, as indicated by the moderate bivariate associations between psychological variables included in the study. These findings are important as they might guide interventions and research in a more effective way (i.e., reducing the number of target variables due to redundancies and selecting the most robust predictors of outcomes). There is evidence to suggest that neuroticism and negative affect share important variance [46], so the burden of assessment and treatment might be reduced by selecting one of the factors only for research and treatment practices (i.e., negative affect according to the present study findings).

4.2. Factors Predicting Postpartum Depressive Symptoms

Consistent with past research [47], our bivariate analyses revealed that the association between psychosocial factors and depressive symptoms decreased with time. Affective ambivalence and positive affect did contribute to depressive symptoms prospectively, but only when investigated in a bivariate manner.

There is previous evidence to suggest that affective ambivalence is associated with perinatal depressive symptoms [10]. In a context wherein women are forced to view pregnancy as a positive process [11], negative emotions appear to have no or little place. However, as evidenced by the large number of perinatal women who presented some degree of ambivalence in the present investigation (around 70% of respondents), the reality is quite different. Therefore, normalizing and destigmatizing ambivalence toward motherhood should be not only therapeutic goals, but societal aims, so that false negatives are minimized.

Positive affect was also longitudinally associated with prospective depressive symptoms. There is evidence to suggest that the promotion of positive emotions in perinatal women can be achieved via their participation in pleasant activities [48] and, consistent with the present study findings, this appears to reduce PPD symptoms [49]. Therefore, psychological treatments that encourage the induction of positive emotions or the inclusion of positive-induction modules in existent interventions should be recommended in perinatal women presenting low positive affect.

An interesting longitudinal finding was that only our biological factor, namely age, significantly contributed to PPD above and beyond prenatal depressive symptoms and the remaining psychosocial factors. This is a novel finding which might be attributable to a number of factors that are age-related. For instance, it is possible that older women had unrealistic expectations about motherhood, more difficulties in combining job or house-care duties with maternity, or more risk factor for obstetric and perinatal complications in both the women and the children [50,51], which might lead to increased postpartum depressive symptoms. Because providing information about the changes that occur in the perinatal period appears to be a good intervention for perinatal women [52], adjusting the expectations of older women, anticipating the challenges associated with pregnancy and motherhood, and providing them with abilities to deal with this new situation might be of special interest for older women. Research has shown that women face different stressors during the perinatal period depending on their parity status (i.e., primiparous or multiparous) [53]. Overall, multiparous women appear to experience higher concerns about their lack of social support, while primiparous are more worried about negative body changes or the maternal role [54]. Therefore, the information that should be provided to them and the adjustment of their expectations during pregnancy should consider the woman's parity status.

Our results showed that, when all biopsychosocial factors are included in a single model, only age and prenatal depressive symptoms were significant predictors of PPD. As anticipated and in line with previous research [8,9], prenatal depressive symptoms were the best predictors of PPD. What these findings suggest is that the intensity of depressive symptoms might remain relatively stable across time [17], so early detection and management should be a priority. Women regularly attend visits with the midwives during the perinatal period, so these appointments would represent good opportunities for mental health assessment and referral to a specialized mental health service when necessary.

Two of the strengths of the present investigation were the implementation of a longitudinal design and the use of technology for assessment. Current clinical practice guidelines recommended longitudinal assessments to detect and identify women at risk for PPD [6]. However, the high costs associated with extensive longitudinal evaluations make the implementation of such screening programs in the current public health systems difficult. While there is some promising evidence on the utility of ICT in this field to overcome dissemination- and cost-related barriers [55], there are research gaps in programs of these characteristics, as the technologies used tend to be old-fashioned (i.e., SMS texts or phone calls) and little research has been conducted in the prenatal period [56]. The use of app-based or web-based screening and treatment methods should be encouraged in this population to maximize the benefits associated with the use of technology, especially during the prenatal period to ensure an early detection and treatment of this problem.

4.3. Limitations

The present study certainly has limitations. In our sample, the women were Spanish, well-educated, and predominantly were in a stable couple, so our results may not be generalized to all pregnant women populations. Sample size and dropout rates were also a problem. In this study, the participants were initially 266 perinatal women, but the longitudinal nature of the investigation and the number of included measures likely influence negatively the response rates (i.e., some women responding to a part of the assessment only) and dropouts. In fact, one of the present study goals was to explore whether communalities between constructs exist. This represents important information for reducing assessment protocols to a more manageable set. Another solution to long assessments is the validation of single-item measures against full-length traditional scales, which appears to be feasible and important when using technology (i.e., apps) for repeated assessment [57]. Gamification or gift cards are additional methods to increase adherence to longitudinal assessments. It is important to note that several measures exist to assess depressive symptoms during the perinatal period. Some authors found that the BDI-II, the measure used in the present study, could overestimate the prevalence of depressive symptoms in this population due to its extensive assessment of somatic symptoms [58]. Somatic symptoms are indeed prevalent and underestimated during the perinatal period, which explains why some authors recommended their assessment [59]. Given that both the Edinburgh Postnatal Depression Scale (EPDS) and the BDI-II seem to be accurate in evaluating depressive symptoms [60], future studies should explore whether the prevalence of symptoms in perinatal women is inflated when the BDI-II is administered. An additional limitation in the study was the focus on self-report measures. While this is a frequent practice and provides important information about the subjective state of the individual, the fidelity of the data (i.e., honesty, bias, or understanding and interpretation of items) cannot be guaranteed. This is important when assessing sensitive information, such as ambivalence. However, it is also possible that the assessment procedure used (i.e., online as opposed to face-to-face) actually promoted a sense of anonymity and, thus, enhanced honesty. Another potential problem in the study refers to the use of post hoc questions. The majority of questionnaires administered were full-length scales validated in Spanish populations. However, an important construct, namely pregnancy ambivalence, was measured using an ad hoc item. This practice might represent a threat to the comparability of results. Finally, it is important to note that, despite the fact that a set of important biopsychosocial factors associated with perinatal depressive symptoms was selected, the list is far from complete. For example, biological factors, such as reproductive and stress hormones, psychological variables, such as beliefs and perceived anxiety control, social factors such as marital satisfaction and peer support, and contextual information (i.e., seasonal time frame or seasonal light exposure), have also been linked with depressive symptomatology in perinatal research [15,61], but were not included in the present study for feasibility reasons.

5. Conclusions

The assessment of a set of biopsychosocial factors in the present study provides a broader picture of the relationship between biological (age), psychological (affective ambivalence and personality characteristics), and social (social support) factors, and concurrent and prospective depressive symptoms in perinatal women. Our results confirm the need to repeatedly evaluate depressive symptoms in perinatal women. Our SEM analyses revealed that (a) prenatal depressive symptoms were the best biopsychosocial predictors of PPD, (b) for adult women (>18 years old), being younger appears to be a protective factor against perinatal depressive symptoms, especially in the postpartum period, (c) ambivalence about pregnancy and negative affect are related to increased concurrent but not prospective depressive symptoms, and (d) positive affect is associated with reduced concurrent depressive symptoms. The study findings suggest that biopsychosocial longitudinal assessments and intervention protocols that begin during pregnancy and continue in the postpartum are required for this population. In the light of our results, such treatment programs should emphasize the importance of emotional regulation strategies to increase positive affect and to reduce negative affect in women. A recent example is the Unified Protocol for the transdiagnostic treatment of emotional disorders [62,63], but it also includes educational components to help adjust the women's expectations and face the challenges associated with motherhood, especially in older women. From this study and past experience, we recommend the use of ICT in such programs (i.e., blinded treatments combining onsite and online treatment and ecological momentary assessment with apps) to minimize some of the dissemination and stigma barriers of traditional assessments methods.

Author Contributions: Conceptualization, J.O., V.M.-B., and L.A.-P.; methodology, C.S.-R.; formal analysis, C.S.-R. and V.M.-B.; writing—original draft preparation, V.M.-B.; writing—review and editing, J.O., C.S.-R. and L.A.-P.; funding acquisition, J.O. All authors have read and agreed to the published version of the manuscript.

Funding: This research was funded by the Universitat Jaume I, grant number PREDOC/2018/43; the Gobierno de Aragon (Departamento de Innovacion, Investigación y Universidad) and Feder 2014–2020 "Construyendo Europa Desde Aragón", research group grant S31_20D; the Conselleria de Sanidad (Agencia Valenciana de Salud), grant number SMP 45/2011; the Fundación Universitaria Antonio Gargallo and the Obra Social Ibercaja, grant numbers 2013/B006 and 2014/B006.

Acknowledgments: We would like to thank all collaborating centers, all healthcare professionals, and all women who voluntarily participated in this study.

Conflicts of Interest: The authors declare no conflict of interest.

References

1. Woody, C.A.; Ferrari, A.J.; Siskind, D.J.; Whiteford, H.A.; Harris, M.G. A systematic review and meta-regression of the prevalence and incidence of perinatal depression. *J. Affect. Disord.* **2017**, *219*, 86–92. [CrossRef] [PubMed]
2. O'Hara, M.; Wisner, K. Perinatal mental illness: Definition, description and aetiology. *Best Pract. Res. Clin. Obstet. Gynaecol.* **2014**, *28*, 3–12. [CrossRef] [PubMed]
3. World Health Organization Maternal and Child Mental Health. Available online: http://www.who.int/mental_health/maternal-child/maternal_mental_health/en/ (accessed on 17 February 2020).
4. Badon, S.E.; Hedderson, M.M.; Hyde, R.J.; Quesenberry, C.P.; Avalos, L.A. Pre- and Early Pregnancy Onset Depression and Subsequent Rate of Gestational Weight Gain. *J. Women's Health* **2019**, *28*, 1237–1245. [CrossRef] [PubMed]
5. Danaher, B.G.; Milgrom, J.; Seeley, J.R.; Stuart, S.; Schembri, C.; Tyler, M.S.; Ericksen, J.; Lester, W.; Gemmill, A.W.; Kosty, D.B.; et al. MomMoodBooster web-based intervention for postpartum depression: Feasibility trial results. *J. Med. Internet Res.* **2013**, *15*, e242. [CrossRef]
6. Byatt, N.; Carter, D.; Deligiannidis, K.M.; Epperson, C.N.; Meltzer-Brody, S.; Payne, J.L.; Robinson, G.; Silver, N.E.; Stowe, Z.; Van Niel, M.S.; et al. Position Statement on Screening and Treatment of Mood and Anxiety Disorders During Pregnancy and Postpartum. *APA Off. Actions* **2018**. Available online: https://www.psychiatry.org/File%20Library/About-APA/Organization-Documents-Policies/Policies/Position-Screening-and-Treatment-Mood-Anxiety-Disorders-During-Pregnancy-Postpartum.pdf (accessed on 14 November 2020).
7. Milgrom, J.; Martin, P.; Negri, L. *Treating Postnatal Depression: A Psychological Approach for Health Care Practicionaers*; John Wiley & Sons, Ltd.: Chichester, UK, 1999.
8. Biaggi, A.; Conroy, S.; Pawlby, S.; Pariante, C.M. Identifying the women at risk of antenatal anxiety and depression: A systematic review. *J. Affect. Disord.* **2016**, *191*, 62–77. [CrossRef]
9. Norhayati, M.N.; Nik Hazlina, N.H.; Asrenee, A.R.; Wan Emilin, W.M.A. Magnitude and risk factors for postpartum symptoms: A literature review. *J. Affect. Disord.* **2015**, *175*, 34–52. [CrossRef]
10. Chatillon, O.; Even, C. Antepartum depression: Prevalence, diagnosis and treatment. *Encephale* **2010**, *36*, 443–451. [CrossRef]
11. Peñacoba-Puente, C.; Marín-Morales, D.; Carmona-Monge, F.J.; Velasco Furlong, L. Post-Partum Depression, Personality, and Cognitive-Emotional Factors: A Longitudinal Study on Spanish Pregnant Women. *Health Care Women Int.* **2016**, *37*, 97–117. [CrossRef]
12. Bos, S.C.; Macedo, A.; Marques, M.; Pereira, A.T.; Maia, B.R.; Soares, M.J.; Valente, J.; Gomes, A.A.; Azevedo, M.H. Is positive affect in pregnancy protective of postpartum depression? *Rev. Bras. Psiquiatr.* **2013**, *35*, 5–12. [CrossRef]
13. Míguez, C.; Fernández, V.; Pereira, B. Depresión postparto y factores asociados en mujeres con embarazos de riesgo 1. *Behav. Psychol./Psicol. Conduct.* **2017**, *25*, 47–64.

14. Hetherington, E.; McDonald, S.; Williamson, T.; Patten, S.B.; Tough, S.C. Social support and maternal mental health at 4 months and 1 year postpartum: Analysis from the All Our Families cohort. *J. Epidemiol. Community Health* **2018**, *72*, 933–939. [CrossRef] [PubMed]
15. Yim, I.S.; Tanner Stapleton, L.R.; Guardino, C.M.; Hahn-Holbrook, J.; Dunkel Schetter, C. Biological and psychosocial predictors of postpartum depression: Systematic review and call for integration. *Annu. Rev. Clin. Psychol.* **2015**, *11*, 99–137. [CrossRef] [PubMed]
16. Adamu, A.F.; Adinew, Y.M. Domestic Violence as a Risk Factor for Postpartum Depression Among Ethiopian Women: Facility Based Study. *Clin. Pract. Epidemiol. Ment. Health* **2018**, *14*, 109–119. [CrossRef] [PubMed]
17. Park, M.; Brain, U.; Grunau, R.; Diamond, A.; Oberlander, T. Maternal depression trajectories from pregnancy to 3 years postpartum are associated with children's behavior and executive functions at 3 and 6 years. *Arch. Womens. Ment. Health* **2018**, *21*, 353–363. [CrossRef]
18. Lara, M.A.; Navarrete, L.; Nieto, L.; Berenzon, S. Acceptability and barriers to treatment for perinatal depression. An exploratory study in Mexican women. *Salud Ment.* **2014**, *37*, 293–301. [CrossRef]
19. Clout, D.; Brown, R. Sociodemographic, pregnancy, obstetric, and postnatal predictors of postpartum stress, anxiety and depression in new mothers. *J. Affect. Disord.* **2015**, *188*, 60–67. [CrossRef]
20. Bennett, H.A.; Einarson, A.; Taddio, A.; Koren, G.; Einarson, T.R. Prevalence of depression during pregnancy: Systematic review. *Obstet. Gynecol.* **2004**, *103*, 698–709. [CrossRef]
21. Takehara, K.; Tachibana, Y.; Yoshida, K.; Mori, R.; Kakee, N.; Kubo, T. Prevalence trends of pre- and postnatal depression in Japanese women: A population-based longitudinal study. *J. Affect. Disord.* **2018**, *225*, 389–394. [CrossRef]
22. Qandil, S.; Jabr, S.; Wagler, S.; Collin, S.M. Postpartum depression in the Occupied Palestinian Territory: A longitudinal study in Bethlehem. *BMC Pregnancy Childbirth* **2016**, *16*, 375. [CrossRef]
23. Harris, R. *A Primer of Multivariate Statistics*, 3rd ed.; LEA: Mahwah, NJ, USA, 2001.
24. Harrell, F. *Regression Modeling Strategies: With Applications to Linear Models, Logistic Regression, and Survival Analysis*; Springer: New York, NY, USA, 2001.
25. Beck, A.; Steer, R.; Brown, G. *Manual for the Beck Depression Inventory-II.*; Psychological Corporation: San Antonio, TX, USA, 1996; ISBN 0158018389.
26. Sanz, J.; Perdigón, A.; Vázquez, C. Adaptación Española del inventario para la depresión de Beck-II (BDI-II): 2. Propiedades psicométricas en población general. *Clínica y Salud* **2003**, *14*, 249–280.
27. Sanz, J.; Gutiérrez, S.; Gesteira, C.; García-Vera, M. Criteria and norms for interpreting the Beck Depression Inventory-II (BDI-II). *Behav. Psychol. Psicol. Conduct.* **2014**, *22*, 37–59.
28. Sandín, B.; Chorot, P.; Lostao, L.; Joiner, T.; Santed, M.; Valiente, R. Escalas PANAS de afecto positivo y negativo: Validación factorial y convergencia transcultural. *Psicothema* **1999**, *11*, 37–51.
29. Watson, D.; Clark, L.; Tellegen, A. Development and validation of brief measures of positive and negative affect: The PANAS scales. *J. Pers. Soc. Psychol.* **1988**, *54*, 1063–1070. [CrossRef] [PubMed]
30. Eysenck, H.; Eysenck, S. *Manual of Eysenck Personality Questionnaire*; Hodder & Stoughton: London, UK, 1975.
31. Ortet, G.; Ibáñez, M.; Moro, M.; Silva, F. *Cuestionario Revisado de Personalidad de Eysenck: Versiones Completa (EPQ-R) y Abreviada (EPQ-RS)*; TEA Ediciones: Madrid, Spain, 2001.
32. Landeta, O.; Calvete, E. Adaptación y validación de la escala multidimensional de apoyo social percibido. *Ansiedad y Estrés* **2002**, *8*, 173–182.
33. Zimet, G.D.; Dahlem, N.W.; Zimet, S.G.; Farley, G.K. The Multidimensional Scale of Perceived Social Support. *J. Pers. Assess.* **1988**, *52*, 30–41. [CrossRef]
34. Hooper, D.; Coughlan, J.; Mullen, M. Structural equation modelling: Guidelines for determining model fit. *Electron. J. Bus. Res. Methods* **2008**, *6*, 53–59. [CrossRef]
35. Cupani, M. Análisis de Ecuaciones Estructurales: Conceptos, etapas de desarrollo y un ejemplo de aplicación. *Tesis* **2012**, *1*, 186–199.
36. Hu, L.; Bentler, P.M. Cutoff criteria for fit indexes in covariance structure analysis: Conventional criteria versus new alternatives. *Struct. Equ. Model. Multidiscip. J.* **1999**, *6*, 1–55. [CrossRef]
37. DiStefano, C.; Morgan, G.B. A Comparison of Diagonal Weighted Least Squares Robust Estimation Techniques for Ordinal Data. *Struct. Equ. Model. Multidiscip. J.* **2014**, *21*, 425–438. [CrossRef]
38. Rubin, M. Do p values lose their meaning in exploratory analyses? It depends how you define the familywise error rate. *Rev. Gen. Psychol.* **2017**, *21*, 269–275. [CrossRef]
39. Beck, C. Predictors of postpartum depression: An update. *Nurs. Res.* **2001**, *50*, 275–285. [CrossRef] [PubMed]

40. Strelow, B.; Fellows, N.; Fink, S.R.; O'Laughlin, D.J.; Radke, G.; Stevens, J.; Tweedy, J.M. Postpartum depression in older women. *J. Am. Acad. Physician Assist.* **2018**, *31*, 15–18. [CrossRef] [PubMed]
41. Moeller, S.B.; Lars Kessing, P.B.; Mortensen, E.L. A Psychometric Validation Analysis of Eysenck's Neuroticism and Extraversion Scales in a Sample of First Time Depressed Patients. *J. Depress. Anxiety* **2015**, *4*, 1–6. [CrossRef]
42. Guardino, C.M.; Dunkel-Schetter, C. Coping during pregnancy: A systematic review and recommendations. *Health Psychol. Rev.* **2014**, *8*, 70–94. [CrossRef]
43. Milgrom, J.; Hirshler, Y.; Reece, J.; Charlene, C.H.; Gemmill Alan, A.W. Social support—A protective factor for depressed perinatal women? *Int. J. Environ. Res. Public Health* **2019**, *16*, 1426. [CrossRef]
44. Doraiswamy, S.; Jithesh, A.; Chaabane, S.; Abraham, A.; Chaabna, K.; Cheema, S. Perinatal mental illness in the middle east and North Africa region—A systematic overview. *Int. J. Environ. Res. Public Health* **2020**, *17*, 5487. [CrossRef]
45. Leahy-Warren, P.; Newham, J.; Alderdice, F. Perinatal social support: Panacea or a pitfall. *J. Reprod. Infant Psychol.* **2018**, *36*, 219–221. [CrossRef]
46. Saeed Abbasi, I.; Rattan, N.; Kousar, T.; Khalifa Elsayed, F. Neuroticism and Close Relationships: How Negative Affect is Linked with Relationship Disaffection in Couples. *Am. J. Fam. Ther.* **2018**, *46*, 139–152. [CrossRef]
47. Hain, S.; Oddo-Sommerfeld, S.; Bahlmann, F.; Louwen, F.; Schermelleh-Engel, K. Risk and protective factors for antepartum and postpartum depression: A prospective study. *J. Psychosom. Obstet. Gynecol.* **2016**, *37*, 119–129. [CrossRef]
48. Maloni, J.A.; Przeworski, A.; Damato, E.G. Web recruitment and internet use and preferences reported by women with postpartum depression after pregnancy complications. *Arch. Psychiatr. Nurs.* **2013**, *27*, 90–95. [CrossRef]
49. O'Neill, P.; Cycon, A.; Friedman, L. Seeking social support and postpartum depression: A pilot retrospective study of perceived changes. *Midwifery* **2019**, *71*, 56–62. [CrossRef] [PubMed]
50. McMahon, C.A.; Boivin, J.; Gibson, F.L.; Hammarberg, K.; Wynter, K.; Fisher, J.R.W. Older maternal age and major depressive episodes in the first two years after birth: Findings from the Parental Age and Transition to Parenthood Australia (PATPA) study. *J. Affect. Disord.* **2015**, *175*, 454–462. [CrossRef] [PubMed]
51. Nassar, A.H.; Usta, I.M. Advanced Maternal Age. Part II: Long-Term Consequences. *Am. J. Perinatol.* **2009**, *26*, 107–112. [CrossRef] [PubMed]
52. Lara-Cinisomo, S.; Clark, C.T.; Wood, J. Increasing Diagnosis and Treatment of Perinatal Depression in Latinas and African American Women: Addressing Stigma Is Not Enough. *Women's Health Issues* **2018**, *28*, 201–204. [CrossRef] [PubMed]
53. Parvin, S.; Sakineh, N.; Seyed, M.; Bahram, G.; Hashem, A. Comparing postpartum stressors and social support level in primiparous and multiparous women. *J. Midwifery Reprod. Health* **2014**, *2*, 71–77.
54. Hung, C.H. The psychosocial consequences for primiparas and multiparas. *Kaohsiung J. Med. Sci.* **2007**, *23*, 352–360. [CrossRef]
55. Donker, T.; Cuijpers, P.; Stanley, D.; Danaher, B. The Future of Perinatal Depression Identification Can Information and Communication Technology Optimize Effectiveness? In *Identifying Perinatal Depression and Anxiety: Evidence-Based Practice in Screening, Psychosocial Assessment, and Management*; Wiley-Blackwell: Oxford, UK, 2015; pp. 240–255. ISBN 978-1-118-50969-2.
56. Martínez-Borba, V.; Suso-ribera, C.; Osma, J. The Use of Information and Communication Technologies in Perinatal Depression Screening: A Systematic Review. *Cyberpsychol. Behav. Soc. Netw.* **2018**, *21*, 741–752. [CrossRef]
57. Suso-Ribera, C.; Castilla, D.; Zaragozá, I.; Ribera-Canudas, M.V.; Botella, C.; García-Palacios, A. Validity, reliability, feasibility, and usefulness of Pain Monitor. A multidimensional smartphone app for daily monitoring of adults with heterogeneous chronic pain. *Clin. J. Pain* **2018**, *34*, 900–908. [CrossRef]
58. Čuržik, D.; Nataša Begić, J. The utility of BDI-II in assessment of pre-and postpartum depression symptoms and their relation to labor pain. *Psychiatr. Danub.* **2012**, *24*, 167–174.
59. Carvalho Bos, S.; Pereira, A.T.; Marques, M.; Maia, B.; Soares, M.J.; Valente, J.; Gomes, A.; Macedo, A.; Azevedo, M.H. The BDI-II factor structure in pregnancy and postpartum: Two or three factors? *Eur. Psychiatry* **2009**, *24*, 334–340. [CrossRef]
60. Darius Tandon, S.; Cluxton-Keller, F.; Leis, J.; Le, H.-N.; Perry, D.F. A comparison of three screening tools to identify perinatal depression among low-income African American women. *J. Affect. Disord.* **2012**, *136*, 155–162. [CrossRef] [PubMed]
61. Goyal, D.; Gay, C.; Torres, R.; Lee, K. Shortening day length: A potential risk factor for perinatal depression. *J. Behav. Med.* **2018**, *41*, 690–702. [CrossRef] [PubMed]

62. Barlow, D.H.; Farchione, T.J.; Fairholme, C.P.; Ellard, K.K.; Boisseau, C.L.; Allen, L.B.; Ehrenreich-May, J.; Fairholme, C.P.; Farchione, T.J.; Boisseau, C.L.; et al. *Unified Protocol for Transdiagnostic Treatment of Emotional Disorders: Therapist Guide*; Treatments that work; Oxford University Press: New York, NY, USA, 2011; ISBN 978-0-19-977266-7. (Paperback).
63. Crespo-Delgado, E.; Martínez-Borba, V.; Osma, J. The Unified Protocol for Transdiagnostic Treatment of Perinatal Depression: A Case Study. *Clin. Case Stud.* **2020**, *19*, 491–508. [CrossRef]

International Journal of
Environmental Research and Public Health

MDPI

Article

States Transitions Inference of Postpartum Depression Based on Multi-State Markov Model

Juan Xiong, Qiyu Fang, Jialing Chen, Yingxin Li, Huiyi Li, Wenjie Li and Xujuan Zheng *

Health Science Center, Shenzhen University, Shenzhen 518060, China; jxiong@szu.edu.cn (J.X.); fangqiyu320@szu.edu.cn (Q.F.); chenjialing0829@163.com (J.C.); Wuwu009lyx@163.com (Y.L.); 18576627549@163.com (H.L.); 2019227013@szu.edu.cn (W.L.)

* Correspondence: zhengxujuan@szu.edu.cn

Abstract: *Background*: Postpartum depression (PPD) has been recognized as a severe public health problem worldwide due to its high incidence and the detrimental consequences not only for the mother but for the infant and the family. However, the pattern of natural transition trajectories of PPD has rarely been explored. *Methods:* In this research, a quantitative longitudinal study was conducted to explore the PPD progression process, providing information on the transition probability, hazard ratio, and the mean sojourn time in the three postnatal mental states, namely normal state, mild PPD, and severe PPD. The multi-state Markov model was built based on 912 depression status assessments in 304 Chinese primiparous women over multiple time points of six weeks postpartum, three months postpartum, and six months postpartum. *Results*: Among the 608 PPD status transitions from one visit to the next visit, 6.2% (38/608) showed deterioration of mental status from the level at the previous visit; while 40.0% (243/608) showed improvement at the next visit. A subject in normal state who does transition then has a probability of 49.8% of worsening to mild PPD, and 50.2% to severe PPD. A subject with mild PPD who does transition has a 20.0% chance of worsening to severe PPD. A subject with severe PPD is more likely to improve to mild PPD than developing to the normal state. On average, the sojourn time in the normal state, mild PPD, and severe PPD was 64.12, 6.29, and 9.37 weeks, respectively. Women in normal state had 6.0%, 8.5%, 8.7%, and 8.8% chances of progress to severe PPD within three months, nine months, one year, and three years, respectively. Increased all kinds of supports were associated with decreased risk of deterioration from normal state to severe PPD (hazard ratio, HR: 0.42–0.65); and increased informational supports, evaluation of support, and maternal age were associated with alleviation from severe PPD to normal state (HR: 1.46–2.27). *Conclusions:* The PPD state transition probabilities caused more attention and awareness about the regular PPD screening for postnatal women and the timely intervention for women with mild or severe PPD. The preventive actions on PPD should be conducted at the early stages, and three yearly; at least one yearly screening is strongly recommended. Emotional support, material support, informational support, and evaluation of support had significant positive associations with the prevention of PPD progression transitions. The derived transition probabilities and sojourn time can serve as an importance reference for health professionals to make proactive plans and target interventions for PPD.

Keywords: multi-state Markov model; postpartum depression; transition probability; proactive prevention

Citation: Xiong, J.; Fang, Q.; Chen, J.; Li, Y.; Li, H.; Li, W.; Zheng, X. States Transitions Inference of Postpartum Depression Based on Multi-State Markov Model. *Int. J. Environ. Res. Public Health* **2021**, *18*, 7449. https://doi.org/10.3390/ijerph18147449

Academic Editor: M.Carmen Míguez Varela

Received: 17 June 2021
Accepted: 10 July 2021
Published: 13 July 2021

1. Introduction

Postpartum depression (PPD) is defined as a non-psychotic depressive episode beginning in or extending to the postpartum period [1]. In addition to the similar symptoms of depression at other times of life such as loss of interest, insomnia, irritability, exhaustion, poor concentration, low self-respect, and thoughts of suicide, women who have PPD also experience guilty feelings about taking care of their new baby [2–5]. Due to the high incidence worldwide, PPD has been recognized as a severe public health problem during the last decades [3,6]. Longitudinal and epidemiological studies have found the at the prevalence of PPD in different countries varied from 10% to more than 25% in the first year postpartum [7–9]. A systematic review reported that the average prevalence of PPD in developed countries was 19.2% among mothers [10], while in low- and middle-income countries, up to 20–25% of women were found to suffer from PPD [11].

In addition to its high incidence, PPD can lead to several detrimental consequences in the longer terms not only for the mother, but for the infant and the family as a whole [12]. First, PPD is associated with the hazards for the mother's mental and physical wellbeing [3,13]. PPD was found to be one of the leading causes of maternal morbidity and mortality in various countries [3]. Second, PPD is related to the impairment of mother–infant attachment [14] and maternal self-efficacy [15,16], which could lead to the longer-term disruption of motional and cognitive development of the infant [14,17]. Additionally, women with PPD are more likely to stop breastfeeding earlier than non-depressed mothers [18,19]. Third, PPD has an adverse effect on the marital relationship and the psychological health of the spouse [20]. For instance, PPD had a considerable burden on close family members, affecting social and leisure activities and posing financial challenges within the family [17].

Extensive studies have identified various risk factors of PPD including biological and psychological categories [21,22]. Biological risk factors of PPD included the endocrine system, the immune system, and genetic factors [23–25]. Psychosocial factors involved previous history of depression and anxiety, marital status, stressful status, social support, etc. [26,27]. From the perspective of risk factor discovery, regression and structural equation analysis have been widely used in PPD studies to explore the factors [3,15,16,28]. However, the above analysis offers little information about the dynamic process of disease evaluation [29].

In the existing literature, the pattern of nature progressive trajectories of PPD from normal status has been poorly explored. Therefore, it would be worth investigating its natural progression for early detection and prevention of PPD. It is noted that multi-state Markov modeling is a modeling technique that has been widely used in the medical field to analyze the progression of a variety of diseases such as high blood pressure, diabetes, and chronic kidney disease [29–31]. Likewise, it can be used to analyze the transition from a normal (non-disease) state, through a mild state to a severe and/or death state [32]. In this study, we were interested in estimating the average transition rates between depression states, and also wanted to investigate potential factors related to the rates of transition. The depression statuses are represented as Markov states, and the depression status changes are shown as transition probabilities between states. Thereby, a multi-state Markov model was used in this research to explore the PPD progression process, providing information on the transition probability, hazard ratio, and the mean sojourn time in each state to fill the research gap.

2. Materials and Methods

2.1. Study Design and Participants

A quantitative longitudinal study was conducted to uncover the state transitions of PPD based on the multi-state Markov model among Chinese primiparous women. Ethical approval of this research was conducted in the Health Science Center at Shenzhen University. Women were eligible to enroll in the study if they were married; aged 18 years or above; first-time mothers with healthy baby; and able to respond to the questionnaires. Women were excluded from the study if they or their infants had serious diseases. From January to December 2020, a total of 644 participants were recruited in the Department of Obstetrics and Gynecology of the three public hospitals in China. Flow of participants through the study is illustrated in Figure 1. Before data collection, all participants provided written informed consent and were informed of the purpose of the study and freedom to withdraw at any time in the research process.

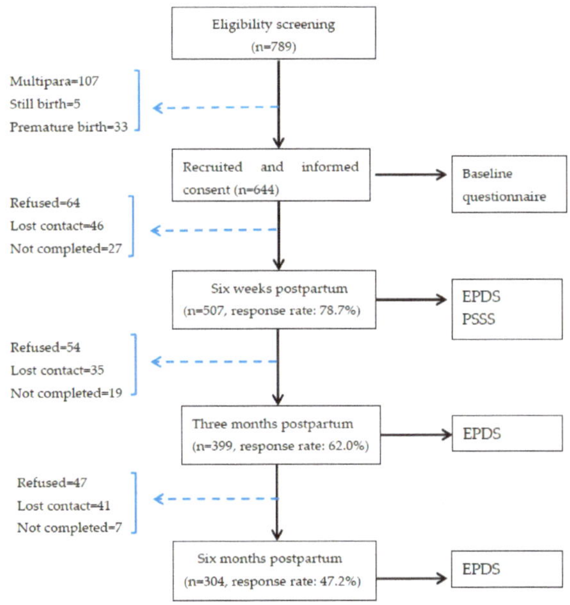

Figure 1. Flow of participants through the study. EPDS: Edinburgh Postnatal Depression Scale; PSSS: Postpartum Social Support Scale.

2.2. Measurements

Data on maternal age, marital status, maternal education, occupation, family income (per person, month), mode of childbirth, whether attending parenting training, baby gender, baby health, and baby fussiness via self-report by new mothers were collected by baseline questionnaires developed by the researchers.

The researchers measured the depressive symptoms by the Edinburgh Postnatal Depression Scale (EPDS) [33], which is the most widely used screening tool for PPD, and translated into over 60 different languages [34]. EPDS is a comprehensive, easy to administer, self-reporting scale of ten short items, where responses are scored from 0 to 30 based on the symptom severity. The higher score indicates the worse mental health status women have. The reported Cronbach's alpha coefficient of Chinese version EPDS was 0.87, and its concurrent validity with the BDI (Beck Depression Inventory) was 0.79 [35]. In the present study, the internal consistency of the EPDS was 0.87. According to the maximized combined sensitivity and specificity of this tool, a 0–9 score was categorized as "normal state", scores of 10–12 were categorized as "mild PPD", and those more than 13 were listed as "severe PPD" in mainland China [35–37].

Postpartum Social Support Scale (PSSS) in the Chinese version was used to assess the various supports received by primiparous women after childbirth. The 20-item instrument includes four kinds of postnatal support including emotional support (five items), material support (five items), informational support (five items), and evaluation of support (five items). The scale uses the 4-point Likert score type and ranges from 0 to 3 points depending on the response options of "never", "rarely", "sometimes", and "often". A higher score the mother obtains, the more postnatal support she receives. The Cronbach's alpha coefficient of this tool was 0.89 [38]. The internal consistency of PSSS was 0.90 in the current research.

2.3. Data Collection Procedure

Baseline questionnaires and contact details of participants were collected in the Department of Obstetrics and Gynecology by the research team face to face on the third to the fifth day postpartum. The electronic documents of EPDS and PSSS were sent to participants via WeChat or email at six weeks postpartum. The follow up electronic EPDS was likewise distributed to these women at three months postpartum, and six months postpartum, respectively. The WeChat or call reminders were given to participants before and after one week, and one day of the three different time points to improve the response rate.

2.4. Data Analysis

Descriptive statistics were used to describe the social-demographic characteristics and clinical variables by mean (M), standard deviation (SD), and frequency proportions. Hazard ratios (HRs) and corresponding 95% confidence intervals (CIs) were used in the statistical analysis. The multi-state Markov model was built using the msm package of R software.

In the Markov model, there were three PPD states of interest: state 1 (normal state), state 2 (mild PPD), and state 3 (severe PPD). Figure 2 illustrates nine possible transitions among the three transient states. For example, a new mother can stay in the current state or transit to any of the other states such as normal → normal, normal→ mild, normal → severe, mild → mild, mild → severe, mild → normal, severe → severe, severe → mild, severe → normal. The sojourn time means the average length of time staying in a transient state before transiting to a new state.

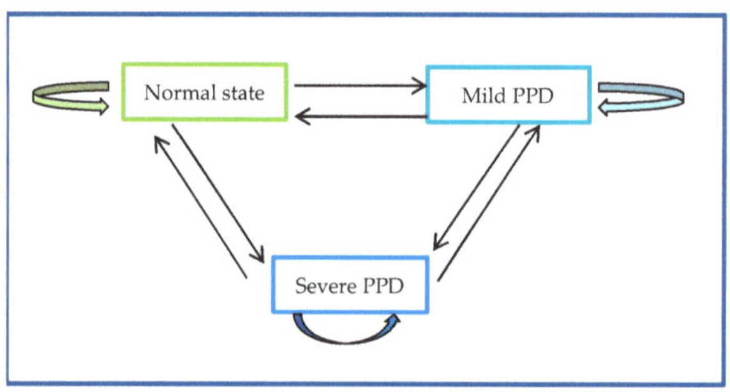

Figure 2. Three PPD state transitions in the Markov model.

3. Results

3.1. Social-Demographic and Clinical Characteristics of the Participants

There were 304 participants who completed the questionnaires at six weeks postpartum, three months postpartum, and six months postpartum. These social-demographic and clinical characteristics of primiparous women are summarized in Table 1. For example, the average age of these participants was 24.8 (2.89) years and all of them were married.

Table 1. Social-demographic and clinical characteristics of the participants.

Variables	Total (n = 304)
Age, mean (SD)	24.8 (2.89)
Marital status, n (%)	
Married	304 (100.0%)
Divorced	0 (0.0%)
Single	0 (0.0%)
Education, n (%)	
Middle school or lower	78 (25.6%)
High school or junior college	123 (40.5%)
University or higher	103 (33.9%)

Table 1. *Cont.*

Variables	Total (n = 304)
Occupation, n (%)	
Professional	10 (3.3%)
Skilled	25 (8.2%)
Unskilled	181 (59.5%)
Unemployed	88 (29.0%)
Family income (per person, month), n (%)	
<3000 yuan (US$420)	73 (24.0%)
3001—5000 yuan (US$420–700)	144 (47.4%)
>5000 yuan (US$700)	87 (28.6%)
Delivery mode, n (%)	
Natural childbirth	218 (71.7%)
Assisted childbirth	46 (15.1%)
C-section	40 (13.2%)
Whether attending parenting train, n (%)	
Yes	157 (51.6%)
No	147(48.4%)
Baby gender, n (%)	
Boy	181 (59.5%)
Girl	123 (40.5%)
Baby health, mean (SD)	80.5 (15.49)
Baby fussiness, mean (SD)	69.6 (19.89)
Emotional support, mean (SD)	10.2 (2.72)
Material support, mean (SD)	9.9 (3.43)
Informational support, mean (SD)	6.8 (3.14)
Evaluation of support, mean (SD)	8.4 (2.92)

3.2. Observed Numbers of PPD Status Transitions from One Visit to the Next Visit

Among the 912 depression status assessments in the 304 women over the period 6–24 weeks postpartum, 304 measurements were taken in the initial visit (T1: six weeks postpartum) and 608 measurements were taken at follow-up visits (T2: three months postpartum, T3: six months postpartum). Table 2 shows the number of transitions from one visit (given by the row state) to the next one (given by the column state). Of the 608 transitions, 6.2% (38/608) showed deterioration of mental status from the level at the previous visit, while 40.0% (243/608) showed improvement at the next visit, and 53.8% (327/608) showed no change. For example, there were 155 transitions where the participant had no PPD (normal state) and remained in the normal state at the next visit, and nine cases where a participant in normal state developed mild PPD at the next visit. There were ten cases where participants in the normal state developed severe PPD. Similarly, there were 33 occurrences where participants remained in mild PPD and 19 cases where participants progressed from mild PPD to severe PPD at the following visit.

Table 2. Observed number of PPD transitions from one visit to the next visit.

From\To	Normal State n (%)	Mild PPD n (%)	Severe PPD n (%)
T1 Normal state	155(25.5%)	9 (1.5%)	10 (1.6%)
T2 Mild PPD	88 (14.5%)	33 (5.4%)	19 (3.1%)
T3 Severe PPD	63 (10.3%)	92 (15.1%)	139 (22.9)

Note: State 1: Normal state (EPDS < 10); State 2: Mild PPD (EPDS $\geq$ 10); State 3: Severe PPD (EPDS $\geq$ 13); Time points: T1 (6 weeks), T2 (3 months), T3 (6 months). PPD: Postpartum depression; EPDS: Edinburgh Postnatal Depression Scale.

3.3. PPD State Transition Probabilities

Table 3 presents the model estimated probability of the next transition if and when a subject transitions from the current state at an examination, and the estimated sojourn time while in each state. For example, a subject in normal state who does transition then has a probability of 49.8% of worsening to mild PPD, and 50.2% to severe PPD. The subject with mild PPD who does transition has an 80.0% chance of improving to normal state or 20.0% chance of worsening to severe PPD. A subject with severe PPD is more likely to improve to mild PPD than developing to the normal state. On average, subjects remained in a normal state for 64.12 weeks before transitions to other states (sojourn time), remained in mild PPD for 6.29 weeks, and in severe PPD for 9.37 weeks.

Table 3. PPD state transition probabilities.

From\To	Normal PPD	Mild PPD	Severe PPD
Normal state	-	0.498	0.502
Mild PPD	0.800	-	0.200
Severe PPD	0.064	0.936	-
Sojourn Time (weeks)	64.12	6.29	9.37

Note: The sojourn time means the average length of time staying in a transient state before transiting to a new state.

3.4. Model-Estimated Transition Probabilities over a Given Follow-Up Interval

On the basis of the probabilities of transitions from state to state, the researchers computed the probabilities over a given follow-up interval of deterioration progress (state 1 through 2 to state 3) and alleviation progress (state 3 through 2 to state 1). Probability over a follow-up interval of one month to three years is shown in Table 4 and Figure 3. For example, women in normal state (state 1) had 6.0%, 8.5%, 8.7%, and 8.8% chance of progress to severe PPD (state 3) if the next checkup was performed after the interval of three months, nine months, one year, and three years, respectively. In contrast, women with severe PPD had 40.7%, 76.9%, 80.1%, and 81.6% chance of alleviation to normal state within three months, nine months, one year, and three years, respectively.

Table 4. Model-estimated transition probabilities over a given follow-up interval.

Interval of Follow-Up	State 1 to State 3 Percent (95% CI)	State 2 to State 3 Percent (95% CI)	State 3 to State 1 Percent (95% CI)	State 2 to State 1 Percent (95% CI)
1 month	0.028 (0.015, 0.059)	0.085 (0.050, 0.149)	0.104 (0.086, 0.143)	0.390 (0.332, 0.445)
3 month	0.060 (0.036, 0.108)	0.114 (0.080, 0.171)	0.407(0.351, 0.473)	0.680 (0.600, 0.735)
6 month	0.079 (0.050, 0.144)	0.101 (0.073, 0.157)	0.673(0.601, 0.721)	0.782 (0.700, 0.826)
9 month	0.085 (0.054, 0.150)	0.093 (0.063, 0.152)	0.769 (0.681, 0.818)	0.806 (0.709, 0.859)
1 year	0.087 (0.057, 0.161)	0.090 (0.059, 0.162)	0.801 (0.694, 0.851)	0.813 (0.700, 0.866)
2 year	0.088 (0.054, 0.149)	0.088 (0.054, 0.149)	0.816(0.712, 0.873)	0.816 (0.712, 0.873)
3 year	0.088 (0.056, 0.147)	0.088 (0.056, 0.147)	0.816 (0.718, 0.871)	0.816 (0.718, 0.871)

Note: Interval of follow-up refers to the time to the next examination for women in a given state at the beginning of the interval. State 1: Normal state (EPDS < 10); State 2: Mild PPD (EPDS ≥ 10); State 3: Severe PPD (EPDS ≥ 13).

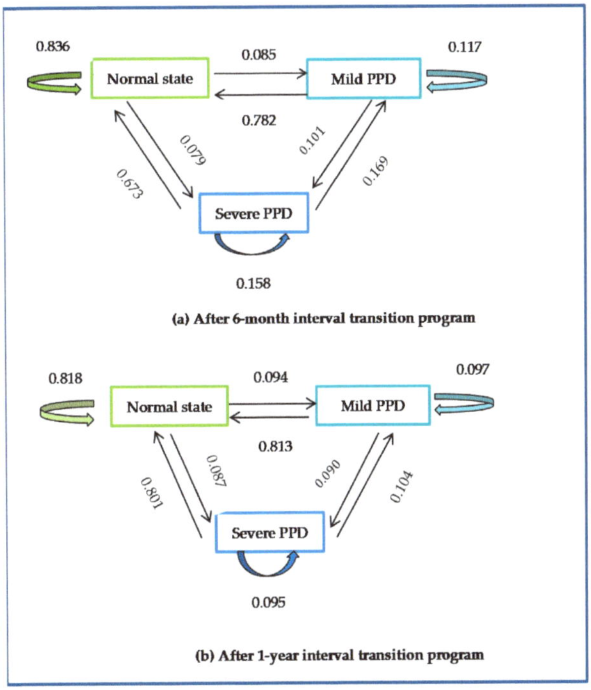

Figure 3. State transition diagrams.

3.5. Covariate Effects and Patient-Specific Risks

The covariates in the research included maternal age, marital status, maternal education, occupation, family income (per person, month), mode of childbirth, whether attending parenting training, baby gender, baby health, baby fussiness, emotional support, material support, informational support, and evaluation of support. The effects of covariates on PPD transition intensity with statistical significance are summarized in Tables 5 and 6. Emotional support, material support, informational support, evaluation of support, and maternal age had some significant unadjusted associations with possible transitions. For example, increase in all kinds of support was associated with decreased risk of deterioration from the normal state (state 1) to severe PPD (state 3), and increased informational supports and evaluation of support were associated with alleviation from severe PPD to normal state.

Table 5. The effects of covariates on PPD worsening transition.

Worsening Transition	Hazard Ratio (95% CI)
State 1 to State 3	
Emotional support	0.48 (0.33, 0.70)
Material support	0.65 (0.51, 0.82)
Informational support	0.57 (0.42, 0.76)
Evaluation of support	0.42 (0.22, 0.82)

Note: State 1: Normal state (EPDS < 10); State 2: Mild PPD (EPDS $\geq$ 10); State 3: Severe PPD (EPDS $\geq$ 13).

Table 6. The effects of covariates on PPD bettering transition.

Bettering Transition	Hazard Ratio (95% CI)
State 3 to State 1	
Informational support	1.59 (1.15, 2.19)
Evaluation of support	2.27 (1.12, 4.58)
Maternal age	1.46 (1.15, 1.86)
State 3 to State 2	
Evaluation of support	1.14 (1.04, 1.26)

Note: State 1: Normal state (EPDS < 10); State 2: Mild PPD (EPDS ≥ 10); State 3: Severe PPD (EPDS ≥ 13).

4. Discussion

Due to the high incidence and the severe consequence for mothers, infants, and families, PPD has become a severe public health problem worldwide during the last decades [3,6,12]. Thus, it was of significant importance to explore transition patterns in different PPD states and the risk factors relating to postnatal mental status alleviation and deterioration. Previous studies have investigated that primiparous women were more prone to suffer from PPD than multipara, and therefore worthy of more attention and investigation [15,16]. In the current research, a time-homogeneous continuous Markov model was used to explore the three PPD state transition probabilities, the mean sojourn time in each state, and the risk factors affecting the progression or regression of PPD in Chinese primiparous women, which has not been explored in the existing literature.

The present study found that of the 608 transitions, 6.2% (38/608) showed deterioration of PPD state from the level at the previous visit. In contrast, 40.0% (243/608) showed alleviation of PPD state at the next visit. It was consistent with the previous studies that indicated PPD symptoms in some women would remit with the passage to time [9,10,39]. However, a subject in normal state who does transition was found to have a probability of 49.8% of worsening to mild PPD and 50.2% to severe PPD; a subject with mild PPD had 20.0% chance of worsening to severe PPD; and a subject with severe PPD was more likely to improve to mild PPD than developing to a normal state. The results of PPD state transition probabilities have caused more attention and awareness about regular PPD screening for postnatal women and the timely intervention for women with mild or severe PPD. Health agencies in developed countries such as in the USA and the EU have recommended the regular screening of postpartum women to detect PPD symptoms [40–42].

Additionally, the transition probabilities over a 1-month to 3-year period were first estimated in the study. For instance, women in the normal state had 6.0%, 8.5%, 8.7%, and 8.8% chance of progress to severe PPD within three months, nine months, one year, and three years, respectively. Even though women with normal state had a low probability of developing PPD in the first postpartum year, the probability of maternal depression will increase substantially within three years. The findings well align with a prior study that found that PPD might persist for up to three years after childbirth [43]. The previous research showed approximately 25% of women had depressive symptoms at some point in the three years postpartum, and some women had increasing depressive symptoms over the three years [43]. Therefore, the preventive actions on PPD should be conducted at the early stages and three yearly; at least one yearly checkup or screening is strongly recommended, not merely during the period of pregnancy and postpartum visiting [44].

In terms of covariate effects, increase in all kinds of social supports was associated with decreased risk of deterioration from normal state to severe PPD (HR: 0.42–0.65) and increased informational supports and evaluation of support were associated with alleviation from severe PPD to the normal state (HR: 1.59–2.27). The previous research likewise identified that social support significantly affects the postnatal mental status for new mothers [15,16,45]. However, Chinese first-time mothers were reported to receive insufficient social support after childbirth, and particularly lacked adequate informational and appraisal support from health professionals [15,16]. It was almost not available for single support provider to offer all kinds of support [9]. Women's family and friends are expected to offer them great emotional support and material support such as love, trust, time, and money; and health professionals could be appropriate to supply women with much more informational support and evaluation of support (i.e., professional advice and instructions on PPD prevention and treatment) [9,45]. Thus, in order to improve mental health outcomes, the family members of women and health professionals should supply new mothers with increased support to improve outcomes. Health professionals also need to play a more active and significant role in PPD alleviation transitions by offering professional informational and appraisal support.

In summary, there are key contributions in the research. First, a multi-state Markov model was used to explore the state transition dynamics of three PPD states and investigate how various support types affected the progression or alleviation of PPD in the Chinese population. Furthermore, through the developed model, the sojourn time in each PPD state and the transition probabilities from one state to other state were estimated, thereby providing statistical foundations for regularly screening and time targeted interventions. However, some limitations of this study can be summarized as follows. First, recognizing the belief of "domestic shame should not be made public" [46], the percent of women with PPD could be underestimated. Second, women's lifestyles may change dramatically over such a long period, which could violate the model's assumption on time homogeneity, and it could lead to biases. Third, the potential effect of confounding covariates or interaction among covariates was not investigated in this study. Fourth, EPDS was the only screening tool of PPD used in the research, and the other commonly used depression measures such as the Beck Depression Inventory (BDI) and Montgomery-Asberg Depression Rating Scale (MADRS) could be used to test the results in further study.

5. Conclusions

The results of the PPD state transition probabilities have created more attention and awareness about regular PPD screening for postnatal women and the timely intervention for women with mild or severe PPD. The preventive actions on PPD should be conducted at the early stages and three yearly; at least one yearly checkup or screening is strongly recommended, not merely during the period of pregnancy and postpartum visiting. All kinds of support including emotional support, material support, informational support, and evaluation of support had significant positive associations with the prevention of PPD progression transitions. The derived transition probabilities and sojourn time can serve as an importance reference for health professionals to make proactive plans and targeted interventions for PPD.

Author Contributions: Conceptualization, X.Z. and J.X.; Investigation, Q.F., J.C., Y.L., H.L., and X.Z.; Data entry and analysis, J.X., W.L., and X.Z.; Writing—original draft preparation, X.Z.; Writing—review and editing, X.Z. and J.X.; Project administration, X.Z. All authors have read and agreed to the published version of the manuscript.

Funding: Xujuan Zheng (X.Z.) was supported by the National Natural Science Foundation of China youth project (grant no. 81703234), the Medical Science and Technology Research Fund Project of Guangdong Province (grant no. A2018335), the Basic Research Free Exploration Project of Shenzhen City (grant no. JCYJ20180305163459491), and the General Program of Stable Support Plan for Universities in Shenzhen City (grant no. 20200804101756002). Juan Xiong (J.X.) was supported by the National Natural Science Foundation of China (grant no. 81903412).

Institutional Review Board Statement: The study was conducted according to the guidelines of the Declaration of Helsinki, and approved by the Ethics Committee of Health Science Center, Shenzhen University (date of approval 30 October 2017).

Informed Consent Statement: Informed consent was obtained from all subjects involved in the study.

Data Availability Statement: The data presented in this study are available on request from the corresponding author. The data are not publicly available due to privacy restrictions.

Acknowledgments: We would like to thank all participants who voluntarily participated in this study.

Conflicts of Interest: The authors declare no conflict of interest.

References

1. Cox, J.L.; Murray, D.; Chapman, G. A Controlled Study of the Onset, Duration and Prevalence of Postnatal Depression. *Br. J. Psychiatry* **1993**, *163*, 27–31. [CrossRef] [PubMed]
2. Craig, M.; Howar, L. Postnatal depression. *Clin. Evid.* **2009**, *1*, 1407.
3. Radzi, W.M.; Jenatabadi, H.S.; Samsudin, N. Postpartum depression symptoms in survey-based research: A structural equation analysis. *BMC Public Health* **2021**, *21*, 27.
4. El-Gilany, A.H.; Elkhawaga, G.O.; Sarraf, B.B. Depression and its associated factors among elderly: A community-based study in Egypt. *Arch. Gerontol. Geriatr.* **2018**, *77*, 103–107. [CrossRef] [PubMed]
5. Zeng, N.; Pope, Z.; Lee, J.; Gao, Z. Virtual reality exercise for anxiety and depression: A preliminary review of current re-search in an emerging field. *J. Clin. Med.* **2018**, *7*, 42. [CrossRef] [PubMed]
6. Daley, A.; Jolly, K.; MacArthur, C. The effectiveness of exercise in the management of post-natal depression: Systematic re-view and meta-analysis. *Fam. Prac.* **2009**, *26*, 154–162. [CrossRef]
7. Zejnullahu, V.A.; Ukella-Lleshi, D.; Zejnullahu, V.A.; Miftari, E.; Govori, V. Prevalence of postpartum depression at the clinic for obstetrics and gynecology in Kosovo teaching hospital: Demographic, obstetric and psychosocial risk factors. *Eur. J. Obstet. Gynecol. Reprod. Biol.* **2021**, *256*, 215–220. [CrossRef] [PubMed]
8. Goweda, R.; Metwally, T. Prevalence and associated risk factors of postpartum depression: A cross sectional study. *Arch. Clin. Psychiatry* **2020**, *47*, 106–109. [CrossRef]
9. Zheng, X.; Morrell, J.; Watts, K. Changes in maternal self-efficacy, postnatal depression symptoms and social support among Chinese primiparous women during the initial postpartum period: A longitudinal study. *Midwifery* **2018**, *62*, 151–160. [CrossRef]
10. Gavin, I.N.; Gaynes, N.B.; Lohr, N.K.; Meltzer-Brody, N.S.; Gartlehner, N.G.; Swinson, N.T. Perinatal depression a systematic review of prevalence and incidence. *Obstet. Gynecol.* **2005**, *106*, 1071–1083. [CrossRef]
11. Dadi, A.F.; Miller, E.R.; Mwanri, L. Postnatal depression and its association with adverse infant health outcomes in low- and middle-income countries: A systematic review and meta-analysis. *BMC Pregnancy Childbirth* **2020**, *20*, 1–15. [CrossRef]
12. Chew-Graham, C.; Sharp, D.; Chamberlain, E.; Folkes, L.; Turner, K.M. Disclosure of symptoms of postnatal depression, the perspectives of health professionals and women: A qualitative study. *BMC Fam. Prac.* **2009**, *10*, 7. [CrossRef] [PubMed]
13. Oates, M.R.; Cox, J.L.; Neema, S.; Asten, P.; Glangeaud-Freudenthal, N.; Figueiredo, B.; Gorman, L.L.; Hacking, S.; Hirst, E.; Kammerer, M.; et al. Postnatal depression across countries and cultures: A qualitative study. *Br. J. Psychiatry* **2004**, *184*, s10–s16. [CrossRef] [PubMed]
14. Peñacoba Puente, C.; Suso-Ribera, C.; Blanco Rico, S.; Marín, D.; San Román Montero, J.; Catalá, P. Is the association between postpartum depression and early maternal–infant relationships contextually determined by avoidant coping in the Mother? *Int. J. Environ. Res. Public Health* **2021**, *18*, 562. [CrossRef] [PubMed]
15. Zheng, X.; Morrell, J.; Watts, K. A quantitative longitudinal study to explore factors which influence maternal self-efficacy among Chinese primiparous women during the initial postpartum period. *Midwifery* **2018**, *59*, 39–46. [CrossRef] [PubMed]
16. Wang, Q.; Zhang, Y.; Li, X.L.; Ye, Z.W.; Huang, L.L.; Zhang, Y.; Zheng, X.J. Exploring maternal self-efficacy of first-time mothers among rural-to-urban floating women: A quantitative longitudinal study in China. *Int. J. Environ. Res. Public Health* **2021**, *18*, 2793. [CrossRef] [PubMed]
17. Woldeyohannes, D.; Tekalegn, Y.; Sahiledengle, B.; Ermias, D.; Ejajo, T.; Mwanri, L. Effect of postpartum depression on exclusive breast-feeding practices in sub-Saharan Africa countries: A systematic review and meta-analysis. *BMC Pregnancy Childbirth* **2021**, *21*, 1–10. [CrossRef]
18. Adewuya, A.O.; Ola, B.O.; Aloba, O.O.; Mapayi, B.M.; Okeniyi, J.A. Impact of postnatal depression on infants' growth in Nigeria. *J. Affect. Disord.* **2008**, *108*, 191–193. [CrossRef]
19. Dennis, C.-L.; McQueen, K. Does maternal postpartum depressive symptomatology influence infant feeding outcomes? *Acta Paediatr.* **2007**, *96*, 590–594. [CrossRef]
20. Wilkinson, R.B.; Mulcahy, R. Attachment and interpersonal relationships in postnatal depression. *J. Reprod. Infant Psychol.* **2010**, *28*, 252–265. [CrossRef]
21. Shi, X.; Ying, Y.; Yu, Z.; Xing, M.; Zhu, J.; Feng, W.; Xu, D.; Zhang, W.; Zhou, M.; Wang, J.; et al. Risk factors for postpartum depression in Chinese women: A cross-sectional study at 6 weeks postpartum. *J. Psychosom. Res.* **2021**, *140*, 110295. [CrossRef] [PubMed]
22. Ceriani Cernadas, J.M. Postpartum depression: Risks and early detection. *Arch. Argent. Pediatr.* **2020**, *118*, 154–155.
23. Bloch, M.; Daly, R.C.; Rubinow, D.R. Endocrine factors in the etiology of postpartum depression. *Compr. Psychiatry* **2003**, *44*, 234–246. [CrossRef]
24. Brummelte, S.; Galea, L.A. Depression during pregnancy and postpartum: Contribution of stress and ovarian hormones. *Prog. Neuro-Psychopharmacol. Biol. Psychiatry* **2010**, *34*, 766–776. [CrossRef]
25. Corwin, E.J.; Kohen, R.; Jarrett, M.; Stafford, B. The heritability of postpartum depression. *Biol. Res. Nurs.* **2010**, *12*, 73–83. [CrossRef]
26. Robertson, E.; Grace, S.; Wallington, T.; Stewart, D.E. Antenatal risk factors for postpartum depression: A synthesis of recent literature. *Gen. Hosp. Psychiatry* **2004**, *26*, 289–295. [CrossRef]

27. Yim, I.S.; Tanner Stapleton, L.R.; Guardino, C.M.; Hahn-Holbrook, J.; Dunkel Schette, C. Biological and psychosocial predictors of postpartum depression: Systematic review and call for integration. *Annu. Rev. Clin. Psychol.* **2015**, *11*, 99–137. [CrossRef]
28. Martínez-Borba, V.; Suso-Ribera, C.; Osma, J.; Andreu-Pejó, L. Predicting Postpartum Depressive Symptoms from Pregnancy Biopsychosocial Factors: A Longitudinal Investigation Using Structural Equation Modeling. *Int. J. Environ. Res. Public Health* **2020**, *17*, 8445. [CrossRef]
29. Yang, J.; Liu, F.; Wang, B.; Chen, C.; Church, T.; Dukes, L.; Smith, J.O. Blood Pressure States Transition Inference Based on MultiState Markov Model. *IEEE J. Biomed. Health Inform.* **2021**, *25*, 237–246. [CrossRef]
30. Wong, L.Y.; Toh, M.P.H.S.; Tham, L.W.C. Projection of prediabetes and diabetes population size in singapore using a dynamic-markovmodel. *J. Diabetes* **2017**, *9*, 65–75. [CrossRef]
31. Grover, G.; Sabharwal, A.; Kumar, S.; Thakur, A.K. A multi-state markov model for the progression of chronic kidney disease. *Türkiye Klin. Biyoistatistik* **2019**, *11*, 1–14. [CrossRef]
32. Srikanth, P. Using Markov Chains to predict the natural progression of diabetic retinopathy. *Int. J. Ophthalmol.* **2015**, *8*, 132–137. [CrossRef] [PubMed]
33. Cox, J.L.; Holden, J.M.; Sagovsky, R. Detection of postnatal depression: Development of the 10-Item Edinburgh Postnatal Depression Scale. *Br. J. Psychiatry* **1987**, *150*, 782–786. [CrossRef]
34. Cox, J.; Holden, J. *Perinatal Mental Health: A Guide to the Edinburgh Postnatal Depression Scale (EPDS)*; Gaskell: London, UK, 2003.
35. Wang, Y.; Guo, X.; Lau, Y.; Chan, K.S.; Yin, L.; Chen, J. Psychometric evaluation of the Mainland Chinese version of the Edinburgh Postnatal Depression Scale. *Int. J. Nurs. Stud.* **2009**, *46*, 813–823. [CrossRef] [PubMed]
36. Levis, B.; Negeri, Z.; Sun, Y.; Benedetti, A.; Thombs, B. Accuracy of the Edinburgh Postnatal Depression Scale (EPDS) for screening to detect major depression among pregnant and postpartum women: Systematic review and meta-analysis of individual participant data. *BMJ* **2020**, *371*, m4022. [CrossRef]
37. O'Connor, E.; Rossom, R.C.; Henninger, M.; Groom, H.C.; Burda, B.U. Primary care screening for and treatment of depression in pregnant and postpartum women: Evidence report and systematic review for the US Preventive Services Task Force. *JAMA* **2016**, *315*, 388–406. [CrossRef]
38. Lu, H.; Zheng, X.X. The relationship between social support and postnatal depression of primiparous women. *Chin. J. Nurs.* **2001**, *36*, 731–733. (In Chinese)
39. Hewitt, C.; Gilbody, S.; Brealey, S.; Paulden, M.; Palmer, S.; Mann, R.; Green, J.; Morrell, J.; Barkham, M.; Light, K.; et al. Methods to identify postnatal depression in primary care: An integrated evidence synthesis and value of information analysis. *Health Technol. Assess.* **2009**, *13*, 1. [CrossRef]
40. National Collaborating Centre for Mental Health. *Antenatal and Postnatal Mental Health: Clinical Management and Service Guidance*, Updated ed.; British Psychological Society: Leicester, UK, 2014.
41. Force, U.P.S.T. Screening for Depression in Adults: U.S. Preventive Services Task Force Recommendation Statement. *Ann. Intern. Med.* **2009**, *151*, 784–792. [CrossRef]
42. Austin, M.-P.; Highet, N. Guidelines Expert Advisory Committee. Clinical Practice Guidelines for Depression and Related DisOrders—Anxiety, Bipolar Disorder and Puerperal Psychosis—In the Perinatal Period. In *A Guideline for Primary Care Health Professionals*; The National Depression Initiative; Beyondblue: Melbourne, Australia, 2013.
43. National Institute of Child Health and Human Development (NICHD). Postpartum depression may persist three years after giving birth. *JAMA* **2020**, *324*, 2475.
44. General Office of the National Health Commission. Notice of the General Office of the NationalHealth Commission on Exploring the Implementation of Special Services for the Prevention and Treatment of Depression and Senile Dementia. Available online: http://www.nhc.gov.cn/jkj/s7914/202009/a63d8f82eb53451f97217bef0962b98f.shtml (accessed on 3 March 2021).
45. Zheng, X.J.; Morrell, J.; Watts, K. An Exploration of Factors which Influence Maternal Self-Efficacy in Primiparous Women in China during the Initial Postnatal Period. Ph.D. Thesis, The University of Nottingham, Nottingham, UK, 2015.
46. Gong, W.; Jin, X.; Cheng, K.; Caine, E.; Lehman, R.; Xu, D. Chinese women's acceptance and uptake of referral after screening for perinatal depression. *Int. J. Environ. Res. Public Health* **2020**, *17*, 8686. [CrossRef]

International Journal of
Environmental Research and Public Health

MDPI

Article

The Psychometric Properties of the Patient Health Questionnaire-4 for Pregnant Women

María de la Fe Rodríguez-Muñoz [1,*], Natalia Ruiz-Segovia [1], Cristina Soto-Balbuena [2], Huynh-Nhu Le [3], María Eugenia Olivares-Crespo [4] and Nuria Izquierdo-Méndez [4]

1 Department of Psychology, Universidad Nacional de Educación a Distancia (UNED), 28040 Madrid, Spain; nataliaruizseg@gmail.com
2 Deparment of Gynecology and Obstetrics, Hospital Universitario Central de Asturias, 33011 Oviedo, Spain; cristsobal@yahoo.es
3 Department of Psychology, George Washington University, Washington, DC 20052, USA; hnle@gwu.edu
4 Deparment of Gynecology and Obstetrics, Instituto de Salud de la Mujer José Botella Llusiá, Hospital Clínico San Carlos, Faculty of Medicine Universidad Complutense de Madrid, 28040 Madrid, Spain; meolivares@cop.es (M.E.O.-C.); nuriaizquierdo4@gmail.com (N.I.-M.)
* Correspondence: mfrodriguez@psi.uned.es

Received: 14 September 2020; Accepted: 16 October 2020; Published: 19 October 2020

check for updates

Abstract: *Background:* Perinatal anxiety and depression are common complications during pregnancy. The purpose of this study was to examine the item characteristics, reliability, validity, and factorial structure of the four-item Patient Health Questionnaire-4 (PHQ-4) and to determine the associations between scale scores and sociodemographic factors in a sample of pregnant women from Spain. *Method:* A total of 845 pregnant women were recruited from two public hospitals in Spain between 2014 and 2016. Participants completed a self-report questionnaire that included Patient Health Questionnaire-4, including the two-item Patient Health Questionnaire and the two-item Generalized Anxiety Disorder Screener. *Results:* Exploratory and confirmatory factor analysis and scale inter-correlations between the PHQ-4 and PHQ-9 revealed that the PHQ-4 has a bivariate structure and adequately assesses the dimensions of antenatal anxiety and depression. *Conclusion*: The PHQ-4 is a reliable and valid instrument to screen for depression and anxiety during pregnancy. The PHQ-4 is an ultra-brief measure that can be used to screen for antenatal depression and anxiety to prevent the negative consequences associated with these mental health conditions among mothers and infants.

Keywords: depression; anxiety; pregnancy; PHQ-4; assessment tools

1. Introduction

Depression is the most common complication during pregnancy [1,2]. Studies have been conducted in both clinical and non-clinical samples of pregnant women, demonstrating wide prevalence, ranging from 6.9% to 12.4% [3,4]. In Spain, the prevalence of antenatal depressive symptoms lies between 10.3% and 14.8% [5,6]. Depression is also highly comorbid with anxiety [2]. The systematic review and meta-analysis conducted by Dennis et al. (2017) [7] found that the prevalence of anxiety symptoms was 18.2% in the first-, 19.1% in the second-, and 24.6% in the third trimester of pregnancy. In Spain, Soto-Balbuena et al. (2018) [8] also found a high prevalence of anxiety during pregnancy: 19.5%, 16.8%, and 17.2% in the first-, second-, and third trimester, respectively.

Antenatal depression and anxiety have well-documented negative consequences on women and infants. Antenatal depression is associated with having a preterm birth, and low infant birthweight [9,10]. The single best predictor of major depression in the postpartum period is the presence of depressive symptoms during pregnancy [9–11]. Antenatal anxiety is associated with low adherence to medical advice, inadequate nutrition, and substance abuse [12]. Therefore, there is need to screen for symptoms of depression and anxiety during pregnancy to prevent these deleterious effects for women and their infants [13].

Pregnancy presents an opportunity to screen for depressive symptomatology as women are more likely to seek medical care during this period than any other period in their lives. To implement screening, it is necessary to have a good assessment tool [14]. The nine-item Patient Health Questionnaire (PHQ-9) demonstrates good psychometric properties in screening for depression during pregnancy [15]. The two-item Patient Health Questionnaire (PHQ-2), the ultra-short version of the PHQ-9, is the most validated screener for depressive symptomatology, with good criterion and convergent validity, with good sensitivity and specificity values [16]. The PHQ-2 is a psychometrically sound screening tool for major depression in adults and pregnant and postpartum women [17,18]. The seven-item Generalized Anxiety Disorder Scale (GAD-7) was validated to detect symptoms of anxiety during the antenatal period and has demonstrated high reliability and good construct validity in general population [19] and among pregnant women [10]. The two-item Generalized Anxiety Disorder Scale (GAD-2), the shortest version of the GAD-7 [20], includes the two core criteria for GAD, which have also been shown to be effective screening items for panic, social anxiety, and post-traumatic stress disorders. A validation study with primary care patients indicated good criterion validity of the GAD-2 [20].

The PHQ-2 and the GAD-2 have been combined to create a composite ultra-brief screening instrument called the Patient Health Questionnaire-4 (PHQ-4). The PHQ-4 can reliably and validly assess depressive and anxious symptomatology in the general population [21], clinical samples [22], and pregnant woman [23]. The results of the confirmatory factor analysis (CFA) revealed the best fit to be an oblique two-factor structure, which included depression and anxiety [21,24–26].

Some research groups have used the PHQ-4 in Spanish-speaking samples [25,26] and one with a Spanish- and English-speaking sample of pregnant women [23]. The evidence supports the validity of the two-factor PHQ-4 as a measure of anxiety and depression in the general population [2] and as a brief measure of psychological distress among pregnant women [23,27]. Its brevity is useful on clinical contexts, such as obstetric settings. However, to our knowledge, no study has used this instrument with only Spanish-speaking pregnant women.

The purpose of this study was to examine the item characteristics, reliability, validity, and factorial structure of the four-item Patient Health Questionnaire-4 (PHQ-4), and to determine the associations between scale scores and sociodemographic factors in a sample of pregnant women from Spain. We examined the item characteristics, reliability, factor structure, and construct validity of the PHQ-2, the GAD-2, and the PHQ-4. A second aim was to investigate the associations between scale scores and socio-demographic factors and to determine the relationship with the presence of anxious and depressive symptoms during pregnancy.

2. Materials and Methods

2.1. Study Population

The sample included 845 pregnant women receiving antenatal care in two Spanish hospitals: San Carlos Clinic Hospital and Central University Hospital of Asturias. Inclusion criteria included receiving care at one of these hospitals beginning in their first trimester and Spanish fluency (reading, writing, speaking). Acceptance and rejection rates are presented in Figure 1. After obtaining informed consent, participants completed self-reported questionnaires on sociodemographic characteristics, depression and anxiety symptoms, and associated risk factors. This study was approved by the ethics committees from both hospitals (14/060 HOSPITAL CLINICO SAN CARLOS and 128/15 HOSPITAL CENTRAL DE ASTURIAS).

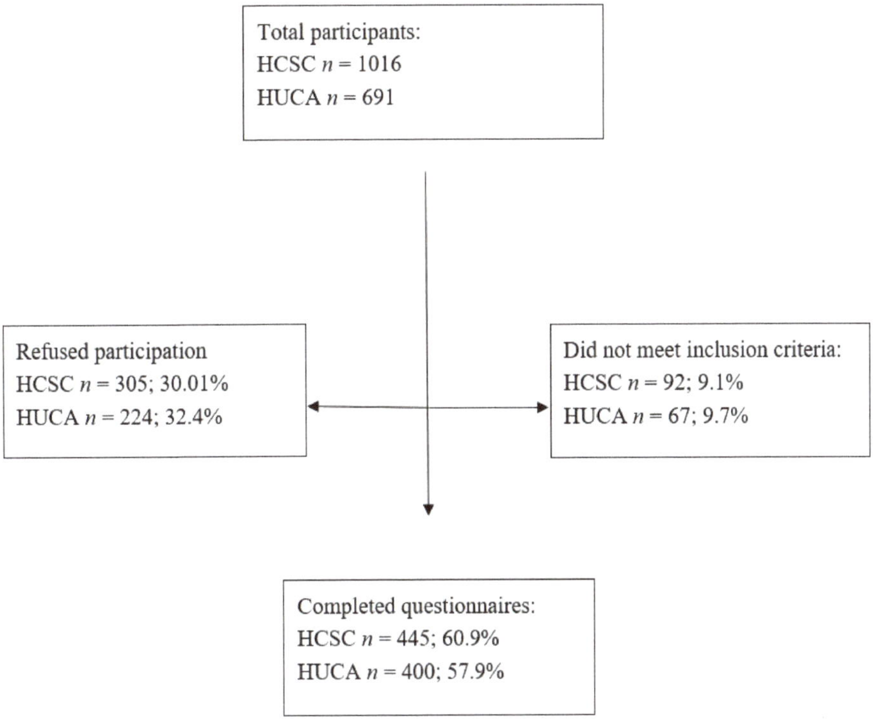

Figure 1. Participants. Note: HCSC = Hospital Clínico San Carlos, HUCA = Hospital Universitario Central de Asturias.

2.2. *Data Collection and Variable Specification*

Participants completed a sociodemographic questionnaire, including questions about education, employment status, marital status, illness, number of children, medication, substance use, history of medical and depression conditions.

2.3. *Instruments*

2.3.1. The Patient Health Questionnaire (PHQ-2)

Whereas the PHQ-9 assesses each of the nine specific symptoms of Major Depressive Disorder (MDD) based on DSM-IV criteria, the PHQ-2 [28] includes the two core criteria for MDD: "little interest or pleasure in doing things" and "feeling down, depressed or hopeless." The total PHQ-2 scores range from 0 to 6 [28]; scoring ≥ 2 is considered an appropriate cut-off score to detect depression during pregnancy in a sample from Spain [17].

2.3.2. The Generalized Anxiety Disorder Scale (GAD-2)

The GAD-2 [21] measures two core criteria for generalized anxiety disorder, including "feeling nervous, anxious or on edge" and "not being able to stop or control worrying". The total scores on the GAD-2 range from 0 to 6 [21]; scoring ≥ 3 indicates an appropriate cut-off point to indicate risk of developing anxiety in an English and Spanish-speaking population [26]. To date, no studies have examined the GAD-2 in Spanish-speaking sample.

2.3.3. The Patient Health Questionnaire (PHQ-4)

These measures (PHQ-2 and GAD-2) were combined to form a composite four-item scale called PHQ-4 [24]. Equivalent to the parent scales, the PHQ-4 begins with the stem question: "Over the last 2 weeks, how often have you been bothered by the following problems?" Response options are "not at all", "several days", "more than half the days", and "nearly every day", scored as 0, 1, 2, and 3, respectively. The total score ranges from 0 to 12, 6 being the moderate cut-off point, and 9 the cut-off point for "red alert" for depressive-anxious symptoms in an English-speaking sample. The internal consistencies of the PHQ-4, PHQ-2 and GAD-2 were acceptable ($\alpha = 0.78$, $\alpha = 0.75$, and $\alpha = 0.82$), respectively [21].

2.3.4. Statistical Analyses Overview

The internal consistency of the PHQ-4 and its subscales were assessed to examine reliability. Specifically, item characteristics of the PHQ-4, including item means, item-intercorrelations, and corrected item-total correlations and Cronbach's alpha without the respective item were examined.

To examine the factor structure of the PHQ-4, we conducted both exploratory and confirmatory analyses. Exploratory Factor Analyses (EFA) examined one- and two-dimensional factor constraints and were analyzed to determine the underlying individual item loadings for each model. Based upon the results of the EFA with SPSS (Version 24), using principal component solutions with varimax rotation to maximize fit, one-factor and two-factor were then analyzed using Analysis of Moment Structures (AMOS) version 24 software. In order to evaluate the dimensionality of the PHQ-4, CFAs were performed on the original two-dimensional structure of the PHQ-4 as well as a one-dimensional structure representing the PHQ-4 total score. To evaluate the fit of these structures, several indices were examined: (a) the root mean square error of approximation (RMSEA), (b) the normed fit index (NFI), (c) the comparative fit index (CFI); (d) the Akaike information criterion (AIC), (e) expected cross-validation index (ECVI), and (f) parsimonious normed fit index (PNFI).

For construct validity, we investigated the inter-correlations among the PHQ-4, GAD-2, PHQ-2, and the PHQ-9. To investigate the relationship between the sociodemographic variables and anxious and depressive symptomatology, we examined the associations between the PHQ-4, PHQ-2, and GAD-2 scores and sociodemographic characteristics (age, nationality, education level, employment and marital status and history of medical illness) that have been found to be possible risk factors for antenatal depressive and anxious symptomatology [29].

The PHQ-2, GAD-2, and PHQ-4 scores had skewed (but unimodal) distributions as dependent variables; therefore, the rank transformation of each dependent variable was performed for each model, and Bonferroni-adjustment was conducted due to multiple testing.

3. Results

3.1. Participant Characteristics

Table 1 shows the socio-demographic characteristics, lifestyle, and general health data of the pregnant women. Participants of the total sample were generally young (60%) and well educated, with most women reporting having a secondary (31.0%) or university level education (51.7%). Approximately half were first time mothers (54.2%). The majority were living with a partner (85%), employed (83.2%), and mostly native Spaniards (78.1%). Most of the participants did not report a previous history of depression (97.5%) and history of medical illness (83.2%).

Table 1. Demographic characteristics of sample.

	n = 845 %	HCSC (n = 445) n (%)	HUCA (n = 400) n (%)	χ^2	p-Value
Age group				1.166	0.125
16–25 years	8.6	41 (10.0)	29 (7.3)		
26–36 years	60.0	234 (56.8)	253 (63.4)		
36–45 years	31.3	137 (33.3)	117 (29.3)		
Nationality				68.239	0.000
Spanish	78.1	297 (66.9)	361 (90.5)		
Other	21.9	147 (33.1)	38 (9.5)		
Education level				18.163	0.000
Primary	17.3	55 (12.4)	91 (22.9)		
Secondary	31.0	155 (34.8)	106 (26.6)		
University level	51.7	235 (52.8)	201 (50.5)		
Employment status				1.714	0.190
Unemployed	25.6	105 (23.8)	110 (27.7)		
Employed	74.4	337 (76.2)	287 (72.3)		
Marital Status				8.891	0.003
Single	11.5	65 (14.6)	32 (8.1)		
Partnered	88.5	379 (85.4)	365 (91.9)		
History medical illness				0.321	0.571
No	83.2	357 (82.4)	334 (83.9)		
Yes	16.8	76 (14.6)	64 (16.1)		
Previous depression history				0.170	0.680
No	97.5	420 (97.7)	385 (97.2)		
Yes	2.5	10 (2.3)	11 (2.8)		
First-time mother				0.130	0.719
No	54.2	232 (54.4)	204 (51.1)		
Yes	45.8	211 (47.6)	195 (48.9)		

Comparing the sociodemographic characteristics of women between two hospital sites (HCSC and HUCA), results showed significant differences with respect to nationality ($\chi^2 = 68.2$, $p < 0.01$), education level ($\chi^2 = 18.2$, $p < 0.01$), and marital status ($\chi^2 = 8.9$, $p < 0.01$). Generally, women receiving services from HUCA were more likely to be Spanish natives (90.5%) and partnered (91.9%). At HCSC, there was a higher percentage of women from other nationalities (33.1%) and with higher educational levels (52.8% university level, 34.8% secondary level). There were no significant differences between sites for age, employment status, medical illness, previous depression history, and being a first-time mother.

3.2. Reliability

Descriptive characteristics of the items, correlation of each item with the global scale, and reliability indices are displayed in Table 2. The two items from PHQ-2 were positively correlated ($r = 0.52$). Similarly, the two items from the GAD-2 were positively correlated ($r = 0.60$). Item-intercorrelations with items from the other subscale ranged between $r = 0.30$ and $r = 0.49$. The PHQ-2 items were positively correlated with the GAD-2 items ($r = 0.50$). All the above-mentioned correlations were significant at $p < 0.001$. The PHQ-4 total score ranges from 0 to 12, and the sample reported a score lower than the cut-off point ($M = 2.47$; $SD = 2.40$). The Cronbach's alphas were all in the acceptable range (PHQ-4 $\alpha = 0.77$, the PHQ-2 $\alpha = 0.70$ and the GAD-2 $\alpha = 0.75$).

3.3. Factor Analyses

The initial analysis of the one- and two-factor models supported the appropriateness of conducting the present EFA (Kaiser–Meyer–Olkin, KMO = 0.713, and Bartlett's sphericity test was 922.07, $p < 0.001$).

The EFA indicated that the one-factor structure (anxiety-depression) of the PHQ-4 explained 59.63% of the total variance. In contrast, the two-factor solution explained 79.50% of the total variance. Factor 1 (i.e., anxiety) explained 59.63%, and Factor 2 (i.e., depression) explained 19.87% of the total variance. The items that loaded on Factors 1 and 2 showed acceptable internal consistency, $\alpha = 0.75$ and $\alpha = 0.70$, respectively. The item loadings on the corresponding factors are shown in Table 3. The depression factor was negatively associated with the anxiety factor (Spearman $r = -0.15$, $p < 0.01$).

Table 2. Characteristics of the PHQ-4 items and subscales in the Spanish pregnant population.

Item	*n*	*M*	*SD*	r^a	α
Depression items (PHQ-2)	824				
Little interest or pleasure in doing things		0.84	0.86	0.74 **	
Feeling down, depressed, or hopeless		0.50	0.76	0.79 **	
lePHQ-2 sum score		1.35	1.41		0.70
Anxiety items (GAD-2)	814				
Feeling nervous, anxious or on edge		0.67	0.80	0.75 **	
Not being able to stop or control worrying		0.42	0.71	0.80 **	
GAD-2 sum score		1.13	1.36		0.75
Total scale score (PHQ-4)	806	2.47	2.40		0.77

** Correlation significant at $p < 0.01$; *n* = sample size; *M* = mean; *SD* = standard deviation; r^a Corrected item-total correlation; α = Cronbach's alpha.

Table 3. One-factor and two-factor solution matrix of confirmatory factor analysis with varimax rotation for the PHQ-4 during pregnancy.

	One-Factor	Two-Factor	
Item	Anxiety-Depression	Factor 1-Anxiety	Factor 2-Depression
1. Little interest or pleasure in doing things	0.714		0.909
2. Feeling down, depressed, or hopeless	0.799		0.769
3. Feeling nervous, anxious or on edge	0.753	0.906	
4. Not being able to stop or control worrying	0.818	0.812	

CFA were conducted to test the one and two factor structures of the PHQ-4. The results of the CFA (Table 4) indicated excellent fit (RMSEA = 0.069, CFI = 0.99, NFI = 0.90). The value of AIC = 31.006 in the two-factor model versus the AIC = 128.127 in the one-factor model indicated greater parsimony of the two-factor structure. The expected cross-validation index (ECVI) and parsimonious normed fit index (PNFI) were evaluated with models that generated lower values and considered superior. Based on the principle of parsimony and the proportion of total explained variance, the two-factor model was determined to be superior to the one-factor model.

Table 4. Goodness-of-fit indices for the PHQ-4 one-factor and two-factor models.

Model	X^2	X^2/df	RMSEA	CFI	NFI	AIC	ECVI	PNFI
Two-factor	5.006	5.006	0.069	0.99	0.91	31.006	0.037	0.09
One-factor	104.127	52.063	0.246	0.89	0.88	128.127	0.152	0.178

Note: NFI = Normed Fit Index, CFI = Comparative Fit Index, RMSEA = Root mean square error of approximation, AIC = Akaike information criterion, ECVI = Expected Cross-Validation Index, PNFI = Parsimonious Normed Fit Index.

3.4. Construct Validity

The intercorrelations between the PHQ-4 and the PHQ-9 was $r = 0.76$. Similarly, the intercorrelations between the PHQ-2 and the PHQ-9 was $r = 0.67$. Finally, the intercorrelation between the GAD-2 and the

PHQ-9 was $r = 0.63$. These results were all significant at $p < 0.01$, suggesting good construct validity of the PHQ-4.

3.5. Analysis of Variance

The independent samples *t*-test and analysis of variance (ANOVA) were used to determine whether the results of the instrument differed statistically based on participants' demographic characteristics (Table 5). The association between the PHQ-4 and its subscale scores with demographic characteristics is shown in Table 5. Results indicate that younger women had more depressive symptoms than older women. Regarding educational level, women with more education obtained the lowest scores on the PHQ-4 compared to women with less education. Unemployed women exhibited more depressed symptoms compared to partnered women. Additionally, women who reported having a history of medical illness and smokers also report having higher levels of depressive symptoms compared to those without a history of medical illness. Similarly, participants with a history of previous depression reported having higher levels of anxious and depressive symptoms compared to those without a history of depression or tobacco use.

Table 5. Association of the PHQ-2, the GAD-2 and the PHQ-4 with sociodemographic characteristics.

	PHQ-2, $n = 824$		GAD-2, $n = 814$		PHQ-4, $n = 806$	
	M (*SD*)	Group Differences *p*-Value	*M* (*SD*)	Group Differences *p*-Value	*M* (*SD*)	Group Differences *p*-Value
Age group		0.026		0.580		0.063
16–25	1.82 (1.67)		1.29 (1.53)		3.15 (2.78)	
26–35	1.32 (1.41)		1.15 (1.36)		2.47 (2.45)	
36–45	1.33 (1.37)		1.09 (1.32)		2.37 (2.45)	
Education level		0.000		0.017		0.000
Primary	1.59 (1.61)		1.26 (1.48)		2.83 (2.66)	
Secondary	1.60 (1.57)		1.29 (1.45)		2.90 (2.71)	
University	1.14 (1.22)		1.00 (1.26)		2.12 (2.07)	
Employment status		0.049		0.234		0.074
Unemployed	1.53 (1.60)		1.23 (1.44)		2.75 (2.73)	
Employed	1.29 (1.34)		1.10 (1.33)		2.37 (2.28)	
Marital Status		0.089		0.468		0.437
Single	1.63 (1.67)		1.24 (1.51)		2.86 (2.72)	
Partnered	1.32 (1.38)		1.12 (1.34)		2.42 (2.36)	
History of medical illness		0.031		0.268		0.059
No	1.30 (1.34)		1.10 (1.31)		2.38 (2.24)	
Yes	1.63 (1.70)		1.26 (1.57)		2.89 (2.99)	
Smoking		0.029		0.47		0.046
No	1.37 (1.43)		1.26 (139)		2.61 (2.41)	
Yes	1.80 (1.73)		1.38 (1.49)		3.20 (2.86)	
Previous depression history		0.013		0.001		0.01
No	1.31 (1.37)		1.08 (1.30)		2.37 (2.30)	
Yes	2.63 (2.09)		2.78 (1.90)		5.53 (3.33)	

Group differences were examined using analysis of variance and *t*-tests. All group differences remained significant after Bonferroni-adjustment for multiple testing.

4. Discussion

The results of this study suggest that the PHQ-4 is a reliable and valid instrument that can be used to assess anxious and depressive symptoms during the antenatal period. To our knowledge, this is the first study that examined the psychometric properties and structure factor of the PHQ-4 in a sample of pregnant women in Spain.

Our first goal was to determine the psychometric characteristics of the screening measure, including the reliability, validity, and structure factor of the PHQ-4. Similar to previous studies [21,23,24,26], we used CFA to determine the most appropriate model for this population. The results provide good fit indices for the two-factor solution (anxiety, depression) of the PHQ-4. This finding is consistent with previous research conducted with samples from the general population [21,24,30] which determined that the PHQ-4 adequately assessed the dimensions of anxiety and depression. However, given that the one-factor solution explains more than half of the total variance (59.63%), the use of the total score on the PHQ-4 is justified [21]. A score greater than 6 on the PHQ-4 does not determine a diagnosis, but it does suggest the presence of anxious and/or depressive symptoms [21]. In this study, 86.1% of the pregnant women did not attain a score higher than the cut-off point on the PHQ-4.

The second goal of this study was to determine the relationship between the scale scores and the demographic characteristics of the sample. Results indicate that younger women (<25 years) had more depressive symptoms than older women (>35). These data are not consistent with a systematic review [31], which concluded that there is no consensus among researchers about the influence of age as a risk factor for antenatal depressive symptomatology. This systematic review examined psychosocial risk factors associated with antenatal depression and anxiety based on 97 international studies (the total sample was not reported). Similar to the systematic review [31], our study found that women with higher education levels obtained the lowest scores on the PHQ-4. Other studies highlight the lack of social support, low perceived levels of social support, and not having a partner as risk factors for the development of antenatal depression [28,31]. Consistent with these findings, the present study found that single women were more likely to be depressed compared to partnered women. In addition, this study found a higher prevalence of depressive symptoms among pregnant smokers, consistent with previous research [28,31]. In this study, women who reported having a history of medical illness also reported having higher levels of depressive symptoms compared to those without a history of medical illness. Similarly, pregnant women with a depression history reported having higher levels of anxious and depressive symptoms compared to those without a depression history. These findings are consistent with previous research [28,31,32].

Our study had some limitations. First, the cross-sectional design only provides information about the first trimester of pregnancy. Second, we did not perform a clinical interview to determine the construct validity of the PHQ-4, but instead, we used the PHQ-9 scores. Third, there were significant sociodemographic differences in nationality, education, marital status among pregnant women between the two hospitals. Nevertheless, results from two large hospital sites increases the generalizability of these results. Future research can adjust the cut-off points in the PHQ-4 in pregnant women because it has been observed that changes in anxious and depressive symptomatology can occur throughout the nine months of pregnancy, and longitudinal studies are important and needed in this field [17].

5. Conclusions

Results from our study suggest that the antenatal period provides a good opportunity to assess the mental health of women, given the regular and multiple contacts they have with the health care setting. The National Institute for Health and Care Excellence [33] in the United Kingdom and the American College of Obstetrician and Gynecologist [34] in the United States recommend screening for antenatal symptoms of depression and anxiety during routine follow-up visits. Because it is common for symptoms of anxiety and depression to be co-occur with pregnancy [35], it is essential for providers to have the necessary knowledge and tools to discriminate these symptoms adequately. In addition, given the comorbidity of depression and anxiety, the PHQ-4 could be an appropriate and short instrument to screen for both conditions. In the health care setting, providers have limited time to interact with their patients, and the PHQ-4 is a good instrument to perform a fast, reliable, and valid screening. In addition, it is important for health providers to assess sociodemographic risk factors associated with higher scores in depressive and anxious symptoms, such as smoking or a history of depression and medical illness. The PHQ-4 evaluation should also be followed-up with a more exhaustive evaluation if the pregnant women exceeds the cut-off point (>6).

Previous studies have used the PHQ-4 with Spanish-speaking samples [25,26] or Spanish- and English-speaking pregnant samples [23], but to our knowledge, this is the first study that used the PHQ-4 in a pregnant women from Spain. Our findings indicate that the PHQ-4 is a good screening tool during pregnancy that can enable appropriate follow up interventions to improve the lives of mothers and babies.

Author Contributions: Conceptualization: M.d.l.F.R.-M. and N.R.-S.; Methodology and formal analyses, M.d.l.F.R.-M. and N.R.-S.; writing—original draft preparation: M.d.l.F.R.-M., N.R.-S., C.S.-B. and H.-N.L.; writing—review and editing, M.d.l.F.R.-M., N.R.-S., C.S.-B., H.-N.L., M.E.O.-C., and N.I.-M. All authors have read and agreed to the published version of the manuscript.

Funding: This research received no external funding.

Conflicts of Interest: The authors declare that they have no conflict of interest.

References

1. Caparrós-González, R.A.; Rodríguez Muñoz, M.F. Depresión posparto paterna: Visibilidad e influencia en la salud infantil. [Paternal postpartum depression: Visibility and influence on child health]. *Clínica Salud* **2020**. [CrossRef]
2. Bauer, A.; Knapp, M.; Parsonage, M. Lifetime costs of perinatal anxiety and depression. *J. Affect. Disord.* **2016**, *192*, 83–90. [CrossRef]
3. Andersson, L.; Sundström-Poromaa, I.; Bixo, M.; Wulff, M.; Bondestam, K.; Åström, M. Point prevalence of psychiatric disorders during the second trimester of pregnancy: A population-based study. *Am. J. Obstet. Gynecol.* **2003**, *189*, 148–154. [CrossRef]
4. Banti, S.; Mauri, M.; Oppo, A.; Borri, C.; Rambelli, C.; Ramacciotti, D.; Montagnani, M.; Camilleri, V.; Cortopassi, S.; Rucci, P.; et al. Prevalence, incidence, recurrence and new onset of depression durin pregnancy. Results from the perinatal depression-research & screening unit (PND-RESCU) study. *Eur. Psychiatry* **2010**, *25*, 1389.
5. Escribà-Agüir, V.; Gonzalez-Galarzo, M.C.; Barona-Vilar, C.; Artazcoz, L. Factors related to depression during pregnancy: Are there gender differences? *J. Epidemiol. Community Health* **2008**, *62*, 410–414. [CrossRef]
6. Rodríguez-Muñoz, M.F.; Le, H.N.; Vargas, I.; Olivares, M.E.; Izquierdo, N. Feasibility of screening and prevalence of prenatal depression in an obstetric setting in Spain. *Eur. J. Obs. Gynecol. Reprod. Biol.* **2017**, *215*, 101–105. [CrossRef]
7. Dennis, C.L.; Kobra, F.H.; Shiri, R. Prevalence of antenatal and postnatal anxiety: Systematic review and meta-analysis. *Br. J. Psychiatry* **2017**, *210*, 315–323. [CrossRef]
8. Soto-Balbuena, C.; Rodríguez, M.F.; Escudero-Gomis, A.I.; Ferrer, F.J.; Le, H.N.; Grupo PMB-HUCA. Incidence, prevalence and risk factors related to anxiety symptoms during pregnancy. *Psicothema* **2018**, *30*, 257–263.
9. Field, T. Prenatal depression effects on early development: A review. *Infant Behav. Dev.* **2011**, *34*, 1–14. [CrossRef]
10. Zhong, Q.; Gelaye, B.; Zaslavsky, A.; Fann, J.; Ronden, M.; Sánchez, S.; Williams, M. Diagnostic validity of the generalized anxiety disorder-7 (GAD-7) among pregnant women. *PLoS ONE* **2015**, *10*, e0125096. [CrossRef]
11. Vázquez, M.B.; Míguez, M.C. Spanish brief version of the Pregnancy Related Anxiety Questionnaire: PRAQ-20. *Clínica Salud* **2020**. [CrossRef]
12. Dunkel, C.; Tanner, L. Anxiety, depression and stress in pregnancy: Implications for mothers, children, research, and practice. *Curr. Opin. Psychiatry* **2012**, *25*, 141–148. [CrossRef]
13. Garcia-Esteve, L.; Valdés, M. *Manual de Psiquiatría Perinatal: Guía Para el Manejo de los Trastornos Mentales Durante el Embarazo, Postparto y Lactancia. [Perinatal Psychiatry Manual: Guide for the Management of Mental Disorders during Pregnancy, Postpartum and Lactation]*; Panamericana: Madrid, Spain, 2017.
14. Rodríguez-Muñoz, M.F.; Izquierdo, N.; Olivares, M.E.; Picos, M.C.; Rodríguez, M.I.; Herráiz, M.A.; Le, H.N.; Fonseca, J. Postpartum Depression Screening Scale Short Form: Is it possible to use it for antenatal depression? *Clínica Salud* **2018**, *29*, 147–150. [CrossRef]

15. Marcos-Nájera, R.; Le, H.N.; Rodríguez-Muñoz, M.F.; Olivares, M.E.; Izquierdo, N. The structure of the Patient Health Questionnaire-9 in pregnant women in Spain. *Midwifery* **2018**, *62*, 36–41. [CrossRef]
16. Lowë, B.; Kroenke, K.; Gräfe, K. Detecting and monitoring depression with a two-item questionnaire (PHQ-2). *J. Psychosom. Res.* **2005**, *58*, 163–171. [CrossRef]
17. Rodríguez-Muñoz, M.F.; Castelao, P.C.; Olivares, M.E.; Soto, C.; Izquierdo, N.; Ferrer, J.; Le, H.N. PHQ-2 como primer instrumento de cribado de la depresión prenatal. *Rev. Española Salud Pública* **2017**, *91*, 1–8.
18. Smith, M.; Gotman, N.; Lin, H.; Yonkers, K. Do the PHQ-8 and the PHQ-2 accurately screen for depressive disorders in a sample of pregnant women? *Gen. Hosp. Psychiatry* **2010**, *32*, 544–548. [CrossRef]
19. Spitzer, R.L.; Kroenke, K.; Willians, J.B.; Lowe, B. A brief measure for assessing generalized anxiety disorder, the GAD-7. *Arch. Intern. Med.* **2006**, *166*, 1092–1097. [CrossRef]
20. Kroenke, K.; Spitzer, R.L.; Williams, J.B.W.; Monahan, P.; Löwe, B. Anxiety disorders in primary care: Prevalence, impairment, comorbidity, and detection. *Ann. Intern. Med.* **2007**, *146*, 317–325. [CrossRef]
21. Löwe, B.; Wahl, I.; Rose, M.; Spitzer, C.; Glaesmer, H.; Winterfeld, K.; Schneider, A.; Brähler, E. A 4-item measure of depression and anxiety: Validation and standardization of the patient health questionnaire-4 (PHQ-4) in the general population. *J. Affect. Disord.* **2010**, *122*, 86–95. [CrossRef]
22. Penlington, C.; Araújo-Soares, V.; Durham, J. Predicting Persistent Orofacial Pain: The role of illness perceptions, anxiety, and depression. *JDR Clin. Transl. Res.* **2020**, *5*, 40–49. [CrossRef]
23. Barrera, A.Z.; Moh, Y.S.; Nichols, A.; Le, H.N. The factor reliability and convergent validity of the patient health questionnaire-4 among an international sample of pregnant women. *J. Womens Health* 2020. [CrossRef]
24. Kroenke, K.; Spitzer, R.; Williams, J.; Löwe, B. An ultra-brief screening scale for anxiety and depression: The PHQ-4. *Psychosomatics* **2009**, *50*, 613–621.
25. Koncalevent, R.; Finck, C.; Jimenez-Leal, W.; Sautier, L.; Hinz, A. Standardization of the Colombian version of the PHQ-4 in the general population. *BMC Psychiatry* **2014**, *14*, 205.
26. Mills, S.D.; Fox, R.S.; Pan, T.M.; Malcarne, V.L.; Roesch, S.C.; Robins Sadler, G. Psychometrics evaluation of the patient health questionnaire-4 in Hispanic Americans. *Hisp. J. Behav. Sci.* **2015**, *37*, 560–571. [CrossRef]
27. Wubetu, A.D.; Habte, S.; Dagne, K. Prevalence of risky alcohol use behavior and associated factors in pregnant antenatal care attendees in Debre Berhan, Ethiopia, 2018. *BMC Psychiatry* **2019**, *19*, 250. [CrossRef]
28. Kroenke, K.; Spitzer, R.L.; Williams, J.B. The Patient Health Questionnaire-2: Validity of a two-item depression screener. *Med. Care* **2003**, *41*, 1284–1292. [CrossRef]
29. Clout, D.; Brown, R. Sociodemographic, pregnancy, obstetric, and postnatal predictors of postpartum stress, anxiety and depression in new mothers. *J. Affect. Disord.* **2015**, *188*, 60–67. [CrossRef]
30. Cano-Vindel, A.; Muñoz-Navarro, R.; Medrano, L.A.; Ruiz-Rodríguez, P.; González-Blanch, C.; Gómez-Castillo, M.D.; Capafons, A.; Chacón, F.; Santolaya, F. A computerized version of the Patient Health Questionnaire-4 as an ultra-brief screening tool to detect emotional disorders in primary care. *J. Affect. Disord.* **2018**, *234*, 247–255. [CrossRef]
31. Biaggi, A.; Corno, S.; Pawlby, S.; Pariante, C. Identifying the women at risk of antenatal anxiety and depression: A systematic review. *J. Affect. Disord.* **2016**, *191*, 62–77. [CrossRef]
32. Lancaster, C.A.; Gold, K.J.; Flynn, H.A.; Yoo, H.; Marcus, S.M.; Davis, M.M. Risk factors for depressive symptoms during pregnancy: A systematic review. *J. Gen. Intern. Med.* **2010**, *202*, 5–14. [CrossRef]
33. NICE. Antenatal and Postnatal Mental Health: Clinical Management and Service Guidance. 2014. Available online: https://www.nice.org.uk/guidance/cg192 (accessed on 1 September 2020).
34. ACOG. Screening for Perinatal Depression. *Obstet. Gynecol.* **2015**, *132*, e208–e212. [CrossRef]
35. Somerville, S.; Dedman, K.; Hagan, R. The Perinatal Anxiety Screening Scale: Development and preliminary validation. *Arch. Womens Ment. Health* **2014**, *17*, 443–454. [CrossRef]

International Journal of
Environmental Research and Public Health

Article

Validity and Reliability of the Caregiver Strain Index Scale in Women during the Puerperium in Spain

David Feligreras-Alcalá, María del Pilar Cazalilla-López, Rafael del-Pino-Casado * and Antonio Frías-Osuna

Department of Nursing, Faculty of Health Sciences, University of Jaén, 23071 Jaén, Spain; dfa00001@red.ujaen.es (D.F.-A.); mpcl0008@red.ujaen.es (M.d.P.C.-L.); afrias@ujaen.es (A.F.-O.)
* Correspondence: rdelpino@ujaen.es; Tel.: +34-953-212021

Abstract: Background: The objective of this study is to determine the validity and reliability of the Caregiver Strain Index (CSI) for women during the postpartum period. Methods: This is a validation study of a measurement instrument. This study includes 212 women over the age of 19 who gave birth from March to September 2019 in Maternal and Child Hospital of Jaén (Spain). The items of the CSI were adapted for newborn care. Content validity was measured by five experts, calculating the index of agreement (Aiken's V). Criterion validity was assessed by correlations with scores of other tools that measure constructs related to burden (Edinburgh Postpartum Depression Scale, State-Trait Anxiety Questionnaire, SOC-13 and Duke-UNC-11). Construct validity was determined by the known-groups method. Internal consistency was measured using Cronbach's Alpha, and stability was analysed using the intraclass correlation coefficient (ICC). Results: Regarding content validity, an Aiken's V of 1.00 ($p = 0.032$) was obtained. Regarding criterion validity, the correlation analyses showed statistically significant coefficients between the scores of the questionnaire and those of the sense of coherence ($r = -0.447$, $p < 0.001$), depressive symptoms ($r = 0.429$, $p < 0.001$), social support ($rho = -0.379$, $p < 0.001$) and anxiety symptoms ($r = 0.532$, $p < 0.001$). The known-groups method showed statistically significant differences in the mean of subjective burden between the groups (depressive symptoms, anxiety symptoms, sense of coherence and social support). The total scale obtained a Cronbach's alpha value of 0.710. The ICC was 0.979. Conclusions: The adapted CSI is a valid and reliable screening tool for the subjective burden in women during the puerperium. The adapted CSI can play an important role as a guide to detect the subjective burden in women during the puerperium.

Keywords: subjective burden; caregiver strain index; puerperium; postpartum depression; validity; reliability

check for updates

Citation: Feligreras-Alcalá, D.; Cazalilla-López, M.d.P.; del-Pino-Casado, R.; Frías-Osuna, A. Validity and Reliability of the Caregiver Strain Index Scale in Women during the Puerperium in Spain. *Int. J. Environ. Res. Public Health* **2021**, *18*, 3602. https://doi.org/10.3390/ijerph18073602

Academic Editor: M.Carmen Míguez Varela

Received: 4 February 2021
Accepted: 27 March 2021
Published: 30 March 2021

1. Introduction

The process of pregnancy, childbirth and puerperium constitutes an important event in a woman's life, where she faces significant changes in her cognitive, behavioural and social spheres [1]. Sometimes, this process can be perceived as stressful [2,3], which can lead to an increase in the subjective burden on newborn care [4,5]. The subjective burden has been defined based on the model of the General Theory of Stress. In this model, the caregiver must face certain stressors, and the caregiver's response will be conditioned by psychological processes that include emotional impact, the perception of social support and coping strategies [6]. On the other hand, according to the Lazarus and Folkman Stress Transactional Model, the consequences of stress are measured according to the way in which caregivers perceive, evaluate and manage the care process [7].

Thus, subjective burden is considered a state characterised by stress, fatigue and difficulties in adapting to the role of caregiver, caused by a negative evaluation of the caregiver's situation that threatens their physical, psychological and emotional health [8]. The term subjective burden refers to the assessment by the caregiver that the care situation surpasses the skills that the caregiver possesses to deal with the situation adequately [9]. In this sense, it can also refer to the perception that women have of feeling bewildered, burdened, trapped, resentful and excluded [9]. The objective burden is considered to reflect the daily and practical aspects of the provision of care that capture quantitative dimensions of the caregiver function, such as the level of care needs and the hours of care provision [10].

The presence of caregiver burden can be associated with the appearance of disorders such as depressive symptoms [11] and anxiety [12]. In this context, we could consider the puerperium as a stage in which the subjective burden is significant. Some authors affirm that women with high levels of care burden could have a greater tendency to develop health problems during the puerperium. The investigation of factors associated with the presence of negative consequences related to the subjective burden during the postpartum period, takes on special importance in the early detection and prevention of these factors, such as anxiety [13] or depressive symptoms [14].

Several studies have been carried out to explore the possible association of subjective burden and depressive symptoms in caregivers of the elderly [15–17]. In relation to the presence of postpartum depression (PPD), there are studies that suggest that a higher level of subjective burden regarding newborn care could be associated with a higher level of stress and an increase in depressive symptoms [18,19]. Similarly, Leung et al. [14] show the importance of stress with newborn care as an important predictor of the appearance of PPD. Postpartum depression has a prevalence of 12–13% at 6 weeks of postpartum in industrialised countries [20,21]; in Spain, the studies carried out place it between 10% and 23% [22–25].

In this sense, it would be especially useful to have a measurement instrument adapted to women in the puerperium, which allows a more specific assessment of the construct of the subjective burden of care in this population. The Caregiver Strain Index (CSI) is an instrument designed to measure the subjective burden of caregivers of dependent family members. It is a simple scale, which requires little time to complete, and offers the possibility of an empathic approach towards the caregiver [26]. Robinson validated this instrument in 1983 in the United States (U.S.) in caregivers of patients, after hospital discharge, with atherosclerotic heart disease or with implantation of a hip prosthesis [27].

The CSI scale has been widely used and adapted to diverse populations, cultural contexts and languages [28–30]. In the Spanish population, this scale has been validated with caregivers of patients with chronic, oncological and acute pathologies that required home care [31] and in caregivers of patients diagnosed with dementia [26], with an acceptable internal consistency (Cronbach's alpha of 0.80). This scale is made up of 13 items with a dichotomous response (yes/no) in the context of a semistructured interview whose score ranges from 0 to 13 points [31]. However, no validation study has been found to prove its use in women during the puerperium.

Thus, the adaptation of this CSI scale would have enormous clinical applicability. On the one hand, it would allow the detection of subjective burden in these types of caregivers and early identification of women with high levels of subjective burden in care and therefore with a tendency towards postpartum depression or anxiety, among other associated complications. On the other hand, it would allow improving the treatment of these health problems with a more specific and individualised approach. Thus, this scale would become a useful tool for detecting the subjective burden in care in puerperal women. The aim of this study is to determine the validity and reliability of the CSI in women during the puerperium.

2. Materials and Methods

2.1. Questionnaire Adaptation

To carry out this work, the items of the CSI scale (Spanish version validated by López Alonso et al. [31]) were adapted for newborn care, after consensus of a working group formed by the authors of the present study.

2.2. Content Validation by Experts

Content validity was measured by five experts from the Department of Nursing of the University of Jaén, with extensive academic experience in the study area and other complementary areas. The index of agreement that should exist to determine this validity was established using the Validity Coefficient V of Aiken [32,33].

2.3. Pilot Test

A pilot test was conducted to determine the comprehension and applicability of the scale through semistructured interviews with 40 women during the puerperium, during which they were asked if they adequately understood the items of the scale. Subsequently, an analysis and interpretation of the responses obtained was carried out, identifying possible aspects that were not well understood.

2.4. Clinical Validation

Clinical validation was carried out through a descriptive cross-sectional study in women during the puerperium in the province of Jaén, Spain, using the data collected by Feligreras et al. [34]. Two-hundred-and-twelve women who gave birth at the Maternal-Infant Hospital of Jaén were recruited by random sampling between March and September 2019.

The sample size analysed allows us to affirm, for a 13-item scale, that the calculated Cronbach's alpha is significantly higher than the value of 0.7, with a statistical power of 80% and a significance level of 5%, taking the value of the null hypothesis at 0.6 (calculations performed with PASS 11). The aforementioned sample size also allows us to detect differences of at least 1.1 points out of 13 (8.5%) with a power of 80% and a significance level of 5%, taking as a reference a standard deviation of 2.76 (calculations made with EpiDat 4.2).

The exclusion criteria were age equal to or less than 19 years, previous and/or current personal history of psychiatric pathology, serious illness or death of the newborn, not understanding the Spanish language, not accepting participation in the study or not signing the informed consent.

For the characterisation of the sample, the following variables were collected: age, marital status, educational level, employment situation, family income, pregnancy search, number of pregnancies, type of delivery, sex of the newborn and family history of psychiatric pathology.

2.4.1. Criterion Validity

Criterion validity was assessed by correlations with the scores of other instruments that measure constructs related to subjective burden. These measurement instruments were the Edinburgh Postpartum Depression Scale (EPDS) for the depression construct [35], the state-trait anxiety scale STAI for the anxiety construct [36], the Antonovsky SOC scale for the construct of sense of coherence [37] and the Duke-UNC-11 scale for the construct of social support [38].

Depressive symptoms were measured using the EPDS [35]. This scale is used to detect depressive states in the postpartum period. It is a self-administered scale of 10 items, with four possible response alternatives, scored from 0 to 3, depending on the severity of symptoms. Scores range from 0 to 30 points (proportional to the level of depressive symptoms). A cut-off point, equal to or greater than 10 points, is considered adequate to detect depressive symptoms in this period, with a sensitivity of 79%, a specificity of 95% and a positive predictive value of 63% [25]. Its use is recommended in the first 6 weeks of postpartum to ensure correct screening for depressive symptoms in puerperium, according to the Ministerio de Sanidad, Consumo y Bienestar Social of Spain [39]. It is validated and widely applied in Spain [25].

Anxiety was measured by STAI state-trait's anxiety questionnaire [36], a self-administered instrument that measures two independent concepts of anxiety: On the one hand, anxiety as a state is referred to as a transient emotional condition; on the other hand, anxiety as a trait is described as a relatively stable anxious propensity. In the development of this research, anxiety status has been evaluated as a specific measure of anxiety during this study period. This subscale consists of 20 items, with 4-point, Likert responses (proportional to intensity of anxiety). Total subscale scores range from 0 to 60 points, with the 75th percentile recommended as a cut-off point in adult women [36]. This questionnaire is validated in the Spanish population, presenting a Cronbach's alpha coefficient of 0.94 [40].

The sense of coherence was collected using the SOC-13 Sense of Coherence scale [37]. This scale assesses three dimensions of sense of coherence: compressibility, manageability and significance, which are closely related. It consists of 13 items that are answered on a Likert scale with seven scores, ranging from 1 (always) to 7 (never), where a higher score indicates a greater sense of coherence. This scale is validated in the Spanish population, presenting a Cronbach's alpha of 0.80 [41].

Perceived social support was measured by the Duke-UNC-11 questionnaire [38], a self-administered instrument that measures social support both in its affective dimension (i.e., referring to expressions of love, appreciation, sympathy or belonging) and its confidential dimension (i.e., that through which people can receive information, advice or guidance). It consists of 11 items along with a 5-point, Likert response scale, ranging from 1 (Much less than I want) to 5 (As much as I want). Scoring for the total questionnaire ranges from 11 to 55 points (directly proportional to the level of perceived social support). This questionnaire has been validated in the Spanish population with adequate psychometric properties (e.g., Cronbach's alpha coefficient of 0.93) [42].

These measurement instruments were chosen because there is sufficient scientific evidence that relates the subjective burden with a higher incidence of depression in post-partum women [19], with higher levels of anxiety in caregivers of patients at the hospital level [43], with a lower sense of coherence in caregivers of dependent elderly relatives [11] and with less social support in caregivers of adults with schizophrenia [44].

We used the Pearson bivariate correlations between the scores of the adapted CSI and the scores of the questionnaires of the variables that fulfilled the assumptions of normality (depressive symptoms, anxiety and sense of coherence), and bivariate Spearman correlations in social support; this was a similar analysis to that carried out in the validation of the CSI in our country [31].

2.4.2. Construct Validity

To evaluate the construct validity, the known-groups method was performed. Difference of means tests were carried out using the Student's t-test and the magnitude of the effect was measured using Cohen's d. The hypotheses tested were, according to the scientific literature on subjective burden, (1) the greater the presence of depressive symptoms, the higher the subjective burden level in women in the puerperium [19]; (2) the greater the presence of anxiety symptoms, the higher the level of subjective burden in women in the puerperium [43]; (3) the lower the sense of coherence, the higher the level of subjective burden [11]; and (4) the less social support, the higher the level of subjective burden in women in the puerperium [44]. The cut-off points proposed by each author in the scales used for depressive symptoms, anxiety symptoms and social support were used, whereas we used the median in the case of the sense of coherence.

2.4.3. Reliability

Internal Consistency

To determine internal consistency, Cronbach's alpha was analysed. For the assessment of this coefficient, the recommendations of George and Mallery [45] were used, who show that an acceptable internal consistency has values greater than 0.70.

Stability (Test–Retest)

Stability was measured with the intraclass correlation coefficient (ICC). To do this, the scale was administered again after one week to a sample of 20 women. Following the Fleiss recommendations [46], values above 0.75 represent excellent reliability.

To carry out the analyses, the level of statistical significance was set at 0.05. The relationships between the proposed variables were examined with the help of the SPSS v. 22.0 (IBM International Business Machines Corporation, Armonk, NY, USA) program.

3. Results

3.1. Definitive Questionnaire and Pilot Test

In adapting the questionnaire, the examples that the authors provided in the original version for chronic, oncological and acute patients requiring home care were replaced with examples related to newborn care. In addition, item number 10 has been adapted to a newborn care situation. The final questionnaire (the CSI adapted to newborn care) is showed in Appendix A, and its translation into English is presented in Appendix B.

Regarding content validity, the five experts obtained a Validity Coefficient V of Aiken of 1.00 ($p = 0.032$) for the total of the items of the questionnaire [32,33]. Therefore, according to the recommendations of Aiken, we can show the maximum agreement among the experts, avoiding random coincidences. There were no changes derived from the performance of the content validity analysis in the questionnaire.

After conducting the pilot test, an adequate understanding of the item statements was verified.

3.2. Clinical Validation

Descriptive data of the sample are shown in Table 1. The mean age of the participating women was 32 years, with a minimum age of 19 and a maximum age of 47 years. Most of the women were married (78.3%) with an active employment situation, self-employed or employed (69.4%). Forty-seven percent of the participants had university studies, and 90.1% of the women reported that the pregnancy had been wanted.

Table 1. Description of the studied sample.

Variables		n (%)	M (SD)	CI 95%
Age			32.670 (4.58)	32.06–33.26
Marital Status	Single	8 (3.8)		1.40–6.60
	Married	166 (78.3)		72.60–83.50
	With couple	35 (16.5)		11.80–21.70
	Separated or divorced	3 (1.4)		0.00–3.30
Education level	Primary	18 (8.5)		4.70–12.30
	Secondary	21 (9.9)		6.10–14.20
	High School	12 (5.7)		2.40–9.00
	FP Middle degree	36 (17.0)		12.30–22.20
	FP Higher degree	24 (11.3)		7.10–15.60
	University	101 (47.6)		41.00–54.20
Employment situation	Student	3 (1.40)		0.00–3.30
	Active or own account	39 (18.4)		13.70–23.60
	Asset	108 (50.9)		43.90–57.10
	Unemployed	47 (22.2)		16.50–27.80
	Domestic work	15 (7.1)		4.20–10.80
Family income	<from 500€	1 (0.5)		0.00–1.40
	From 500 to <1000€	27 (12.7)		8.50–17.00
	From 1000 to <1500€	60 (28.3)		22.60–34.40
	From 1500 to <2000€	54 (25.5)		19.80–31.60
	From 2000 to <2500€	29 (13.7)		9.00–17.90
	From 2500 to <3000€	28 (13.2)		9.00–17.90
	From 3000 to <5000€	10 (4.7)		1.90–8.00
	>from 5000€	3 (1.4)		0.0–3.30

Table 1. *Cont.*

Variables		*n* (%)	M (SD)	CI 95%
Pregnancy wanted	Yes	191 (90.1)		85.80–93.90
	No	21 (9.9)		6.10–14.20
No. of pregnancies			1.835 (0.986)	1.71–1.97
Type of delivery	Eutocic	141 (66.5)		60.80–73.10
	Instrumental	32 (15.1)		10.40–20.30
	Caesarean section	39 (18.4)		13.20–23.60
Sex of newborn	Male	112 (52.8)		46.20–59.90
	Female	100 (47.2)		40.10–53.80
Family history of psychiatric pathology	Yes	13 (6.1)		3.30–9.40
	No	199 (93.6)		90.60–96.70

Source: self-made.

The minimum CSI score obtained was 0 and the maximum score was 13, the mean score being 5.23 (SD: 2.76). The correlations between the different items and the overall result were higher than 0.2 in all cases [47], and the ICC for the agreement between items was 0.71 [48].

3.3. Criterion Validity

The correlation analyses showed statistically significant coefficients between the scores of the adapted CSI questionnaire and those of sense of coherence (r = −0.447, $p < 0.001$), depressive symptoms (r = 0.429, $p < 0.001$), social support (rho = −0.379, $p < 0.001$) and anxiety symptoms (r = 0.532, $p < 0.001$).

3.4. Construct Validity

We proceeded to perform the known-groups method. There were statistically significant differences in the mean of subjective burden between the groups analysed: (1) presence or not of depressive symptoms (6.68 vs. 4.69; d: 0.77; 95% CI: 0.45, 1.08), (2) presence or absence of anxiety symptoms (7.08 vs. 4.51; d: 1.02; 95% CI: 0.71, 1.34), (3) presence or not of sense of coherence (4.28 vs. 6.21; d: −0.76; 95% CI: −1.04, −0.48) and (4) presence or not of social support (4.88 vs. 7.00; d: −0.81; 95% CI: −1.18, −0.43) (Table 2).

Table 2. Differences in means of subjective burden in the subgroups of women with and without depressive symptoms, anxiety, sense of coherence and social support.

Variable	Mean (SD)	Significance	Cohen's d	95% CI
Depressive symptoms	Yes: 6.68 (2.72) No: 4.69 (2.58)	$p < 0.0001$	0.77	(0.45, 1.08)
Anxiety	Yes: 7.08 (2.62) No: 4.51 (2.47)	$p < 0.0001$	1.02	(0.71, 1.34)
Sense of coherence	Yes: 4.28 (2.56) No: 6.21 (2.62)	$p < 0.0001$	−0.76	(−1.04, −0.48)
Social support	Yes: 4.88 (2.67) No: 7.00 (2.52)	$p < 0.0001$	−0.81	(−1.18, −0.43)

Source: self-made.

3.5. Reliability

In relation to internal consistency, Cronbach's alpha was determined for the total scale, obtaining a value of 0.710 (acceptable internal consistency). Regarding the stability of the test, the Intraclass Correlation Coefficient (ICC) was measured, reaching a value of 0.979 (95% CI = 0.949–0.992) (excellent stability).

4. Discussion

In this study, we presented the adaptation and validation of the CSI in order to measure the subjective burden in women during the puerperium. The CSI adapted to newborn care was quick and easy to administer in the population studied. The study participants adequately understood each of the items both in the pilot test and in the final application of this measurement instrument. The adapted scale obtains adequate psychometric properties at the level of criterion validity and construct validity, internal consistency and stability, which shows an adequate validity and reliability of the measurement instrument.

Criterion validity was assessed using bivariate correlations with scores from other instruments that measured constructs related to subjective burden. López-Alonso et al. [29] in the CSI validation in the Spanish population carried out a similar analysis, correlating the subjective burden with other similar areas included in the original validation of the scale.

Regarding the construct validity, we confirmed all the hypotheses tested in the known-groups method, which reinforces the construct validity of the instrument in measuring subjective burden in women during the puerperium.

Regarding internal consistency, we can find some coincidences of our study with other studies on CSI in other types of caregiver populations. Thus, Ugur et al. [49] carried out an adaptation of this scale in the Turkish population, finding a Cronbach's alpha value of 0.77. Ramasamy et al. [50] in Malaysia obtained an internal consistency of 0.75. The Chinese version [51] showed high reliability with a Cronbach's alpha of 0.91, the same result as that obtained in the Portuguese population [52]. In our study, we obtained an internal consistency of 0.710. Therefore, our results in this regard are similar to those available in the literature.

Regarding the measurement of stability, the adapted CSI was administered again one week after the first measurement in the puerperium; the time elapsed between both applications should not be too long (variation of the phenomenon studied) nor too short (learning effect) [53]. The ICC for test–retest reliability was 0.979, higher than the 0.88 obtained by Thornton and Travis in the modified version of the CSI [54]. Both in the original validation of the CSI [27] and in the validation of the CSI in our country [31], test–retest reliability was not calculated. Following Fleiss [46], values above 0.75 show excellent reliability. These data confirm the stability of the CSI adapted to newborn care.

To date, in the scientific literature there was no validation of the CSI scale in women during the puerperium. In this way, with the adaptation and validation of this scale, we obtain a measurement instrument that has enormous clinical applicability. This scale allows us to measure in a more specific way the construct of the subjective burden of care in women during the puerperium. In this sense, the adapted CSI in the puerperal population offers us the possibility of early diagnosis of women with high levels of subjective burden and, therefore, with a possible higher risk of developing PPD or anxiety (among other associated complications). Therefore, this scale constitutes a useful tool for detecting the subjective burden of newborn care in puerperal women.

The study has the limitation that the entire sample obtained for the study comes from a single hospital centre. Another limitation is that the study does not fully comprise some perinatal factors and circumstances associated with delivery, which might affect the evaluation of the criterion validity.

5. Conclusions

According to the findings obtained in this research, the CSI adapted to newborn care is a valid and reliable screening tool for the subjective burden in women during the puerperium. This study can play an important role as a guide to detect the subjective burden in women during the puerperium, in order to plan preventive and health promotion actions in those women with a risk profile of subjective burden in newborn care.

Author Contributions: Conceptualisation, D.F.-A., M.d.P.C.-L., R.d.-P.-C. and A.F.-O.; methodology, D.F.-A., M.d.P.C.-L., R.d.-P.-C. and A.F.-O.; validation, D.F.-A.; and M.d.P.C.-L.; formal analysis, R.d.-P.-C. and A.F.-O.; investigation, D.F.-A., M.d.P.C.-L. and R.d.-P.-C.; resources, R.d.-P.-C.; data curation, D.F.-A., M.d.P.C.-L., R.d.-P.-C. and A.F.-O.; writing—original draft preparation, R.d.-P.-C. and A.F.-O.; writing—review and editing, D.F.-A., R.d.-P.-C. and A.F.-O.; visualisation, R.d.-P.-C. and

A.F.-O.; supervision, R.d.-P.-C. and A.F.-O.; project administration, R.d.-P.-C. All authors have read and agreed to the published version of the manuscript.

Funding: This research received no external funding.

Institutional Review Board Statement: This study was approved by the Jaén Research Ethics Committee of the SSPA (Andalusian Public Health System) on April 5, 2017 with code 0262-M1-17. Informed consent was requested as a guarantee of respect for the bioethical principle of Autonomy, in accordance with the provisions of Spanish Law 41/2002, of 14 November, regulating the basic autonomy of the patient and rights and obligations regarding information and clinical documentation. The study was carried out in accordance with state legislation and the principles established in the Declaration of Helsinki of 1964. The confidentiality and privacy of the data obtained were guaranteed, in accordance with Spanish Organic Law 15/1999, of 13 December, Protection of Personal Data. The possibility of the participants both to refuse to participate and to abandon the study at any time was indicated verbally and in writing.

Informed Consent Statement: Informed consent was obtained from all subjects involved in the study. Written informed consent has been obtained from the patients to publish this paper.

Data Availability Statement: The data presented in this study are available on request from the corresponding author. The data are not publicly available due to their containing information that could compromise the privacy of research participants.

Acknowledgments: The authors would like to thank the women interviewed for their participation in the study.

Conflicts of Interest: The authors declare no conflict of interest.

Appendix A. Caregiver Strain Index Adapted to Newborn Care (In Spanish)

Ítems	**Sí = 1**	**No = 0**
1. Tiene trastornos de sueño (p. ej., porque su hijo/a se despierta por la noche).		
2. Es un inconveniente (p. ej., porque el cuidado consume mucho tiempo o se tarda mucho en proporcionarlo).		
3. Representa un esfuerzo físico.		
4. Supone una restricción (p. ej., porque el cuidado limita el tiempo libre).		
5. Ha habido modificaciones en la familia (p. ej., porque el cuidado ha roto la rutina o no hay intimidad).		
6. Ha habido cambios en los planes personales (p. ej., se tuvo que rechazar un trabajo o no se pudo ir de vacaciones).		
7. Ha habido otras exigencias de mi tiempo (p. ej., por parte de otros miembros de la familia).		
8. Ha habido cambios emocionales (p. ej., causa de fuertes discusiones).		
9. Algunos comportamientos son molestos (p. ej., el llanto, los despertares nocturnos …).		
10. Es molesto darse cuenta de que la situación ha cambiado tanto comparada con la de antes.		
11. Ha habido modificaciones en el trabajo (p. ej., a causa de la necesidad de dedicar tiempo para el cuidado).		
12. Es una carga económica.		
13. Nos ha desbordado totalmente (p. ej., por la preocupación sobre cómo cuidar a su hijo/a).		
Puntuación total (contar respuestas afirmativas)		

Appendix B. Caregiver Strain Index Adapted to Newborn Care (English Translation of the Spanish Version)

Items	Yes = 1	No = 0
1. Sleep is disturbed (e.g., because your child wakes up at night).		
2. It is inconvenient (e.g., because helping takes so much time or it is a long drive over to help).		
3. It is a physical strain.		
4. It is confining (e.g., helping restricts free time).		
5. There have been family adjustments (e.g., because helping has disrupted routine or there has been no privacy).		
6. There have been changes in personal plans (e.g., had to turn down a job or could not go on vacation).		
7. There have been other demands on my time (e.g., from other family members).		
8. There have been emotional adjustments (e.g., because of severe arguments).		
9. Some behaviour is upsetting (e.g., crying, night awakenings).		
10. It is upsetting to find the situation has changed so much compared to before.		
11. There have been work adjustments (e.g., because of having to take time off).		
12. It is a financial strain.		
13. Feeling completely overwhelmed (e.g., because of concern about how to care for your child).		
Total Score (count yes responses)		

References

1. Don, B.P.; Chong, A.; Biehle, S.N.; Gordon, A.; Mickelson, K.D. Anxiety across the transition to parenthood: Change trajectories among low-risk parents. *Anxiety Stress Coping* **2014**, *27*, 633–649. [CrossRef] [PubMed]
2. Lee, H.; Kim, K.-E.; Kim, M.-Y.; Park, C.G.; Han, J.Y.; Choi, E.J. Trajectories of Depressive Symptoms and Anxiety during Pregnancy and Associations with Pregnancy Stress. *Int. J. Environ. Res. Public Health* **2021**, *18*, 2733. [CrossRef]
3. Razurel, C.; Kaiser, B.; Sellenet, C.; Epiney, M. Relation between perceived stress, social support, and coping strategies and maternal well-being: A review of the literature. *Women Health* **2013**, *53*, 74–99. [CrossRef]
4. Hasanjanzadeh, P.; Faramarzi, M. Relationship between maternal general and specific-pregnancy stress, anxiety, and depression symptoms and pregnancy outcome. *J. Clin. Diagn. Res.* **2017**, *11*, VC04. [CrossRef] [PubMed]
5. Nelson, A.M. Transition to motherhood. *J. Obstet. Gynecol. Neonatal Nurs.* **2003**, *32*, 465–477. [CrossRef]
6. Zarit, S.H.; Birkel, R.C.; Malone-Beach, E. *Family Involvement in the Treatment of the Frail Elderly*; Goldstein, M.Z., Ed.; American Psychiatric Press: Washington, DC, USA, 1989.
7. Lazarus, R.S.; Folkman, S. *Stress, Appraisal, and Coping*; Springer Publishing Company: New York, NY, USA, 1984.
8. Kim, H.; Chang, M.; Rose, K.; Kim, S. Predictors of caregiver burden in caregivers of individuals with dementia. *J. Adv. Nurs.* **2012**, *68*, 846–855. [CrossRef] [PubMed]
9. Crespo, M.; López, J. *El Estrés en Cuidadores de Mayores Dependientes. Cuidarse para Cuidar*; Psicología Pirámide: Madrid, Spain, 2007.
10. Domingues, N.S.; Verreault, P.; Hudon, C. Reducing Burden for Caregivers of Older Adults with Mild Cognitive Impairment: A Systematic Review. *Am. J. Alzheimer's Dis. Demen.* **2018**, *33*, 401–414. [CrossRef] [PubMed]
11. del-Pino-Casado, R.; Espinosa, A.; Lopez, C.; Orgeta, V. Sense of coherence, burden and mental health in caregiving: A systematic review and meta-analysis. *J. Affect. Disord.* **2019**, *242*, 14–21. [CrossRef] [PubMed]
12. Cooper, C.; Balamurali, T.; Livingston, G. A systematic review of the prevalence and covariates of anxiety in caregivers of people with dementia. *Int. Psychogeriatr.* **2007**, *19*, 175–195. [CrossRef]
13. Britton, J.R. Maternal anxiety: Course and antecedents during the early postpartum period. *Depress. Anxiety* **2008**, *25*, 793–800. [CrossRef]

14. Leung, S.S.; Martinson, I.M.; Arthur, D. Postpartum depression and related psychosocial variables in Hong Kong Chinese women: Findings from a prospective study. *Res. Nurs. Health* **2005**, *28*, 27–38. [CrossRef] [PubMed]
15. Geng, H.M.; Chuang, D.M.; Yang, F.; Yang, Y.; Liu, W.M.; Liu, L.H.; Tian, H.M. Prevalence and determinants of depression in caregivers of cancer patients: A systematic review and meta-analysis. *Medicine* **2018**, *97*, e11863. [CrossRef]
16. Watson, B.; Tatangelo, G.; McCabe, M. Depression and Anxiety among Partner and Offspring Carers of People with Dementia: A Systematic Review. *Gerontologist* **2019**, *59*, e597–e610. [CrossRef] [PubMed]
17. Zhu, W.; Jiang, Y. A Meta-analytic Study of Predictors for Informal Caregiver Burden in Patients with Stroke. *J. Stroke Cerebrovasc. Dis.* **2018**, *27*, 3636–3646. [CrossRef] [PubMed]
18. Nurbaeti, I.; Deoisres, W.; Hengudomsub, P. Association between psychosocial factors and postpartum depression in South Jakarta, Indonesia. *Sex. Reprod. Healthc.* **2019**, *20*, 72–76. [CrossRef] [PubMed]
19. Poo, F.A.; Espejo, S.C.; Godoy, P.C.; Gualda, C.M.; Hernandez, O.T.; Perez, H.C. Prevalence and risk factors associated with postpartum depression in puerperal women consulting in primary care. *Rev. Med. Chil.* **2008**, *136*, 44–52.
20. Shorey, S.; Yin, C.C.; Debby, E.; Yiong, C.; Wai, W.T.; Seng, C.Y. Prevalence and incidence of postpartum depression among healthy mothers: A systematic review and meta-analysis. *J. Psychiatr. Res.* **2018**, *104*, 235–248. [CrossRef]
21. Fiala, A.; Švancara, J.; Klánová, J.; Kašpárek, T. Sociodemographic and delivery risk factors for developing postpartum depression in a sample of 3233 mothers from the Czech ELSPAC study. *BMC Psychiatry* **2017**, *17*, 104. [CrossRef]
22. Marín-Morales, D.; Toro-Molina, S.; Peñacoba-Puente, C. Relationship between postpartum depression and psychological and biological variables in the initial postpartum period. *Matern. Child Health J.* **2018**, *22*, 866–873. [CrossRef]
23. Míguez, M.C.; Fernández, V.; Pereira, B. Depresión postparto y factores asociados en mujeres con embarazos de riesgo. *Rev. Int. Psicol. Clin. Salud.* **2017**, *25*, 47–64.
24. Escribà-Agüir, V.; Artazcoz, L. Gender differences in postpartum depression: A longitudinal cohort study. *J. Epidemiol. Community Health* **2011**, *65*, 320–326. [CrossRef]
25. Garcia, L.; Ascaso, C.; Ojuel, J.; Navarro, P. Validation of the Edinburgh postnatal depression scale (EPDS) in Spanish mothers. *J. Affect. Disord.* **2003**, *75*, 71–76. [CrossRef]
26. Odriozola, M.; Vita, A.; Maiz, B.; Zialtzeta, L.; Bengoetxea, L. Índice de esfuerzo del cuidador: Test diagnóstico de sobrecarga en cuidadores de enfermos con demencia. *Semergen* **2008**, *34*, 435–438. [CrossRef]
27. Robinson, B.C. Validation of a caregiver strain index. *J. Gerontol.* **1983**, *38*, 344–348. [CrossRef]
28. López, O.; Lorenzo, A.; Santiago, P. Morbilidad en cuidadores de pacientes confinados en su domicilio. *Aten. Prim.* **1999**, *24*, 404–410.
29. Gómez, M.J.; González, F.M. El cuidador del paciente con demencia: Aplicación del test Índice del Esfuerzo del Cuidador. *Rev. Esp. Geriatr. Gerontol.* **2004**, *39*, 154–159. [CrossRef]
30. Moral, M.S.; Ortega, J.J.; López, M.J.; Pellicer, P. Perfil y riesgo de morbilidad psíquica en cuidadores de pacientes ingresados en su domicilio. *Aten. Prim.* **2003**, *32*, 77–83. [CrossRef]
31. López, S.R.; Moral, M.S. Validación del Índice de Esfuerzo del Cuidador en la población española. *Enferm. Comun.* **2005**, *1*, 12–17.
32. Escurra, L. Cuantificación de la validez de contenido por criterio de jueces. *Rev Psicol.* **1988**, *6*, 103–111.
33. Aiken, L.R. Three coefficients for analyzing the reliability and validity of ratings. *Educ. Psychol. Meas.* **1985**, *45*, 131–142. [CrossRef]
34. Feligreras-Alcalá, D.; Frías-Osuna, A.; del-Pino-Casado, R. Personal and Family Resources Related to Depressive and Anxiety Symptoms in Women during Puerperium. *Int. J. Environ. Res. Public Health* **2020**, *17*, 5230. [CrossRef]
35. Cox, J.L.; Holden, J.M.; Sagovsky, R. Detection of postnatal depression: Development of the 10-item Edinburgh Postnatal Depression Scale. *Br. J. Psychiatry* **1987**, *150*, 782–786. [CrossRef]
36. Buela, G.; Guillén, A.; Seisdedos, N. *Manual del Cuestionario de Ansiedad Estado-Rasgo (STAI)*; TEA Ediciones: Madrid, Spain, 1982.
37. Antonovsky, A. The structure and properties of the sense of coherence scale. *Soc. Sci. Med.* **1993**, *36*, 725–733. [CrossRef]
38. Broadhead, W.E.; Gehlbach, S.H.; De-Gruy, F.V.; Kaplan, B.H. The Duke-UNC Functional Social Support Questionnaire: Measurement of social support in family medicine patients. *Med. Care* **1988**, *26*, 709–723. [CrossRef]
39. Ministry of Health, Social Services and Equality. *Clinical Practice Guide for Pregnancy and Puerperium Care*; Ministry of Health, Social Services and Equality: Madrid, Spain, 2014.
40. Guillén, A.; Buela, G. Actualización psicométrica y funcionamiento diferencial de los items en el State Trait Anxiety Inventory (STAI). *Psicothema* **2011**, *23*, 510–515.
41. Virués, J.; Martínez, P.; del Barrio, J.L.; Lozano, L.M. Validación transcultural de la Escala de Sentido de Coherencia de Antonovsky (OLQ 13) en ancianos mayores de 70 años. *Med. Clin.* **2007**, *128*, 486–492. [CrossRef]
42. Bellón, J.S.; Delgado, A.S.; del-Castillo, J.D.; Lardelli, P.C. Validity and reliability of the Duke-UNC-11 questionnaire of functional social support. *Aten. Prim.* **1996**, *18*, 153–163.
43. del-Pino-Casado, R.; Priego-Cubero, E.; López-Martínez, C.; Orgeta, V. Subjective caregiver burden and anxiety in informal caregivers: A systematic review and meta-analysis. *PLoS ONE* **2021**, *16*, e0247143. [CrossRef] [PubMed]
44. Peng, M.M.; Zhang, T.M.; Liu, K.Z.; Gong, K.; Huang, C.H.; Dai, G.Z.; Hu, S.H.; Lin, F.R.; Chan, S.K.; Ng, S.; et al. Perception of social support and psychotic symptoms among persons with schizophrenia: A strategy to lessen caregiver burden. *Int. J. Soc. Psychiatry* **2019**, *65*, 548–557. [CrossRef] [PubMed]

45. George, D.; Mallery, P. *SPSS for Windows Step by Step: A Simple Study Guide and Reference, 17.0 Update*, 10th ed.; Allyn & Bacon: Boston, MA, USA, 2010.
46. Fleiss, J.L. *Reliability of Measurement. The Design and Analysis of Clinical Experiments*; John Wiley and Sons: New York, NY, USA, 1986.
47. Frías, D. *Apuntes de Consistencia Interna de las Puntuaciones de un Instrumento de Medida*; Universidad de Valencia: Valencia, Spain, 2019.
48. Mandeville, P.B. *El Coeficiente de Correlación Intraclase (CCI)*; Universidad Autónoma de Nuevo León: Nuevo León, Mexico, 2005.
49. Ugur, O.; Fadiloglu, C. Caregiver Strain Index validity and reliability in Turkish society. *Asian Pac. J. Cancer Prev.* **2010**, *11*, 1669–1675. [PubMed]
50. Ramasamy, M.S.; Ibrahim, R.; Madon, Z.; Arshat, Z. A validity study of Malay-translated version of the Modified Caregivers Strain Index Questionnaire (M-CSI-M). *J. Bus. Soc. Rev. Emerg. Econ.* **2017**, *3*, 217–226.
51. Chan, W.C.; Chan, C.L.; Suen, M. Validation of the Chinese version of the Modified Caregivers Strain Index among Hong Kong caregivers: An initiative of medical social workers. *Health Soc. Work* **2013**, *38*, 214–221. [CrossRef] [PubMed]
52. Ribeiro, O.; Brandão, D.; Oliveira, A.F.; Martín, I.; Teixeira, L.; Paúl, C. The Modified Caregiver Strain Index: Portuguese version. *J. Health Psychol.* **2019**. [CrossRef]
53. Yébenes, M.; Rodríguez, F.; Carmona, L. Validación de cuestionarios. *Reumatol. Clin.* **2009**, *5*, 171–177.
54. Thornton, M.; Travis, S.S. Analysis of the reliability of the modified caregiver strain index. *J. Gerontol. Soc. Sci.* **2003**, *58*, 127–132. [CrossRef] [PubMed]

International Journal of
Environmental Research and Public Health

MDPI

Article

Effects of Pregnancy Loss on Subsequent Postpartum Mental Health: A Prospective Longitudinal Cohort Study

David C. Reardon [1,*] and Christopher Craver [2]

[1] Elliot Institute, St. Peters, MO 63376, USA
[2] Charlotte Lozier Institute, Arlington, VA 22206, USA; ccraver@lozierinstitute.org
* Correspondence: elliotinstitute@gmail.com

Abstract: Pregnancy loss, natural or induced, is linked to higher rates of mental health problems, but little is known about its effects during the postpartum period. This study identifies the percentages of women receiving at least one postpartum psychiatric treatment (PPT), defined as any psychiatric treatment (ICD-9 290-316) within six months of their first live birth, relative to their history of pregnancy loss, history of prior mental health treatments, age, and race. The population consists of young women eligible for Medicaid in states that covered all reproductive services between 1999–2012. Of 1,939,078 Medicaid beneficiaries with a first live birth, 207,654 (10.7%) experienced at least one PPT, and 216,828 (11.2%) had at least one prior pregnancy loss. A history of prior mental health treatments (MHTs) was the strongest predictor of PPT, but a history of pregnancy loss is also another important risk factor. Overall, women with a prior pregnancy loss were 35% more likely to require a PPT. When the interactions of prior mental health and prior pregnancy loss are examined in greater detail, important effects of these combinations were revealed. About 58% of those whose first MHT was after a pregnancy loss required PPT. In addition, over 99% of women with a history of MHT one year prior to their first pregnancy loss required PPT after their first live births. These findings reveal that pregnancy loss (natural or induced) is a risk factor for PPT, and that the timing of events and the time span for considering prior mental health in research on pregnancy loss can significantly change observed effects. Clinicians should screen for a convergence of a history of MHT and prior pregnancy loss when evaluating pregnant women, in order to make appropriate referrals for counseling.

Keywords: perinatal mental health; postpartum psychiatric treatments; pregnancy loss; abortion; miscarriage

check for updates

Citation: Reardon, D.C.; Craver, C. Effects of Pregnancy Loss on Subsequent Postpartum Mental Health: A Prospective Longitudinal Cohort Study. *Int. J. Environ. Res. Public Health* **2021**, *18*, 2179. https://doi.org/10.3390/ijerph18042179

Academic Editor: M. Carmen Míguez Varela

Received: 12 January 2021
Accepted: 17 February 2021
Published: 23 February 2021

Publisher's Note: MDPI stays neutral with regard to jurisdictional claims in published maps and institutional affiliations.

1. Introduction

Pregnancy loss (natural or induced) is associated with an increased risk of mental health problems [1–4]. Self-reports and clinical experience suggest that unresolved and suppressed feelings regarding prior pregnancy losses may be aggravated or triggered by subsequent pregnancies [5,6]. At least some women report that their feelings of joy regarding a pregnancy they are carrying to term are comingled with a feelings of loss, impacted grief, and or guilt regarding prior pregnancy losses [5]. Others report heightened fears about losing the subsequent pregnancy and/or fears of being unworthy to be a mother, and other anxieties which sometimes impede bonding [5]. These anecdotal observations of a link between pregnancy loss and subsequent mental health problems during the antenatal and postpartum periods of subsequent pregnancies are supported by statistical evidence from a small number of studies. These studies have revealed that pregnancy loss is associated with higher rates of mental health treatments during both the antenatal [7–10] and the postpartum period [11–16]. Moreover, at least one study has revealed that fear of childbirth is a significant risk factor for postpartum depression [14], which is consistent with reports of heightened fears surrounding subsequent wanted pregnancies among women with a history of induced abortions [5]. Most studies examining the effects of pregnancy loss on maternal mental health, however, are limited to relatively small sample sizes and often lack a comprehensive control for prior mental health issues. Therefore, the primary purpose of this study is to examine both the effects of pregnancy loss and prior mental health on treatment rates for postpartum mental illness in a large population of primiparous women. Since early intervention can ameliorate the symptoms of perinatal depression [17], screening for a history of pregnancy loss may lead to earlier referrals to address unresolved mental health issues.

A secondary purpose is to examine the differences associated with the time frames used for considering the effects of prior mental on mental health.To date, there does not appear to be an evidence-based standard for determining which, if any, time frames are best suited for understanding the effects of prior mental health on mental health during and after a subsequent pregnancy. The choice of time frames used to consider prior mental health appears to vary widely, jumping about from nine months [18] to one year [19] or two years [20], even among research teams employing the same individuals. Therefore, our secondary purpose in this paper is to investigate different time frames before, between, and during pregnancy, in order to better understand how the choice of time frame may affect findings and the interpretation of results relative to reproductive mental health issues.

2. Materials and Methods

2.1. Study Population

Data was obtained from the United States Centers for Medicare and Medicaid Services (CMS) using the data submitted to CMS from the 17 states (Alaska, Arizona, California, Connecticut, Hawaii, Illinois, Maryland, Massachusetts, Minnesota, Montana, New Jersey, New Mexico, New York, Oregon, Vermont, Washington, and West Virginia) where Medicaid coverage included all reproductive health care options, including induced abortion, during the years 1999 through at least 2012, inclusive. Data for each beneficiary was rolled in beginning in 1999 or the year of each woman's 14th birthday, whichever was later. The study population was limited to all women born in 1983 or later who had at least one live birth over the age of 13 between 1999 and June of 2012 inclusive, and had been eligible for Medicaid coverage for at least 12 months between 1999 and 2012. Using these selection criteria, wherein the oldest women in the cohort were 16 years of age in 1999 and 29 years of age in 2012, maximized the likelihood that our data captured the first pregnancy outcome for the vast majority of our study population.

2.2. Study Variables

The primary outcome variable was any postpartum psychiatric treatment (PPT), defined as any treatment code associated with the International Classification of Diseases (ICD-9) codes 290–316 occurring within six months of each woman's first known live birth. In addition, beneficiaries who had at least one inpatient PPT or one emergency room PPT were identified for a subgroup analysis.

In addition, for each woman, her race, age at first live birth, and the date and outcomes of all pregnancies prior to and including her first live birth, were also extracted. To address the secondary analysis examining the effects of time frames used to control for prior mental health, any occurrence of a mental health treatment (MHT), defined as any ICD-9 codes 290–316, was identified for each of the following periods: one year before the first conception date, one year prior to the first pregnancy outcome, one year prior to the first live birth, any time prior to the first conception, any time prior to the first pregnancy outcome, any time prior to the first live birth, between first conception and the first live birth, and any time after the first conception but prior to the first live birth.

2.3. Identification of Pregnancies and Conception Dates

Pregnancy outcomes were identified using diagnostic ICD-9 codes and clarified with Current Procedural Terminology (CPT) codes and Healthcare Common Procedure Coding System (HCPS codes. Multiple diagnostic or treatment codes for any pregnancy within

30 days of other pregnancy codes were collapsed into a single pregnancy outcome, using the first date associated with that cluster of Medicaid claims. Pregnancy outcomes were segregated into four categories: live birth; induced abortion; natural fetal loss (miscarriage, ectopic pregnancy, molar pregnancy, or stillbirth); and indeterminate loss, wherein the latter combined missed abortion (ICD 632; $n = 28{,}859$), unspecified abortion (ICD 637; $n = 12{,}655$), illegally induced abortion (ICD 636; $n = 271$), and failed attempted abortion (ICD 638; $n = 0$). All women with any history of an induced abortion, natural loss, or indeterminate loss prior to their first live birth were identified as having a pregnancy loss. Also, to address coding errors or other conflicts with the data, coding indicating an abortion within 36 weeks prior to a live birth was excluded, as well as any data indicating an abortion or natural loss within four weeks of an induced abortion. The estimated date of conception was calculated for each pregnancy by subtracting 290 days from the date of a livebirth and 84 days from the date of a pregnancy loss.

2.4. Statistical Analyses

Logistic regression analyses were conducted to compare the subsets of women who experienced PPT to those women who did not. Covariates included age, race, type and number of losses, and history of MHTs. Regarding the history of MHTs, several models were run to examine any differences between each of the following time frames: one year prior to first conception; any time prior to first conception; one year prior to first pregnancy outcome; any time prior to first pregnancy outcome; one year prior to first live birth; any time prior to first live birth; and for the interval between the first conception and first live birth.

3. Results

Using the selection criteria for young Medicaid beneficiaries described above, we identified the first live birth of 1,939,078 Medicaid beneficiaries. Of these women, 207,654 (10.7%) experienced at least one postpartum psychiatric treatment (PPT) within 6 months of the delivery, and 216,828 (11.2%) had at least one pregnancy loss prior to their first live birth. Overall, younger women experienced higher rates of PPT, 12.9%, 9.7%, and 8.6% for women aged 14–19, 20–24, and 25–29, respectively, but the risk of PPT following an earlier pregnancy loss increased with age. There were even more significant variations relative to race. Overall, Hispanic women had the lowest rate of PPT, at 5.5% compared to 15.9%, 9.3%, and 7.8% for whites, Blacks, and other races, respectively.

Table 1 shows the rates of PPT in various subgroups segregated by exposure to a pregnancy loss prior to the first birth. Overall, the 216,828 women with one or more pregnancy losses prior to their first live births were about 35% more likely to require PPTs than women who delivered their first pregnancies. Relative to race, the risk of PPT associated with pregnancy loss increased 19% for Black women, 32% for white women, 59% for Hispanic women, and 48% for other races. Overall, PPT treatment was twice as likely to occur within the first 90 days after delivery compared to the next 90 days, but a history of pregnancy loss was associated with a 42% increased risk of PPT within the first three months and a 21% increased risk in the second three months. In addition, while most women experiencing PPT received outpatient treatment only, the risk of inpatient treatment was 83% higher for those with a history of pregnancy loss. There was also a 22% higher risk that PPT treatment was sought at emergency room.

Table 2 shows the treatment rates between the two groups relative to their history of receiving mental health treatments (MHTs) prior to their first live birth. To address our secondary research objective, multiple time frames were examined. The time frames of interest are illustrated in Figure 1. The mean average age of at first conception was 19.8 (standard deviation: SD = 3.0) for those whose first pregnancy was a loss, and 20.2 (SD = 2.9) for those whose first pregnancy was delivered. The average age of first live birth was 23.4 (SD = 3.8) for those with a history of one or more losses, and 20.9 (SD = 2.8) for those without a history of loss. The average age of women as they were rolled into the data cohort was approximately 13.5 years of age. Therefore, the time frame for "any time" prior to a specific date in Tables 2–4 includes the time between 13.5 years of ag and the specified reference date.

Table 2 reveals that the choice of time frame (see Figure 1) can significantly change the strength of associations between pregnancy loss and the outcome variable. For example, among women with at least one MHT during the year prior to their first live birth, nearly half required PPT regardless of pregnancy loss history. However, when the period of observation of prior MHT was one year prior to their first pregnancy loss, nearly 100% of women required PPT following their first live birth.

Among women with no history of mental health problems in the selected time frames, pregnancy loss was positively associated with PPT (OR > 1) in all but one case. The one exception was in the comparison of women with no history of MHT any time prior to their first live birth. With this subgroup, women with and without a history of pregnancy loss had nearly identical rates of PPT (7.03–7.05%). However, for those with any history of MHT, the risk of PPT was four times higher (27.69–30.73%). Notably, with the exception of two cases, among women with a history of MHT pregnancy loss was inversely associated with PPT (odds ratio:OR < 1). These findings may indicate either that women with a pregnancy loss are more likely to have a successful history of mental health care, which helps to reduce the need for PPT, or these findings may reflect an emotional boost or healing effect associated with experiencing a successful birth following a pregnancy loss. Of the two exceptions, only one is notable, but it is very notable: MHT one year prior to a first pregnancy ending in a loss was almost perfectly correlated with PPT (99.97%).

Table 1. Total of all women by subgroup with percentages of total receiving postpartum psychiatric treatment (PPT) rates relative to first pregnancy (Pg) outcome, population differences, timing, and type of treatment.

Characteristics of Study Population	No Prior Pg Loss n = 1,722,250		Yes Prior Pg Loss n = 216,828		Crude Odds Ratio
	% Receiving PPT	Total	% Receiving PPT	Total	
Total	10.36%	1,722,250	13.50%	216,828	1.35
Age at live birth (years)					
14–19	12.65%	603,925	14.24%	96,119	1.15
20–24	9.34%	885,674	13.13%	97,343	1.47
25–29	8.29%	232,651	12.03%	23,366	1.51
Calendar year of live birth					
2000–2002	9.98%	638,645	13.69%	36,350	1.43
2003–2005	10.50%	448,784	13.69%	51,142	1.35
2006–2008	10.64%	472,841	13.26%	58,188	1.28
2009–2011	10.62%	161,980	13.47%	71,148	1.31
Race					
White	15.43%	696,577	19.38%	84,731	1.32
Black	9.08%	315,128	10.60%	62,161	1.19
Hispanic	5.22%	485,319	8.05%	46,334	1.59
Other	7.52%	225,226	10.74%	23,602	1.48
First occurrence of PPT					
Within 90 Days	7.30%	1,665,464	10.05%	208,498	1.42
Within 91–183 Days	3.55%	1,600,662	4.25%	195,878	1.21
Severity of Disorder					
Inpatient Treatment	0.44%	1,550,677	0.80%	189,063	1.83
Outpatient Only	10.00%	1,715,449	12.90%	215,313	1.33
Emergency Room	0.18%	3083	0.22%	473	1.22

Pg: first pregnanacy; PPT: postpartum psychiatric treatment.

Table 2. Women with postpartum psychiatric treatments (PPT) relative to first pregnancy outcome (birth or loss) and history of mental health treatments (MHTs) prior to specific pregnancy associated dates.

	Time Frame for Identifying Any History of MHT	No Prior Pg Loss		Prior Pg Loss		Crude OR
		n = 1,722,250		n = 216,828		
		% PPT	Total	% PPT	Total	
One Year	MHT one year prior to first live birth					
	No	7.91%	1,617,780	9.03%	192,511	1.16
	Yes	48.32%	104,470	48.91%	24,317	1.02
	MHT one year prior to first pregnancy outcome					
	No	7.91%	1,617,780	10.42%	209,354	1.35
	Yes	48.32%	104,470	99.97%	7474	>999
	MHT one year prior to first concception					
	No	8.41%	1,630,781	12.47%	209,255	1.55
	Yes	45.06%	91,471	42.00%	7573	0.88
Anytime	MHT any time prior to first conception					
	No	7.07%	1,510,083	8.35%	155,292	1.20
	Yes	33.77%	212,167	26.52%	61,536	0.71
	MHT any time prior to first pregnancy outcome					
	No	7.05%	1,481,689	10.23%	175,053	1.50
	Yes	30.73%	240,561	27.22%	41,775	0.84
	MHT any time prior to first live birth					
	No	7.05%	1,481,689	7.03%	148,891	1.00
	Yes	30.73%	240,561	27.69%	67,937	0.86
Other	MHT between first conception and first live birth					
	No	7.13%	1,614,965	9.38%	196,393	1.35
	Yes	58.99%	107,285	53.09%	20,435	0.79
	Women with MHT prior to first live birth and first MHT					
	Prior to first conception	33.77%	212,167	26.52%	61,536	0.71
	After first conception	8.03%	28,394	38.90%	6401	7.30

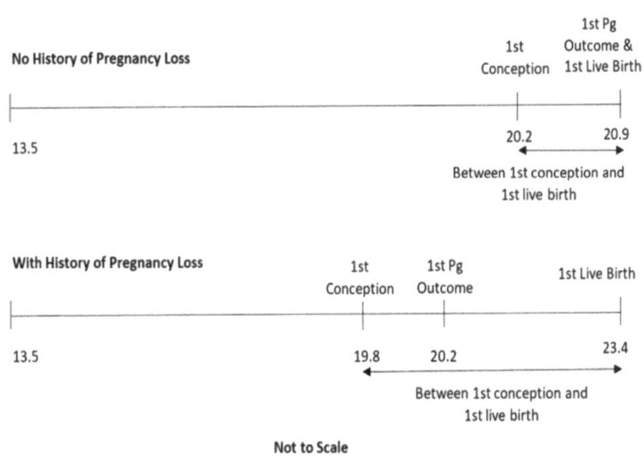

Figure 1. Mean average age of women at entry into cohort, first conception, first pregnancy (Pg) outcome, and first live birth, segregated by any history of pregnancy loss. Not to scale.

Table 3. PPT risk regression models for all women (n = 1,939,078) controlling for first pregnancy outcome, age, race, and years of live birth, as well as history of mental health treatments (MHT).

Independent Variables Used in Logistic Regression	% PPT	Total	Model 1 Adjuted Odds Ratio (95% Confidence Interval)	Model 2 Adjusted Odds Ratio (95% Confidence Intervall)
History of pregnancy loss				
No	10.36%	1,722,250	Ref	Ref
Yes	13.50%	216,828	1.27 (1.25–1.29)	1.10 (1.08–1.12)
Age at live birth (years)				
14–19	12.87%	90,065	Ref	Ref
20–24	9.71%	95,491	0.66 (0.65–0.68)	0.92 (0.90–0.94)
25–29	8.63%	22,098	0.50 (0.50–0.51)	0.82 (0.80–0.83)
Calandar year of live birth				
2000–2002	10.18%	68,717	Ref	Ref
2003–2005	10.83%	54,118	1.01 (1.00–1.03)	0.88 (0.87–0.90)
2006–2008	10.93%	58,032	1.02 (1.00–1.03)	0.82 (0.81–0.83)
2009–2011	11.49%	26,787	1.00 (0.99–1.02)	0.74 (0.72–0.75)
Race				
White	15.86%	123,904	Ref	Ref
Black	9.33%	35,197	0.51 (0.51–0.52)	0.52(0.51–0.52)
Hispanic	5.47%	29,079	0.30 (0.30–0.30)	0.37 (0.37–0.38)
Other	7.83%	19,474	0.45 (0.44–0.46)	0.50 (0.50–0.51)
MHT any time prior to first conception				
No	7.19%	119,683	N/A	Ref
Yes	32.14%	87,971	N/A	5.09 (4.99–5.20)
MHT any time prior to first pregnancy outcome				
No	7.39%	122,353	N/A	Ref
Yes	30.21%	85,301	N/A	1.07 (1.03–1.11)
MHT any time prior to first live birth				
No	7.05%	114,914	N/A	Ref
Yes	30.06%	92,740	N/A	2.13 (2.04–2.22)
MHT occurred between first conception and prior to live birth				
No	7.37%	133,514	N/A	Ref
Yes	58.05%	74,140	N/A	13.39 (13.16–13.62)

MHT = mental health treatment; Ref = reference for comparision in calculating the adjusted odds ratio shown below the reference. Adjusted odds ratio are odds ratios adjusted for the independent variables shown in column one.

Table 3 shows the results of two regression analyses examining the risk of PPT in the entire population studied. Model 1 examines the effects of a history of pregnancy loss and demographic characteristics. This analysis revealed that the experience of a prior pregnancy loss increased risk of PPT by 27% (adjusted OR = 1.27; 95% CI = 1.25–1.29), non-white women had half, or less, of the PPT rates compared to white women, and younger women were at greater risk of PPT. Model 2 includes additional variables relative to the women's prior history of mental health treatments. Notably, Model 2 shows that a history of MHT between a first conception (which may end in a pregnancy loss) and a first live birth has the strongest effect (adjusted OR = 13.39; CI = 13.16–13.62). This strong effect is at least in part explained by the fact that women with a pregnancy loss had a much longer period of time in which MHT may have been provided than women who carried their first pregnancies to term.

Table 4. PPT risk regression models for women with a history of pregnancy loss (n = 216,828), controlling for age, race, year of live birth (LB), number of losses, type of first loss, pregnancy interval, and history of MHT.

Independent Variables Used in Logistic Regression	% PPT	Total	Model 3	Model 4
			Adj OR (95% CI)	Adj OR (95% CI)
Age at live birth (years)				
14–19	14.24%	96,119	Ref	Ref
20–24	13.13%	97,343	1.11 (1.04–1.18)	1.00 (0.95–1.05)
25–29	12.03%	23,366	1.11 (1.00–1.22)	0.97 (0.92–1.01)
Calendar Year of Live Birth				
2000–2002	13.69%	36,350	Ref	Ref
2003–2005	13.69%	51,142	0.87 (0.83–0.91)	0.83 (0.80–0.87)
2006–2008	13.26%	58,188	0.77 (0.74–0.81)	0.72 (0.69–0.75)
2009–2011	13.47%	71,148	0.69 (0.66–0.72)	0.61 (0.59–0.64)
Race				
White	19.38%	84,731	Ref	Ref
Black	10.60%	62,161	0.54 (0.52–0.56)	0.55 (0.53–0.57)
Hispanic	8.05%	46,334	0.46 (0.44–0.48)	0.45 (0.44–0.47)
Other	10.74%	23,602	0.56 (0.53–0.59)	0.58 (0.55–0.61)
Number of Prior Pregnancy Losses				
1	13.24%	163,993	Ref	Ref
2	14.17%	37,506	1.05 (1.01–1.09)	1.03 (1.00–1.07)
3	14.46%	11,177	1.10 (1.03–1.17)	1.04 (0.98–1.11)
>3	15.20%	4152	1.17 (1.06–1.30)	1.10 (1.00–1.21)
Interval Between First Pg Loss and First LB				
<24 months	13.44%	98,447	Ref	Ref
2–4 years	13.43%	57,669	1.07 (1.03–1.11)	0.97 (0.94–1.01)
4–6 years	13.36%	31,292	1.10 (1.05–1.16)	0.95 (0.91–1.00)
>6 years	14.01%	29,420	1.17 (1.12–1.24)	0.96 (0.91–1.01)
First loss identified as				
Natural loss	13.08%	51,822	Ref	Ref
Induced abortion	13.69%	70,394	0.98 (0.95–1.01)	0.96 (0.93–0.99)
Indeterminate loss	12.70%	41,777	0.98 (0.95–1.02)	0.97 (0.94–1.01)
MHT one year prior to first live birth				
No	9.00%	192,511	Ref	N/A
Yes	48.91%	24,317	1.75 (1.58–1.92)	N/A
MHT one year prior to first conception				
No	12.47%	209,255	Ref	N/A
Yes	42.00%	7573	1.32 (1.25–1.38)	N/A
MHT one year prior to first Pg outcome				
No	10.42%	209,354	Ref	N/A
Yes	99.97%	7474	>999.999	N/A
MHT between first conception and first live birth				
No	12.42%	211,781	Ref	Ref
Yes	59.04%	5047	3.90 (3.53–4.31)	7.25 (6.95–7.56)
MHT any time prior to first live birth				
No	7.03%	148,891	N/A	Ref
Yes	27.69%	67,937	N/A	1.11 (1.03–1.19)
MHT any time prior first conception				
No	8.35%	155,292	N/A	Ref
Yes	26.52%	61,536	N/A	2.29 (2.14–2.45)
MHT any time prior first Pg outcome				
No	10.23%	17,909	N/A	Ref
Yes	27.22%	11,371	N/A	1.09 (1.05–1.14)

Table 4 shows the results of two additional regression models examining the subset of women with a history of pregnancy loss. Both models examine the effects of demographics, the number of pregnancy losses, the interval between the first pregnancy loss and the first live birth, and the type of the first pregnancy loss on PPT rates. Model 3 also examines the effects relative to one-year periods prior to the first live birth, first conception, first pregnancy outcome, and the time period between the first conception and first live birth. In order to examine a longer time span of prior mental health, alternatively, Model 4 controls for any time prior to first live birth, any time prior to first conception, any time prior to the first pregnancy outcome, and the time period between the first conception and first live birth. Both models reveal that the number of losses and type of loss had little effect. The shorter interval between the first pregnancy loss and first live birth (<24 months) had a small but significant effect in Model 3, but this significance was not present by Model 4. The time periods for examining MHT that had the highest adjusted odds ratios were one year prior to the first live birth (1.75), one year prior to the first pregnancy outcome (>999.999), the interval between first conception and first live birth (3.9 in Model 3 and 7.25 in Model 4), and any time prior to the first conception (2.29).

4. Discussion

Our findings reveal that prior pregnancy loss and a history of prior mental health treatments (MHT), individually and especially in combination, are risk factors for postpartum psychiatric treatments (PPT). Overall, pregnancy loss prior to a first live birth increases the risk of postpartum psychiatric disorders, both before and after controlling for prior mental health history. This risk is most elevated in the first 90 days postpartum (OR = 1.42) and for inpatient treatments (OR = 1.83). These findings are consistent with the only other population study we could identify that examined both pregnancy loss and prior mental health as risk factors for postpartum depression [14].

Among women with no history of MHT, pregnancy loss is consistently associated with elevated risk of PPT (Table 2). Still, the strongest observed predictor of PPT is a history of MHT. Yet, for women with a history of MHT, the relationship with PPT is complicated by any exposure to pregnancy loss and specific time frames in which prior MHT are considered.

Our use of multiple models demonstrates that both the recency of MHT (Model 3) and any history of MHT (Model 4) show significant effects that would have been missed if only a single model was employed. For example, MHT one year prior to the first pregnancy outcome (including losses) was almost perfectly correlated to PPT following a first live birth, but MHT any time prior to the first pregnancy outcome was only weakly correlated (Adj OR = 1.09). Conversely, any time prior to first conception was nearly twice as predictive as one year prior to first conception.

Another notable finding revealed by our use of multiple time frames was that the risk of PPT is modestly reduced among women with a history of both MHT and pregnancy loss (see Table 2). This may be due to either a successful history of mental health treatments that prepare some women to handle postpartum stress. or to positive effects associated with giving birth following a pregnancy loss. A very notable exception was found in cases where mental health treatments were provided within one year prior to the pregnancy loss, in which case nearly 100 percent of the women required PPT. When examining only women with PPT, Model 4 (Table 4) shows that the strongest effect was correlated to a history of MHT in the interval between conception of a first pregnancy and a first live birth (Adj OR = 7.25), which includes not only the nine months of a pregnancy (indicating the importance of recency) but also the period of time following any pregnancy losses preceding the birth. Notably, this time between first conception and first birth was the second most powerful predictor in Model 3.

These findings are especially important in regard the interpretation of existing literature on postpartum psychiatric disorders. In general, insufficient attention has been given to the impact of pregnancy loss on subsequent postpartum psychiatric events [16,17].

Furthermore, as seen in Tables 2–4, the choice of time frame used for consideration of prior MHT can profoundly change results. Meaningful effects may be missed, or obscured, in studies [18–20] that fail to distinguish between MHT events both before and after prior pregnancy losses. Therefore, research into the interactions between reproductive and mental health should include the consideration of multiple time frames regarding prior history of mental health treatments. These time frames account for recency of prior mental health issues, lifetime exposure to mental health treatments, and the history of any mental health treatments following pregnancy loss(es).

A number of limitations apply to this study. First, a history of seeking mental health care is likely an indicator of a greater willingness to seek postpartum mental health care. Conversely, many women who may benefit from MHT may simply not seek it either before or after their first live birth. Similarly, the differences observed in relation to race may be artifacts of different levels of cultural acceptance of MHT. Second, the available data was limited to low-income women. In part, this is an advantage, since it eliminates the likelihood that the differences observed are due to socioeconomic factors. Still, additional research is necessary to confirm that the differences observed exist across all income classes. Third, Medicaid eligibility changes with age, circumstance, across states, and across different fiscal years, which can create data gaps. The effects of such churning, however, were reduced by excluding women with less than 12 months of eligibility. Moreover, since pregnancy increases eligibility for Medicaid, it is likely that most pregnancies subject to any medical treatment were identified in the medical records for women in this economic group. Fourth, early miscarriages can often occur without any medical treatment. However, unless early miscarriages are linked with a significantly decreased risk of PPT, which is unlikely, more complete data on miscarriages would likely strengthen rather than weaken the findings regarding elevated risk of PPT when there is a history of pregnancy loss. Fifth, this study only examines PPT risks following a first live birth. While it seems likely that similar effects would be observed following subsequent live births, additional research is necessary to address the effects relative to the number of live births.

Given the limitations on our data, it would be beneficial in future research to examine the effects of relationship status, education, employment, pregnancy intention, and risk factors relevant to induced abortion, such as coercion or emotional attachment to the pregnancy [18]. Additional research should also be conducted to investigate specific diagnoses associated with PPT relative to prior pregnancy loss. Another research objective should be the evaluation of interventions and counseling programs for pregnancy loss that may ameliorate the increased risk of PPT following a live birth.

5. Conclusions

A history of pregnancy loss is an independent risk factor for postpartum psychiatric illness. This risk is heightened by a co-occurring history of mental health treatments. Important differences are observed in relation to the timing of mental health treatments occurring before and after a pregnancy loss and the relative risk of subsequent PPT.

Important clinical implications arise from this study. Both a history of mental health treatments and prior pregnancy loss are risk factors for PPT, especially when both are present. Clinicians should be alert to these findings, in order to better identify and refer women at higher risk to appropriate counseling. Moreover, for mental health counselors, the appearance of postpartum disorders may present an opportunity to help patients address underlying issues. The clinical experience of grief counselors has revealed that many women will not offer to discuss prior pregnancy losses unless invited to do so [19]. A simple, "Do you have any unresolved feelings about any prior pregnancy losses that you would like to discuss?" may serve as the invitation some women may need to open up about sensitive or difficult topics.

Author Contributions: Conceptualization, D.C.R.; methodology, D.C.R. and C.C.; formal analysis, C.C.; data curation, United Stated Centers for Medicare and Medicaid Services; writing—original draft preparation, D.C.R.; writing—review and editing, D.C.R. and C.C.; funding acquisition, D.C.R. and C.C. All authors have read and agreed to the published version of the manuscript.

Funding: This research was funded by the Charlotte Lozier Institute.

Institutional Review Board Statement: Sterling IRB, 15 March, 2019.

Informed Consent Statement: Not applicable.

Data Availability Statement: The data used is available from the United States Centers for Medicare and Medicaid Services.

Conflicts of Interest: The authors declare no conflict of interest. The funders had no role in the design of the study; in the collection, analyses, or interpretation of data; in the writing of the manuscript, or in the decision to publish the results.

References

1. Jacob, L.; Gerhard, C.; Kostev, K.; Kalder, M. Association between induced abortion, spontaneous abortion, and infertility respectively and the risk of psychiatric disorders in 57,770 women followed in gynecological practices in Germany. *J. Affect. Disord.* **2019**, *251*, 107–113. [CrossRef] [PubMed]
2. Reardon, D.C. The abortion and mental health controversy: A comprehensive literature review of common ground agreements, disagreements, actionable recommendations, and research opportunities. *SAGE Open Med.* **2018**, *6*, 205031211880762. [CrossRef] [PubMed]
3. Sullins, D.P. Abortion, substance abuse and mental health in early adulthood: Thirteen-year longitudinal evidence from the United States. *SAGE Open Med.* **2016**, *4*, 11. [CrossRef] [PubMed]
4. Farren, J.; Mitchell-Jones, N.; Verbakel, J.Y.; Timmerman, D.; Jalmbrant, M.; Bourne, T. The psychological impact of early pregnancy loss. *Hum. Reprod. Update* **2018**, *24*, 731–749. [CrossRef] [PubMed]
5. Burke, T.; Reardon, D.C. *Forbidden Grief: The Unspoken Pain of Abortion*; Acorn Books: Springfield, IL, USA, 2007; ISBN 978-0964895799.
6. Stotland, N.L. Abortion: Social context, psychodynamic implications. *Am. J. Psychiatry* **1998**, *155*, 964–967. [CrossRef] [PubMed]
7. Zegeye, A.; Alebel, A.; Gebrie, A.; Tesfaye, B.; Belay, Y.A.; Adane, F.; Abie, W. Prevalence and determinants of antenatal depression among pregnant women in Ethiopia: A systematic review and meta-analysis. *BMC Pregnancy Childbirth* **2018**, *18*, 462. [CrossRef] [PubMed]
8. Gong, X.; Hao, J.; Tao, F.; Zhang, J.; Wang, H.; Xu, R.; Sedgh, G.; Henshaw, S.K.; Singh, S.; Bankole, A.; et al. Pregnancy loss and anxiety and depression during subsequent pregnancies: Data from the C-ABC study. *Eur. J. Obstet. Gynecol. Reprod. Biol.* **2013**, *166*, 30–36. [CrossRef] [PubMed]
9. Chojenta, C.; Harris, S.; Reilly, N.; Forder, P.; Austin, M.-P.; Loxton, D.; Kersting, A.; Wagner, B.; Lok, I.; Yip, A.; et al. History of Pregnancy Loss Increases the Risk of Mental Health Problems in Subsequent Pregnancies but Not in the Postpartum. *PLoS ONE* **2014**, *9*, e95038. [CrossRef] [PubMed]
10. Coleman, P.K.; Reardon, D.C.; Rue, V.M.; Cougle, J. A history of induced abortion in relation to substance abuse during subsequent pregnancies carried to term. *Am. J. Obstet. Gynecol.* **2002**, *187*, 1673–1678. [CrossRef] [PubMed]
11. Giannandrea, S.A.M.; Cerulli, C.; Anson, E.; Chaudron, L.H. Increased risk for postpartum psychiatric disorders among women with past pregnancy loss. *J. Womens Health* **2013**, *22*, 760–768. [CrossRef] [PubMed]
12. Meltzer-Brody, S.; Maegbaek, M.L.; Medland, S.E.; Miller, W.C.; Sullivan, P.; Munk-Olsen, T. Obstetrical, pregnancy and socio-economic predictors for new-onset severe postpartum psychiatric disorders in primiparous women. *Psychol. Med.* **2017**, *47*, 1427. [CrossRef] [PubMed]
13. Montmasson, H.; Bertrand, P.; Perrotin, F.; El-Hage, W. Facteurs prédictifs de l'état de stress post-traumatique du postpartum chez la primipare. *J. Gynécol. Obs. Biol. Reprod.* **2012**, *41*, 553–560. [CrossRef] [PubMed]
14. Räisänen, S.; Lehto, S.M.; Nielsen, H.S.; Gissler, M.; Kramer, M.R.; Heinonen, S. Fear of childbirth predicts postpartum depression: A population-based analysis of 511 422 singleton births in Finland. *BMJ Open* **2013**, *3*, e004047. [CrossRef] [PubMed]
15. Al-Shami, N.; Moawed, S.E.A. Identification of Factors Associated with Postpartum Depression among Saudi Females in Riyadh City. Master's Thesis, King Saud University, Riyadh, Saudi Arabia, 2010.
16. Devore, N.E. The relationship between previous elective abortions and postpartum depressive reactions. *JOGN Nurs.* **1979**, *8*, 237–240. [CrossRef] [PubMed]
17. Goodman, S.H.; Dimidjian, S. The Developmental Psychopathology of Perinatal Depression: Implications for Psychosocial Treatment Development and Delivery in Pregnancy. *Can. J. Psychiatry* **2012**, *57*, 530–536. [CrossRef]
18. Munk-Olsen, T.; Laursen, T.M.; Pedersen, C.B.; Lidegaard, Ø.; Mortensen, P.B. Induced first-trimester abortion and risk of mental disorder. *N. Engl. J. Med.* **2011**, *364*, 332–339. [CrossRef] [PubMed]

19. Munk-Olsen, T.; Bech, B.H.; Vestergaard, M.; Li, J.; Olsen, J.; Laursen, T.M. Psychiatric disorders following fetal death: A population-based cohort study. *BMJ Open* **2014**, *4*, 1–6. [CrossRef] [PubMed]
20. Munk-Olsen, T.; Pedersen, H.S.; Laursen, T.M.; Fenger-Grøn, M.; Vedsted, P.; Vestergaard, M. Use of primary health care prior to a postpartum psychiatric episode. *Scand. J. Prim. Health Care* **2015**, *33*, 127–133. [CrossRef] [PubMed]

International Journal of
Environmental Research and Public Health

MDPI

Article

Perinatal Depression, Birth Experience, Marital Satisfaction and Childcare Sharing: A Study in Russian Mothers

Vera Yakupova [1,*] and Liudmila Liutsko [2]

[1] Psychological Institute, Russian Academy of Education, 125009 Moscow, Russia
[2] Faculty of Psychology, Lomonosov Moscow State University, 125009 Moscow, Russia; liudmila_liutsko@yahoo.es
* Correspondence: vera.a.romanova@gmail.com; Tel.: +7-(903)-530-47-83

Abstract: Background: Over 300,000 women in Russia face perinatal depressive disorders every year, according to the data for middle-income countries. This study is the first attempt to perform a two-phase study of perinatal depressive disorders in Russia. The paper examines risk factors for perinatal depressive symptoms, such as marital satisfaction, birth experience, and childcare sharing. Methods: At 15–40 gestational weeks (M = 30.7, SD = 6.6), 343 Russian-speaking women, with a mean age of 32 years (SD = 4.4), completed the Edinburgh Postnatal Depression Scale, Couples Satisfaction Index, Birth Satisfaction Scale, and provided socio-demographic data. Two months after childbirth, 190 of them participated in the follow-up. Results: The follow-up indicated that 36.4% of participants suffered from prenatal depression and 34.3% of participants had postnatal depression. Significant predictors of prenatal depression were physical well-being during pregnancy ($\beta = -0.25$; $p = 0.002$) and marital satisfaction during pregnancy ($\beta = -0.01$; $p = 0.018$). Birth satisfaction ($\beta = -0.08$; $p = 0.001$), physical well-being at two months after delivery ($\beta = -0.36$; $p < 0.01$), and marital satisfaction during pregnancy ($\beta = 0.01$; $p = 0.016$) and after delivery ($\beta = -0.02$; $p < 0.01$) significantly predicted postnatal depression at 2 months after delivery. Conclusion: Our study identified that physical well-being during pregnancy and marital satisfaction during pregnancy significantly predicted prenatal depression. Birth satisfaction, physical well-being at 2 months after delivery, and marital satisfaction during pregnancy and after delivery significantly predicted postnatal depression. To our knowledge, this is the first study of perinatal depressive disorders in the context of marital satisfaction and birth satisfaction in the Russian sample. The problem of unequal childcare sharing is widely spread in Russia. Adjusting spousal expectations and making arrangements for childcare may become the focus of psychological work with the family. The availability of psychological support during pregnancy and labor may be important in the context of reducing perinatal depression risks.

Keywords: prenatal depression; postnatal depression; perinatal disorders; birth satisfaction; marital satisfaction

Citation: Yakupova, V.; Liutsko, L. Perinatal Depression, Birth Experience, Marital Satisfaction and Childcare Sharing: A Study in Russian Mothers. *Int. J. Environ. Res. Public Health* **2021**, *18*, 6086. https://doi.org/10.3390/ijerph18116086

Academic Editors: Marco Scarselli and M. Carmen Míguez Varela

Received: 10 March 2021
Accepted: 31 May 2021
Published: 4 June 2021

1. Introduction

Perinatal depression is highly prevalent in low-income and middle-income countries, affecting approximately 25% of women during pregnancy, and about 19% of women after childbirth [1]. It translates to over 300,000 women in Russia facing perinatal depressive disorders each year. Women suffering from prenatal and postnatal depression are at risk for suicide [2], eating disorders, and body dissatisfaction [3]. They tend to have lower self-efficacy and poor self-esteem [4]. Prenatal depression is a risk factor for premature births, low birth weights, and negatively correlates with the length of breastfeeding [5,6]. Furthermore, prenatal depression is a significant predictor of postpartum depression [7]. Depression during pregnancy and after delivery has a negative impact on the development of the emotional and social intelligence of the offspring [8–11]. Moreover, it may endanger not only the mother's life but also the health and life of her child [12]. There are risk factors predicting higher rates of prenatal and postnatal depression, such as a history of depressive episodes [7], experience of childhood abuse [13], hypothalamic-pituitary-adrenal dysregulation [14], and physical health problems during pregnancy [15]. In this study, we focused on marital satisfaction and birth experience, because Russia has some specific features concerning family life and delivery practices. According to the Russian Federal Agency for Statistics, most couples who divorce and have children do so in the first years of their child's life [16]. Today, Russia is transitioning from the extended family to the nuclear one. Most young families with small children used to live in a parental home 20 years ago, whereas today the number of young families living independently is on the rise [17]. Childcare responsibilities are shared between the spouses rather than members of the extended family. According to data from the Ministry of Labor of the Russian Federation, only 2% of fathers take paternity leave to take care of their children. Thus, it is primarily the mother who takes maternity leave and bears the main burden of childcare, which may affect both the quality of the marital relationship and the emotional well-being of the mother [18].

However, there is a growing generation of "involved fathers" who participate in childcare from the birth of the child [19]. Studies show marital satisfaction to be a strong factor in reducing the risk of depression during pregnancy and after childbirth [20–22]. This is true not only for women but also for men [23].

There is evidence linking experiences of loneliness and partner dissatisfaction to depression symptoms during pregnancy [24]. An ambivalent attachment type and constant relationship anxiety are highly correlated with the risk of developing depression after childbirth [16].

Birth experience has been shown to be an important factor associated with the risk of postnatal depression [25]. A traumatic birth experience with intensive pain is associated with higher postpartum depression risk [26]. In Russia, most births take place in a maternity hospital solely in the presence of hospital staff, and unaccompanied by a partner or individual assisting specialists [27].

The presence of a partner or other family member during labor was not allowed in state-run hospitals until 2012. In many Russian cities, state maternity hospital management is still against doula or personal midwife labor assistance. A conservative Soviet approach is still widely spread and includes a paternalistic style of communication, a lack of ethical concern, outdated medical practices, and the extended medicalization of birth [28].

Research into perinatal mental disorders and their interrelations with marital satisfaction, the childcare sharing between partners, and birth satisfaction in Russia is scarce. To our knowledge, this is the first study to address prenatal depressive disorders in a Russian sample.

The aim of this research is to explore the risk factors for prenatal and postnatal depression, such as satisfaction with the birth process, marital satisfaction during pregnancy and after delivery, planned childcare sharing during pregnancy, and real childcare sharing after delivery, and the adjustment to physical well-being both during pregnancy and after delivery.

2. Materials and Methods

2.1. Phases of the Study

The first phase of the study (T1) included screening during pregnancy. The inclusion criteria were as follows: aged over 18 years, a pregnancy at 15 to 40 weeks of gestation, and the ability to read and speak the Russian language. Such a dispersion in the gestational age was chosen to explore the possible associations between the gestational age and risk for prenatal depression, postnatal depression, and marital satisfaction during pregnancy and after delivery. The gestational period of 15 weeks was chosen as the period when a woman can start feeling the baby's movements and contacting with it [29].

The second phase of the study (T2) included the follow-up screening of the participants 2 months after delivery. This time-point was chosen because postnatal symptoms tend to develop during the first months after delivery [30]. The same set of questionnaires was sent to all of the participants who took part in the first phase of the study. Those who experienced antenatal or neonatal loss were excluded from the study ($n = 1$).

2.2. Recruitment of the Participants

The data collection lasted from June 2018 to February 2019. Information about the study was placed in thematic online and offline communities and courses for parents-to-be and new parents. Women who were interested in the participation left their contact information and received an invitation to take part in the study by e-mail. They confirmed the terms of participation in the online form and filled out the questionnaires in the online form as well. Participants demonstrating high scores for perinatal depression were informed about the options to acquire psychological support.

2.3. Sample

In the first phase (T1) of the study, 343 women took part and 190 of them participated in the follow-up 2 months after delivery (T2). Of the participants, 100% were Caucasian, spoke the Russian language, and lived in big cities (population over 500,000). The detailed characteristics of the sample are shown in Table 1.

Table 1. Characteristics of the sample.

		T1 (n = 343)			**T2 (n = 190)**			
		M/N	**±SD/%**	**Range**	**M/N**	**±SD/%**	**Range**	***p*-Value**
Age at testing (years)		32	4.4	19–46	32	4.3	19–46	
Education	Upper secondary/College	32	9.3%		16	8.4%		
	Tertiary/University	311	90.7%		174	91.6%		
Family status	Married	284	82.8%		158	83%		
	Cohabiting with a partner	49	14.3%		27	14.5%		
	Single	10	2.9%		5	2.5%		
Time passed after the childbirth (months)					1.9	0.22	1.7–2.1	
Gestation week		30.7	6.6	15–40				
Week of birth					39.4	1.6	37–42	
Parity	primiparous	139	40.4%	82	43%			
	multiparous	204	59.6%	108	57%			
Delivery mode	Vaginal				139	73%		
	Emergency Cesarean				23	12%		
	Elective Cesarean				28	15%		
Mode of birth support	No support				69	36.1%		
	Partner				75	39.3%		
	Doula/Private midwife				15	8.2%		
	Partner + Doula/Private midwife				8.2%	16.4%		

Table 1. *Cont.*

	T1 (n = 343)			T2 (n = 190)			
	M/N	±SD/%	Range	M/N	±SD/%	Range	p-Value
EPDS score	8.5	5.4	0–28	7.9	2.3	0–21	$p = 0.568$
CSI score	62.4	17.3	0–81	60.4	17.9	0–81	$p < 0.001$
Physical well-being during pregnancy/2 months after delivery	3.6	0.9	1–5	4.2	0.8	2–5	$p < 0.001$
Maternal share of childcare planned/real	71.9	14.4	0–100	78.9	14.4	40–100	$p < 0.001$
BSSR-RI score				7.3	2.2	0–10	

Legend: EPDS, postnatal depression (measured using the Edinburgh Postnatal Depression Scale); CSI, marital satisfaction (measured using the Couples Satisfaction Index); BSS-RI, birth satisfaction (measured using the Birth Satisfaction Scale Revised). Where p shows statistical differences between the first phase of the study (T1) (n = 343) and the follow-up (T2) (n = 190).

2.4. Data Collection Tools

The Russian version of the Edinburgh Postnatal Depression Scale (EPDS) [31] was used to measure the intensity of pre- and postnatal depression. It is a 10-question scale that indicates how the mother has felt during the previous week. A 4-point Likert scale is used for each question. A score of 10 and higher is suggested to indicate possible depression (Cronbach's α = 0.838).

The Couples Satisfaction Index (CSI) is a 16-item questionnaire that is used to measure satisfaction in a relationship with four subscales (partner's support, respect, the pleasure of interaction, quality of relationships) [32]. A 6-point Likert scale is used for each question, the last block is a semantic differential scale with 6-point rating options. A total score lower than 50 may indicate relationship dissatisfaction (Cronbach's α = 0.817).

The participants were asked to measure their expectations of childcare sharing with their partner in percentages (0–100%, where 100% is all of the baby's needs) in answer to the following question: "How much of the childcare do you plan to share with the father of the child?" We asked the participants to assess their state of physical well-being at the time of the first screening during pregnancy using a 5-point Likert scale (1 = "very poor", 5 = "very good"). We also collected data on the socio-demographics, the number of children, etc.

At the second stage of the study, we repeated the questionnaires used during the first phase and, in addition, we used the following ones. A Birth Satisfaction Scale-Revised Indicator (BSS-RI)-short 6-item self-report questionnaire to assess birth satisfaction (the subscales are the level of stress and anxiety, feeling of control, medical staff support) [33]. A 3-point Likert scale is used for each question (range 0–2). While higher scores represent greater birth satisfaction, a total score lower than 50 is supposed to show relationship dissatisfaction (Cronbach's α = 0.701). We asked the participants to assess their state of health at the time of the second screening (2 months after delivery) using a 5-point Likert scale (1 = "very poor", 5 = "very good"). The participants were asked to measure the childcare sharing with the partner in percentages in answer to the following question: "How much of the childcare do you share with the father of the child?". We asked the participants about the mode of delivery and type of delivery support, place and time of delivery, and gestational age.

2.5. Data Analysis

The main variables of the study were prenatal and postnatal depression (EPDS), marital satisfaction during pregnancy and after delivery (CSI), childcare share during pregnancy and after delivery, physical well-being during pregnancy and after delivery, and birth satisfaction (BSSR-RI).

The Mann–Whitney U-test was used to examine the difference between the group that took the invitation to participate in the second phase of the study and the group that did not answer the invitation. Spearman's correlation coefficient was used to measure the associations between pre- and postnatal depression, marital satisfaction, birth satisfaction, physical well-being during pregnancy and after delivery, and childcare sharing.

A dependent sample t-test was used to describe the changes in the level of depression, childcare sharing, and marital satisfaction during pregnancy and after delivery. In order to examine the factors predicting prenatal and postnatal depression, we conducted linear regression analysis. The dependent variable in model one was prenatal depression, and the independent variables were gestational age, marital satisfaction during pregnancy, physical well-being during pregnancy, and maternal planned childcare share, whilst controlling for age also. The dependent variable in model two was postnatal depression (EPDS scores), and the independent variables were marital satisfaction during pregnancy and after delivery, physical well-being 2 months after delivery, gestational age at birth, birth satisfaction, and maternal real childcare share, whilst controlling for age also.

We used the Kruskal–Wallis test to assess the differences in the levels of prenatal and postnatal depression between the groups with different forms of labor assistance (alone, with a partner, with a doula or a midwife and a partner, and with a doula or a midwife without a partner) and the mode of delivery. All analyses were performed using SPSS Statistics 22 (IBM SPSS Statistics, Russian Federation).

2.6. Ethical Consideration

This study was conducted in accordance with the recommendations of the Declaration of Helsinki. The protocol was approved by the Ethical Committee of the Russian Psychological Society. The study was approved by the Ethics Committee of the Faculty of Psychology at Lomonosov Moscow State University (approval code #18/1102).

3. Results

In the first phase of the study (T1), 36.4% (n = 125) of participants had prenatal depression. At the follow-up (T2), 34.3% (n = 65) of participants had postnatal depression.

The women who responded to the invitation to take part in the follow-up (T2) showed lower depression levels during pregnancy (U = 12.179, p = 0.007) in comparison to the women who took part in the first phase of the study (T1) but did not respond to the invitation to participate in the follow-up two months after delivery (T2). No statistically significant differences in age, gestational age, education level, or marital satisfaction level were found between the two groups.

The levels of depression did not differ significantly 2 months after delivery compared to that during pregnancy (t = −0.557, p = 0.568). No statistically significant correlations were found between the gestational age and the levels of prenatal and postnatal depression and marital satisfaction before and after delivery. The descriptive statistics of the main variables during T1 and T2 of the study are shown in Table 2.

Table 2. Correlations between the main variables of the study.

	EPDS T2	BSSR-RI	Physical Well-Being T1	Physical Well-Being T2	CSI T1	CSI T2	Maternal Planned Childcare Share	Maternal Real Childcare Share
EPDS T1	0.48 **	0.01	−0.20 **	−0.08	−0.04	−0.07	−0.02	−0.034
EPDS T2		−0.28 **	−0.18 **	−0.39 **	−0.25 **	−0.43 **	0.19 **	0.22 **
BSSR_RI				0.07	0.23 **	0.26 **	−0.16 *	−0.19
Physical well-being T2						0.20 *	−0.08	−0.05
CSI T1						0.80 **	−0.30 **	−0.24 **
CSI T2							−0.32 **	−0.41 **

Legend: rho, ** $p < 0.01$, * $p < 0.05$.

3.1. Satisfaction with the Birth Process and Perinatal Depression

Satisfaction with the birth process negatively correlates with postnatal depression (rho = −0.28, $p < 0.01$). No statistically significant relationships were found to exist between the delivery modes, vaginal birth (VB), emergency C-section (ECS), and elective C-section (ELCS), and the level of pre- and postpartum depression (H = 2.444, $p = 0.295$; H = 0.033, $p = 0.983$). The groups based on birth support (partner, doula or private midwife, no support) did not differ significantly in the levels of prenatal and postnatal depression (H = 1.464, $p = 0.691$; H = 3.270, $p = 0.352$).

3.2. Marital Satisfaction and Perinatal Depression

Marital satisfaction significantly decreased 2 months after delivery compared to that during pregnancy (t = 4.429, $p < 0.001$). We found a significant correlation between marital satisfaction and after delivery (rho = −0.43, $p < 0.01$).

During pregnancy, the expected childcare share was 70% for the mother and 30% for the father (when 100% means all of the baby's needs). After childbirth, the woman's real burden proves to be higher, averaging at about 80% (t = −6.572, $p < 0.001$), and the man's burden proves lower, at about 20% (t = −6.296, $p < 0.001$). After delivery, a higher planned mother's childcare share and real maternal childcare share are associated with higher rates of depression (rho = 0.195, $p < 0.01$; rho = 0.219, $p < 0.01$).

3.3. Physical Well-Being and Perinatal Depression

The severity of prenatal depression and postpartum depression symptoms is associated with lower scores of well-being during pregnancy (rho = −0.20, $p < 0.01$; rho = −0.18, $p < 0.01$. Lower scores of postpartum depression correlate with a higher quality of well-being 2 months after delivery (rho =−0.39, $p < 0.01$).

3.4. Linear Regression Analysis for Predicting Prenatal and Postnatal Depression

We performed a linear regression including prenatal depression as a dependent variable. Physical well-being during pregnancy, gestational age, marital satisfaction, and planned childcare sharing were the independent variables (see Table 3). The analysis revealed that these variables contributed significantly to the regression model F (5, 143) = 10.96, $p < 0.001$ and accounted for 27.7% of the variance in prenatal depression. The significant predictors of prenatal depression were physical well-being ($\beta = -0.25$; $p = 0.002$) and marital satisfaction during pregnancy ($\beta = -0.01$; $p = 0.018$).

Table 3. Linear regression results examining associations with prenatal depression at phase one and postnatal depression at phase two of the longitudinal study.

	β	Std β	R^2	ΔR^2
	Phase one (Prenatal Depression)			
CSI (pregnancy)	−0.01 *	0.004	0.28	0.25
Physical well-being in the III trimester	−0.246 **	0.8		
	Phase two (Postnatal Depression)			
CSI (pregnancy)	0.016 *	0.005	0.35	0.33
CSI (postpartum)	−0.02 ***	0.005		
Physical well-being (2 months after delivery)	−0.36 ***	0.06		
Birth satisfaction	−0.07 **	0.02		

Legend: * $p < 0.05$, ** $p < 0.01$, *** $p < 0.001$.

The second linear regression model included postnatal depression as a dependent variable, and marital satisfaction during pregnancy and after delivery, real maternal childcare share, prenatal depression, gestational age at birth, birth satisfaction and physical well-being two months after delivery as independent variables. These variables contributed significantly to the regression model F (7, 176) = 13.64, $p < 0.001$ and accounted for 35.2% of the variance in postnatal depression. The significant predictors of postnatal depression were marital satisfaction during pregnancy ($\beta = 0.013$; $p = 0.016$), marital satisfaction after delivery ($\beta = -0.022$; $p < 0.001$), physical well-being 2 months after delivery ($\beta = -0.362$; $p < 0.001$), and birth satisfaction ($\beta = -0.075$; $p = 0.001$).

4. Discussion

Our study identified that physical well-being during pregnancy and marital satisfaction during pregnancy significantly predicted prenatal depression. Birth satisfaction, physical well-being 2 months after delivery, and marital satisfaction during pregnancy and after delivery significantly predicted postnatal depression. The results of our study in the Russian sample are consistent with other research on the problem and show that perinatal disorders are a complex, multi-component phenomenon [21,34]. In our study, 36.4% of the participants had prenatal depression and 34.3% of the participants had postnatal depression, which seems to be higher than the statistics for middle-income countries [1].

Studies show a decrease in marital satisfaction after childbirth [35,36]. The data obtained in our research showed an unexpected result in the linear regression model for postnatal depression. Higher levels of marital satisfaction during pregnancy predicted higher postnatal depression scores. It turns out that the women who had high CSI scores during pregnancy and low CSI scores after delivery are at higher risk of postnatal depression. There is a possibility that, for these women, the negative changes in the partner relationships themselves are a factor for depression development, rather than the low marital satisfaction after delivery. The changes in marital satisfaction and their relations with depression after delivery might be a direction for further research investigation could also be carried out regarding The topic of the further research could concern the Couples' Satisfaction index. Six points of each item might reflect the idealization of marriage. For example: 1. "Please, indicate the degree of happiness of your relationship", the six-score answer is "Perfect". 2. "In general, how often do you think that things between you and your partner are going well?", the six-score answer is "All the time". We can assume that women with higher scores tend to idealize their marriage during pregnancy and experience more hard feelings about the changes in their marital relationship after delivery.

In our study, a father's actual involvement in childcare is far from being equal and is short of the mother's expectations. The childcare share variable did not show significant associations with prenatal and postnatal depression in the linear regression models. However, it is associated with marital satisfaction during pregnancy and after delivery. The traditional distribution of childcare duties (when a mother is the main caregiver) is still widely spread [37], but our data suggests that it no longer satisfies the expectations of women with higher education living in big cities. The study of parental burnout in 42 countries [38] shows that Russia is approaching Europe and North America in the growing trend of "intensive parenting". The demands on the parent are high, the support of the extended family is low. In these new circumstances, the balance of childcare needs revision. It may be important to perform more detailed research on the variable of the childcare share, for example, by adding a question about the mother's satisfaction with the distribution of the childcare duties and about other members of the family taking part in childcare.

Adjusting spousal expectations and making arrangements for childcare may become the focus of psychological work with the family before and during pregnancy [39,40]. Psychological education and work on the quality of relationships in couples are generally associated with greater marital satisfaction after delivery, empathy, and mutual support [41].

Our findings are consistent with evidence that psychologically and physically traumatic childbirth experiences may become a serious risk factor for postpartum depression [25,34,42]. There is an increasing number of partner births in Russia. According to our results, the rates of birth alone at the hospital and partner birth are practically equal. Partner birth may help enhance relationship functioning and partner involvement in childcare [43,44]. There is evidence that men who were present at the delivery are more likely to show empathy and emotional support for their spouse [45]. Higher birth satisfaction significantly predicts lower postpartum depression scores 2 months after delivery. Hospital administrations start focusing on psychological comfort and support availability during labor, but this process is still at its very beginning [46]. A major issue during childbirth in Russia today is partner accompaniment and assistance from specialists, such as an individual midwife or a doula, at childbirth because these practices are far from being typical of every city and maternity hospital.

5. Conclusions

Our study identified that physical well-being during pregnancy and marital satisfaction during pregnancy predicted prenatal depression significantly. Birth satisfaction, physical well-being 2 months after delivery, and marital satisfaction during pregnancy and after delivery significantly predicted postnatal depression. To our knowledge, this is the first study of perinatal depressive disorders in the context of marital satisfaction and birth satisfaction in the Russian sample. The problem of unequal childcare sharing is widely spread in Russia. Adjusting spousal expectations and making arrangements for childcare may become the focus of psychological work with a family as early as it plans and expects a child. The study results raise the question of the importance of psychological support for the mother during pregnancy, especially if the woman is experiencing issues with her physical well-being. The availability of support and psychological comfort during labor may be crucial in the context of reducing postpartum depression risks.

Study Limitations and future research: One of this study's limitations is that we used only self-reporting techniques that are less reliable in comparison to clinical examinations. It is important to mention that 45% of participants dropped out of the study and did not take part in the follow-up. This resulted in biased data, since women with lower levels of prenatal depression tended to participate in the second phase of the study. Women with higher rates of prenatal depression might be in a less resourceful state after delivery and less willing to take part in the next phase of the study. The gestational age from 15 to 40 weeks of pregnancy is wide and may also result in data biases. The construct of childcare sharing needs further detailed research. Our data was not normally distributed and does not allow us to drive the conclusions about the prevalence of perinatal depression in the Russian population. In addition, the sample size of this study does not allow us to perform analysis by group (levels of EPDS and/or CSI) to detect significant effects in some subgroups. For these reasons, to explore the effects in detail, further studies are needed with a larger sample size. More studies are needed on the effects of this interventional work prior to pregnancy on the overall well-being of women during pregnancy and after delivery.

Author Contributions: V.Y. conceived of the study, collected, verified, and analyzed the data, and drafted the manuscript. L.L. contributed to concretizing the design of the study and supervised the statistical analyses and the final draft of the manuscript. The authors provided critical revision of the manuscript for important intellectual content. All authors have read and agreed to the published version of the manuscript.

Funding: No funds, grants, or other support was received.

Institutional Review Board Statement: This study was performed in line with the principles of the Declaration of Helsinki. Approval was granted by the Ethics Committee of the Russian Psychological Society (approval number 18/1102).

Informed Consent Statement: Informed consent was obtained from all subjects involved in the study.

Data Availability Statement: The datasets used and/or analyzed during the current study are available from the corresponding author upon request.

Conflicts of Interest: The authors declare no conflict of interest.

References

1. Gelaye, B.; Rondon, M.B.; Araya, R.; Williams, M.A. Epidemiology of maternal depression, risk factors, and child outcomes in low-income and middle-income countries. *Lancet Psychiatry* **2016**, *3*, 973–982. [CrossRef]
2. Gressier, F.; Guillard, V.; Cazas, O.; Falissard, B.; Glangeaud-Freudenthal, N.M.-C.; Sutter-Dallaye, A.-L. Risk factors for suicide attempt in pregnancy and the post-partum period in women with serious mental illnesses. *J. Psychiatr. Res.* **2017**, *84*, 284–291. [CrossRef]
3. Riquin, E.; Lamas, C.; Nicolas, I.; Lebigre, C.D.; Curt, F.; Cohen, H.; Legendre, G.; Corcos, M.; Godart, N. A key for perinatal depression early diagnosis: The body dissatisfaction. *J. Affect. Disord.* **2019**, *245*, 340–347. [CrossRef]
4. Zheng, X.; Morrell, J.; Watts, K. Changes in maternal self-efficacy, postnatal depression symptoms and social support among Chinese primiparous women during the initial postpartum period: A longitudinal study. *Midwifery* **2018**, *62*, 151–160. [CrossRef] [PubMed]
5. Grigoriadis, S.; VonderPorten, E.H.; Mamisashvili, L.; Tomlinson, G.; Dennis, C.L.; Koren, G.; Steiner, M.; Mousmanis, P.; Cheung, A.; Radford, K.; et al. The impact of maternal depression during pregnancy on perinatal outcomes: A systematic review and meta-analysis. *J. Clin. Psychiatry* **2013**, *74*, 321–341. [CrossRef]
6. Jarde, A.; Morais, M.; Kingston, D.; Giallo, R.; MacQueen, G.M.; Giglia, L.; Beyene, J.; Wang, Y.; McDonald, S.D. Neonatal Outcomes in Women With Untreated Antenatal Depression Compared With Women Without Depression: A Systematic Review and Meta-analysis. *JAMA Psychiatry* **2016**, *73*, 826–837. [CrossRef] [PubMed]
7. McMahon, C.; Boivin, J.; Gibson, F.L.; Hammarberg, K.; Wynter, L.; Fisher, J. Older maternal age and major depressive episodes in the first two years after birth: Findings from the Parental Age and Transition to Parenthood Australia (PATPA) study. *J. Affect. Disord.* **2015**, *175*, 454–462. [CrossRef]
8. Madigan, S.; Oatley, H.; Racine, N.; Fearon, R.M.P.; Schumacher, L.; Akbari, E.; Cooke, J.E.; Tarabulsy, G.M. A Meta-Analysis of Maternal Prenatal Depression and Anxiety on Child Socioemotional Development. *J. Am. Acad. Child Adolesc. Psychiatry* **2018**, *57*, 645–657.e8. [CrossRef] [PubMed]
9. Drury, S.; Scaramella, L.; Zeanah, C. The Neurobiological Impact of Postpartum Maternal Depression: Prevention and Intervention Approaches. *Child Adolesc. Psychiatr. Clin. N. Am.* **2016**, *25*, 179–200. [CrossRef]
10. Burmenskaya, G.V. Child's Attachment to Mother as the Basis of Mental Development Typology. *Psychol. Russ. State Art.* **2009**, *2*, 385–403. [CrossRef]
11. Evans, J.; Melotti, R.; Heron, J.; Ramchandani, P.; Wiles, N.; Murray, L. The timing of maternal depressive symptoms and child cognitive development: A longitudinal study. *J. Child Psychol. Psychiatry* **2012**, *53*, 632–640. [CrossRef] [PubMed]
12. Jacques, N.; Loret de Mola, C.; Joseph, G.; Mesenburg, M.A.; Silveira, M.F. Prenatal and postnatal maternal depression and infant hospitalization and mortality in the first year of life: A systematic review and meta-analysis. *J. Affect. Disord.* **2019**, *243*, 201–208. [CrossRef]
13. Wosu, A.C.; Gelaye, B.; Williams, M.A. History of Childhood Sexual Abuse and Risk of Prenatal and Postpartum Depression or Depressive Symptoms: An Epidemiologic Review. *Arch. Women Ment. Health* **2015**, *18*, 659–671. [CrossRef]
14. Yim, I.S.; Stapleton, L.R.T.; Guardino, C.M.; Hahn-Holbrook, J.; Schetter, C.D. Biological and Psychosocial Predictors of Postpartum Depression: Systematic Review and Call for Integration. *Annu. Rev. Clin. Psychol.* **2015**, *11*, 99–137. [CrossRef] [PubMed]
15. Pace, R.; Rahme, E.; Da Costa, D.; Dasgupta, K. Association between gestational diabetes mellitus and depression in parents: A retrospective cohort study. *Clin. Epidemiol.* **2018**, *10*, 1827–1838. [CrossRef] [PubMed]
16. Marques, R.; Monteiro, F.; Canavarro, M.C.; Fonseca, A. The role of emotion regulation difficulties in the relationship between attachment representations and depressive and anxiety symptoms in the postpartum period. *J. Affect. Disord.* **2018**, *238*, 39–46. [CrossRef]
17. Eliseeva, I.I. Evolution of the Structure of Russian Households: A Tentative Explanation. *Petersb. Sociol. Today* **2016**, *7*, 216–242. (In Russian)
18. Lin, W.-C.; Chang, S.-Y.; Chen, Y.-T.; Lee, H.-C.; Chen, Y.-H. Postnatal paternal involvement and maternal emotional disturbances: The effect of maternal employment status. *J. Affect. Disord.* **2017**, *219*, 9–16. [CrossRef]
19. Noskova, A.V. New Methodological Approaches, Research Tricks, Discussion Problems of Family Sociology. *Sociol. Stud.* **2015**, *10*, 177–185. (In Russian)
20. Yakupova, V.A. The Impact of Psychological and Physiological Conditions of Motherhood on Postnatal Depression. *Russ. J. Psychol.* **2018**, *15*, 8–23. [CrossRef]
21. Yusuff, A.S.M.; Tang, L.; Binns, C.W.; Lee, A.H. Prevalence and risk factors for postnatal depression in Sabah, Malaysia: A cohort study. *Women Birth* **2015**, *28*, 25–29. [CrossRef]
22. Shi, P.; Ren, H.; Li, H.; Dai, Q. Maternal depression and suicide at immediate prenatal and early postpartum periods and psychosocial risk factors. *Psychiatry Res.* **2018**, *261*, 298–306. [CrossRef] [PubMed]
23. Da Costa, D.; Danieli, C.; Abrahamowicz, M.; Dasgupta, K.; Sewitch, M.; Lowensteyn, I.; Zelkowitz, P. A prospective study of postnatal depressive symptoms and associated risk factors in first-time fathers. *J. Affect. Disord.* **2019**, *249*, 371–377. [CrossRef] [PubMed]
24. Luoma, I.; Korhonen, M.; Puura, K.; Salmelin, R.K. Maternal loneliness: Concurrent and longitudinal associations with depressive symptoms and child adjustment. *Psychol. Health Med.* **2018**, *5*, 1–13. [CrossRef]

25. Bell, A.F.; Andersson, E. The birth experience and women's postnatal depression a systematic review. *Midwifery* **2016**, *39*, 112–123. [CrossRef] [PubMed]
26. Ponti, L.; Smorti, M. Mediating Role of Labor on the Relationship Between Prenatal Psychopathologic Symptoms and Symptoms of Postpartum Depression in Women Who Give Birth Vaginally. *J. Obstet. Gynecol. Neonatal Nurs.* **2019**, *48*, 627–634. [CrossRef]
27. Borozdina, E.; Novkunskaya, A. Patient-centered care in Russian maternity hospitals: Introducing a new approach through professionals' agency. *Health Interdiscip. J. Soc. Study Health Illn. Med.* **2020**. [CrossRef]
28. Temkina, A.A. Medicalization of childbirth: Fight for control. *J. Soc. Policy Res.* **2014**, *12*, 321–336. (In Russian)
29. Zakharova, E.I. Developmental psychology and psychological support during the transition to parenting period. *World Psychol.* **2016**, *4*, 227–236. (In Russian)
30. Anokye, R.; Acheampong, E.; Budu-Ainooson, A.; Obeng, E.I.; Akwasi, A.G. Prevalence of postpartum depression and interventions utilized for its management. *Ann. Gen. Psychiatry* **2018**, 17–18. [CrossRef]
31. Yakupova, V.A.; Bukhalenkova, D.A. Prenatal Depression: Risk factors and ways of prevention. *Issues Psychol.* **2019**, *2*, 154–161. (In Russian)
32. Funk, J.L.; Rogge, R.D. Testing the ruler with item response theory: Increasing precision of measurement for relationship satisfaction with the Couples Satisfaction Index. *J. Fam. Psychol.* **2007**, *21*, 572–583. [CrossRef] [PubMed]
33. Martin, C.R.; Martin, H.C.; Redshaw, M. The Birth Satisfaction Scale-Revised Indicator (BSS-RI). *BMC Pregnancy Childbirth* **2017**, *17*, 277. [CrossRef]
34. Mohammad, K.I.; Gamble, J.; Creedy, D.K. Prevalence and factors associated with the development of antenatal and postnatal depression among Jordanian women. *Midwifery* **2011**, *27*, 238–245. [CrossRef] [PubMed]
35. Delicate, A.; Ayers, S.; McMullen, S. A systematic review and meta-synthesis of the impact of becoming parents on the couple relationship. *Midwifery* **2018**, *61*, 88–96. [CrossRef] [PubMed]
36. Doss, B.D.; Rhoades, G.K. The transition to parenthood: Impact on couples' romantic relationships. *Curr. Opin. Psychol.* **2017**, *13*, 25–28. [CrossRef] [PubMed]
37. Temkina, A.A. Childbearing and Work-Family Balance among contemporary Russian women. *Finish Yearb. Popul. Res.* **2010**, *XLV*, 83–103. [CrossRef]
38. Roskam, I.; Aguiar, J.; Akgun, E.; Arikan, G.; Artavia, M.; Avalosse, H.; Aunola, K.; Bader, M.; Bahati, C.; Barham, E.J.; et al. Parental Burnout Around the Globe: A 42-Country Study. *Affect. Sci.* **2021**, *2*, 58–79. [CrossRef] [PubMed]
39. Shockley, K.M.; Allen, T.D. It's not what I expected: The association between dual-earner couples' met expectations for the division of paid and family labor and well-being. *J. Vocat. Behav.* **2018**, *104*, 240–260. [CrossRef]
40. Cho, H.J.; Kwon, J.H.; Lee, J.J. Antenatal cognitive-behavioral therapy for prevention of postpartum depression: A pilot study. *Yonsei Med. J.* **2008**, *49*, 553–562. [CrossRef] [PubMed]
41. Suto, M.; Takehara, K.; Yamane, Y.; Ota, E. Effects of prenatal childbirth education for partners of pregnant women on paternal postnatal mental health: A systematic review and meta-analysis protocol. *J. Affect. Disord.* **2016**, *210*, 115–121. [CrossRef] [PubMed]
42. Dikmen-Yildiz, P.; Ayers, S.; Phillips, L. Factors associated with post-traumatic stress symptoms (PTSS) 4-6 weeks and 6 months after birth: A longitudinal population-based study. *J. Affect. Disord.* **2017**, *221*, 238–245. [CrossRef] [PubMed]
43. Daley-McCoy, C.; Rogers, M.; Slade, P. Enhancing relationship functioning during the transition to parenthood: A cluster-randomised controlled trial. *Arch. Women Ment. Health* **2015**, *18*, 681–692. [CrossRef] [PubMed]
44. Gambrel, L.E.; Piercy, F.P. Mindfulness-based relationship education for couples expecting their first child–part 1: A randomized mixed-methods program evaluation. *J. Marital Fam.* **2015**, *41*, 5–24. [CrossRef] [PubMed]
45. Coutinho, E.C.; Vilaça, J.G.; Antunes, C.; Duartea, J.C.; Parreirac, V.C.; Chaves, C.M.B.; Nelas, P.A.B. Benefits for the Father from their Involvement in the Labour and Birth Sequence. *Procedia Soc. Behav. Sci.* **2016**, *217*, 435–442. [CrossRef]
46. Ozhiganova, A.A. Active mistrust of doctors: A case study of legal support during childbirth. Medical anthropology research. *Sib. Hist. Res.* **2020**, *4*, 195–216. (In Russian) [CrossRef]

International Journal of *Environmental Research and Public Health*

MDPI

Article

Is the Association between Postpartum Depression and Early Maternal–Infant Relationships Contextually Determined by Avoidant Coping in the Mother?

Cecilia Peñacoba Puente [1], Carlos Suso-Ribera [2], Sheila Blanco Rico [1], Dolores Marín [3], Jesús San Román Montero [1] and Patricia Catalá [1,*]

[1] Department of Psychology, Rey Juan Carlos University, Avda. de Atenas s/n, 28922 Madrid, Spain; cecilia.penacoba@urjc.es (C.P.P.); sheila.blanco.rico@urjc.es (S.B.R.); jesus.sanroman@urjc.es (J.S.R.M.)

[2] Department of Basic and Clinical Psychology and Psychobiology, Jaume I University, 12071 Castellon, Spain; susor@uji.es

[3] Hospital Universitario de Fuenlabrada, 28944 Madrid, Spain; dolores.marin@salud.madrid.org

* Correspondence: patricia.catala@urjc.es

Abstract: This study analyzes the moderating role of avoidant coping (in early pregnancy) in the relationship between postpartum depressive (PPD) symptoms and maternal perceptions about mother–baby relations and self-confidence. Participants were 116 low-risk obstetric mothers (mean age = 31.2 years, SD = 3.95, range 23–42) who received care and gave birth at a Spanish public hospital. Measurements were made at two points in time: at first trimester of pregnancy (maternal avoidance coping) and four months after childbirth (PPD and maternal perceptions). Avoidant coping was associated with the perception of the baby as irritable and unstable ($p = 0.003$), including irritability during lactation ($p = 0.041$). Interaction effects of avoidant coping and postpartum depression were observed on the perception of the baby as irritable ($p = 0.031$) and with easy temperament ($p = 0.002$). Regarding the mother's self-confidence, avoidant coping was related to a lack of security in caring for the baby ($p < 0.001$) and had a moderating effect between PPD and mother's self-confidence (i.e., lack of security in caring for the baby, $p = 0.027$; general security, $p = 0.007$). Interaction effects showed that the use of avoidant coping in the mother exacerbated the impact of PPD on the early mother–infant relationship.

Keywords: mother; avoidant coping; post-partum depression; pregnant women; early mother-infant relationship

check for updates

Citation: Peñacoba Puente, C.; Suso-Ribera, C.; Blanco Rico, S.; Marín, D.; San Román Montero, J.; Catalá, P. Is the Association between Postpartum Depression and Early Maternal–Infant Relationships Contextually Determined by Avoidant Coping in the Mother? *Int. J. Environ. Res. Public Health* **2021**, *18*, 562. https://doi.org/10.3390/ijerph18020562

Received: 7 December 2020
Accepted: 7 January 2021
Published: 11 January 2021

Publisher's Note: MDPI stays neutral with regard to jurisdictional claims in published maps and institutional affiliations.

1. Introduction

The process towards motherhood implies a vital change for women. This involves significant psychological, social, and physiological consequences, which ultimately increases their vulnerability for mental diseases [1]. For example, postpartum depression (PPD) prevalence rates can be established around 10–15% [2], even though estimates in low- and middle-income countries have been argued to be up to 25–20% of women [3].

PPD is associated with important consequences for both the mother and the newborn [4,5]. For the mother, it is manifested in symptoms such as low mood, reduced activity and energy, loss of enjoyment, reduced self-esteem, self-harm or suicide thoughts, sadness, guilt, or sleeping and eating disorders, among others [6–8]. In general terms, postpartum depression constitutes a serious public health problem associated with disability, comorbidity, and increased mortality through suicide [4].

In addition to the consequences of PPD on the mother, a topic of growing interest has been the evaluation of the consequences of PPD on the newborn. In particular, PPD is associated with maternal–infant interactions characterized by disengagement, hostility, and intrusion [9–11]. Mothers presenting PPD often exhibit negative thoughts about their confidence with baby care, such as deeming themselves to be insubstantial in taking care of the newborn [6–8]. Related to this, PPD can lead to poor infant feeding practices, which might result in baby malnutrition and reduced infant growth [12,13]. In addition, PPD can affect the mother's capacity to bond with her new-born and depressed mothers may react negatively towards the child [14]. As a consequence of the previous, PPD has shown to negatively impact the cognitive and emotional development of the newborn later during infancy and childhood [15,16].

Given the relevance of PPD as a public health problem, the study of its risk variables is essential to establish preventive actions. As noted earlier, the relationship between PPD and negative maternal–infant interactions has been established. Nevertheless, this association is also complex and dynamic, and depends on the mother–infant interaction indicator that has been chosen [10]. For example, stronger effects have been found for PPD on behavioral child outcomes than on cognitive development such as language and intelligence quotient [10]. Furthermore, the effect of previous, chronic, or recurrent depression in the mother needs to be controlled, because in some reviews, it has been shown that they play a more relevant role than postpartum depression per se [10]. Finally, the relationship between maternal depression and early maternal–infant relationships might be moderated by maternal variables such as involvement in childcare; therefore, it would be necessary to adopt a multifactorial and prospective approach [5].

However, studies that investigate the impact of certain psychological variables in this relationship are limited [17]. Specifically, coping strategies constitute highly relevant variables within Lazarus and Folkman's transactional model of stress and coping [18]. Coping is defined as a combination of "thoughts and behaviors used to manage the internal and external demands of situations that are appraised as stressful" [19]. Becoming a mother can certainly be a stressful situation, which requires the implementation of coping strategies. Numerous coping classifications exist. However, the distinction between approach and avoidance coping is probably the most widely used [20]. Approach and avoidance have been described as being "cognitive and emotional activity that is oriented either toward or away from threat", respectively [21]. Approach coping involves reducing distress by taking steps to directly remove the stressor or reduce its impact, whereas avoidance coping intends to reduce distress by taking actions to avoid direct contact with the stressor [22]. Both strategies can be adaptive in the short term [23]. However, when exploring their influences in the long term, approach coping predicts improved psychological health and well-being, whereas avoidance has been related to a decrease in the outcome [24].

In this context, avoidance coping has stimulated greater interest in the literature owing to its maladaptive long-term effects on health-disease processes in both clinical and non-clinical populations [25–27]. Research has linked the use of avoidance coping with worse mental health, both during pregnancy and in the postpartum period [28]. Use of avoidance coping strategies is associated with decreased responsiveness to positive environmental stimuli [29]. Understanding coping energy and efforts as a finite resource, the investment of significant resources in avoidance may hinder efforts to engage in pleasurable activities, cultivate a mindful and present-focused demeanor, and recognize one's innate strengths [30]. Avoidance of such thoughts and emotions may inhibit the individual from adopting more adaptive perceptions by preventing disconfirming evidence from being recognized or explored [31], thereby hampering the emergence of new learning experiences [24,32]. Studies have also investigated the mediating role of avoidant coping. For example, the use of avoidant coping was found to explain why perceived the neighborhood environment influenced depressive symptoms in pregnant African-American women [17]. What remains unclear is whether the implementation of avoidant strategies in combination with depressed mood can exacerbate the negative impact of PPD on the mother–baby relationship. This is important because avoidant coping is frequent, but not unique of depressed individuals. That is, not all mentally distressed individuals avoid to the same extent and individual differences in avoidant coping also exist in healthy individuals [33]. Therefore, the exploration of both their unique and combined impacts on baby–infant outcomes might provide new insights into therapeutic goals in this population (i.e., whether both constructs contribute independently to poor outcomes and whether their combinations lead to an even worse status).

Therefore, the present study focuses on the analysis of avoidance coping (in early pregnancy; first trimester) as a moderating variable in the relationship between PPD and early maternal–infant interactions (four months after delivery). The hypotheses are difficult to anticipate based on previous research. We expect, however, that PPD and avoidant coping will share variance in the prediction of baby–mother relationships. We also anticipate that the impact of PPD will be exacerbated by the use of avoidant coping when depressed.

2. Materials and Methods

2.1. Design and Sample

Women who received care and gave birth at the University Hospital of Fuenlabrada in Madrid, Spain, were recruited to participate in the study. The Ethics Committee of the Hospital approved the study protocol and the evaluation procedures. Women were eligible to participate if they met the following criteria: (a) were aged 18 years or older, (b) understood oral and written Spanish adequately, (c) did not have a multiple pregnancy, (d) did not have a serious or hormonal medical condition that could interfere with the pregnancy or dictate the type of delivery, (e) had a pregnancy that did not involve a severe fetal pathology, and (f) had not been diagnosed with a psychological disorder previously.

A prospective design was used. Women were assessed at two time points: first trimester of pregnancy and four months after delivery. At the beginning of pregnancy (during their first-trimester ultrasound), pregnant women that met the inclusion criteria were informed of the nature of the investigation and the conditions for their participation, and voluntarily agreed to participate. Women were excluded from the study if they completed the questionnaires improperly. At this first assessment (first trimester of pregnancy), a total of 287 pregnant women completed the avoidance coping measure. Of them, 116 women kept their participation four months after delivery. At this second assessment, both post-partum depression and maternal self-perception about early maternal–infant relationships measures were administered. Therefore, the final sample was composed of 116 low-risk obstetric mothers. The age of the participants ranged from 23 to 42 years (mean = 31.4; SD = 3.96). Half of them were new mothers (50.8%). Regarding educational level, 23.3% of the participants completed primary studies, 48.3% completed secondary studies, and 28.3% completed university studies. In total, 27.7% of the participants had history of at least one previous miscarriage. The majority of the women were employed during pregnancy (65%). Most pregnancies were planned (85%). The mean gestational age at delivery was 277.93 weeks (SD = 8.92; range, 253–299). The percentage of women who had vaginal, cesarean, and instrumental delivery was 62.5%, 17.9%, and 19.6%, respectively. Regarding the type of anesthesia, the women received epidural (66.4%), local (5.2%), spinal (7.8%), general (1.7%), and no anesthesia (18.9%). In spite of the high attrition rate, no significant differences were found for any of the sociodemographic or clinical variables considered between the initial sample (first trimester, n = 287) and the final sample (four months after delivery, n = 116): age (p = 0.38), educational level (p = 0.53), employed during pregnancy (p = 0.96), planning pregnancy (p = 0.49), previous pregnancies (p = 0.61), previous miscarriages (p = 0.87), gestational age at delivery (p = 0.78), type of delivery (p = 0.48), and type of anesthesia (p = 0.47). Regarding the outcome variables, no statistically significant differences were found between the samples for avoidance coping at the first trimester (p = 0.46).

2.2. Variables and Instruments

2.2.1. First Trimester of Pregnancy

Avoidance coping. The avoidance the coping scale of the Coping Strategies Questionnaire (CAE) [34] was used. Items are rated on a five-point Likert-like scale ranging from

0 (never) to 4 (almost always). The CAE allows the assessment of seven basic independent styles of coping, including problem-solving coping, negative auto-focused coping, positive reappraisal, overt emotional expression, social support seeking, religious coping, and avoidance coping. The latter was used for the purpose of the present study. This scale contains seven items (e.g., "I tried not to think about the problem" or "I went to the movies, to dinner, for a walk, etc., to forget about the problem"). The minimum score for the avoidant subscale is 0 and the maximum is 24. Higher scores indicate higher avoidance coping. The questionnaire has been used in various studies and it has good indices of reliability and validity [35,36].

2.2.2. Four Months after Childbirth

Post-partum depression. The Spanish version of the Edinburg Postnatal Depression Scale (EPDS) was used [37]. This scale consists of 10 multiple choice items (4 options each) concerning the respondent's mood in the past 7 days. The total score can range from 0 to 30. Higher scores indicate higher PPD. Psychometric studies of the test have shown an alpha value of 0.87, a sensitivity of 85%, a specificity of 77%, and a positive predictive value of 83% [38,39].

Maternal perceptions about mother–baby relations. The "Mother and Baby Scales" scale (MABS) [40], which is a self-report instrument, was used to assess the mothers' perceptions about her relationship with the newborn. Two types of maternal perceptions are particularly relevant in the MABS structure: (1) newborn behavior and (2) confidence in caring for the baby. The first (newborn behavior) contains 39 items that are grouped into five dimensions: Alert-Interest (8 items; "When I talk to my baby s/he seems to take notice"); Unstable-Irregular (15 items; "My baby has fussed before settling down"); Irritable During Lactation (8 items; "During feeds my baby has tended to fuss or cry"); Alert During Lactation (5 items; "After feeds my baby's mood has been awake and alert"); and Easy Temperament (3 items; "Overall how difficult is your baby?"). Items are presented in a six-point Likert-type response format ranging from 0 (not at all/never) to 5 (a lot/frequently) for dimensions Alert-Interest, Unstable-Irregular, Irritable During Lactation, and Alert During Lactation, respectively, and 7 points for Easy Temperament. The second MABS dimension (i.e., maternal perceptions about confidence in caring for the baby) includes three subscales, namely, lack of confidence in care, lack of confidence in lactation, and general level of safety. These three areas are represented by 24 items: lack of confidence in care—13 items ("I've felt unsure whether I've been doing the right thing whilst looking after my baby"); lack of confidence in lactation—8 items ("I felt I haven't always had enough milk to satisfy my baby"); and general level of safety—3 items ("Overall how stressful do you find it looking after your baby?"). A six-point Likert-type response format ranging from 0 (not at all/never) to 5 (a lot/frequently) is used in lack of confidence in care and lack of confidence in lactation. Seven points are used in the general level of safety scale. Studies so far support the validity of the MABS to measure maternal perceptions about mother–baby relations [40,41].

2.3. *Procedure*

This study is part of a larger investigation that aims to analyze the evolution of maternal psychosocial variables during pregnancy, delivery, and postpartum (FIS ISCIII PI07/0571).

A midwife participating in the study contacted the participants personally at the antenatal clinic during their first-trimester ultrasound. For eligibility reasons, she checked the electronic record to approach the women who met the inclusion criteria. These women then received information regarding the study and were invited to participate. In total, 320 women were found to be eligible during a period of 18 months. Of these, 287 women decided to participate (89.68%) and signed the informed consent form. After being enrolled in the study, the participants completed the avoidance coping instrument and returned it directly to the researcher. Four months after delivery, a questionnaire that included postpartum depression and maternal self-perception of both her baby and her own confidence as a mother was sent by mail. These were returned and correctly completed by 116 (39%) women from the initial sample.

2.4. Statistical Analysis

The SPSS 22 statistical package was used to perform all the analyses [42]. Descriptive analyses and internal consistency analyses (Cronbach's alpha coefficients) were conducted as a first step. Means, standard deviations, and Pearson's correlations were calculated for all study variables. Finally, the moderation analyses were carried out with model 1 of the PROCESS Macro version 3.4 [43]. PPD was set as the independent variable, maternal perceptions of early relationship and newborn behavior as dependent variables, and avoidant coping as the moderator. In the post-hoc analyses, non-centered variables were used to facilitate the interpretation of the results (centered variables were used elsewhere). Statistical significance was established at an alpha level of 0.05.

3. Results

3.1. Means, Standard Deviations, and Pearson Correlations between Study Variables

Table 1 shows the Cronbach alphas, means, standard deviations, and Pearson correlations between the study variables. The dimensions assessed show adequate values for internal consistency, and acceptable values in the case of the Alert-Interest—perception of the baby- (0.69) and lack of confidence in lactation (0.68). No significant associations were observed between avoidance coping at the end of the first trimester during pregnancy and PPD. Pregnancy avoidance coping was also unrelated to the mother's perception of the baby or the lack of safety in lactation at the postpartum. Pregnancy avoidance coping, however, was significantly associated with less safety with baby care and general safety at the postpartum. Regarding the associations of PPD with postpartum maternal–infant relationships, a significant and negative association was observed between PPD and alert during lactation and with the general level of security. A positive association was found for PPD in relation to three mothers' perceptions at postpartum (perception of the baby as Unstable-Irregular and Irritable During Lactation, and lack of self-confidence in lactation).

Table 1. Means, standard deviations, and Pearson correlations between study variables.

Variable	Cronbach alpha	Mean (SD)	2.	3.	4.	5.	6.	7.	8.	9.	10.
1.Avoidance	0.72	9.15 (3.71)	0.09	0.06	0.13	−0.04	−0.16	0.13	0.30 **	0.08	−0.23 *
2. PPD	0.88	6.08 (4.86)		−0.13	0.22 *	−0.10	−0.25 **	0.30 **	0.51 **	0.30 **	−0.43 **
3. Alert-Interest	0.69	32.18 (4.64)			0.09	0.08	0.06	0.02	−0.12	−0.03	0.12
4. Unstable-Irregular	0.78	27.84 (11.92)				−0.74 **	-0.13	0.69 **	0.55 **	0.09	−0.46 **
5. Easy Temperament	0.80	14.85 (2.97)					0.07	−0.52 **	−0.39 **	−0.02	0.48 **
6. ADL	0.79	16.01 (4.63)						−0.05	−0.27 **	0.08	0.40 **
7. IDL	0.80	7.02 (5.38)							0.46 **	0.29 **	−0.37 **
8. LCC	0.78	14.73 (9.66)								0.25 **	−0.67 **
9. LCL	0.68	7.43 (6.22)									−0.21 *
10.GLS	0.81	15.03 (3.05)									

PPD: post-partum depression; ADL: Alert During Lactation; IDL: Irritable During Lactation; LCC: lack of confidence in care; LCL: lack of confidence in lactation; GLS: general level of safety. * $p < 0.05$; ** $p < 0.01$.

3.2. Moderation Analysis and Multivariate Linear Regression

The results of the regression analyses, including the moderation analyses, are presented in Table 2. Significant associations were observed between PPD and general safety level (Beta = −0.26, $p < 0.001$, 95% CI = [−0.37, −0.15]), lack of confidence in lactation

(Beta = 0.39, p = 0.009, 95% CI = [0.10, 0.67]), lack of confidence in caring for the baby (Beta = 1.01, p < 0.001, 95% CI = [0.71, 1.32]), the perception of the baby as being alert during lactation (Beta = −0.19, p = 0.044, 95% CI = [−0.37, −0.01]), and the perception of the baby as being irritable during lactation (Beta = 0.32, p = 0.004, 95% CI = [0.10, 0.54]). Significant direct associations of avoidant coping were observed with the perception of the baby as being unstable (Beta = 0.95, p = 0.003, 95% CI = [0.33, 1.56]), the perception of the baby as being irritable during lactation (Beta = 0.31, p = 0.041, 95% CI = [0.01, 0.60]), and the lack of confidence in baby care (Beta = 0.81, p < 0.001, 95% CI = [0.37, 1.24]). Regarding the moderation analyses, the results revealed that avoidant coping moderated the relationship between PPD and the perception of the baby as being unstable (Beta = 0.16, p = 0.031, 95% CI = [0.01, 0.30]), easy temperament (Beta = −0.06, p = 0.002, 95% CI = [−0.09, −0.02]), lack of security in baby care (Beta = 0.11, p = 0.027, 95% CI = [0.01, 0.21]), and general safety level (Beta = −0.05, p = 0.007, 95% CI = [−0.09, −0.01]). The models accounted for 15%, 14%, 40%, and 28% of variance, respectively.

Table 2. Prospective prediction of maternal perceptions about mother–baby relationships from postpartum depression, avoidance coping, and their interaction.

Variable	R^2	F	p	Beta	t	p	95% CI
DV = A	0.08	2.29	0.083				
PPD				−0.17	−1.80	0.074	−0.36, 0.02
Avoidance				0.26	1.80	0.063	−0.01, 0.511
Interaction				−0.01	−0.40	0.689	−0.07, 0.05
DV = UI	0.15	4.84	0.003				
PPD				0.39	1.73	0.086	−0.06, 0.83
Avoidance				0.95	3.03	0.003	0.33, 1.56
Interaction				0.16	2.19	0.031	0.01, 0.30
DV = ET	0.14	3.72	0.015				
PPD				−0.06	−0.92	0.358	−0.18, 0.07
Avoidance				−0.11	−1.31	0.191	−0.28, 0.06
Interaction				−0.06	−3.10	0.002	−0.09, −0.02
DV = ADL	0.10	3.17	0.028				
PPD				−0.19	−2.04	0.044	−0.37, −0.01
Avoidance				−0.18	−1.40	0.164	−0.44, 0.08
Interaction				0.04	1.23	0.221	−0.02, 0.09
DV = IDL	0.16	5.14	0.002				
PPD				0.32	2.91	0.004	0.10, 0.54
Avoidance				0.31	2.06	0.041	0.01, 0.60
Interaction				0.07	1.90	0.060	−0.01, 0.14
DV = LCL	0.08	2.40	0.073				
PPD				0.39	2.66	0.009	0.10, 0.67
Avoidance				−0.06	−0.31	0.760	−0.46, 0.33
Interaction				−0.01	.20	0.845	−0.11, 0.09
DV = LCC	0.40	18.71	<0.001				
PPD				1.01	6.48	<0.001	0.71, 1.32
Avoidance				0.81	3.66	<0.001	0.37, 1.24
Interaction				0.11	2.25	0.027	0.01, 0.21
DV = GLS	0.28	8.67	<0.001				
PPD				−0.26	−4.74	<0.001	−0.37, −0.15
Avoidance				−0.08	−0.93	0.355	−0.24, 0.09
Interaction				−0.05	−2.73	0.007	−0.09, −0.01

PPD: post-partum depression; A: Alert-Interest; UI: Unstable-Irregular; ET: Easy Temperament ADL: Alert During Lactation; IDL: Irritable During Lactation; LCC: lack of confidence in care, LCL: lack of confidence in lactation; GLS: general level of safety; DV: Dependent Variable; CI: Confidence interval.

As noted earlier, post-hoc analyses were planned to analyze significant moderations in more detail. These were calculated and are presented in Table 3.

Table 3. Conditional effects of PPD on maternal perceptions about newborn behavior and confidence in caring for the baby.

Variable	Avoidance	Beta (PPD)	t	p	95% CI
UI					
	−3.77	−0.20	−0.63	0.528	−0.83, 0.43
	−0.77	0.27	1.21	0.229	−0.17, 0.70
	4.22	1.05	2.59	0.011	0.24, 1.85
ET					
	−3.77	0.16	1.86	0.067	−0.01, 0.33
	−0.77	−0.01	−0.23	0.819	−0.14, 0.11
	4.22	−0.30	−2.75	0.007	−0.52, −0.08
LCC					
	−3.77	0.59	2.64	0.009	0.15, 1.03
	−0.77	0.93	6.00	<0.001	0.62, 1.23
	4.22	1.49	5.25	<0.001	0.93, 2.05
GLS					
	−3.71	−0.08	−0.96	0.338	−0.23, 0.08
	−0.71	−0.23	−4.18	<0.001	−0.33, 0.12
	3.28	−0.43	−4.76	<0.001	−0.61, −0.25

PPD: post-partum depression; UI: Unstable-Irregular; ET: Easy Temperament; LCC: lack of confidence in care; GLS: general level of safety.

Figure 1 shows the moderation of avoidance coping in the relationship between PPD and the perception of baby as unstable. Specifically, the analyses indicated that PPD was positively associated with the perception of the baby as being unstable when avoidant coping was high ($p = 0.011$). When these were low, however, PPD and the perception of the baby as being unstable were no longer related ($p > 0.05$).

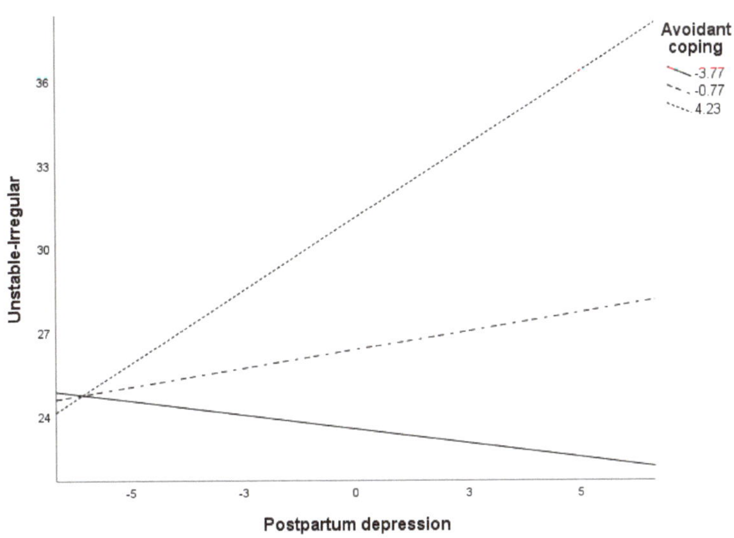

Figure 1. Conditional effects of post-partum depression (PPD) on perception of baby as unstable at values of avoidance.

Figure 2 shows the moderation of avoidant coping in the relationship between PPD and the perception of the baby as having easy temperament. Specifically, the results indicated that

PPD was negatively associated with the perception of the baby having an easy temperament when avoidant coping was high ($p = 0.007$). When avoidant coping was low, there was no relationship between PPD and mother perceptions about the baby ($p > 0.05$).

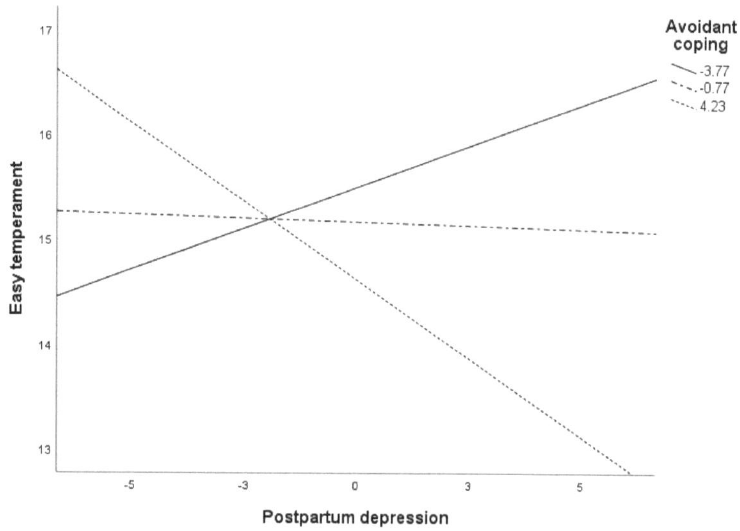

Figure 2. Conditional effects of PPD on perception of baby with easy temperament at values of avoidance.

Figure 3 shows the moderation of avoidant coping in the relationship between PPD and lack of security in baby care. Specifically, the relationship between these variables increased with higher levels of avoidant coping ($p < 0.001$). The relationship between PPD and lack of safety in baby care, however, was significant across all avoidant coping levels.

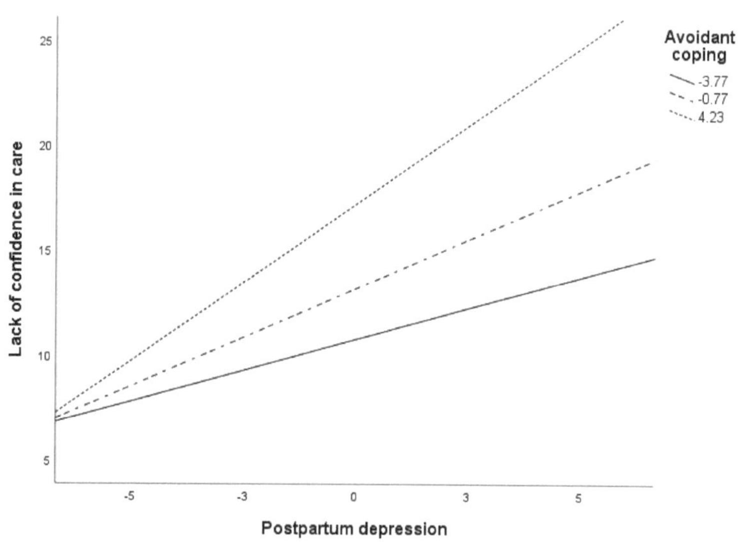

Figure 3. Conditional effects of PPD on lack of security in baby care at values of avoidance.

Figure 4 shows the moderation of avoidant coping in the relationship between PPD and general safety level. Specifically, PPD was negatively associated with maternal safety when avoidant coping was high or medium ($p < 0.001$). When avoidant coping was low, the relationship between PPD and general safety was not significant.

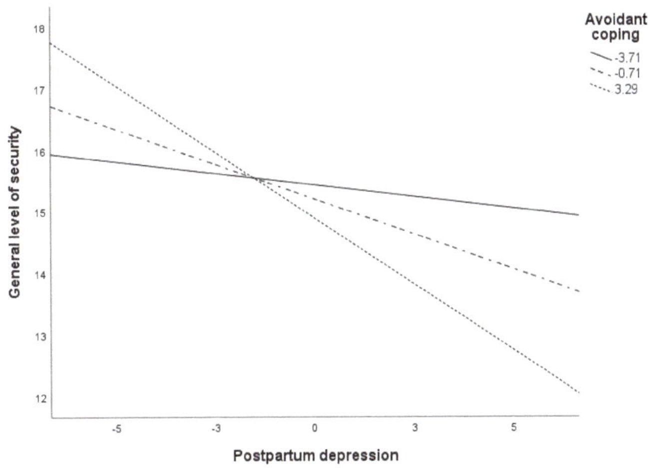

Figure 4. Conditional effects of PPD on maternal general level of safety at values of avoidance.

4. Discussion

The aim of the present study was to explore the moderating role of avoidant coping during early pregnancy in the relationship between PPD and maternal–baby relations (i.e., perception of both the baby and herself and confidence as a mother). The relationship between postpartum depression and maternal–infant relationships has been investigated in the literature [5]. Consistent with past research [5,44–46], the results found in the present work revealed significant relationships between PPD and several dimensions of maternal–infant relationships (e.g., perception of the newborn as more unstable). As previous research shows, the association between PPD and maternal–infant relationships might not be linear [5]. In particular, the present investigation pointed to a coping strategy, namely avoidance, as a potential exacerbating factor for the relationship between PPD and maternal–infant relationships. These findings might be important for clinical practice as they point to a coping strategy in the mother that can be targeted to minimize the potentially harmful impact of PPD on maternal–infant relationships. Importantly, because avoidant coping was evaluated early during pregnancy, the findings might be important for prevention purposes. To the best of our knowledge, the exploration of the relationship between avoidant coping and early maternal–baby relationships, as well as its potential moderating role in the relationship between PPD and maternal–infant relationships, is new to the literature. Past research has previously pointed to the deleterious impact of avoidance coping, for example, for maternal stress levels during pregnancy and Apgar scores [47], satisfaction with childbirth [48], and maternal–fetal attachment [49]. This latter study showed that avoidant/disengagement coping and depression scores were negatively correlated with prenatal attachment scores [49]. In line with this study, our results showed that, even when the contribution of PPD was controlled for, avoidant coping in early pregnancy was significantly associated with several variables from maternal-infant relationships. Specifically, avoidant coping was related to the perception of the baby as unstable (in general and during lactation), and with the lack safety in baby care. These results are important as they point to a therapeutic target that might be included in interdisciplinary management programs during pregnancy when aiming to improve mother-infant relationships.

In addition to these direct associations between avoidant coping and mother–infant relationships, a key finding in the present study was that avoidant coping exacerbated the relationship between PPD and the mother–infant relationship. In particular, the moderation occurred with two factors associated with the perception of the baby and two factors related to maternal self-efficacy. In general terms, the results show that, when avoidance levels are high, the relationship between PPD and maternal–baby relationship increases and becomes statistically significant. A previous study [50] carried out among women with childhood trauma showed mediating effects of postpartum depression between trauma and maternal–infant bonding after controlling for covariates and antenatal distress. Maternal avoidance of fearful stimuli emerged as a potential affective mechanism. Although there are no similar previous studies in low obstetric risk samples to which our moderation results can be compared, our findings point in the same direction as previous research indicating the maladaptive role of avoidant coping in the gestation-puerperium process [47–49], including prenatal attachment [49].

A recent review indicated that the relationship between PPD and early maternal–infant relations is complex [5]. In this context, the contributions of certain variables to the aforementioned relationship have been studied, including gynaecological-obstetrics, demographic, infant, social support and parenting, and emotional availability factors. Among these factors, it is striking that the psychological factors related to the mother's personality and coping strategies have received little attention [5]. The current investigation is a step in this direction. We hope that the findings will inspire researchers and clinicians alike.

In addition to the moderation analyses, the present study explored linear associations between PDD and maternal–infant relationships. A number of interesting findings were revealed. For example, a recent review indicated that lactation and maternal perceptions related to it are often omitted in research about the relationship between maternal depression and early baby–mother relations [5]. Our results, therefore, provide relatively novel data in this regard. Particularly, we evidenced that PPD is associated with the perception of the baby as being both less alert and more irritable during lactation. The relationship between breastfeeding problems and depression had been previously reported, especially in the first postpartum days [51,52]. However, the inclusion of maternal perceptions on the baby's attitude towards lactation is new to the literature [53]. Even though the following is only hypothetical at this stage, it is possible that the relationship between PPD and breastfeeding cessation is mediated by perceptions in the mother that have been revealed to be associated with PPD in the present study (perception of the baby as being less alert and more irritable during lactation). These findings open new avenues for research and clinical practice.

Another finding in relation to PPD and maternal–infant relationships refers to the mother's perception of self-efficacy. In the present study, a significant association emerged between depressive symptoms and the lack of security in baby care, the lack of security in lactation, and the general level of security. Self-efficacy, which refers to the confidence individuals have in their abilities to successfully perform their duties, such as parenting [54], has been found to be related to maternal depression and maternal behavior [55–57]. Not surprisingly, several studies have emphasized the role of early diagnosis and treatment of depressive symptoms and promotion of maternal self-efficacy to improve the overall functional status of mothers in the postpartum [57,58]. Maternal depressive symptomatology and self-efficacy have been directly and significantly correlated with infant self-regulation and maternal self-efficacy has been found to mediate the relationship between maternal depressive symptomatology and infant self-regulation [59]. High maternal efficacy has also been shown to buffer the detrimental impact of attachment insecurity and low self-esteem on maternal depression [60]. For example, previous research suggests that breastfeeding self-efficacy at the early postpartum period can predict postpartum depression [61]. In sum, both the present and past research suggest that maternal self-efficacy may be an important protective factor against depression [62].

An interesting finding was that avoidant coping and PPD were not related. The relationship between avoidance and depressive symptoms has been extensively analyzed in both clinical [63,64] and non-clinical samples [26]. Its study in the context of PPD has been less frequent, but studies appear to indicate modest, yet significant associations between avoidant coping in the mothers and PPD [65,66]. One possibility for the non-significant association between avoidant coping and PPD in the present study might lie in the different times at which both variables were collected (first trimester of pregnancy for avoidant coping and four months after delivery for depression). Another possible explanation for the discrepancy between the results could lay in the fact that previous studies have been carried out in high obstetric risk samples (mothers of infants treated in a neonatal intensive care unit) [65,66].

The present study has some limitations that should be mentioned. Regarding the generalizability of the results, for example, it should be noted that participants included a convenience sample made up of pregnant volunteers recruited through a health center. This may indeed limit its representativeness and attempt against the generalizability of these findings to the general population of pregnant women. On the other hand, it must be taken into account that our sample included women of low obstetric risk, which is likely to have resulted in relatively favorable PPD scores. Taking both shortcomings together, it would be interesting to explore to what extent the current study findings are replicated with samples presenting a higher PPD profile. Given the relationship between avoidant coping and PPD [28], it is possible that a reduced variability of avoidant coping scores in high PPD samples would result in a reduction moderating role of avoidant coping in the relationship between PPD and mother–infant relations. Further research is needed to shed light in this regard.

Despite the above limitations, as noted, this study might have some important practical implications. The fact that avoidance coping was evaluated early during the first trimester of pregnancy supports the idea that we could establish prevention strategies to improve the mother's mental health and her relationship with the newborn as early as during the first trimester during pregnancy. Both emotional processing (via emotion-focused techniques integrated within cognitive-behavioral therapy) and cognitive restructuring (via overall cognitive-behavioral therapy techniques) have been shown to be essential elements in the therapy for depression. Assimilating emotion-focused techniques into cognitive-behavioral therapy (CBT) facilitates greater emotional processing during treatment and greater self-efficacy during follow-up. Additionally, cognitive restructuring in either standard CBT or exposure-based CBT leads to increased self-efficacy and reduced avoidant coping [67]. Important for the present study, the reduction of avoidance has been described as a key change mechanism in CBT for depression [68]. Therefore, according to the present and past research, the identification and intervention of avoidant coping early during pregnancy would be important for the promotion of the mother's mental health in the postpartum period, as well as for her relationship with the newborn.

5. Conclusions

PPD is especially associated with the self-perception of security of the mother both in caring for her child and in lactation, but also in relation to the negative perception of the child during lactation. Maternal avoidant coping in early pregnancy has been associated with a lack of confidence in caring for the baby and the perception of the child as unstable and irritable during lactation. The moderating role of maternal avoidant coping in the relationship between PPD and the perception of the baby (unstable and easy temperament), along with the self-perception of security (in baby care and general safety level), are of special interest. When maternal avoidant coping was high, PPD was positively associated with the perception of the baby as being unstable and without an easy temperament. The relation between PPD and lack of safety in baby care increased with higher levels of avoidant coping, and PPD was negatively associated with maternal safety when avoidant coping was high or medium. Therefore, maternal avoidance coping in early pregnancy is suggested to be a risk factor moderating the complex and dynamic associations between

PPD and mother–child relationships, in this case, through maternal perceptions both of the newborn and of their self-confidence as mothers.

Author Contributions: Conceptualization, C.P.P. and D.M.; Data curation, C.S.-R., S.B.R., D.M. and P.C.; Formal analysis, C.P.P., D.M., J.S.R.M. and P.C.; Investigation, C.P.P., C.S.-R. and S.B.R.; Methodology, C.P.P., C.S.-R., J.S.R.M. and P.C.; Project administration, C.P.P.; Resources, S.B.R. and J.S.R.M.; Software, C.S.-R.; Supervision, C.P.P.; Validation, D.M.; Visualization, P.C.; Writing —original draft, C.P.P.; Writing—review & editing, C.P.P., C.S.-R., S.B.R., D.M., J.S.R.M. and P.C. All authors have read and agreed to the published version of the manuscript.

Funding: This work was supported by the Health Research Fund (Fondo de Investigaciones Sanitarias, FIS), Instituto de Salud Carlos III (Spain) [PI07/0571].

Institutional Review Board Statement: The study was conducted according to the guidelines of the Declaration of Helsinki, and approved by the Ethics Committee of Hospital Universitario de Fuenlabrada (protocol code PI07/0571 and date of approval 02/01/2012).

Informed Consent Statement: Informed consent was obtained from all subjects involved in the study.

Data Availability Statement: The data presented in this study are available on request from the corresponding author. The data are not publicly available due to privacy restrictions.

Acknowledgments: The authors gratefully acknowledge all the participants for their collaboration and enthusiasm.

Conflicts of Interest: The authors declare no conflict of interest.

References

1. Law, K.H.; Dimmock, J.; Guelfi, K.J.; Nguyen, T.; Gucciardi, D.; Jackson, B. Stress, Depressive Symptoms, and Maternal Self-Efficacy in First-Time Mothers: Modelling and Predicting Change across the First Six Months of Motherhood. *Appl. Psychol. Health Well-Being* **2019**, *11*, 126–147. [CrossRef]
2. Hammer, P.; Hageman, I.; Garde, A.; Begtrup, L.; Flachs, E.; Hansen, J.; Hansen, Å.; Hougaard, K.; Kolstad, H.; Larsen, A.; et al. Night work and postpartum depression: A national register-based cohort study. *Scand. J. Work. Environ. Health* **2019**, *45*, 577–587. [CrossRef] [PubMed]
3. Dadi, A.F.; Miller, E.R.; Mwanri, L. Postnatal depression and its association with adverse infant health outcomes in low- and middle-income countries: A systematic review and meta-analysis. *BMC Pregnancy Childbirth* **2020**, *20*, 416. [CrossRef] [PubMed]
4. Slomian, J.; Honvo, G.; Emonts, P.; Reginster, J.Y.; Bruyère, O. Consequences of maternal postpartum depression: A systematic review of maternal and infant outcomes. *Women's Health* **2019**, *15*, 1745506519844044. [CrossRef] [PubMed]
5. Śliwerski, A.; Kossakowska, K.; Jarecka, K.; Świtalska, J.; Bielawska-Batorowicz, E. The Effect of Maternal Depression on Infant Attachment: A Systematic Review. *Int. J. Environ. Res. Public Health* **2020**, *17*, 2675. [CrossRef]
6. Turkcapar, A.F.; Kadıoğlu, N.; Aslan, E.; Tunc, S.; Zayıfoğlu, M.; Mollamahmutoğlu, L. Sociodemographic and clinical features of postpartum depression among Turkish women: A prospective study. *BMC Pregnancy Childbirth* **2015**, *15*, 108. [CrossRef]
7. Spinelli, M.G. Postpartum Psychosis: Detection of Risk and Management. *Am. J. Psychiatry* **2009**, *166*, 405–408. [CrossRef]
8. Guo, N.; Bindt, C.; Te Bonle, M.; Appiah-Poku, J.; Hinz, R.; Barthel, D.; Koffi, M.; Posdzich, S.; Deymann, S.; Barkmann, C.; et al. Association of Antepartum and Postpartum Depression in Ghanaian and Ivorian Women With Febrile Illness in Their Offspring: A Prospective Birth Cohort Study. *Am. J. Epidemiol.* **2013**, *178*, 1394–1402. [CrossRef]
9. Cicchetti, D.; Rogosch, F.A.; Toth, S.L. Maternal depressive disorder and contextual risk: Contributions to the development of attachment insecurity and behavior problems in toddlerhood. *Dev. Psychopathol.* **1998**, *10*, 283–300. [CrossRef]
10. Grace, S.L.; Evindar, A.; Stewart, D.E. The effect of postpartum depression on child cognitive development and behavior: A review and critical analysis of the literature. *Arch. Womens Ment. Health* **2003**, *6*, 263–274. [CrossRef]
11. Kurstjens, S.; Wolke, D. Effects of Maternal Depression on Cognitive Development of Children Over the First 7 Years of Life. *J. Child Psychol. Psychiatry* **2001**, *42*, 623–636. [CrossRef]
12. Anoop, S. Maternal depression and low maternal intelligence as risk factors for malnutrition in children: A community based case-control study from South India. *Arch. Dis. Child.* **2004**, *89*, 325–329. [CrossRef] [PubMed]
13. Rahman, A.; Harrington, R.; Bunn, J. Can maternal depression increase infant risk of illness and growth impairment in developing countries? *Child Care Health Dev.* **2002**, *28*, 51–56. [CrossRef]
14. World Health Organization. Maternal Mental Health and Child Health and Development in Low and Middle-Income Countries: Report of the Meeting, Geneva, Switzerland, 30 January–1 February 2008. Available online: https://apps.who.int/iris/handle/10665/43975 (accessed on 23 November 2020).
15. Zhu, P.; Sun, M.-S.; Hao, J.-H.; Chen, Y.-J.; Jiang, X.-M.; Tao, R.-X.; Huang, K.; Tao, F.-B. Does prenatal maternal stress impair cognitive development and alter temperament characteristics in toddlers with healthy birth outcomes? *Dev. Med. Child Neurol.* **2014**, *56*, 283–289. [CrossRef]

16. Conroy, S.; Pariante, C.M.; Marks, M.N.; Davies, H.A.; Farrelly, S.; Schacht, R.; Moran, P. Maternal Psychopathology and Infant Development at 18 Months: The Impact of Maternal Personality Disorder and Depression. *J. Am. Acad. Child Adolesc. Psychiatry* **2012**, *51*, 51–61. [CrossRef] [PubMed]
17. Giurgescu, C.; Zenk, S.N.; Templin, T.N.; Engeland, C.G.; Dancy, B.L.; Park, C.G.; Kavanaugh, K.; Dieber, W.; Misra, D.P. The Impact of Neighborhood Environment, Social Support, and Avoidance Coping on Depressive Symptoms of Pregnant African-American Women. *Women's Health Issues* **2015**, *25*, 294–302. [CrossRef] [PubMed]
18. Lazarus, R.S.; Folkman, S. *Stress, Appraisal, and Coping*; Springer Publishing Company: New York, NY, USA, 1984; ISBN 0-8261-4191-9.
19. Folkman, S.; Moskowitz, J.T. Coping: Pitfalls and Promise. *Annu. Rev. Psychol.* **2004**, *55*, 745–774. [CrossRef]
20. Kato, T. Frequently Used Coping Scales: A Meta-Analysis. *Stress Health* **2015**, *31*, 315–323. [CrossRef]
21. Roth, S.; Cohen, L.J. Approach, avoidance, and coping with stress. *Am. Psychol.* **1986**, *41*, 813–819. [CrossRef]
22. Carver, C.S.; Connor-Smith, J. Personality and Coping. *Annu. Rev. Psychol.* **2010**, *61*, 679–704. [CrossRef]
23. Lazarus, R.S.; Folkman, S. Transactional theory and research on emotions and coping. *Eur. J. Pers.* **1987**, *1*, 141–169. [CrossRef]
24. Arble, E.; Arnetz, B.B. A Model of First-responder Coping: An Approach/Avoidance Bifurcation. *Stress Health* **2017**, *33*, 223–232. [CrossRef] [PubMed]
25. Brooks, M.; Graham-Kevan, N.; Robinson, S.; Lowe, M. Supplemental Material for Trauma Characteristics and Posttraumatic Growth: The Mediating Role of Avoidance Coping, Intrusive Thoughts, and Social Support. *Psychol. Trauma Theory Res. Pr. Policy* **2019**, *11*, 232–238. [CrossRef]
26. Bartone, P.T.; Homish, G.G. Influence of hardiness, avoidance coping, and combat exposure on depression in returning war veterans: A moderated-mediation study. *J. Affect. Disord.* **2020**, *265*, 511–518. [CrossRef] [PubMed]
27. Gauthier-Duchesne, A.; Hébert, M.; Daspe, M.-È. Culpabilité chez les enfants victimes d'agression sexuelle. *Criminologie* **2017**, *50*, 181–201. [CrossRef] [PubMed]
28. Aneja, J.; Chavan, B.S.; Huria, A.; Goel, P.; Kohli, N.; Chhabra, P. Perceived stress and its psychological correlates in pregnant women: An Indian study. *Int. J. Cult. Ment. Health* **2018**, *11*, 268–279. [CrossRef]
29. Litz, B.T.; Orsillo, S.M.; Kaloupek, D.; Weathers, F. Emotional processing in posttraumatic stress disorder. *J. Abnorm. Psychol.* **2000**, *109*, 26–39. [CrossRef]
30. Kashdan, T.B.; Breen, W.E.; Julian, T. Everyday strivings in war veterans with posttraumatic stress disorder: Suffering from a hyper-focus on avoidance and emotion regulation. *Behav. Ther.* **2010**, *41*, 350–363. [CrossRef]
31. Barlow, D.H. Unraveling the mysteries of anxiety and its disorders from the perspective of emotion theory. *Am. Psychol.* **2000**, *55*, 1247–1263. [CrossRef]
32. Hayes, S.C.; Luoma, J.B.; Bond, F.W.; Masuda, A.; Lillis, J. Acceptance and commitment therapy: Model, processes, and outcomes. *Behav. Res. Ther.* **2006**, *44*, 1–25. [CrossRef]
33. Nielsen, E.; Sayal, K.; Townsend, E. Functional coping dynamics and experiential avoidance in a community sample with no self-injury vs. Non-suicidal self-injury only vs. those with both non-suicidal self-injury and suicidal behaviour. *Int. J. Environ. Res. Public Health* **2017**, *14*, 575. [CrossRef]
34. Sandín, B.; Chorot, P. Cuestionario de afrontamiento del estrés (CAE): Desarrollo y validación preliminar. *Rev. Psicopatol. Y Psicol. Clín.* **2003**, *8*. [CrossRef]
35. Quezada-Berumen, L.; Moral de la Rubia, J.; Ibarra-González, L.D.; González-Ramírez, M.T. Estudio de validación del Cuestionario de Afrontamiento del Estrés en personas trans de México. *Rev. Psicopatol. Y Psicol. Clín.* **2018**, *23*, 121. [CrossRef]
36. Melendez, J.C.; Satorres, E.; Delhom, I. Personalidad y afrontamiento. ¿Qué rasgos predicen las estrategias adaptativas? *Ann. Psicol.* **2019**, *36*, 39–45. [CrossRef]
37. Garcia-Esteve, L.; Ascaso, C.; Ojuel, J.; Navarro, P. Validation of the Edinburgh Postnatal Depression Scale (EPDS) in Spanish mothers. *J. Affect. Disord.* **2003**, *75*, 71–76. [CrossRef]
38. Jairaj, C.; Fitzsimons, C.M.; McAuliffe, F.M.; O'Leary, N.; Joyce, N.; McCarthy, A.; Cassidy, E.; Donnelly, J.; Tully, E.; Imcha, M.; et al. A population survey of prevalence rates of antenatal depression in the Irish obstetric services using the Edinburgh Postnatal Depression Scale (EPDS). *Arch. Womens Ment. Health* **2019**, *22*, 349–355. [CrossRef]
39. Loscalzo, Y.; Giannini, M.; Contena, B.; Gori, A.; Benvenuti, P. The Edinburgh Postnatal Depression Scale for Fathers: A contribution to the validation for an Italian sample. *Gen. Hosp. Psychiatry* **2015**, *37*, 251–256. [CrossRef]
40. Wolke, D.; James-Roberts, I.S. Multi-Method Measurement of the Early Parent-Infant System with Easy and Difficult Newborns. *Adv. Psychol.* **1987**, *46*, 49–70.
41. Meier, P.; Wolke, D.; Gutbrod, T.; Rust, L. The influence of infant irritability on maternal sensitivity in a sample of very premature infants. *Infant Child Dev.* **2003**, *12*, 159–166. [CrossRef]
42. IBM Corp. *IBM Corp IBM SPSS Statistics for Windows, Version 22.0*; IBM Corp: Armonk, NY, USA, 2017.
43. Hayes, A.F. *Introduction to Mediation, Moderation, and Conditional Process Analysis Second Edition A Regression-Based Approach*; Guilford Publications: New York, NY, USA, 2017; ISBN 9781462534654.
44. Lefkovics, E.; Rigó, J.; Kovács, I.; Talabér, J.; Szita, B.; Kecskeméti, A.; Szabó, L.; Somogyvári, Z.; Baji, I. Effect of maternal depression and anxiety on mother's perception of child and the protective role of social support. *J. Reprod. Infant Psychol.* **2018**, *36*, 434–448. [CrossRef]
45. Thomason, E.; Flynn, H.A.; Himle, J.A.; Volling, B.L. Are women's parenting-specific beliefs associated with depressive symptoms in the perinatal period? Development of the rigidity of maternal beliefs scale. *Depress. Anxiety* **2015**, *32*, 141–148. [CrossRef]

46. Kerstis, B.; Engström, G.; Edlund, B.; Aarts, C. Association between mothers' and fathers' depressive symptoms, sense of coherence and perception of their child's temperament in early parenthood in Sweden. *Scand. J. Public Health* **2013**, *41*, 233–239. [CrossRef]
47. Penengo, C.; Colli, C.; Garzitto, M.; Driul, L.; Cesco, M.; Balestrieri, M. Validation of the Italian version of the Revised Prenatal Coping Inventory (NuPCI) and its correlations with pregnancy-specific stress. *BMC Pregnancy Childbirth* **2020**, *20*, 466. [CrossRef]
48. Catala, P.; Peñacoba, C.; Carmona, J.; Marin, D. Do maternal personality variables influence childbirth satisfaction? A longitudinal study in low-risk pregnancies. *Women Health* **2020**, *60*, 197–211. [CrossRef]
49. Ozcan, H.; Ustundag, M.F.; Yilmaz, M.; Aydinoglu, U.; Ersoy, A.O.; Yapar Eyi, E.G. The Relationships between Prenatal Attachment, Basic Personality Traits, Styles of Coping with Stress, Depression, and Anxiety, and Marital Adjustment Among Women in the Third Trimester of Pregnancy. *Eurasian J. Med.* **2019**, *51*, 232–236. [CrossRef]
50. Choi, K.W.; Sikkema, K.J.; Vythilingum, B.; Geerts, L.; Faure, S.C.; Watt, M.H.; Roos, A.; Stein, D.J. Maternal childhood trauma, postpartum depression, and infant outcomes: Avoidant affective processing as a potential mechanism. *J. Affect. Disord.* **2017**, *211*, 107–115. [CrossRef]
51. Onat, G.; Karakoç, H. Three spirals: Breastfeeding problems, growth spurts, and postpartum depression. *Perspect. Psychiatr. Care* **2020**. [CrossRef]
52. Koutra, K.; Vassilaki, M.; Georgiou, V.; Koutis, A.; Bitsios, P.; Kogevinas, M.; Chatzi, L. Pregnancy, perinatal and postpartum complications as determinants of postpartum depression: The Rhea mother–child cohort in Crete, Greece. *Epidemiol. Psychiatr. Sci.* **2018**, *27*, 244–255. [CrossRef]
53. Limas, E.A. Social Context of Breastfeeding: The Intersection between Attitudes and Postpartum Depression. Ph.D. Thesis, Indiana University, Bloomington, IN, USA, 2018.
54. Bandura, A.; Pastorelli, C.; Barbaranelli, C.; Caprara, G.V. Self-efficacy pathways to childhood depression. *J. Pers. Soc. Psychol.* **1999**, *76*, 258–269. [CrossRef]
55. Razurel, C.; Kaiser, B.; Antonietti, J.-P.; Epiney, M.; Sellenet, C. Relationship between perceived perinatal stress and depressive symptoms, anxiety, and parental self-efficacy in primiparous mothers and the role of social support. *Women Health* **2017**, *57*, 154–172. [CrossRef]
56. Martini, J.; Petzoldt, J.; Einsle, F.; Beesdo-Baum, K.; Höfler, M.; Wittchen, H.-U. Risk factors and course patterns of anxiety and depressive disorders during pregnancy and after delivery: A prospective-longitudinal study. *J. Affect. Disord.* **2015**, *175*, 385–395. [CrossRef]
57. Fathi, F.; Mohammad-Alizadeh-Charandabi, S.; Mirghafourvand, M. Maternal self-efficacy, postpartum depression, and their relationship with functional status in Iranian mothers. *Women Health* **2018**, *58*, 188–203. [CrossRef]
58. Santos, H.P.; Kossakowski, J.J.; Schwartz, T.A.; Beeber, L.; Fried, E.I. Longitudinal network structure of depression symptoms and self-efficacy in low-income mothers. *PLoS ONE* **2018**, *13*, e0191675. [CrossRef]
59. Bates, R.A.; Salsberry, P.J.; Justice, L.M.; Dynia, J.M.; Logan, J.A.R.; Gugiu, M.R.; Purtell, K.M. Relations of Maternal Depression and Parenting Self-Efficacy to the Self-Regulation of Infants in Low-Income Homes. *J. Child Fam. Stud.* **2020**, *29*, 2330–2341. [CrossRef]
60. Lee, J.-S.; Koo, H.J. The relationship between adult attachment and depression in Korean mothers during the first 2years postpartum: A moderated mediation model of self-esteem and maternal efficacy. *Pers. Individ. Dif.* **2015**, *79*, 50–56. [CrossRef]
61. Minamida, T.; Iseki, A.; Sakai, H.; Imura, M.; Okano, T.; Tanii, H. Do postpartum anxiety and breastfeeding self-efficacy and bonding at early postpartum predict postpartum depression and the breastfeeding method? *Infant Ment. Health J.* **2020**, *41*, 662–676. [CrossRef]
62. Koury, A.J.; Dynia, J.; Dore, R.; Logan, J.A.R.; Purtell, K.M.; Joy, E.; Salsberry, P. Food Insecurity and Depression among Economically Disadvantaged Mothers: Does Maternal Efficacy Matter? *Appl. Psychol. Health Well-Being* **2020**, *12*, 432–448. [CrossRef]
63. Haskell, A.M.; Britton, P.C.; Servatius, R.J. Toward an assessment of escape/avoidance coping in depression. *Behav. Brain Res.* **2020**, *381*, 112363. [CrossRef]
64. Siepsiak, M.; Sobczak, A.M.; Bohaterewicz, B.; Cichocki, Ł.; Dragan, W.Ł. Prevalence of Misophonia and Correlates of Its Symptoms among Inpatients with Depression. *Int. J. Environ. Res. Public Health* **2020**, *17*, 5464. [CrossRef]
65. Belanger, R.L. Risk and Resilience for Postpartum Depression in Mothers of Infants Who Required Neonatal-Intensive-Care-Unit Hospitalization. Ph.D. Thesis, University of Maryland, College Park, MD, USA, 2018.
66. Lasheras, G.; Farré-Sender, B.; Porta, R.; Mestre-Bach, G. Risk factors for postpartum depression in mothers of newborns admitted to neonatal intensive care unit. *J. Reprod. Infant Psychol.* **2020**, 1–15. [CrossRef]
67. Gómez Penedo, J.M.; Coyne, A.E.; Constantino, M.J.; Krieger, T.; Hayes, A.M. Theory-specific patient change processes and mechanisms in different cognitive therapies for depression. *J. Consult. Clin. Psychol.* **2020**, *88*, 774–785. [CrossRef] [PubMed]
68. Chou, W.-P.; Yen, C.-F.; Liu, T.-L. Predicting Effects of Psychological Inflexibility/Experiential Avoidance and Stress Coping Strategies for Internet Addiction, Significant Depression, and Suicidality in College Students: A Prospective Study. *Int. J. Environ. Res. Public Health* **2018**, *15*, 788. [CrossRef] [PubMed]

International Journal of *Environmental Research and Public Health*

MDPI

Article

Exploring Maternal Self-Efficacy of First-Time Mothers among Rural-to-Urban Floating Women: A Quantitative Longitudinal Study in China

Qun Wang, Yao Zhang, Xilin Li, Ziwen Ye, Lingling Huang, Yan Zhang and Xujuan Zheng *

Health Science Centre, Shenzhen University, Shenzhen 518060, China; qunwang@szu.edu.cn (Q.W.); zhangyao@szu.edu.cn (Y.Z.); xy_11991@163.com (X.L.); y673817550@126.com (Z.Y.); huanglingling@szu.edu.cn (L.H.); xiahzhang@szu.edu.cn (Y.Z.)

* Correspondence: zhengxujuan@szu.edu.cn

Abstract: (1) Background: China has the highest number of rural-to-urban floating women in the world, and the majority of them are of childbearing age. However, few studies have focused on maternal self-efficacy (MSE) for these women. This research aims to explore MSE and its influencing factors for primiparous women among the rural-to-urban floating population in China. (2) Methods: A quantitative longitudinal study was conducted, and primiparous women from the floating population were recruited in China. Face-to-face demographic questionnaires were collected from obstetric wards by the researchers, three days postpartum. The 6-week and 12-week questionnaires, including the Self-efficacy in Infant Care Scale (SICS), the Edinburgh Postnatal Depression Scale (EPDS), and the Postpartum Social Support Scale (PSSS), were sent to participants by wechat or email to measure MSE, postnatal depression, and social support, respectively. The completed 6-week and completed 12-week questionnaires were returned to the researchers. (3) Results: The mean MSE scores at 6 and 12 weeks postpartum were 67.16 (SD = 14.35) and 68.71 (SD = 15.00). The variables of social support, postnatal depression, whether women attended parenting training, baby fussiness, baby health, maternal educational level, occupation, and family income affected MSE at the two time points. (4) Conclusions: Primiparous women among the rural-to-urban floating population had a low MSE level. As a vulnerable and special group, more attention should be paid to the negative parenting status of floating women by health workers and family members. Effective measures must be taken to improve the floating women's accessibility to parenting training from health services to strengthen their social support and alleviate postpartum depression. Health professionals should be more concerned with floating women with relatively low MSE levels, such as new mothers with lower education, poor working and living conditions, unhealthy babies, and babies with fussy temperaments.

Keywords: postpartum women; self-efficacy; floating women; postnatal depression; Mainland China

check for updates

Citation: Wang, Q.; Zhang, Y.; Li, X.; Ye, Z.; Huang, L.; Zhang, Y.; Zheng, X. Exploring Maternal Self-Efficacy of First-Time Mothers among Rural-to-Urban Floating Women: A Quantitative Longitudinal Study in China. *Int. J. Environ. Res. Public Health* **2021**, *18*, 2793. https://doi.org/10.3390/ijerph18062793

Academic Editors: Paul B. Tchounwou and M. Carmen Míguez Varela

Received: 26 January 2021
Accepted: 7 March 2021
Published: 10 March 2021

Publisher's Note: MDPI stays neutral with regard to jurisdictional claims in published maps and institutional affiliations.

1. Introduction

With the rapid development of the economy and urbanization in China, a large portion of the population has moved from the countryside to cities in the last three decades; these people are called the "floating population" or "internal migrants" [1,2]. According to a report on the development of the Chinese floating population, there were approximately 247 million people in the floating population in 2020, more than one-sixth of the total population of China [3], and Shenzhen city had eight million floating people, accounting for more than 60% of the inhabitants. A national survey on the floating population by the Health Commission of China in 2018 said that nearly half of the floating population were female, and the majority of them were of childbearing age [3–5].

These rural-to-urban floating women play an important role in economic development by meeting the social needs of the industrialized urban areas of China [4–6]. However, there are many healthcare benefits and social welfare only available to local city residents [1]. This denial restrains the access of floating women to the full benefits available to city residents and creates social inequality [7]. Studies have shown that health disparities exist between the female floating population and city residents, owing to the lack of social support and unbalanced allocation of health resources [8,9]. Floating women of childbearing age were reported to have poor utilization of reproductive health services and to use fewer perinatal outpatient health services than resident women in terms of prenatal care and postpartum visits [5,6]. For instance, the utilization of reproductive health (RH) services have been found to be poor in floating women; only a minority of migrant women could access RH policies (39.3%), RH education (36.4%), RH counseling (27.4%), gratis contraceptives (36.0%), and free RH examinations (38.9%) [6]. For example, 5372 married rural-to-urban migrant women, aged 20–34, who delivered a baby, were recruited in a large national survey; it was found that many young rural-to-urban migrant women reported no prenatal care in the first trimester of pregnancy and an inadequate number of prenatal visits during their latest pregnancy [5]. Thus, the well-being of women in the reproductive period has drawn significant attention from researchers [1,6].

Transition to motherhood brings great challenges to women, who need to acquire parenting knowledge and skills, adjust to the new household relationship, and accept the maternal role [10]. Many women find it difficult to manage these physical, social, and psychological challenges in early motherhood [11]. Owing to the lack of previous parenting experience, these problems are particularly prominent for first-time mothers [12]. Research findings [13,14] indicate that primiparous women, confronted with many parenting troubles during infancy, such as negative mother–infant interactions and unsuccessful parenting tasks, are negatively impacted in terms of the well-being of infants and mothers.

As an important indicator of parenting outcomes, maternal self-efficacy (MSE) is the perceived ability of a mother to hold up her organization and performance of various parenting tasks [15]. Women with a high level of MSE are identified to conduct positive parenting [16,17]. Considering MSE's important impacts, an increasing number of researchers have focused on this domain, and related studies of MSE have been undertaken in various countries of the world [18–22]. However, the critical limitations of previous research on MSE were that most studies were limited to a homogeneous sample of well-educated and employed women, and conflicting evidence of what factors affect MSE has been presented in the literature [13,23,24].

In mainland China, the studies relating to MSE have been limited to only first-time mothers among local city residents [14,24]; few studies have focused on MSE for Chinese floating women. Therefore, this research was conducted to firstly explore MSE and its influencing factors for Chinese primiparous women among the rural-to-urban floating population during the initial postnatal period to fill the research gap.

2. Materials and Methods

2.1. Study Design

Research of quantitative longitudinal design was conducted to explore MSE and its influencing factors on first-time mothers among the Chinese rural-to-urban floating population in the initial postpartum period.

2.2. Setting and Sample

The research was conducted in the obstetric wards of two hospitals in Shenzhen City, Guangdong Province. There are over 4000 annual live births in each study hospital. Recruitment took place from March to December of 2019 via recruiting posters and leaflets. The inclusion criteria were as follows: being a first-time mother with a healthy baby, over 18 years of age; rural-to-urban floating women; being able to respond to the questionnaires in Chinese. Exclusion criteria were women or their children being seriously ill or having died.

A suitable sample size in multivariate analysis would be tenfold of the number of independent variables [25]. In the research, the maximum number of independent variables that could possibly impact MSE would be 20; hence, the appropriate sample size would be 200. According to previous research, an average attrition rate for postnatal women was about 30–45% at one time point by email [14,24,26]. In this study, a 45% loss at follow-up was conservatively estimated at every time point; it means that a 55% response rate at the first time point of follow-up and 30% response rate at the second time point of follow-up, so the predetermined recruited sample size was calculated to be 200/30% = 667.

2.3. Measures

A demographic questionnaire was developed to collect participant information of maternal age, marital status, educational level, occupation, family income, mode of birth, whether attended parenting training from health services, baby gender, baby health, and baby fussiness via the women's self-report. Baby health refers to a baby with a good health status. Baby health scores were reported by their mothers from 0 (very unhealthy) to 100 (very healthy). A higher baby health score indicates a higher level of baby health, rated by the mother. Baby fussiness means a baby with a negative or difficult temperament, which has characteristics such as irritability and low soothability and manageability. Baby fussiness scores were reported by their mothers from 0 (extreme fussy) to 100 (not at all). A higher baby fussiness score indicates a lower level of baby fussiness, rated by the mother.

MSE was measured using the Self-efficacy in Infant Care Scale (SICS) [27], a 46-item scale comprising four dimensions. Each item indicates one parenting task; the higher the score, the higher the self-efficacy. For instance, women were asked to rate their degree of confidence in performing designated tasks/situations; a score ranging from 0 to 100 was assigned, depending on their confidence response from "not confident at all to do it" to "definitely confident I can do it". The scale is scored by summing the numerical ratings for each task and dividing the result by the number of tasks. The reported internal consistency was 0.96 for the total scale and ranged from 0.86–0.96 for its dimensions [27]. The test–retest reliability coefficient for the total scale was 0.93. The Cronbach's alpha coefficient of the SICS was 0.94 in the present study sample.

Postnatal depression was measured by the Edinburgh Postnatal Depression Scale (EPDS) [28], which is a 10-item four-point Likert instrument. The sum score of the self-report scale ranges between 0–30, and a higher score indicates a worse health status. The Cronbach's alpha coefficient of the Chinese version of EPDS was 0.87; the concurrent validity with the Beck Depression Inventory was 0.79 [29]. In this research, the Cronbach's alpha coefficient of the EPDS was 0.85.

Postnatal social support was assessed using the Postpartum Social Support Scale (PSSS), developed for Chinese women to measure their perceived social support after childbirth [30]. A 20-item 4-point Likert scale was used, and a score ranging from 0 to 3 was assigned, depending on response options of "never", "rarely", "sometimes", and "often". Its total score is in the range of 0–60, and a higher score means more social support. The Cronbach's alpha coefficient of the PSSS was 0.89, and the content validity of this tool was 0.90 [30]. The test–retest reliability coefficient for the total scale was 0.92. The Cronbach's alpha coefficient of the PSSS was 0.90 in the current study.

2.4. Data Collection

The demographic questionnaires and participants' contact details were collected by the researchers face to face in obstetric wards at three days postpartum. The 6-week questionnaires comprised of SICS, EPDS, PSSS, baby health, and baby fussiness, and the 12-week questionnaires, including SICS, EPDS, PSSS, baby health, and baby fussiness, were sent to the participants by wechat or email at 6 and 12 weeks postpartum, respectively. The completed questionnaires were returned to the researchers by wechat or email. In order to improve the response rate, polite wechat reminders were sent to participants one week and one day before and after the 6-week and 12-week postpartum periods, respectively.

2.5. Data Analysis

SPSS Statistics 21.0 was used for statistical analysis. Descriptive statistics were conducted to describe the sociodemographic characteristics of floating women by means and standard deviations (SDs), frequencies, and proportions. Multiple linear regression analysis was used to explore the potential factors influencing MSE [25]. In this study, the MSE scores are the dependent variable, and the other variables as independent variables were entered into the multiple linear regression model (a_{entry} = 0.05, $a_{removal}$ = 0.10) to explore the influencing factors of MSE for these primiparous women in the floating population at – and 12 weeks postpartum, respectively. Diagnostic tests for assumptions, including linearity, normality, homoscedasticity, independence, and model specification, were completed, and these assumptions were met for the multiple linear regression models in the analysis [25].

2.6. Ethical Considerations

This study was approved by the Research Ethics Committee of Health Science Centre, Shenzhen University. Information sheets were distributed to all eligible women to introduce the purposes and process of this research before recruitment. Informed consent was obtained from every participant before data collection. Participants were informed of their freedom to withdraw at any time and were assured of anonymity through the use of special code numbers to identify them. All collected data were treated anonymously and confidentially.

3. Results

3.1. Recruitment and Participant Flow

Recruitment and participant flow in the research are shown in Figure 1.

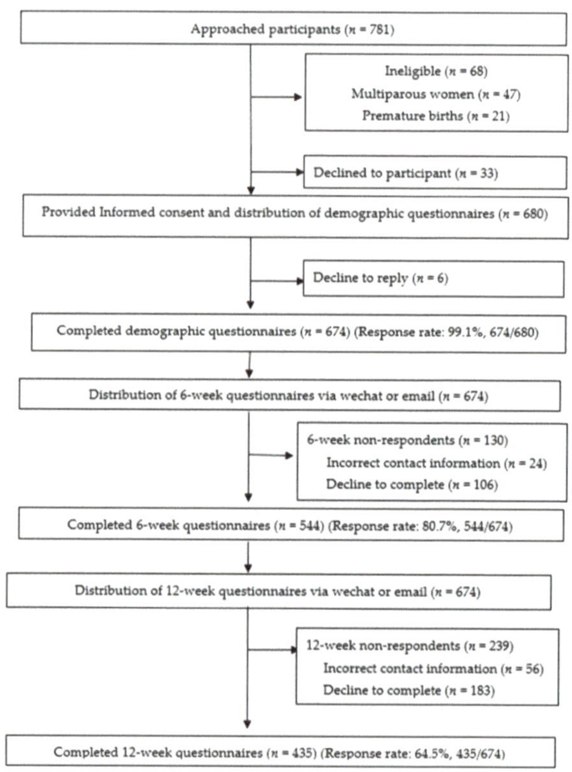

Figure 1. Recruitment and participant flow in this study.

3.2. Demographic Characteristics of the Participants

In total, 680 Chinese first-time mothers from the population of floating women were recruited, and 674 women completed the demographic questionnaires. Demographic data revealed the mean age of these floating women was 25.82 (SD = 3.38), and all of them were married. About 1/3 of respondents (27.0%, 182/674) had a university or college degree, and 61.6% (415/674) of them had an unskilled occupation; 42.4% of participants (286/674) had a family income of ¥3000–5000 (USD420–700)/per month per person. These participants had a higher proportion of vaginal delivery (61.4%, 417/674) than cesarean section (20.5%, 138/674), and over half of them (58.2%, 392/674) had a boy. Compared with first-time mothers among city residents (mean age of 27.28, 61.3% with tertiary education, 4.8% having an unskilled job, and 42.1% with a monthly family income more than ¥5000) [14,24], these primiparous women of the floating population had characteristics of younger childbearing age, lower educational levels, and poor living and working environments.

3.3. Mean Maternal Self-Efficacy (MSE), Postnatal Depression (PPD), Social Support, Baby Health, and Fussiness Scores at 6 and 12 Weeks Postpartum

The mean MSE scores at 6 and 12 weeks postpartum were 67.16 (SD = 14.35) and 68.71 (SD = 15.00), respectively. The mean social support score increased from 37.04 (SD = 10.15) at 6 weeks postpartum to 38.68 (SD = 10.46) at 12 weeks postpartum, while the mean EPDS score was kept almost stable, from 11.19 (SD = 4.89) at 6 weeks postpartum to 11.18 (SD = 5.34) at 12 weeks postpartum. Mean baby health scores were 83.01 (SD = 14.34) and 83.74 (13.74) at 6 and 12 weeks postpartum, respectively, and the mean baby fussiness scores were 72.83 (SD = 19.06) and 72.66 (SD = 16.72) at the two time points.

3.4. Coding Independent Variables in the Multiple Linear Regression Model

According to the requirements of coding, the independent variables in multiple regression models and the continuous independent variables retain the original numerical value as an assigned coding in the model. In relating to dichotomous variables, one variable is coded as 0, and the other is coded as 1. In terms of polytomous independent variables (more than two categories), they were established as dummy variables to represent different comparison groups [25]. To create the set of dummy variables, a reference group or category was firstly decided. Then, dummy variables were created for the remaining groups (excluding the reference group) and coded 1 for participants who were in that group; all others were coded 0. Therefore, there are (k − 1) dummy variables needed for k categories [25]. The coding of independent variables in the regression model is shown in Table 1.

Table 1. The coding of independent variables in the regression model.

Independent Variables	Methods of Coding
Maternal age	Original numerical value
Education level (* middle school or lower)	
Education level 1	Middle school or lower = 0, High school = 0, University/College = 0, Master's degree or higher = 1
Education level 2	Middle school or lower = 0, High school = 0, University/College = 1, Master's degree or higher = 0
Education level 3	Middle school or lower = 0, High school = 1, University/College = 0, Master's degree or higher = 0
Occupation (* unemployed status)	
Occupation 1	Unemployed status = 0, Professional occupation = 0, Skilled occupation = 0, Unskilled occupation = 1

Table 1. *Cont.*

Independent Variables	Methods of Coding
Occupation 2	Unemployed status = 0, Professional occupation = 0, Skilled occupation = 1, Unskilled occupation = 0
Occupation 3	Unemployed status = 0, Professional occupation = 1, Skilled occupation = 0, Unskilled occupation = 0
Family income (* >5000)	
Family income 1	<3000 = 1, 3001—5000 = 0, >5000 = 0
Family income 2	<3000 = 0, 3001—5000 = 1, >5000 = 0
Mode of birth (* normal vaginal birth)	
Mode of birth 1	Normal vaginal birth = 0, Assisted delivery = 0, Caesarean section = 1
Mode of birth 2	Normal vaginal birth = 0, Assisted delivery = 1, Caesarean section = 0
Whether attended parenting training	No = 0, Yes = 1
Baby gender	Girl = 0, Boy = 1
Baby health scores	Original numerical value
Baby fussiness scores	Original numerical value
Postnatal depression (EPDS scores)	Original numerical value
Social support (PSSS scores)	Original numerical value

* Reference group. EPDS: Edinburgh Postnatal Depression Scale; PSSS: Postpartum Social Support Scale.

3.5. The Regression Results of MSE Scores at Six Weeks Postpartum

The regression results (Table 2) show that seven variables affected MSE (*t*-test, $p < 0.05$); and these variables explained 63.1% of the variance in MSE at six weeks postpartum (adjusted R2 = 0.631, F = 91.225, $p < 0.001$).

Table 2. The regression results of maternal self-efficacy (MSE) scores at six weeks postpartum ($n = 544$).

Variables	Unstandardized Coefficients B	Unstandardized Coefficients Std. Error	Standardized Coefficients Beta (Descending)	t	p
Constant	48.233	2.949		16.36	< 0.001
Social support (PSSS) scores	0.540	0.045	0.382	11.92	< 0.001
EPDS scores	−0.804	0.095	−0.274	−8.47	< 0.001
Family income 2	−6.895	1.099	−0.238	−6.27	<0.001
Baby fussiness scores	0.161	0.022	0.214	7.35	< 0.001
Education 3	4.797	0.940	0.150	5.10	<0.001
Whether attended parenting training	3.700	0.834	0.128	4.39	<0.001
Family income 1	−3.593	1.199	−0.119	−3.00	0.003
Occupation 3	7.787	1.969	0.107	3.95	< 0.001
Education 1	7.335	2.165	0.094	3.39	0.001

F = 91.23, $p < 0.001$, adjusted R2 = 0.631. MSE: maternal self-efficacy; EPDS: Edinburgh Postnatal Depression Scale; PSSS: Postpartum Social Support Scale.

3.6. The Regression Results of MSE Scores at 12 Weeks Postpartum

At 12 weeks postpartum, 8 variables were statistically significant factors influencing MSE (*t*-test, $p < 0.05$); these variables explained 73.5% of variance in MSE (adjusted R2 = 0.735, F = 134.410, $p < 0.001$; Table 3).

Table 3. The regression results of MSE scores at 12 weeks postpartum (n = 435).

Variables	Unstandardized Coefficients B	Std. Error	Standardized Coefficients Beta (Descending)	t	p
Constant	34.195	3.413		10.02	<0.001
EPDS scores	−0.997	0.090	−0.355	−11.12	<0.001
PSSS scores	0.444	0.048	0.309	9.20	<0.001
Baby fussiness scores	0.176	0.026	0.196	6.86	<0.001
Baby health scores	0.196	0.032	0.179	6.17	<0.001
Family income 2	−4.897	1.037	−0.163	−4.72	<0.001
Family Income 1	−4.223	1.207	−0.132	−3.50	0.001
Education 2	3.184	0.873	0.105	3.65	<0.001
Whether attended parenting training	2.548	0.814	0.085	3.13	0.002
Occupation 3	4.790	1.865	0.065	2.57	0.011

F = 134.41, $p < 0.001$, adjusted R2 = 0.735. MSE: maternal self-efficacy; EPDS: Edinburgh Postnatal Depression Scale; PSSS: Postpartum Social Support Scale.

4. Discussion

4.1. The MSE of First-Time Mothers among Rural-to-Urban Floating Women

In this study, the mean MSE scores of primiparous women in the floating population were 67.16 (SD = 14.35) at six weeks postpartum and 68.71 (SD = 15.00) at 12 weeks postpartum, which are significantly lower than previous findings from first-time mothers of city residents in China, whose MSE scores were 74.92 (SD = 11.05) and 77.78 (SD = 11.13) at the same time points [14,24]. These scores are also obviously lower than the MSE score of 80.02 (SD = 11.70) in a sample of Thai women using the same measurement of SICS [31]. The results indicated that these first-time mothers of floating women had a low MSE level.

There are some reasons that could explain this phenomenon. Firstly, parenting a baby is not only a significant matter for a Chinese mother but also an important issue for the whole family; retired grandparents have more time and will volunteer to help new mothers look after their babies [32]. One survey result of 20,083 seniors showed that 80% of urban elderly females participate in raising grandchildren [33]. These urban grandmothers have rich experiences in child-rearing and easily translate past experiences into current parenting practices for new urban mothers, which could definitely improve these women's MSE levels [34]. However, many floating women lacked the babies' grandparents' involvement in child-rearing because most of their parents live in relatively poor and underdeveloped rural areas and rarely move to urban areas to live together in consideration of the economic burden. Secondly, under China's longstanding household registration system, these floating women have an inevitably institutional barrier in accessing social welfare and healthcare benefits due to the absence of official local residence and medical insurance [1]. It means that compared with city residents, these rural-to-urban migrants acquire less health care and social support [8,9], which negatively affect their parenting confidence. Thirdly, as a transmigration group between urban and rural areas, floating women have relatively low educational levels and poor living and working environments [35]. Researchers [24,36] found that mothers with lower educational levels, worse occupations, and lower family incomes were prone to having a lower mean MSE score, which is likewise supported by this research finding.

As a vulnerable and special group, the negative parenting status of primiparous women in the floating population should be paid more attention to by the Chinese government, researchers, and health professionals. It is strongly recommended that future effective intervention should be conducted to improve these first-time mothers' MSE levels, which significantly impacted maternal well-being and child development [16,17].

4.2. Factors Influencing MSE for Chinese Floating Women

4.2.1. Social Support

According to the results of this study, social support was the main influencing factor of MSE at the two time points, which is consistent with most prior studies in different countries [21,24,26,36,37]. The result highlighted that women receiving more social support, in their perception, were more likely to have a higher level of MSE.

Some factors probably accounted for this result. Bandura [34] identified four major elements that affected self-efficacy: previous experience, vicarious experience, verbal persuasion, and physiological and emotional states. Social support could influence MSE level through the last three elements. First of all, support providers would give new mothers more vicarious parenting experience through observational learning from other women [16]. For instance, new mothers may observe successful parenting performance from obstetric nurses, midwives, and family members to learn or model their effective parenting behaviors. Secondly, supporters may give first-time mothers wonderful advice, information, and evaluation of child-rearing that positively impact their MSE levels through verbal persuasion [16]. Thirdly, social supporters may supply women with emotional and material support, such as encouragement, concern, financial assistance, and time to help them have a good physiological and emotional recuperation from childbirth, which increased new mothers' parenting competence.

4.2.2. Postnatal Depression

The study findings identified that postnatal depression was an important factor affecting MSE at 6 and 12 weeks postpartum, which is consistent with previous research [20,24,32,36]. The following evidence may explain how postnatal depression of women negatively influences their MSE levels. One reason is that depressed mothers often suffer from lack of energy, feeling exhausted and sleepy, and the worse physical status makes it difficult for them to bond with and take care of their babies. Furthermore, women with postnatal depression usually experience a persistent feeling of sadness, irritability, guilty conscience, and hopelessness, and these negative mental conditions seriously suppress new mothers' parenting confidence and capability [38].

4.2.3. Whether Attended Parenting Training from Health Services

In this study, whether floating women attended parenting training impacted their MSE. It highlights that attending parenting training from health services plays a significant role in the improvement of MSE levels for the sample of Chinese floating women by teaching them professional and scientific parenting skills and information.

By comparison, in the research of Zheng et al. [24], this variable did not enter the multiple linear regression model of MSE at the two time points. The reason for the inconsistent results was probably that the sample of Zheng et al. [24] focused on female city residents, and most (63%) of them attended parenting training from hospitals, while only 40% of floating women attended the related training in this research. It likewise confirmed that the floating women have less access to healthcare sources compared with their counterparts in city residents [8,9].

4.2.4. Baby Fussiness and Baby Health

In the present study, baby fussiness affected MSE levels at the two time points. Past research conducted in Western countries [18,39] revealed consistent evidence that new mothers with less fussy and irritable infants were reported to have a higher MSE level. Babies with fussy temperament are characterized by slow adaptability, negative mood, and intense reaction. Thus, taking care of these infants increases the difficulty of parenting tasks and leads to more challenges in the achievement of maternal role expectancy and more unsuccessful parenting experiences [40].

The interesting finding in this study was that baby health only remained in the multiple linear regression model at 12 weeks postpartum but not in the regression model at 6 weeks postpartum. This result implies that compared with other major influencing factors such as postnatal depression and social support, baby health does not have an important effect on MSE in the shorter term. However, with the passage of time, baby health conditions significantly influence maternal physical and emotional status, which impact MSE, according to the theory of Bandura [34]. The result was in accord with other research findings, with a longer follow-up period [24,41,42], that noted that women with a self-reported healthier baby tended to score higher on MSE at three and six months postpartum. For example, some Hong Kong mothers expressed that witnessing their infants' well-being increased their maternal role competence at six months postpartum [42]. One mother said, "I was quite competent in mothering because my child was healthy and did not have any problem" [42]. Thus, a conclusion can be drawn that baby health affects MSE for rural-to-urban floating women in the longer term, but not in the shorter term.

4.2.5. Maternal Educational Level, Occupation, and Family Income

The other three influencing factors of MSE among floating women in this study were maternal educational level, occupation, and family income at 6 and 12 weeks postpartum. Indeed, these three variables are interrelated and interact with each other [26].

The findings indicate that mothers with a higher educational level have a higher MSE score. Past research [24,43] agrees that women with at least a tertiary education will score higher on MSE than women with a high or middle school degree. The explanation may be that better-educated mothers have a stronger independent learning capability to acquire more parenting information and knowledge than lower-educated mothers [24]. In contrast, the other research has shown that maternal education level was not related to MSE in a sample of Singaporean women [37] and Chinese urban women in Guangdong City [44]. The main reason causing the inconsistent findings that the majority (80%) sample of the two studies had a university degree or higher, and the skewed education level groups may have led to selection bias.

In this study, mothers with professional occupations had the highest MSE scores in comparison with mothers with other work and the unemployed, which is consistent with previous study findings among female city residents in China [24]. Another study undertaken in a Western country [45] had similar results; women with professional jobs had greater MSE than women with casual jobs because women with professional occupations tend to be mothers with better education levels, which positively influences their parenting confidence, as shown by various studies [24,43].

The present study found that higher family income was one predictor of higher MSE scores for these rural-to-urban floating women. The research by Shorey et al. [36], conducted in Singapore, also demonstrated that higher family income was associated with a higher MSE level for women with infants. Mothers with low family income often suffer from financial problems that cause them to be more stressed, depressed, or irritable, which can negatively affect their parenting confidence. However, Zheng et al. [24] found that family income did not correlate with MSE scores of city residents, which is consistent with previous studies undertaken in different countries [26,36,44]. These conflicting results could be attributed to the different family and social backgrounds. For example, 42.4% of participants in this study had a family income of ¥3000–5000 (USD420–700)/per month per person. In contrast, almost 42.5% of the women in the study of Zheng et al. [24] had a family income of more than ¥5000 per month per person, so they probably did not have any severe economic burden that suppresses their maternal confidence.

Compared with city residents, first-time mothers among floating women had the characteristics of lower educational levels and poor living and working environments, which indeed negatively affect their parenting self-efficacy.

In summary, China has the highest number of rural-to-urban floating women in the world, and the majority of them are of childbearing age. However, few studies have focused on the maternal self-efficacy (MSE) of these women. The research aimed to explore MSE and its influencing factors for primiparous women in the rural-to-urban floating population in China. The study findings indicate that first-time mothers in the rural-to-urban floating population have a low MSE level; the variables of social support, postnatal depression, whether women attended parenting training, baby fussiness, baby health, maternal educational level, occupation, and family income were identified to influence MSE in the initial postpartum period. According to the results, the negative parenting status of first-time mothers among rural-to-urban floating women should be the cause of more concern from the Chinese government, researchers, and health professionals. Future tailored intervention is strongly recommended to be designed and conducted to improve these first-time mothers' MSE levels, which significantly affect the well-being of women and children.

5. Conclusions

In this study, we found that primiparous women in the rural-to-urban floating population have a low MSE level in the initial postpartum period. As a vulnerable group, these floating women's negative parenting status should be paid more attention by researchers and health professionals; this highlights the urgent need for further interventions tailored to the factors affecting MSE. Effective measures must be taken to improve the floating women's accessibility to parenting training from health services, strengthen their social support, and alleviate postpartum depression. Health professionals and family members should be more concerned with floating women with relatively low MSE levels, such as new mothers with lower education, poor working and living conditions, unhealthy babies, and babies with fussy temperament.

However, several limitations need to be noted. First, the variables in the research were assessed by self-report tools and may have led to a social desirability bias owing to the traditional belief of "domestic shame should not be made public". Second, this study did not include female city residents as a comparison group for direct comparison. Third, research findings in one city may not generalize to floating women in other regions of China. Fourth, there was no further follow-up after three months postpartum because of time and financial constraints. Therefore, future research could use multiple methods such as interviews and observation to measure variables more accurately. In consideration of regional diversity, this study could be replicated in other cities or regions of China. In order to gain a better understanding of MSE and its influencing factors on floating women, a further longer-term study could be conducted. Furthermore, in the cause of helping rural-to-urban floating women cope better with parenting tasks, future intervention strategies need to be specifically tailored to the identified factors affecting MSE for these women.

Author Contributions: Conceptualization, X.Z.; methodology, X.Z.; investigation, Q.W., Y.Z. (Yan Zhang), Z.Y., L.H., X.L., Y.Z. (Yao Zhang), and X.Z.; writing—original draft preparation, X.Z. and Q.W.; writing—review and editing, X.Z.; project administration, X.Z.; funding acquisition, X.Z. All authors have read and agreed to the published version of the manuscript.

Funding: This research was funded by the Natural Science Foundation of China youth project (grant no. 81703234), the Medical Science and Technology Research Fund project of Guangdong Province (grant no. A2018335), the Basic Research Free Exploration Project of Shenzhen City (grant no. JCYJ20180305163459491), the General Program of Stable Support Plan for Universities in Shenzhen City (grant no. 20200804101756002), and the SZU Top Ranking Project (grant no. 86000000210).

Institutional Review Board Statement: The study was conducted according to the guidelines of the Declaration of Helsinki, and approved by the Ethics Committee of Health Science Centre, Shenzhen University (date of approval 17 February 2017).

Informed Consent Statement: Informed consent was obtained from all subjects involved in the study.

Data Availability Statement: The data presented in this study are available on request from the corresponding author. The data are not publicly available due to privacy restrictions.

Acknowledgments: We would like to thank all collaborating centers and all women who voluntarily participated in this study.

Conflicts of Interest: The authors declare no conflict of interest.

References

1. Zhao, Y.J.; Kang, B.; Liu, Y.W.; Li, Y.C.; Shi, G.Q.; Shen., T.; Jiang, Y.; Zhang, M.; Zhou, M.G.; Wang, L.M.; et al. Health insurance coverage and its impact on medical cost: Observations from the floating population in China. *PLoS ONE* **2014**, *9*, e111555. [CrossRef]
2. Davis, D. The emergence of a new urban China: Insider's perspectives. *Contemp. Sociol. J. Rev.* **2013**, *42*, 860–861. [CrossRef]
3. National Health Commission of the People's Republic of China. Report on the Development of Chinese Floating Population in 2018. Available online: https://www.dyhzdl.cn/k/doc/c504711cbc23482fb4daa58da0116c175e0e1e73.html (accessed on 7 January 2021).
4. Luo, Y.; Li, M.L. Research progress on the current situation of reproductive health knowledge-attitude-practice and its influencing factors of female floating population. *Chin. J. Mod. Nurs.* **2016**, *22*, 2499–2502.
5. Zong, Z.H.; Huang, J.Y.; Sun., X.M.; Mao, J.S.; Shu, X.Y.; Hearst, N. Prenatal care among rural to urban migrant women in China. *BMC Pregnancy Childbirth* **2018**, *18*, 301. [CrossRef] [PubMed]
6. Zhou, Y.H.; Wang, T.; Fu, J.X.; Chen., M.Z.; Meng., Y.T.; Luo., Y. Access to reproductive health services among the female floating population of childbearing age: A cross-sectional study in Changsha, China. *BMC Health Serv. Res.* **2019**, *19*, 54. [CrossRef]
7. Shi, Q.J.; Liu, T. Glimpsing China's future urbanization from the geography of a floating population. *Environ. Plan. A Econ. Space* **2019**, *51*, 817–819. [CrossRef]
8. Luo, X.Q.; Gui, J.F. Analysis on the practice and cause factors of participation in medical insurance program for urban workers by migrants in cities. *Popul. Dev.* **2014**, *6*, 43–50.
9. Cai, X.Z.; Yang, F.; Bian, Y. Gap analysis on hospitalized health service utilization in floating population covered by different medical insurances: Case study from Jiangsu Province, China. *Int. Equity Health.* **2019**, *18*, 84. [CrossRef]
10. Salonen, A.H.; Kaunonen, M.; Astedt-Kurki, P.; Järvenpää, A.L.; Isoaho, H.; Tarkka, M.T. Effectiveness of an internet-based intervention enhancing Finnish parents' parenting satisfaction and parenting self-efficacy during the postnatal period. *Midwifery* **2011**, *27*, 832–841. [CrossRef]
11. Law, K.H.; Dimmock, J.; Guelfi, K.J.; Jackson, B. Stress, depressive symptoms, and maternal self-efficacy in first-time mothers: Modelling and predicting change across the first six months of motherhood. *Appl. Psychol. Health Well Being* **2019**, *11*, 126–147. [CrossRef]
12. Leahy-Warren, P.; McCarthy, G. Maternal parental self-efficacy in the postpartum period. *Midwifery* **2011**, *27*, 802–810. [CrossRef]
13. Zheng, X.J.; Morrell., J.; Watts, K. An Exploration of Factors Which Influence Maternal Self-Efficacy in Primiparous Women in China during the Initial Postnatal Period. Ph.D. Thesis, The University of Nottingham, Nottingham, UK, 2015.
14. Zheng, X.J.; Morrell, J.; Watts, K. Changes in maternal self-efficacy, postnatal depression symptoms and social support among Chinese primiparous women during the initial postpartum period: A longitudinal study. *Midwifery* **2018**, *62*, 151–160. [CrossRef]
15. Montigny, F.; Lacharite, C. Perceived parental self-efficacy: Concept analysis. *J. Adv. Nurs.* **2005**, *49*, 387–396. [CrossRef] [PubMed]
16. Haslam, D.M.; Pakenham, K.I.; Smith, A. Social support and postpartum depressive symptomatology, the mediating role of maternal self-efficacy. *Infant Ment. Health J.* **2006**, *27*, 276–291. [CrossRef] [PubMed]
17. Li, X.W.; Liu, Y. Parent-Grandparent Coparenting Relationship, maternal parenting self-efficacy, and young children's social competence in Chinese urban families. *J. Child Fam. Stud.* **2019**, *28*, 1145–1153. [CrossRef]
18. Fulton, J.M.; Mastergeorge, A.M.; Steele, J.S.; Hansen, R. Maternal perceptions of the infant: Relationship to maternal self-efficacy during this first six week's postpartum. *Infant Ment. Health J.* **2012**, *33*, 329–338. [CrossRef] [PubMed]
19. Salonen, A.H.; Oommen, H.; Kaunonen, M. Primiparous and multiparous mothers' perceptions of social support from nursing professionals in postnatal wards. *Midwifery* **2014**, *30*, 476–485. [CrossRef] [PubMed]
20. Kohlhoff, J.; Barnett, B. Parenting self-efficacy: Links with maternal depression, infant behaviour and adult attachment. *Early Hum. Dev.* **2013**, *89*, 249–256. [CrossRef]
21. Leahy-Warren, P.; McCarthy, G.; Corcoran, P. First-time mothers: Social support, maternal parental self-efficacy and postnatal depression. *J. Clin. Nurs.* **2012**, *21*, 388–397. [CrossRef] [PubMed]
22. Yap, D.F.F.; Nasir, N.; Tan, K.S.M.; Lau, L.H.S. Variables which predict maternal self-efficacy: A hierarchical linear regression analysis. *J. Appl. Res. Intellect. Disabil.* **2019**, *32*, 841–848. [CrossRef] [PubMed]
23. Azmoude, E.; Jafarnejade, F.; Mazlom, S.R. The predictors for maternal self-efficacy in early parenthood. *J. Midwifery Reprod. Health* **2015**, *3*, 368–376.
24. Zheng, X.J.; Morrell, J.; Watts, K. A quantitative longitudinal study to explore factors which influence maternal self-efficacy among Chinese primiparous women during the initial postpartum period. *Midwifery* **2018**, *59*, 39–46. [CrossRef]
25. Li, K.; He, J. *Medical Statistics*, 6th ed.; People's Medical Publishing House Co, LTD: Beijing, China, 2013; pp. 44–87.
26. Zang, S.M.; Sheng, Y. Study on influencing factors of maternal self-efficacy in primiparous women. *Chin. J. Mod. Nurs.* **2010**, *16*, 2980–2982.
27. Prasopkittikun, T.; Tilokskulchai, F. Self-efficacy in Infant Care Scale: Revision and further. *Nurs. Health Sci.* **2010**, *12*, 450–455. [CrossRef]

28. Cox, J.L.; Holden, J.M.; Sagovsky, R. Detection of postnatal depression: Development of the 10-item Edinburgh postnatal depression scale. *Br. J. Psychiatry* **1987**, *150*, 782–786. [CrossRef] [PubMed]
29. Wang, Y.Q.; Guo, X.J.; Lau, Y.; Chan, K.S.; Yin, L.; Chen, J. Psychometric evaluation of the Mainland Chinese version of the Edinburgh postnatal depression scale. *Int. J. Nurs. Stud.* **2009**, *46*, 813–823. [CrossRef]
30. Lu, H.; Zheng, X.X. The relationship between social support and postnatal depression of primiparous women. *Chin. J. Nurs.* **2001**, *36*, 731–733.
31. Prasopkittikun, T.; Tilokskulchai, F.; Sinsuksai, N.; Sitthimongk, Y. Self-efficacy in infant care scale: Development and psychometric testing. *Nurs. Health Sci.* **2006**, *8*, 44–50. [CrossRef]
32. Gao, L.L.; Chan, S.W.; Sun, K. Effects of an interpersonal-psychotherapy-oriented childbirth education program for Chinese first-time childbearing women at 3-month follow-up: Randomized controlled trial. *Int. J. Nurs. Stud.* **2012**, *49*, 274–281. [CrossRef]
33. China Research Center on Aging. *A Compilation of Survey Data on the System of Elderly Support for the Elderly in China*; Huangling Press: Beijing, China, 2012; Volume 132.
34. Bandura, A. *Self-Efficacy: The Exercise of Control*, 1st ed.; Freeman and Co.: New York, NY, USA, 1997.
35. Liu, H.; Wang, Q.; Lu, Z.X.; Liu, J.N. Reproductive health service use and social determinants among the floating population: A quantitative comparative study in Guangzhou City. *BMC Health Serv. Res.* **2014**, *14*, 502. [CrossRef]
36. Shorey, S.; Chan, S.W.; Chong, Y.S.; He, H.G. Predictors of maternal parental self-efficacy among primiparous women in the early postnatal period. *West. J. Nurs. Res.* **2015**, *37*, 1604–1622. [CrossRef] [PubMed]
37. Shorey, S.; Chan, S.W.; Chong, Y.S.; He, H.G. Maternal parental self-efficacy in newborn care and social support needs in Singapore: A correlational study. *J. Clin. Nurs.* **2014**, *23*, 2272–2283. [CrossRef] [PubMed]
38. Murray, L.; Cooper, P.; Hipwell, A. Mental health of parents caring for infants. *Arch. Womens Ment. Health* **2003**, *6* (Suppl. 2), 71–77. [CrossRef] [PubMed]
39. Troutman, B.; Moran, T.E.; Arndt, S.; Johnson, R.; Chmiele, M. Develop of parenting self-efficacy in mothers of infants with high negative emotional. *Infant Ment. Health J.* **2012**, *33*, 45–54. [CrossRef]
40. Liu, C.C.; Chen, Y.C.; Yeh, Y.P.; Hsieh, Y.S. Effects of maternal confidence and competence on maternal parenting stress in newborn care. *J. Adv. Nurs.* **2012**, *68*, 908–918. [CrossRef] [PubMed]
41. Salonen, A.H.; Kaunonen, M.; Astedt-KurkipK, P.; Järvenpää, A.L.; Isoaho, H.; Tarkka, M.T. Parenting self-efficacy after childbirth. *J. Adv. Nurs.* **2009**, *65*, 2324–2336. [CrossRef] [PubMed]
42. Ngai, F.W.; Chan, S.W.C.; Holroyd, E. Chinese primiparous women's experiences of early motherhood: Factors affecting maternal role competence. *J. Clin. Nurs.* **2011**, *20*, 1481–1489. [CrossRef]
43. Green, B.L.; Rodgers, A. Determinants of social support among low-income mothers: A longitudinal analysis. *Am. J. Community Psychol.* **2001**, *29*, 419–441. [CrossRef] [PubMed]
44. Gao, L.L.; Sun, K.; Chan, S.W. Social support and parenting self-efficacy among Chinese women in the perinatal period. *Midwifery* **2014**, *30*, 532–538. [CrossRef]
45. Koniak-Griffin, D.; Logsdon, M.C.; Hines-Martin, V.; Turner, C.C. Contemporary mothering in a diverse society. *J. Obstet. Gynecol. Neonatal Nurs.* **2006**, *35*, 671–678. [CrossRef]

International Journal of
Environmental Research and Public Health

MDPI

Article

Effects of Tobacco Consumption and Anxiety or Depression during Pregnancy on Maternal and Neonatal Health

Beatriz Pereira [1], Bárbara Figueiredo [2], Tiago Miguel Pinto [2] and M. Carmen Míguez [1,*]

1 Department of Clinical Psychology and Psychobiology, Faculty of Psychology, Campus Vida, University of Santiago de Compostela, 15782 Santiago de Compostela, Spain; beatriz.pereira@usc.es

2 Campus de Gualtar, School of Psychology, University of Minho, 4710-057 Braga, Portugal; bbfi@psi.uminho.pt (B.F.); tmpinto@psi.uminho.pt (T.M.P.)

* Correspondence: mcarmen.miguez@usc.es

Received: 12 September 2020; Accepted: 2 November 2020; Published: 4 November 2020

Abstract: This study analyzed the possible interaction effects between tobacco consumption and anxiety or depression during pregnancy on maternal and neonatal health. We recruited a sample of 807 pregnant Spanish women from public healthcare services. Women completed a questionnaire on sociodemographic variables, health status and tobacco consumption (continuous, quitting or no consumption) in the first and third trimester of pregnancy and at 2 months postpartum, and self-reported measures of anxiety and depression in the first trimester. Abstinence of tobacco consumption was verified through biochemical measurements. Interaction effects between tobacco consumption and anxiety were found for delivery ($p < 0.001$), neonatal health complications ($p = 0.026$) and gestational age at birth ($p = 0.029$). Interaction effects between tobacco consumption and depression were found for pregnancy ($p = 0.032$), delivery complications ($p < 0.001$) and weeks of gestation at birth ($p = 0.031$). This study suggests that there are different kinds of interaction effects between tobacco consumption and anxiety or depression. Smokers with high anxiety presented more delivery complications compared to quitters and non-smokers with high anxiety. There is a cumulative effect of anxiety on the effects of tobacco consumption on maternal health. The results highlighted the beneficial impact of quitting smoking during pregnancy to reduce the risk of suffering anxiety, depression and health complications.

Keywords: tobacco consumption; anxiety; depression; pregnancy complications; delivery complications; neonate's health problems; low birth weight

1. Introduction

Maternal tobacco consumption during pregnancy has been linked with several maternal and infant health complications. Particularly, maternal tobacco consumption during pregnancy was associated with an increased risk of placental pathologies, such as ruptures or premature detachment of the membranes [1], placenta previa [2–4], ectopic pregnancy [5–7] and miscarriage [8,9]. Tobacco consumption during pregnancy is also a risk factor for neonatal health. Premature birth [10,11] and low birth weight are usually present, as the neonates of mothers who smoked during pregnancy weigh approximately 150–250 g less than those of non-smoking mothers [12]. Additionally, the risk of intrauterine growth restriction, fetal death, perinatal mortality (e.g., sudden death syndrome and respiratory distress syndrome), malformations and developmental delays is also increased in the neonates of mothers who smoked during pregnancy [11,13,14].

Anxiety and/or depression during pregnancy were associated with maternal and infant health complications that were similar to those produced by tobacco consumption, including preeclampsia, fetal distress, forceps delivery and prolonged or preterm labor [15–18]. High levels of maternal anxiety or depression during pregnancy were also associated with neonatal health [19–21], specifically preterm birth and low birth weight [21–25]. As stated by [19], anxiety and depression influence obstetric outcomes.

Anxiety and/or depression have been related to tobacco consumption and smoking cessation in distinct populations, including pregnant women [26–30]. Higher levels of anxiety and/or depression were found in pregnant women who smoke [28,30–33]. Likewise, a recent review found that psychological factors play an important role in smoking cessation, and not suffering from depression is one of the major predictors of quitting during pregnancy [34].

Despite the strong association between tobacco consumption and anxiety or depression during pregnancy, these factors have been concurrently considered a small number of times when their effects on maternal and neonatal health were studied. Few studies have focused on examining the joint effect of maternal tobacco consumption and anxiety or depression during pregnancy, and results are somewhat controversial. Regarding depression, although Schechter et al. [35] found that exposure to tobacco consumption has a higher negative effect on the neonate's birth weight of mothers with co-occurring depression symptoms, no significant cumulative effect on the mother's depression in the effect of smoking during pregnancy was found on premature birth or low birth weight by Quispel et al. [36]. Regarding anxiety, a strong relationship has been independently found between anxiety and smoking and premature birth [37,38]. However, to our knowledge, the only study that evaluated the simultaneous effect of maternal anxiety and tobacco consumption on pregnancy complications showed controversial results, and no significant effect was found between tobacco consumption and pregnancy complications [39].

In sum, tobacco consumption and anxiety or depression have been concurrently considered few times when effects were studied on maternal and neonatal health, despite their similar effects and strong associations.

It is also worth pointing out that most of the studies that evaluate the consequences of smoking during pregnancy on maternal and neonatal health focused on comparing non-smokers and smokers, leaving aside the possible effect of quitting smoking during pregnancy, and the few studies that evaluate this effect focus on the neonate's weight [40,41]. To analyze the effects of quitting smoking on other aspects of maternal and neonatal health can be particularly relevant to promoting more effective health practices, specifically to the decision of health professionals to advise women to reduce or quit smoking during pregnancy, and to motivate pregnant women to quit smoking.

Taking this into consideration, this study aims to analyze the possible interaction effects between tobacco consumption during pregnancy (continuous, quitting and no consumption) and maternal anxiety or depression in the first trimester of pregnancy on maternal and neonatal health (pregnancy complications, delivery complications, neonatal health complications, gestational age and birth weight).

2. Materials and Methods

2.1. Procedure and Participants

The present research was conducted in accordance with the Helsinki Declaration and received previous approval from the Ethical Commission of all institutions involved (Ethical Board consent number 2010/299). This is a longitudinal study with three assessment waves: first trimester of pregnancy (M = 9.94 weeks; SD = 4.22), third trimester of pregnancy (M = 33.28 weeks; SD = 2.05), and 2 months postpartum (M = 7.39 weeks; SD = 0.86). Pregnant women attending primary public healthcare services in the northwest of Spain were recruited in the first trimester of pregnancy ($N = 901$). Women were eligible to participate if they were at least 18 years of age, were in the first trimester of pregnancy and spoke Spanish. The aims and procedures were explained and pregnant women who were willing to participate provided written informed consent. Two trained psychologists conducted the interviews individually.

Women completed a questionnaire on socio-demographic variables, health status, and tobacco consumption, and self-reported measures of anxiety and depression. Maternal anxiety and depression and tobacco consumption status (continuous, quitting or no consumption) were considered in the first trimester of pregnancy, in accordance with recent evidence in the literature indicating that the major adverse effects on fetus health and development may occur in the first trimester of gestation [5]. The first trimester is also the moment in which pregnant women usually decide to quit smoking [28,42]. Tobacco consumption was assessed in the three assessment waves by self-reported and biochemical tests. In the first trimester, socio-demographic data were also collected, while health variables related to pregnancy were evaluated in the third trimester. Information regarding delivery and the neonate's health was collected at 2 months postpartum.

The sample comprises 807 pregnant women (see Figure 1). From the 901 pregnant women recruited in the first trimester of pregnancy, 94 women were lost (10.4%) at 2 months postpartum: 28 had suffered a miscarriage, 29 could not be contacted, 4 refused to continue participating in the study and 33 pregnant women were excluded (23 women for changing consumption status after first trimester of pregnancy and 10 for consuming other substances).

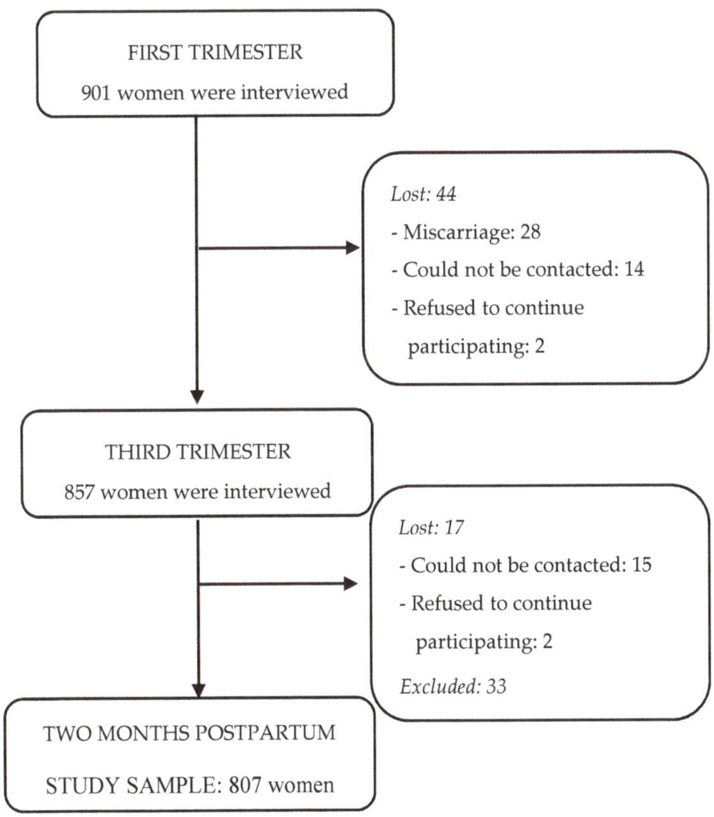

Figure 1. Flow diagram of recruitment and progress through study.

2.2. Measures

2.2.1. Socio-Demographic, Health and Tobacco Consumption Information

A questionnaire was used to collect information regarding socio-demographic and pregnancy-related aspects, consumption information, pregnancy and delivery complications (e.g., threat of abortion, placental problems, threat of premature birth, hemorrhage, fetal suffering), neonate's health problems (e.g., respiratory problems), gestational age at birth and birth weight.

2.2.2. Consumption Status

Pregnant women were classified into three groups based on their self-report of tobacco consumption and the result of the biochemical test: continuous smokers, continuous quitters and non-smokers. Women who maintained their consumption throughout the pregnancy were classified as continuous smokers. Women who reported quitting when they expected or confirmed they were pregnant and who maintained abstinence during pregnancy were classified as continuous quitters. Women who reported no smoking in the past or who reported quitting at least one year before they became pregnant were classified as non-smokers. In the first evaluation, pregnant women were asked if they had ever been smokers and if they had smoked before pregnancy. If the answer was yes, they were requested to indicate the number of cigarettes per day they smoked before pregnancy; if the answer was negative, they were requested to report how long they had gone without smoking. At all times of the evaluation, they were asked what was their current situation in relation to tobacco consumption using multiple answer options: never smoker, currently I do not smoke and I have quit during pregnancy, I am an occasional smoker or I am a daily smoker. At the postpartum evaluation, an alternative answer was added: I quit smoking during pregnancy but started smoking again. Likewise, at all times, it was requested that those who indicated that they had quit smoking, specified in which month they quit, and those women who defined themselves as smokers, indicated the number of cigarettes they smoked. Because the aim of the study was the effects of tobacco consumption status (continuous, quitting or no consumption) during pregnancy on maternal and neonatal health, women reporting changes in their consumption status after the first trimester of pregnancy ($n = 23$) were not included in the analyses.

Self-reports of smoking abstinence were biochemically verified through urinary cotinine by Cotinine Test Medi-marketing (cut-off 200 ng/mL) in the first trimester and through carbon monoxide (CO) in expired air in the third trimester and at 2 months postpartum (cut-off of 5 ppm) using a Carbon Monoxide Monitor (model Smokerlyzer Pico Simple; Bedfont Technical Instruments Ltd., Kent, UK).

2.2.3. Anxiety

The State Anxiety Scale (STAI-S) of the State–Trait Anxiety Inventory [43] was used to assess women's anxiety in the first trimester of pregnancy. The STAI-S consists of a 20-item scale designed to assess the current state of anxiety. The score ranges from 0 to 60 and higher scores indicate higher anxiety symptoms. The STAI-S Spanish version showed good internal consistency and proposed a clinical cut-off >31 to screen for high-anxiety in women. In the present study, the STAI-S showed excellent internal consistency ($\alpha = 0.94$).

2.2.4. Depression

The Edinburgh Postnatal Depression Scale (EPDS) was used to assess women's depression in the first trimester of pregnancy. The EPDS is a 10-item self-reported questionnaire designed to assess the intensity of depression symptoms within the previous 7 days [44]. The EPDS is the most widely used questionnaire to screen pregnancy and postpartum depression symptoms [28,45]. The EPDS Spanish version showed good internal consistency [46]. In the present study, the EPDS showed good internal consistency ($\alpha = 0.85$).

2.3. Data Analysis

Chi-square tests were performed to analyze the associations and the interaction effects between tobacco consumption status, anxiety or depression on pregnancy, delivery and neonatal health complications (dichotomic dependent variables). The MANCOVA was performed to analyze the interaction effects between tobacco consumption status, anxiety or depression (independent variables) on gestational age and birth weight (continuous dependent variables). The sociodemographic variables associated with the independent variables (marital status, parity, educational level and previous consumption) were included in the models as covariates. Pairwise comparisons were applied to assess within-group differences.

Data were analyzed with IBM SPSS 23.0 Windows version (PASW Statistics for Windows, SPSS Inc., Chicago, IL, USA). Statistical significance level was considered at $p < 0.05$.

3. Results

3.1. Participant Sociodemographic Characteristics

Participants' age ranged between 18 and 46 years old (M = 32.74 years; SD = 4.35) and most were married or cohabiting (83.8%). More than half had university studies (53.4%) and were employed (70.9%). In this sample, 28% smoked before pregnancy and their average of previous consumption was 10.88 (*SD* = 6.98). Most of the infants were the firstborn (65.9%), and were born with 37 weeks or more (96.0%) and with a normal weight (94.4%; M = 3274.99 g; SD = 547.50).

3.2. Associations between Tobacco Consumption, Anxiety or Depression, and Sociodemographic Characteristics

Significant associations were found between maternal tobacco consumption status and marital status, parity, educational level, professional status, and socioeconomic level. Significant associations were also found between maternal depression and educational level and between maternal anxiety and marital status (see Table 1).

3.3. Associations between Tobacco Consumption and Anxiety or Depression

Maternal tobacco consumption status was associated with anxiety ($\chi^2 = 15.18$, $p = 0.001$, Cramer's V = 0.14) and depression ($\chi^2 = 12.87$, $p = 0.002$, Cramer's V = 0.13) in the first trimester of pregnancy. Continuous smokers during pregnancy were more likely to present high anxiety (14.8% vs. 8.2% vs. 5.2%) and depression (18.8% vs. 9.2% vs. 8.3%) than continuous quitters and non-smokers. No significant differences were found between continuous quitters and non-smokers during pregnancy in the rates of high anxiety ($Z = 0.3$, $p = 0.748$) and depression ($Z = 0.1$, $p = 0.929$).

Table 1. Maternal socio-demographic characteristics, consumption status, anxiety and depression.

Socio-Demographic Characteristics	Mothers (N = 807)	Consumption Status				Anxiety			Depression		
	%	Continuous Smoker n = 128	Continuous Quitter n = 98	Non-Smoker n = 581	χ^2	Anxiety n = 57	No Anxiety n = 750	χ^2	Depression n = 81	No Depression n = 726	χ^2
Age											
18–34	63.3	64.8	68.4	62.1	1.56	61.4	63.5	0.10	59.3	63.8	0.64
≥35	36.7	35.2	31.6	37.9		38.6	36.5		40.7	36.2	
Marital status											
Single/divorced	16.2	24.2	17.3	14.3	7.71 *	29.8	15.2	8.33 *	34.6	14.2	22.26 ***
Married/living with partner	83.8	75.8	82.7	85.7		70.2	84.8		65.4	85.8	
Parity											
Primiparous	65.9	68.0	79.6	63.2	10.35 *	61.4	66.3	0.56	56.8	66.9	3.34
Multiparous	34.1	32.0	20.4	36.8		38.6	33.7		43.2	33.1	
Educational level											
Non-university (≤12 years)	46.6	75.8	50.0	39.6	55.74 ***	54.4	46.0	1.50	60.5	45.0	6.99 *
University (>12 years)	53.4	24.2	50.0	60.4		45.6	54.0		39.5	55.0	
Professional status											
Unemployed	29.1	39.1	26.5	27.4	7.31 *	31.6	28.9	0.18	32.1	28.8	0.39
Employed	70.9	60.9	73.5	72.6		68.4	71.1		67.9	71.2	
Socioeconomic level											
Medium-low	62.8	73.5	70.1	59.6	9.35 *	69.2	62.3	0.98	64.4	62.7	0.01
Medium-high	37.2	26.5	29.9	40.4		30.8	37.7		35.6	37.3	

* $p < 0.05$; *** $p < 0.001$.

3.4. Associations between Tobacco Consumption, Anxiety or Depression, and the Mother's and the Neonate's Health

Maternal tobacco consumption status was associated with pregnancy ($p = 0.014$, Cramer's V = 0.10) and delivery ($p < 0.001$, Cramer's V = 0.21) complications and neonatal health complications ($p = 0.025$, Cramer's V = 0.10). Continuous smokers during pregnancy were more likely to present pregnancy and delivery complications, and their neonates to present health complications than continuous quitters and non-smokers. No significant differences were found between continuous quitters and non-smokers on the rates of pregnancy (Z = 0.3, $p = 0.781$) and delivery (Z = 0.5, $p = 0.583$) complications, and neonatal health (Z = 0.5, $p = 0.645$) complications (see Table 2).

Significant differences were found in neonatal birth weight in accordance with maternal tobacco consumption status ($F_{(804)} = 5.53$, $p = 0.004$). Neonates of continuous smokers were born with lower weight than neonates of continuous quitters ($p = 0.049$) and neonates of non-smokers ($p = 0.003$), with no significant differences between the weight of neonates born to continuous quitters and non-smokers (3128.36 vs. 3294.39 vs. 3304.03). However, no significant differences were found in gestational age in accordance with tobacco consumption ($F_{(804)} = 5.53$, $p = 0.315$).

Regarding maternal anxiety and depression in the first trimester of pregnancy, high anxiety was associated with more delivery complications ($p = 0.040$, Cramer's V = 0.07) and depression was associated with more pregnancy complications ($p = 0.034$, Cramer's V = 0.08).

Significant differences were found in the neonate's weeks of gestation at birth in accordance with the mother's anxiety ($t_{(805)} = 2.52$, $p = 0.012$) and the mother's depression in the first trimester ($t_{(805)} = 1.35$, $p = 0.045$). Neonates of high anxiety or depressed mothers were born with less weeks of gestation than neonates of low anxiety or non-depressed mothers. No differences were found in birth weight according to the mother's anxiety ($t_{(805)} = 0.37$, $p = 0.713$) or depression ($t_{(805)} = 0.70$, $p = 0.484$) in the first trimester of pregnancy.

3.5. Interaction Effects between Tobacco Consumption Status and Anxiety or Depression on the Health of Mothers and Neonates

No significant interaction effects between maternal tobacco consumption status and anxiety were observed for pregnancy complications ($\chi^2 = 9.31$; $p = 0.097$).

Significant interaction effects between maternal tobacco consumption status and anxiety were observed for delivery complications (see Table 3). Continuous smokers with high anxiety (group 1) had more delivery complications than any other group (groups 2, 3, 4, 5 and 6). Continuous smokers with low anxiety (group 2) had more delivery complications than non-smokers with low anxiety (group 6). Both, continuous smokers with low anxiety (group 2) and continuous quitters with high or low anxiety (groups 3 and 4), had more delivery complications than non-smokers with high anxiety (group 5).

Significant interaction effects between maternal tobacco consumption status and anxiety were also observed for neonatal health complications. Neonates of continuous smokers with high anxiety (group 1) had more health complications than neonates of non-smokers, regardless of their level of anxiety (groups 5 and 6).

Significant interaction effects between maternal tobacco consumption status and anxiety were observed for gestational age at birth (see Table 4). Neonates of continuous smokers with high anxiety (group 1) were born after less gestational weeks than neonates of non-smokers with low anxiety (group 6). No significant interaction effect between maternal tobacco consumption status and anxiety were observed for birth weight ($F_{(802)} = 0.30$, $p = 0.596$).

Table 2. Association between consumption status, anxiety or depression, and health complications.

Health Complications	Consumption Status					Anxiety			Depression			Total
	Continuous Smoker (1)	Continuous Quitter (2)	Non-Smoker (3)	χ^2	Group Comparisons	Anxiety	No Anxiety	χ^2	Depression	No Depression	χ^2	
Pregnancy complications	21.1	9.2	12.4	8.55 *	1 > 2,3	15.8	13.2	0.31	21.0	12.5	4.49 *	13.4
Delivery complications	27.3	13.3	8.3	36.64 ***	1 > 2,3	19.3	11.3	3.2 *	9.9	12.1	0.35	11.9
Neonatal health complications	12.5	10.2	6.0	7.41 *	1 > 3	7.0	7.6	0.03	6.2	7.7	0.25	7.6

* $p < 0.05$; *** $p < 0.001$.

Table 3. Interaction effects between consumption status and anxiety or depression on health complications.

Health Complications	Continuous Smoker		Continuous Quitter		Non-Smoker		χ^2	Group Comparison
	Anxiety $n = 19$ **(1)**	**No Anxiety** $n = 109$ **(2)**	**Anxiety** $n = 8$ **(3)**	**No Anxiety** $n = 90$ **(4)**	**Anxiety** $n = 30$ **(5)**	**No Anxiety** $n = 551$ **(6)**		
Pregnancy complications	26.3	20.2	25.0	8.9	10.0	12.5	9.31	
Delivery complications	52.6	22.0	12.5	13.3	3.3	8.7	49.71 ***	1 > 2,3,4,5,6 2 > 6 2,3,4 > 5
Neonatal health complications	21.1	11.0	12.5	11.1	3.2	6.4	12.69 *	1 > 5,6
Health Complications	**Depression** $n = 24$ **(1)**	**No Depression** $n = 104$ **(2)**	**Depression** $n = 9$ **(3)**	**No Depression** $n = 89$ **(4)**	**Depression** $n = 48$ **(5)**	**No Depression** $n = 533$ **(6)**	χ^2	**Group Comparison**
Pregnancy complications	25.0	20.2	22.2	9.0	20.8	11.6	12.18 *	2 > 4,6
Delivery complications	25.0	26.9	11.1	13.5	2.1	9.0	35.22 ***	1 > 5,6 4 > 5
Neonatal health complications	8.3	13.5	11.1	11.2	8.3	6.0	9.63	

$* p < 0.05$; $*** p < 0.001$.

Table 4. Interaction of consumption status and anxiety or depression on weeks and weight at birth.

	Continuous Smoker		Continuous Quitter		Non-Smoker			
Weeks and Weight at Birth	**Anxiety (1) M (SD)**	**No Anxiety (2) M (SD)**	**Anxiety (3) M (SD)**	**No Anxiety (4) M (SD)**	**Anxiety (5) M (SD)**	**No Anxiety (6) M (SD)**	**F**	**Group Comparison**
Weeks of gestation	38.48 (3.37)	39.34 (1.34)	38.25 (1.91)	39.37 (1.41)	39.27 (1.23)	39.43 (1.50)	6.90 *	1 < 6
Birth weight	3066.84 (546.93)	3139.08 (455.64)	3273.75 (526.01)	3296.22 (550.85)	3358.33 (623.25)	3301.39 (556.25)	0.30	
Weeks and Weight at Birth	**Depression (1)**	**No Depression (2)**	**Depression (3)**	**No Depression (4)**	**Depression (5)**	**No Depression (6)**	**F**	**Group Comparison**
Weeks of gestation	38.40 (1.17)	39.11 (1.95)	38.70 (1.95)	39.38 (1.40)	39.21 (1.32)	39.44 (1.50)	6.21 *	1 < 6
Birth weight	3075.77 (485.40)	3138.68 (472.15)	3321.00 (490.04)	3287.28 (545.49)	3299.58 (575.96)	3304.75 (556.40)	1.08	

* $p < 0.05$.

Significant interaction effects between maternal tobacco consumption status and depression were observed for pregnancy complications (see Table 3). Non-depressed continuous smokers (group 2) had more pregnancy complications than non-depressed continuous quitters (group 4) and non-depressed non-smokers (group 6).

Significant interaction effects between maternal tobacco consumption status and depression were observed for delivery complications. Depressed continuous smokers (group 1) had more delivery complications than depressed (group 5) and non-depressed (group 6) non-smokers. Non-depressed continuous quitters (group 4) had more delivery complications than depressed non-smokers (group 5). No significant interaction effects between maternal tobacco consumption status and depression were observed for neonatal health complications ($\chi^2 = 9.63$; $p = 0.087$).

Likewise, significant interaction effects between maternal tobacco consumption status and depression were observed for weeks of gestation at birth (see Table 4). Neonates of depressed continuous smokers (group 1) were born after less gestational weeks than neonates of non-depressed non-smokers (group 6). No significant interaction effects between maternal tobacco consumption status and depression were found on birth weight ($F_{(802)} = 1.08$, $p = 0.398$).

4. Discussion

This study aimed to analyze the possible interaction effects between tobacco consumption during pregnancy and maternal anxiety or depression in the first trimester of pregnancy on the health of mothers and newborns. An association between maternal tobacco consumption and anxiety or depression in the first trimester of pregnancy was found. Maternal tobacco consumption status was associated with high anxiety as well as with depression, as previously noted in the literature [28,30–33]. Continuous smokers were more likely to present high anxiety and depression than continuous quitters and non-smokers in the first trimester of pregnancy. On the other hand, no significant differences were found between continuous quitters and non-smokers on rates of anxiety or depression. These results highlighted the possible beneficial impact of quitting smoking during pregnancy for the prenatal mental health of mothers.

An independent effect of maternal tobacco consumption, anxiety and depression during pregnancy on the health of mothers and neonates was found. Maternal tobacco consumption during pregnancy was associated with more pregnancy and delivery and neonatal complications, including low birth weight. Interestingly, maternal anxiety in the first trimester of pregnancy was associated with delivery complications, while maternal depression in the first trimester of pregnancy was associated with pregnancy complications.

Several studies have shown that tobacco consumption during pregnancy directly affects the health of both mothers and neonates throughout the perinatal period [2–9,47,48]. Tobacco consumption during pregnancy can lead to epigenetic changes that affect the health of mothers and neonates. One of the main mechanisms is through the impact of tobacco carbon monoxide. This component of tobacco can cause defective vascularization, placental hypertrophy and/or local hypoxia, which reduces uterine blood flow, increasing the risk of complications and restricting fetal growth [3]. Another important action mechanism is the effect of nicotine on the organism. This component has a vasoconstrictor effect and has also been related to the activation of the enzyme phospholipase A2, which is associated with undergoing abortions. However, during the postpartum period, the effects of tobacco on health do not exclusively affect the mother, as the nicotine can be transferred to the neonate through breast milk [11]. These data emphasize the negative effect of tobacco consumption on the course of pregnancy. Contrarily, no significant differences were found between continuous quitters and non-smokers on the studied maternal health complications, neither on neonatal weight at birth nor health complications. These results suggest that early and continued tobacco quitting during pregnancy could decrease maternal risks of suffering health problems during this period of life [40,41]. It should be noted that results (56.6% of women continue to smoke during pregnancy) indicate higher prevalence of smoking than other research carried out in Spain previously (27–42%) [49,50], although similar to the data provided by studies carried out in Europe (57–65%) [51,52]. These differences between prevalence may be due to the methodologies used. Spanish studies are retrospective and based on self-reports (methodology susceptible to bias due to social desirability), whereas the European ones are prospective and use biochemical validation of consumption. As with tobacco consumption, several studies have shown that maternal anxiety and/or depression negatively affect the health of both mothers and neonate throughout the perinatal period [15–18]. This study added that maternal anxiety and depression are specifically associated with different health complications and at different times. Maternal anxiety was found to be associated with complications related to delivery, while maternal depression seems to affect health complications arising during pregnancy. These results contribute to clarify the potential differential impact of maternal anxiety and depression on pregnancy and delivery complications, an issue that remained unclear in the literature [19]. Different underlying epigenetic and endophenotypic mechanisms were suggested to explain the effect of maternal anxiety and/or depression on the emergence of different types of complications. Several studies pointed out that the presence of anxiety or depression can be a stressor for pregnant women, stimulating the activation of different mechanisms, namely the hypothalamic axis (HPA), affecting the course of pregnancy [15,53]. Likewise, it could also affect the physiological development of the newborn by interfering with the levels of cortisol, norepinephrine and dopamine [16]. Experiencing high levels of anxiety or depression during pregnancy may contribute to an increase in hormones such as cortisol and catecholamines, which cause changes in immunologic functioning and uterine blood flow during human pregnancy, thus increasing vulnerability [18].

The results of the interaction effect between maternal consumption status and anxiety or depression suggested that different kinds of interactions were also found. Specifically, three different kinds of interactions were found. First, an interaction in which the fundamental role is of tobacco consumption, such as the results of the interaction effect between maternal consumption status and anxiety or depression on delivery complications. Second, an interaction in which the fundamental role is developed by anxiety or depression. Regarding neonatal health problems, the results of the interaction effect between maternal consumption status and anxiety or depression suggested that effects of tobacco consumption on the gestational age of neonates at birth only emerged when maternal consumption status was associated with anxiety or depression, as no independent effects of maternal consumption status were found. The neonates of continuous smokers with high anxiety or depression were born with fewer weeks than the neonates of non-smokers with no anxiety or no depression.

Finally, an interaction that suggested a cumulative effect of maternal anxiety in the first trimester of pregnancy on the effects of tobacco consumption status (continuous, quitting and no consumption) during pregnancy on the mother's health was also found. Continuous smokers with high-anxiety presented more delivery complications than continuous smokers with low-anxiety. This effect could be explained by the simultaneous activation of the mechanisms activated by tobacco consumption [3,11] and those activated due to the presence of anxiety [15–18]. However, no cumulative effects of anxiety or depression were found on pregnancy complications. This result suggested that the effect of maternal tobacco consumption can be so adverse that anxiety and depression did not increase the risks of pregnancy complications.

Altogether, these data highlighted the close relationship between tobacco consumption, the presence of psychological symptoms (anxiety or depression) and adverse health outcomes [39], being one of the few studies that jointly assess the effect of maternal tobacco consumption, anxiety or depression on health during pregnancy.

This study has certain limitations. Although the selected measures are those of international reference and have shown good internal consistency, anxiety and depression were evaluated with self-reports, which may imply different biases of social desirability, such as the concealment of symptoms. Likewise, pregnancy and delivery complications were evaluated dichotomously (presence or absence of complications), what can lead to bias in the interpretation of results and which does not allow for an in-depth study of these repercussions. In future studies, it would be relevant not only to assess the presence of complications, but also the number, type and severity of the same. Likewise, the sample was collected exclusively in public healthcare centers, which does not allow for the generalization of the results to all pregnant women, since women who attend private healthcare facilities could present different characteristics. Despite these limitations, this study presents several strengths. This is a longitudinal study that followed a large number of women during pregnancy and the early postpartum period. This allowed exploring possible interaction effects between the variables. Moreover, the cumulative effect of anxiety or depression in the effect of tobacco consumption was studied in different relevant aspects related to maternal and infant health in pregnancy and the early postpartum. Moreover, self-reports of tobacco abstinence were validated with biochemical tests. This is particularly relevant in this population due to the social pressure suffered by women not to smoke [54] and this may suppose that some women hide their consumption [55].

The results of this research have practical implications and could help to improve healthcare during pregnancy, as they highlight the importance of evaluating both the presence of tobacco consumption and the level of anxious and depressive symptoms during pregnancy. One of the main reasons for health professionals not to advise pregnant women to quit tobacco is the consideration that anxiety can increase after quitting smoking. However, quitting smoking reduces the risk of suffering anxiety and depression during pregnancy, as well as health risks. These data are proof of how quitting smoking can be beneficial both for the physical and psychological health of pregnant women as well as for the newborn itself. Data highlights the importance of advice during the perinatal period focusing on smoking cessation and not reducing cigarette consumption, since the former would lead to a lower prevalence of health problems (physical and psychological) in both women as well as their children.

5. Conclusions

This study suggests that there are different kinds of interaction effects between tobacco consumption and anxiety or depression on the health of mothers. The likelihood of health problems increases when mothers jointly present tobacco consumption and high anxiety. Specifically, a cumulative effect of anxiety and tobacco consumption on delivery complications was found. Likewise, a beneficial effect of quitting smoking was found both on the physical health of newborns and on the physical and psychological health of women. In particular, quitting smoking during pregnancy reduced the risk of suffering anxiety, depression and health complications.

Author Contributions: Conceptualization, M.C.M. and B.F.; data curation, B.P. and M.C.M.; formal analysis, B.P. and T.M.P.; investigation, B.P. and M.C.M.; methodology, B.P., B.F., T.M.P. and M.C.M.; supervision, B.F. and M.C.M.; writing—original draft, B.P.; writing—review and editing, B.P., B.F., T.M.P. and M.C.M. All authors have read and agreed to the published version of the manuscript.

Funding: This research received no external funding.

Acknowledgments: We would like to express our gratitude to the midwives at the surveyed primary healthcare centers for their valuable assistance. We appreciate the support of the research contract inherent to pre-doctoral research training funded by Axudas de Apoio a Etapa Predoctoral do Plan Galego 2011/2015 (Plan 12C) to the first author (Beatriz Pereira). Moreover, we sincerely appreciate the contribution made by Elizabeth Moss in revising the translation of this manuscript. Lastly, we would like to show our gratitude, especially to the pregnant women for their patience and generous collaboration in this study.

Conflicts of Interest: The authors declare no conflict of interest.

References

1. Homer, L.; Bernard, C.; Collet, M. Management and outcomes of pregnancies complicated by preterm premature rupture of membranes before 26 weeks of gestation. *Gynécol. Obstet. Fertil.* **2014**, *42*, 71–77. [CrossRef]
2. Héquet, D.; Ricbourg, A.; Sebbag, D.; Rossignol, M.; Lubrano, S.; Barranger, E. Placenta accreta: Screening, management and complications. *Gynécol. Obstet. Fertil.* **2013**, *41*, 31–37. [CrossRef]
3. Phelan, S. Smoking cessation in pregnancy. *Obstet. Gynecol. Clin. N. Am.* **2014**, *41*, 255–266. [CrossRef]

4. Shobeiri, F.; Jenabi, E. Smoking and placenta previa: A meta-analysis. *J. Matern. Fetal Neonatal Med.* **2017**, *30*, 2985–2990. [CrossRef]
5. Escobar-Padilla, B.; Perez-López, C.A.; Martínez-Puon, H. Risk factors and clinical features of ectopic pregnancy. *Rev. Med. Inst. Mex. Seguro Soc.* **2017**, *55*, 278–285. [PubMed]
6. Hyland, A.; Piazza, K.; Hovey, K.; Ockene, J.; Andrews, C.; Rivard, C.; Wactawski-Wende, J. Associations of lifetime active and passive smoking with spontaneous abortion, stillbirth and tubal ectopic pregnancy: A cross-sectional analysis of historical data from the women´s health initiative. *Tob. Control* **2015**, *24*, 328–335. [CrossRef]
7. U.S. Department of Health and Human Services. *The Health Consequences of Smoking—50 Years of Progress: A Report of the Surgeon General*; U.S. Department of Health and Human Services: Rockville, MD, USA, 2014.
8. Lee, S.W.; Han, Y.J.; Cho, D.H.; Kwak, H.S.; Ko, K.; Park, M.H.; Han, J.Y. Smoking exposure in early pregnancy and adverse pregnancy outcomes: Usefulness of Urinary Tobacco-Specific Nitrosamine Metabolite 4-(Methylnitrosamino)-1-(3-Pyridyl)-1-Butanol Levels. *Gynecol. Obstet. Investig.* **2018**, *83*, 365–374. [CrossRef]
9. Levy, D.; Jiang, M.; Szklo, A.; Almeida, L.M.; Autran, M.; Bloch, M. Smoking and adverse maternal and child health outcomes in Brazil. *Nicotine Tob. Res.* **2013**, *15*, 1797–1804. [CrossRef] [PubMed]
10. Ion, R.; Bernal, A.L. Smoking and preterm birth. *Reprod. Sci.* **2015**, *22*, 918–926. [CrossRef] [PubMed]
11. U.S. Department of Health and Human Services. *Women and Smoking: A Report of the Surgeon General*; U.S. Department of Health and Human Services: Rockville, MD, USA, 2001.
12. Timur, S.; Hotun, N.; Omac, M. Maternal smoking and newborn sex, birth weight and breastfeeding: A population-based study. *J. Matern. Fetal Neonatal Med.* **2017**, *30*, 2545–2550. [CrossRef]
13. Bruin, J.E.; Gerstein, H.C.; Holloway, A.C. Long-term consequences of fetal and neonatal nicotine exposure: A critical review. *Toxicol. Sci.* **2010**, *116*, 364–374. [CrossRef]
14. Jaddoe, V.; van Duijn, C.; van der Heiden, A.; Makenbach, J.; Moll, H.; Steegers, E.; Hofman, A. The Generation R Study: Design and cohort update 2010. *Eur. J. Epidemiol.* **2010**, *25*, 823–841. [CrossRef]
15. Bayrampour, H.; McDonald, S.; Tough, S. Risk factors of transient and persistent anxiety during pregnancy. *Midwifery* **2015**, *31*, 582–589. [CrossRef]
16. Diego, M.; Field, T.; Hernandez-Reif, M.; Cullen, C.; Schanberg, S.; Kuhn, C. Prepartum, postpartum, and chronic depression effects on newborns. *Psychiatry* **2009**, *67*, 63–80. [CrossRef]
17. Ding, X.X.; Wu, Y.L.; Xu, S.J.; Zhu, R.P.; Jia, X.M.; Zhang, S.F.; Huang, K.; Zhu, P.; Hao, J.H.; Tao, F.B. Maternal anxiety during pregnancy and adverse birth outcomes: A systematic review and meta-analysis of prospective cohort studies. *J. Affect. Disord.* **2014**, *159*, 103–110. [CrossRef]
18. Kelly, R.; Russo, J.; Holt, V.; Danielsen, B.; Zatzick, D.; Walker, E.; Katon, W. Psychiatric and substance use disorders as risk factors for low birth weight and preterm delivery. *Obstet. Gynecol* **2002**, *100*, 297–304. [CrossRef]
19. Alder, J.; Fink, N.; Bitzer, J.; Hösli, L.; Holzgreve, W. Depression and anxiety during pregnancy: A risk factor for obstetric, fetal and neonatal outcome? A critical review of the literature. *J. Matern. Fetal Neonatal Med.* **2007**, *20*, 189–209. [CrossRef] [PubMed]
20. Grote, N.; Bridge, J.; Gavin, A.; Melville, J.; Iyengar, S.; Katon, W. A meta-analysis of depression during pregnancy and the risk of preterm birth, low birth weight and intrauterine growth restriction. *Arch. Gen. Psychiatry* **2010**, *67*, 1012–1024. [CrossRef] [PubMed]
21. Staneva, A.; Bogossian, F.; Pritchard, M.; Wittkoeski, A. The effects of maternal depression, anxiety and perceived stress during pregnancy on preterm birth: A systematic review. *Women Birth* **2015**, *28*, 179–193. [CrossRef]
22. Liu, Y.; Murphy, S.K.; Murtha, A.P.; Fuemmeler, B.F.; Schildkraut, J.; Huang, Z.; Overcash, F.; Kurtzberg, J.; Jirtle, R.; Iversen, E.S.; et al. Depression in pregnancy, infant birth weight and DNA methylation of imprint regulatory elements. *Epigenetics* **2012**, *7*, 735–746. [CrossRef]
23. Fransson, E.; Ortenstrand, A.; Hjelmstedt, A. Antenatal depressive symptoms and preterm birth: A prospective study of a Swedish national sample. *Birth* **2011**, *38*, 10–16. [CrossRef]
24. Doktorchik, C.; Premji, S.; Slater, D.; Wiliamson, T.; Touh, S.; Patten, S. Patterns of change in anxiety and depression during pregnancy predict preterm birth. *J. Affect. Disord.* **2018**, *227*, 71–78. [CrossRef]
25. Shapiro, G.D.; Séquin, J.R.; Muckle, G.; Monnier, P.; Fraser, W.D. Previous pregnancy outcomes and subsequent pregnancy anxiety in a Quebec Prospective cohort. *J. Psychosom. Obstet. Gynecol.* **2017**, *38*, 121–132. [CrossRef]

26. Hauge, L.J.; Torgersen, L.; Vollrath, M. Associations between maternal stress and smoking: Findings from a population-based prospective cohort study. *Addiction* **2012**, *107*, 1168–1173. [CrossRef]
27. Irfan, M.; Hague, A.S.; Shahzad, H.; Samani, Z.A.; Awan, S.; Khan, J.A. Reasons for failure to quit: A cross-sectional survey of tobacco use in major cities in Pakistan. *Int. J. Tuberc. Lung Dis.* **2016**, *20*, 673–678. [CrossRef]
28. Míguez, M.C.; Pereira, B.; Figueiredo, B. Tobacco consumption and spontaneous quitting at the first trimester of pregnancy. *Addict. Behav.* **2017**, *64*, 111–117. [CrossRef]
29. Mykletun, A.; Overland, S.; Edvard, L.; Liabo, H.M.; Stewart, R. Smoking in relation to anxiety and depression: Evidence from a large population survey: The HUNT study. *Eur. Psychiatry* **2008**, *23*, 77–84. [CrossRef]
30. Tong, L.; Shi, H.L.; Zhang, Z.; Yuan, Y.; Xian, Z.J.; Jiang, X.X.; Xiong, X. Mediating effect of anxiety and depression on the relationship between Attention-deficit/hyperactivity disorder symptoms and smoking/drinking. *Sci. Rep.* **2016**, *29*, 21609. [CrossRef]
31. Maxson, P.; Edwars, S.; Ingram, A.; Miranda, M.L. Psychosocial differences between smokers and non-smokers during pregnancy. *Addict. Behav.* **2012**, *37*, 153–159. [CrossRef]
32. Orr, S.T.; Blazer, D.G.; Orr, C.A. Maternal prenatal depressive symptoms, nicotine addiction, and smoking-related knowledge, attitudes, beliefs, and behaviors. *Matern. Child Health J.* **2012**, *16*, 973–978. [CrossRef]
33. Smedberg, J.; Lupattelli, A.; Mardby, A.C.; Overland, S.; Nordeng, H. The relationship between maternal depression and smoking cessation during pregnancy—A cross-sectional study of pregnant women from 15 European countries. *Arch. Womens Ment. Health* **2015**, *18*, 73–84. [CrossRef]
34. Riaz, M.; Lewis, S.; Naughton, F.; Ussher, M. Predictors of smoking cessation during pregnancy: A systematic review and meta-analysis. *Addiction* **2018**, *113*, 610–622. [CrossRef]
35. Schechter, J.; Do, E.; Zhang, J.; Hoyo, C.; Murphy, S.; Kollins, S.; Fuemmeler, B. Effect of prenatal smoke exposure on birth weight: The moderating role of maternal depressive symptoms. *Nicotine Tob. Res.* **2018**, 267. [CrossRef]
36. Quispel, C.; Bangma, M.; Kazemier, B.M.; Steeger, E.A.; Hoogendijk, W.J.; Papatsonis, D.; Paarlberg, K.M.; Lambregtse-Van Den Berg, M.P.; Bonsel, G.J. The role of depressive symptoms in the pathway of demographic and psychosocial risks to preterm birth and small for gestational age. *Midwifery* **2014**, *30*, 919–925. [CrossRef] [PubMed]
37. Grimstad, H.; Schei, B.; Backe, B.; Jacobsen, G. Anxiety, psysical abuse and low birth weight. *Scand. J. Public Health* **1999**, *27*, 296–300. [CrossRef]
38. Pavlov, M.; Steiner, N.; Kessous, R.; Weintraun, A.Y.; Sheiner, E. Obstetric and neonate outcome in patients with anxiety disorders. *J. Matern. Fetal Neonatal Med.* **2014**, *27*, 1339–1342. [CrossRef]
39. Da Costa, D.; Brender, W.; Larouche, J. A prospective study of the impact of psychosocial and lifestile variables on pregnancy complications. *J. Psychosom. Obstet Gynaecol.* **1998**, *19*, 28–37. [CrossRef]
40. Benjamin-Garner, R.; Stotts, A. Impact of smoking exposure change on infant birth weight among a cohort of women in a prenatal smoking cessation study. *Nicotine Tob. Res.* **2013**, *15*, 685–692. [CrossRef]
41. Rode, L.; Kiaergaard, H.; Damm, P.; Ottensen, B.; Hegaard, H. Effect of smoking cessation on postpartum weight gain and neonatal birth weight. *Obstet. Gynecol.* **2013**, *122*, 618–625. [CrossRef]
42. Schneider, S.; Huy, C.; Schütz, J.; Diehl, K. Smoking cessation during pregnancy: A systematic literature review. *Drug Alcohol Rev.* **2010**, *29*, 81–90. [CrossRef]
43. Spielberger, C.D.; Gorsuch, R.L.; Lushene, R. *Manual for the State-Trait Anxiety Inventory*; Consulting Psychologist Press: Palo Alto, CA, USA, 1970; (Spanish version, Ediciones TEA: Madrid, 1982).
44. Cox, J.L.; Holden, J.M.; Sagovsky, R. Detection of postnatal depression: Development of the 10-item Edinburgh Postnatal Depression Scale. *Br. J. Psychiatry* **1987**, *150*, 782–787. [CrossRef]
45. Figueiredo, B.; Conde, A. Anxiety and depression in women and men from early pregnancy to 3-months postpartum. *Arch. Womens Ment. Health* **2011**, *14*, 247–255. [CrossRef]
46. Vázquez, M.B.; Míguez, M.C. Validation of the Edinburgh postnatal depression scale as a screening tool for depression in Spanish pregnant women. *J. Affect. Disord.* **2019**, *246*, 515–521. [CrossRef]

47. Chelchiwska, M.; Gajewska, J.; Maciejewski, T.M.; Mazur, J.; Oltarzewski, M.; Ambroszkiewicz, J. Associations between Maternal and Fetal Levels of Total Adiponectin, High Molecular Weight Adiponectin, Selected Somatomedins, and Birth Weight of Infants of Smoking and Non-Smoking Mothers. *Int. J. Environ. Res. Public Health* **2020**, *17*, 4781. [CrossRef] [PubMed]
48. Míguez, M.C.; Pereira, B. Repercusiones del consumo de tabaco activo y/o pasivo en el embarazo y postparto. [Effects of active and/or passive smoking during pregnancy and the postpartum period]. *Anales Pediatr.* **2020**, *93*. [CrossRef]
49. Cano, J.; Sánchez, M.; García, M.C.; Rabadán, B.; Yep, G. Tabaquismo durante el embarazo en mujeres de la Comunidad de Madrid. [Smoking during pregnancy in women of Madrid]. *Prev. Table* **2007**, *9*, 113–116.
50. Martínez-Frías, M.L.; Rodríguez, E.; Bermejo, E.; Grupo Periférico del ECEMC. Consumo de tabaco durante el embarazo en España: Análisis por años, comunidades autónomas y características maternas. [Tobacco smoking during pregnancy in Spain: An analysis according to years, autonomous communities and mother characteristics]. *Med. Clin.* **2005**, *124*, 86–92. [CrossRef]
51. Orton, S.; Bowker, K.; Cooper, S.; Naughton, F.; Ussher, M.; Pickett, K.; Leonardi-Bee, J.; Sutton, S.; Dhalwani, N.; Coleman, T. Longitudinal cohort survey of women's smoking behaviour and attitudes in pregnancy: Study methods and baseline data. *BMJ* **2014**, *4*, e004915. [CrossRef]
52. Balwicki, L.; Zarzecna-Baran, M.; Wierucki, L.; Jedrzejczyk, T.; Strahl, M.; Wrotkowska, M.; Goniewicz, M.L.; Zdrojewski, T. Smoking among pregnant women in small towns in Poland. *Int. J. Public Health* **2016**, *61*, 111–118. [CrossRef]
53. Pinto, T.M.; Caldas, F.; Nogueira-Silca, C.; Figueiredo, B. Maternal depression and anxiety and fetal-neonatal growth. *J. Pediatr.* **2017**, *93*, 452–459. [CrossRef] [PubMed]
54. Wigginton, B.; Lee, C. Stigma and hostility towards pregnant smokers: Does individuating information reduce the effect? *Psychol. Health* **2013**, *28*, 862–873. [CrossRef] [PubMed]
55. Míguez, M.C.; Pereira, B. Prevalence of smoking in pregnancy: Optimization of the diagnosis. *Med. Clín.* **2018**, *151*, 124–125. [CrossRef]

Publisher's Note: MDPI stays neutral with regard to jurisdictional claims in published maps and institutional affiliations.

International Journal of
Environmental Research and Public Health

MDPI

Article

Effects of Internet-Based Support Program on Parenting Outcomes for Primiparous Women: A Pilot Study

Lingling Huang [1,†], Qu Shen [2,†], Qiyu Fang [1] and Xujuan Zheng [1,*]

[1] Health Science Centre, Shenzhen University, Shenzhen 518060, China; huanglingling@szu.edu.cn (L.H.); fangqiyu320@szu.edu.cn (Q.F.)
[2] Department of Nursing, School of Medicine, Xiamen University, Xiamen 361102, China; shenqumail@163.com
* Correspondence: zhengxujuan@szu.edu.cn
† Lingling Huang and Qu Shen contributed equally for this manuscript.

Abstract: (1) *Background:* Some primiparous women are usually confronted with many parenting problems after childbirth, which can negatively influence the wellbeing of some mothers and infants. Evidence identified that internet interventions can include more tailored information, reach a larger research group, and supply more anonymity than face-to-face traditional interventions. Therefore, the internet-based support program (ISP) was designed to improve the parenting outcomes for Chinese first-time mothers. (2) *Methods*: A multicenter, single-blinded, pilot randomized controlled trial was conducted. From May to October 2020, a total of 44 participants were recruited in the obstetrical wards of two tertiary hospitals in China. Eighteen women in the control group received routine postnatal care; while eighteen women in the intervention group accessed to the ISP and routine postnatal care. The duration of intervention was not less than three months. Intervention outcomes were assessed through questionnaires before randomization (T0), immediately after intervention (T1), and three months after intervention (T2). The Self-efficacy in Infant Care Scale (SICS), Edinburgh Postnatal Depression Scale (EPDS), and Postpartum Social Support Scale (PSSS) were included to measure MSE, postpartum depression (PPD), and social support, respectively. (3) *Results:* No significant difference between the two groups were found in terms of the baseline social-demographic characteristics; and the scores of SICS, EPDS and PSSS at T0 ($p > 0.05$). Repeated measures multivariate analysis of covariance found that women in the intervention group had a higher MSE score at T1 (6.63, $p = 0.007$), and T2 (5.75, $p = 0.020$); a lower EPDS score at T1 (3.11, $p = 0.003$), and T2 (2.50, $p = 0.005$); and a higher PSSS score at T1 (4.30, $p = 0.001$); and no significant difference at T2 (0.35, $p = 0.743$), compared with women in the control group. (4) *Conclusion*: The effect of ISP was evaluated to significantly increase primiparous women's MSE, social support, and to alleviate their PPD symptoms. However, the small sample in pilot study restricted the research results. Therefore, the ISP should be further investigated with a larger, diverse sample to confirm whether it should be adopted as routine postnatal care to support primiparous women on parenting outcomes and mental wellbeing in the early stage of motherhood.

Keywords: pilot study; internet-based intervention; primiparous women; maternal self-efficacy; postpartum depression; social support

Citation: Huang, L.; Shen, Q.; Fang, Q.; Zheng, X. Effects of Internet-Based Support Program on Parenting OutComes for Primiparous Women: A Pilot Study. *Int. J. Environ. Res. Public Health* **2021**, *18*, 4402. https://doi.org/10.3390/ijerph18094402

Academic Editor: M.Carmen Míguez Varela

Received: 6 April 2021
Accepted: 18 April 2021
Published: 21 April 2021

1. Introduction

Due to the lack of parenting experience, some primiparous women frequently suffer from various parenting problems, such as unsuccessful parenting tasks and negative mother–infant interaction in the early stage of motherhood, which can negatively affect the physical and mental wellbeing of some mothers and infants [1–3]. As a significant indicator of parenting outcomes [3], maternal self-efficacy (MSE) refers to the belief that women hold of their capability about the performance of various parenting tasks [4]. Studies found that Chinese primiparous women had a lower level of MSE, compared with the samples in the USA [5], UK [6], Canada [7], and Finland [8,9].

Sound evidence identifies that some factors impact on MSE; and the main variables influencing MSE are postpartum depression (PPD) and social support [2,10,11]. Research showed that in comparison with Western women, Chinese new mothers were more prone to have PPD due to the high expectations of motherhood in Chinese culture and dealing with the sensitive relationship with mothers-in-law [12,13]. In terms of social support, Chinese primiparous women were reported to receive insufficient social support after delivery, and especially lacked adequate informational and appraisal support from health professionals on women's parenting tasks [13].

Some interventions were undertaken in order to improve primiparous women's parenting outcomes and mental health. For instance, the effects of mindfulness intervention on MSE, maternal wellbeing and mental distress were evaluated by a RCT (randomized controlled trial) for Spanish mothers [14]. The intervention was delivered during an eight-week meditation course, with a two-hour session once a week. Research found that primiparous women in the intervention group had a significantly higher MSE score, and experienced significantly less anxiety and stress, than women in the control group. The other RCT conducted in Mainland China was to explore the outcomes of an interpersonal psychotherapy-oriented education program including two 90-min face-to-face educational group meetings and a follow-up telephone during two weeks postpartum. In comparison of the control group, women in the study group were reported to have a significantly higher score of MSE, social support, and a lower score of PPD at 12 weeks postpartum [12,15].

These traditional face-to-face interventions were identified to have an effect in the improvement of parenting outcomes [10]; however, the large number of Chinese primipara, the inadequate funding for maternal health care and the deficiency of Chinese health professionals pose great challenges to the accessibility of these traditional approaches [16]. Therefore, the innovative, effective and feasible intervention methods should be considered. Evidence identified that internet interventions can include more tailored information, approach larger research population, and supply more anonymity than face-to-face traditional interventions [17–21]. In 2020, China News reported that the internet by a device of mobile or computer was available to 61% of the Chinese population [22]. To our knowledge, there has been no RCTS on parenting outcomes in Chinese primiparous women via the Internet [10]. Therefore, the internet-based support program (ISP) was designed to improve the Chinese primiparous women's parenting ability, mental wellbeing, and social support.

2. Materials and Methods

2.1. Study Design

The study protocol was published in JAN [10]. In this study, a multicenter, single-blinded, pilot RCT (randomized controlled trial) was used to assess the effects of ISP for Chinese first-time mothers during the early stage of motherhood, in regarding of the improvements of MSE, and social support; and the alleviation of PPD symptoms.

Ethical approval (2020011) was obtained from Shenzhen University. The trial was registered with the Chinese Clinical Trial Registry (ChiCTR2000033154). The researchers obtained all participants' consent form prior to data collection; and informed them of freedom to withdraw whenever they want. All collected data were kept anonymously and confidentially.

2.2. Participants

Eligible women met the criteria of 18 years old or above; being first-time mothers with healthy babies; having ability to response the questionnaires; and being available to the internet by mobile phone or computer. Women were excluded if they or their infants had serious diseases. From May to October 2020, a total of 98 women were approached, and 30 women were excluded as they did not meet the inclusion criteria, and 24 of them were declined. Finally, 44 participants were recruited when primiparous women admitted in maternity wards of two public tertiary hospitals in China; and were randomly assigned into the control group and the intervention group with allocation ratio as 1:1. Blinding was not possible for the researchers during all the research process; however, the group allocation was masked during the recruitment until the baseline measures are completed. Trial participants, outcome assessors, and data analysts were blinded to the participants' group allocation.

2.3. Intervention

Women in the control group received routine postnatal care; while women in the intervention group accessed to the ISP and routine postnatal care. Routine postnatal care consists of supports from the obstetricians and obstetric nurses during the 3–5 days hospitalization; and home visits from the community doctors on the 3rd, 7th, 14th, and 28th days postpartum [1]. The duration of intervention was not less than three months. Intervention outcomes were investigated via questionnaires before randomization (T0), immediately after the intervention (T1), and three months after the intervention (T2). The CONSORT [23] flowchart was illustrated in Figure 1. The ISP was developed according to the self-efficacy theory and the social exchange theory, which has five components including learning forum, communication forum, ask-the-expert forum, baby home forum, and reminder forum [10]. The detailed contents of the ISP were shown in Table 1. Participants in the intervention group were taught by the researchers to log in and use each components of the ISP. The duration and frequency of the logins were monitored to assess the adherence of participants. Reminder telephones or Wechat were conducted every week for reminding intervention group women to use the ISP, such as frequency logins at least twice one week, and total usage time no less than one hour per week.

2.4. Outcomes

2.4.1. Primary Outcomes

The primary outcome was MSE comparing the intervention and the control group at T1 and T2. MSE was assessed by the Self-efficacy in Infant Care Scale (SICS) [24]. It is a 46-item self-reported tool to assess the belief of women in their capability about the performance of various parenting tasks. Each item means one parenting task ranging from 0-100 points; and the higher mean score of SICS indicates the higher level of MSE. The internal consistency of SICS (Cronbach alpha = 0.95) was good for this study.

2.4.2. Secondary Outcomes

The secondary outcomes of this pilot study were PPD and social support. PPD was evaluated via the Edinburgh Postnatal Depression Scale (EPDS) [25]. The instrument has ten items using four-point Likert score; and its total score ranges from 0 to 30. The lower score means the better mental health status women have. The reported Cronbach's alpha coefficient of Chinese version EPDS was 0.87; and its concurrent validity was 0.79 with the BDI (Beck Depression Inventory) [26]. The internal consistency of the EPDS was 0.85 in the current research.

Social support was measured through the Chinese version of Postnatal Social Support Scale (PSSS). The 20-item instrument was to evaluate women's perception of support after delivery. The total score of PSSS ranges between 0 and 60 points; and a higher score the mother has, indicates the more social support she receives. The internal consistency of this tool was 0.89 [27]. In the present study, the Cronbach's alpha coefficient of PSSS was 0.90.

2.4.3. Other Outcomes

The baseline social-demographic characteristics of participants included the women's age, marital status, education, occupation, monthly family income, delivery mode, whether attending parenting training before childbirth, infant gender, infant health and infant fussiness by women's self-report.

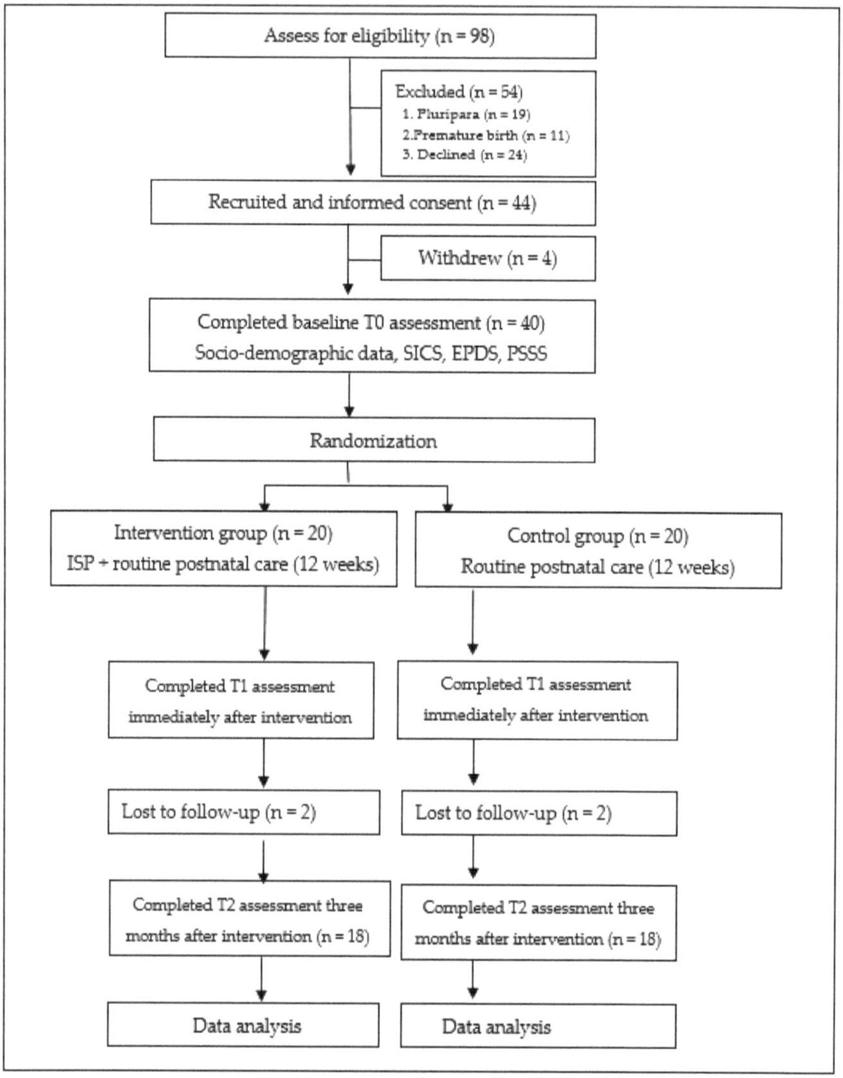

Figure 1. CONSORT (Consolidated Standard of Reporting Trials) flowchart of the Internet-based Support Program (ISP). SICS: the Self-efficacy in Infant Care Scale; EPDS: the Edinburgh Postnatal Depression Scale; PSSS: the Postpartum Social Support Scale.

2.5. Data Collection

The baseline assessment was conducted by the research team, and every participant completed the social-demographic data, SICS, EPDS, and PSSS in the maternity wards. At T1 and T2, the electronically questionnaires of SICS, EPDS, and PSSS were distributed to participants using email or WeChat; and the completed questionnaires were returned to the research team likewise via email or WeChat (Tencent, Shenzhen, China). In order to improve the response rate, participants received a kindly telephone or WeChat reminder before and after one week of T1 and T2 assessment.

Table 1. Contents and functions of the ISP.

Components	Functions	Contents
Learning forum	Educational function	✧ Infant common diseases ✧ First aid and safety care ✧ Daily care of infants ✧ Growth and development ✧ Breastfeeding and bottle feeding ✧ Postnatal care for women
Communication forum	Social function	✧ Parenting feeling, experiences, interactions, etc. ✧ Belonging and resonance of motherhood ✧ Topics discussion, such as doing the month and dealing with the relationship with mother-in-law
Ask-the-expert forum	Answering function	✧ Interaction between experts and mothers ✧ Questions' feedbacks ✧ Baby self-assess tools
Baby home forum	Recording function	✧ Baby growth and development record ✧ Baby early educational multimedia resources
Reminder forum	Reminder function	✧ Learning reminder ✧ Physical examination reminder ✧ Questionnaire filling reminder ✧ Immunization reminder

2.6. Data Analysis

The Statistical Package for Social Sciences (SPSS, IBM Corp, New York, USA) 22.0 was used for the data analysis. Descriptive statistics were used to describe the social-demographic characteristics and clinical variables by mean (M), standard deviation (SD), and frequency, proportions. To detect any significant difference between the intervention group and the control group on the social-demographic characteristics and baseline outcomes, the chi-square ($\chi 2$) for categorical variables and the independent sample t-test for continuous variables were used. The effect of intervention in terms of SICS, EPDS and PSSS was evaluated via repeated measures multivariate analysis of covariance to explore how outcomes has changed between groups; over time, and the interaction between group and time, adjusted through the corresponding baseline values.

3. Results

3.1. Baseline Characteristics

In the pilot study, 44 first-time mothers were recruited, and 40 of them completed baseline assessment and were randomly allocated into the two group. Finally, 18 women in the study group and 18 women in the control group completed the follow-up measurement (response rate: 81.8%).

No significant difference was found between the intervention and the control groups in terms of the baseline social-demographic characteristics; and the scores of SICS, EPDS and PSSS ($p > 0.05$) (Table 2).

3.2. Effectiveness of the ISP

Research found that compared with the control group, women in the intervention group had a higher MSE score at T1 (mean difference = 6.626, $p = 0.007$), and T2 (mean difference = 5.746, $p = 0.020$); a lower EPDS score at T1 (mean difference = 3.111, $p = 0.003$), and T2 (mean difference = 2.500, $p = 0.005$); and a higher social support score at T1 (mean difference = 4.302, $p = 0.001$); and no significant difference at T2 (mean difference = 0.350, $p = 0.743$) (Table 3).

Table 2. Comparison of socio-demographic characteristics and baseline outcomes between the groups.

Variables	Total (n = 40)	Intervention Group (n = 20)	Control Group (n = 20)	t/χ2 Value	p-Value
Maternal age, mean (SD)	27.25 (3.04)	27.15 (3.15)	27.35 (3.00)	0.013	0.908
Marital status, n (%)					
Married	40 (100)	20 (100)	20 (100)	0.000	1.000
Divorced	0 (0)	0 (0)	0 (0)		
Single	0 (0)	0 (0)	0 (0)		
Education, n (%)				0.178	0.915
Middle school or lower	9 (22.5)	5 (25)	4 (20)		
High school	15 (37.5)	7 (35)	8 (40)		
University or higher	16 (40.0)	8 (40)	8 (40)		
Occupation, n (%)				0.443	0.931
Professional	15 (37.5)	8 (40)	7 (35)		
Skilled	7 (17.5)	3 (15)	4 (20)		
Unskilled	11 (27.5)	6 (30)	5 (25)		
Unemployed	7 (17.5)	3 (15)	4 (20)		
Monthly family income, n (%)				0.503	0.778
<3000 yuan (US$420)	5 (12.5)	3 (15)	2 (10)		
3001–5000 yuan (US$420–700)	16 (40.0)	7 (35)	9 (45)		
>5000 yuan (US$700)	19 (47.5)	10 (50)	9 (45)		
Delivery mode, n (%)				0.582	0.748
Natural childbirth	22 (55)	12 (60%)	10 (50)		
Assisted childbirth	10 (25)	4 (20%)	6 (30)		
C-section	8 (20)	4 (20%)	4 (20)		
Whether attending parenting train, n (%)				0.000	1.000
Yes	18 (45)	9 (45)	9 (45)		
No	22 (55)	11(55)	11(55)		
Baby gender, n (%)				0.100	0.752
Boy	21 (52.5)	10 (50)	11 (55)		
Girl	19 (47.5)	10 (50)	9 (45)		
Baby health, mean (SD)	61.42 (18.13)	61.70 (16.76)	61.15 (19.83)	0.701	0.408
Baby fussiness, mean (SD)	49.57 (12.68)	50.20 (12.60)	48.95 (13.05)	1.636	0.209
SICS, mean (SD)	63.61 (7.13)	63.49 (7.17)	63.72 (7.27)	0.023	0.880
EPDS, mean (SD)	5.15 (2.33)	5.05 (2.54)	5.25 (2.15)	0.001	0.982
PSSS, mean (SD)	41.43 (2.78)	41.43 (2.78)	41.43 (2.86)	0.309	0.581

SICS: the Self-efficacy in Infant Care Scale; EPDS: the Edinburgh Postnatal Depression Scale; PSSS: the Postpartum Social Support Scale.

In both two groups, the MSE score of participants increased from T0 to T1, T0 to T2 ($p < 0.01$); and the increase was significantly higher for the intervention group women than for the control group women. There was no significant difference of EPDS score in the intervention group with the passage of time; however, there was the significant increased EPDS score in control group from T0 to T1 (mean difference = 3.889, $p < 0.001$), T0 to T2 (mean difference = 2.944, $p < 0.001$). The social support score in the intervention group had a significant increase from T0 to T1 (mean difference = 4.298, $p < 0.001$), and T0 to T2 (mean difference = 1.488, $p = 0.001$). By comparison, no such increase in social support score was found in control group as time went on. Figure 2 showed a graphical representation of the mean score change in parenting outcomes.

Table 3. Effect of the ISP on outcomes at immediately after the intervention (T1), and three months after the intervention (T2).

ISP Effect	Mean (SD) Intervention Group (n = 18)	Mean (SD) Control Group (n = 18)	Mean Difference (95% CI)	p-Value [a]
Outcomes				
MSE (SICS)				
T1	73.54 (6.38)	66.91 (7.52)	6.63 (1.90 to 11.35)	0.007
T2	72.87 (6.97)	67.12 (7.10)	5.75 (0.98 to 10.51)	0.020
Postpartum depression (EPDS)				
T1	6.11 (2.54)	9.22 (3.30)	−3.11 (−5.11 to −1.12)	0.003
T2	5.78 (2.23)	8.28 (2.66)	−2.50 (−4.17 to −0.83)	0.005
Social support (PSSS)				
T1	45.76 (3.85)	41.45(2.92)	4.30 (1.99 to 6.62)	0.001
T2	42.94 (3.39)	42.59 (3.13)	0.35 (−1.80 to 2.50)	0.743

ISP: Internet-based support program; SICS: Self-efficacy in Infant Care Scale; EPDS: Edinburgh Postnatal Depression Scale; PSSS: Postpartum Social Support Scale; [a]: All P values were calculated using repeated measures multivariate analysis of covariance

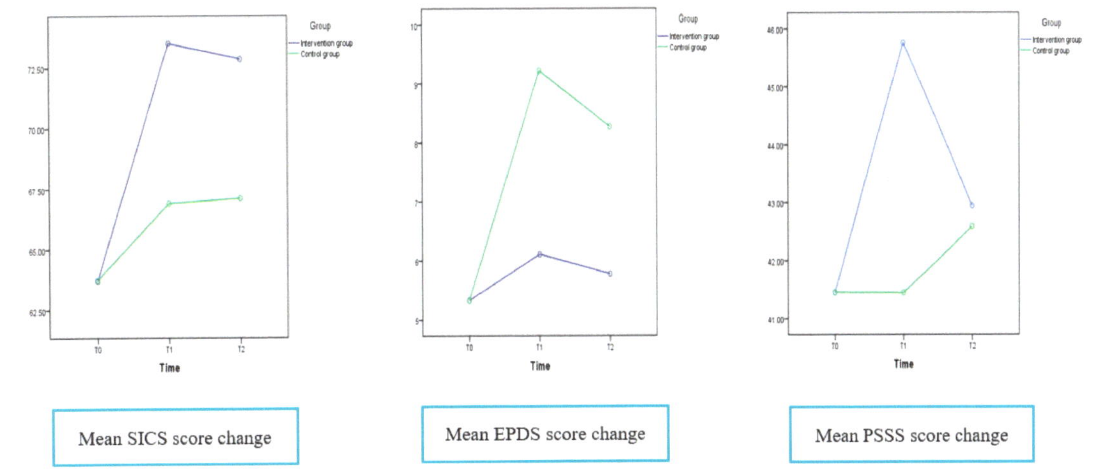

Figure 2. The mean score change in parenting outcomes of MSE, postpartum depression and social support. SICS: the Self-efficacy in Infant Care Scale; EPDS: the Edinburgh Postnatal Depression Scale; PSSS: the Postpartum Social Support Scale.

4. Discussion

The objective of this pilot study was to assess the effects of internet-based support program (ISP) to improve the Chinese primiparous women's parenting ability, mental wellbeing, and social support. Upon completing the ISP, primiparous women in the study group had a higher MSE score at T1 and T2; a lower EPDS score at T1, and T2; and a higher PSSS score at T1, in comparison with women in the control group.

The pilot study suggested that this ISP had the potential to improve the MSE level for primiparous women; and these beneficial effects could be sustained at three months after intervention, in keeping with previous research using face-to-face intervention methods [12,14,15]. Chinese primiparous women were reported to suffer from many parenting problems of unsuccessful parenting tasks and inefficient mother-infant interactions, significantly undermined the physical and mental wellbeing of women and infants [1,2]. In order to improve the parenting outcomes of new mothers, the intervention of ISP includes the various parenting knowledge and skills that taught via attractively multimedia resources from the learning forum and baby home forum; and the sharing parenting feeling and experience from the communication forum; and the instructional feedback from health professionals in the ask-the-expert forum; and the kindly suggestions from other mothers in the communication forum. These learning materials, sharing parenting experiences and various kinds of supports could effectively improve new mothers' parenting ability and confidence, supported by Bandura's theory [28]. The current research showed that in both two groups, the MSE score of participants increased from T0 to T1, T0 to T2, which were consistent with the prior study results that the mean MSE scores of women increased with the passage of time [2,29,30]. However, the increase was significantly higher for the intervention group women than the control group women. The results likewise demonstrated the effect of ISP on the improvement of MSE levels.

The previous studies found that a higher proportion of Chinese primiparous women were prone to have PPD, compared with the women in Western country [1,2]. In this research, the ISP was identified to significantly alleviate PPD for first-time mothers in the intervention group; and the positive outcomes on PPD could be sustained at three months after intervention. As researchers argued that the ISP could improve women's psychological wellbeing by the promotion of mothers' capability to successfully fulfill varied parenting tasks; initiatively mediate their mood and positively deal with the relationship with mother-in-law [10]. In our study, there was the significant increased EPDS score in control group from T0 to T1, and the decreased EPDS score from T1 to T2, which was consistent with the previous research [2,30]. As reported, PPD was identified to have a peak incidence at about six to eight weeks postpartum; and its symptoms would remit with the passage to time [31,32]. However, the alleviation of PPD as time went on was too little to have clinical significance [1,2]. Thus, the ISP is strongly recommended to improve primiparous women 's mental status after childbirth.

In the present study, the ISP was reported to enhance social support level for primiparous women; however, the effects were not sustained at three months after intervention, inconsistent with the prior findings [12,15]. For example, women in the intervention group had a higher social support score at T1 than women in the control group; but no significant difference at T2. No longer-term effects of the ISP on social support for primiparous women may be because the sample of pilots study was too small to identify the outcomes on social support. Moreover, the possible explanation was that women could access the ISP only for three months, and the intervention program could cause little residual advantage on social support at six months postpartum. Therefore, suggesting women to retain the ISP access in longer-term may lead to different social support outcomes [33].

The strengths of the research were the sound theoretical framework of ISP, the rigorous research design, and the methodological rigor in data collection and analysis. However, some limitations need to be noted. Firstly, it was not possible to blind researchers during all the research process, which could produce the potential biases. Secondly, the research only approached the participants who were available to the internet, limiting the generalizability of research results. Thirdly, the pilot sample was small which restricted the results. The larger sample RCT study needs to be conducted to further identify the intervention outcomes.

5. Conclusions

The research contributed to the practical and scientific knowledge of new parenting intervention method. The effect of ISP was evaluated to significantly increase the levels of MSE, social support, and alleviate PPD symptoms for first-time mothers. However, the small sample in pilot study restricted the research results. Therefore, the ISP should be further investigated with a larger, diverse sample to confirm whether it should be adopted as routine postnatal care to support primiparous women on parenting outcomes and mental wellbeing in the early stage of motherhood.

Author Contributions: Conceptualization, X.Z.; methodology, X.Z.; investigation, L.H., Q.S., Q.F. and X.Z.; data analysis, X.Z., L.H. and Q.S.; writing—original draft preparation, X.Z.; writing—review and editing, X.Z.; project administration, X.Z.; funding acquisition, X.Z. All authors have read and agreed to the published version of the manuscript.

Funding: This pilot study was funded by the Natural Science Foundation of China youth project (81703234), the Medical Science and Technology Research Fund project of Guangdong Province (A2018335), the Basic Research Free Exploration Project of Shenzhen City (JCYJ20180305163459491), the General Program of Stable Support Plan for Universities in Shenzhen City (20200804101756002), and the SZU Top Ranking Project (86000000210).

Institutional Review Board Statement: The study was conducted according to the guidelines of the Declaration of Helsinki, and approved by the Ethics Committee of Health Science Centre, Shenzhen University (2020011 and 05.2020).

Informed Consent Statement: Informed consent was obtained from all subjects involved in the study.

Data Availability Statement: The data presented in this study are available on request from the corresponding author. The data are not publicly available due to privacy restrictions.

Acknowledgments: We would like to thank all primiparous women in the research.

Conflicts of Interest: The authors declare no conflict of interest.

References

1. Zheng, X.J.; Morrell, J.; Watts, K. An Exploration of Factors Which Influence Maternal Self-Efficacy in Primiparous Women in China during the Initial Postnatal Period. Ph.D. Thesis, The University of Nottingham, Nottingham, UK, 2015.
2. Zheng, X.J.; Morrell, J.; Watts, K. Changes in maternal self-efficacy, postnatal depression symptoms and social support among Chinese primiparous women during the initial postpartum period: A longitudinal study. *Midwifery* **2018**, *62*, 151–160. [CrossRef]
3. Li, X.W.; Liu, Y. Parent-Grandparent Coparenting Relationship, maternal parenting self-efficacy, and young children's social competence in Chinese urban families. *J. Child Fam. Stud.* **2019**, *28*, 1145–1153. [CrossRef]
4. Montigny, F.; Lacharite, C. Perceived parental self-efficacy: Concept analysis. *J. Adv. Nurs.* **2005**, *49*, 387–396. [CrossRef]
5. Fulton, J.M.; Mastergeorge, A.M.; Steele, J.S.; Hansen, R. Maternal perceptions of the infant: Relationship to maternal self-efficacy during this first six week's postpartum. *Infant. Ment. Health J.* **2012**, *33*, 329–338. [CrossRef]
6. Whittaker, K.A.; Cowley, S. A survey of parental self-efficacy experiences: Maximising potential through health visiting and universal parenting support. *J. Clin. Nurs.* **2012**, *21*, 3276–3286. [CrossRef] [PubMed]
7. Pierce, T.; Boivin, M.; Frenettea, E.; Forget-Duboisa, N.; Dionnea, G.; Tremblayb, R.E. Maternal self-efficacy and hostile-reactive parenting from infancy to toddlerhood. *Infant Behav. Dev.* **2010**, *33*, 149–158. [CrossRef]
8. Salonen, A.H.; Kaunonen, M.; Astedt-Kurkip, P.; Järvenpää, A.L.; Isoaho, H.; Tarkka, M.T. Parenting self-efficacy after childbirth. *J. Adv. Nurs.* **2009**, *65*, 2324–2336. [CrossRef]
9. Salonen, A.H.; Kaunonen, M.; Astedt-Kurki, P.; Järvenpää, A.L.; Isoaho, H.; Tarkka, M.T. Effectiveness of an internet-based intervention enhancing Finnish parents' parenting satisfaction and parenting self-efficacy during the postnatal period. *Midwifery* **2011**, *27*, 832–841. [CrossRef]
10. Zheng, X.J.; Huang, L.L.; Fang, Q.Y.; Zhang, Y.; Zhang, Y.; Li, X.L.; Ye, Z.W.; Wang, Q. Internet-based support program on parenting outcomes for Chinese primiparous women: Study protocol for a randomized controlled trial. *J. Adv. Nurs.* **2020**, *76*, 1–9. [CrossRef]
11. Wang, Q.; Zhang, Y.; Li, X.L.; Ye, Z.W.; Huang, L.L.; Zhang, Y.; Zheng, X.J. Exploring maternal self-efficacy of first-time mothers among rural-to-urban floating women: A quantitative longitudinal study in China. *Int. J. Environ. Res. Public Health* **2021**, *18*, 2793. [CrossRef] [PubMed]
12. Gao, L.L.; Chan, S.W.; Sun, K. Effects of an interpersonal-psychotherapy-oriented childbirth education program for Chinese first-time childbearing women at 3-month follow-up: Randomized controlled trial. *Int. J. Nurs. Stud.* **2012**, *49*, 274–281. [CrossRef]
13. Zheng, X.J.; Morrell, J.; Watts, K. A quantitative longitudinal study to explore factors which influence maternal self-efficacy among Chinese primiparous women during the initial postpartum period. *Midwifery* **2018**, *59*, 39–46. [CrossRef]
14. Perez-Blasco, J.; Viguer, P.; Rodrigo, M.F. Effects of a mindfulness-based intervention on psychological distress, well-being, and maternal self-efficacy in breast-feeding mothers: Results of a pilot study. *Arch. Women Ment. Health* **2013**, *16*, 227–236. [CrossRef]
15. Gao, L.L.; Sun, K.; Chan, S.W. Social support and parenting self-efficacy among Chinese women in the perinatal period. *Midwifery* **2014**, *30*, 532–538. [CrossRef]
16. Zhu, J.M.; Ebert, L.; Liu, X.Y.; Chan, W.C. A mobile application of breast cancer e-support program versus routine care in the treatment of Chinese women with breast cancer undergoing chemotherapy: Study protocol for a randomized controlled trial. *BMC Cancer* **2017**, *17*, 291. [CrossRef]
17. Van den Berg, S.W.; Gielissen, M.F.; Ottevanger, P.B.; Prins, J.B. Rationale of the BREAst cancer e-healTH [BREATH] multicentre randomised controlled trial: An internet-based self-management intervention to foster adjustment after curative breast cancer by decreasing distress and increasing empowerment. *BMC Cancer* **2012**, *12*, 394. [CrossRef]
18. Li, Z.Y.; Tse, M.; Tang, A. The effectiveness of a dyadic pain management program for community-dwelling older adults with chronic pain: A pilot randomized controlled trial. *Int. J. Environ. Res. Public Health* **2020**, *17*, 4966. [CrossRef]
19. Friesen, N.L.; Hadjistavropoulos, D.H.; Schneider, H.L.; Alberts, M.N.; Titov, F.N.; Dear, F.B. Examination of an internet-delivered cognitive behavioural pain management course for adults with fibromyalgia: A randomized controlled trial. *PAIN* **2017**, *158*, 593–604. [CrossRef]
20. Natalie, K.; Jessica, S.; Shivani, U.; Mathew, A.J.; Adrian, R.A.; Gavin, A.; Jill, M.N. Transdiagnostic internet-delivered CBT and mindfulness-based treatment for depression and anxiety: A randomized controlled trial. *Internet Interv.* **2020**, *20*, 100310.
21. Lee, C.S.; Vellone, E.; Lyons, K.S.; Cocchieri, A.; Bidwell, J.T.; D'Agostino, F.; Hiatt, S.O.; Alvaro, R.; Buck, H.G.; Riegel, B. Patterns and predictors of patient and caregiver engagement in heart failure care: A multi-level dyadic study. *Int. J. Nurs. Stud.* **2015**, *52*, 588–597. [CrossRef] [PubMed]
22. China News 2020. Big Data of Chinese Netizens' Behavior. Available online: https://news.sina.cn/2019-02-20/detail-ihqfskcp7055720.d.html (accessed on 7 March 2021). (In Chinese).
23. Schulz, K.F.; Altman, D.G.; Moher, D. CONSORT 2010 statement: Updated guidelines for reporting parallel group randomised trials. *Int. J. Surg.* **2011**, *9*, 672–677. [CrossRef]
24. Prasopkittikun, T.; Tilokskulchai, F. Self-efficacy in Infant Care Scale: Revision and further. *Nurs. Health Sci.* **2010**, *12*, 450–455. [CrossRef]
25. Cox, J.L.; Holden, J.M.; Sagovsky, R. Detection of postnatal depression: Development of the 10-item Edinburgh postnatal depression scale. *Br. J. Psychiatry.* **1987**, *150*, 782–786. [CrossRef]
26. Wang, Y.Q.; Guo, X.J.; Lau, Y.; Chan, K.S.; Yin, L.; Chen, J. Psychometric evaluation of the Mainland Chinese version of the Edinburgh postnatal depression scale. *Int. J. Nurs. Stud.* **2009**, *46*, 813–823. [CrossRef]

27. Lu, H.; Zheng, X.X. The relationship between social support and postnatal depression of primiparous women. *Chin. J. Nurs.* **2001**, *36*, 731–733. (In Chinese)
28. Bandura, A. *Self-Efficacy: The Exercise of Control*, 1st ed.; Freeman and Co.: New York, NY, USA, 1997.
29. Zang, S.M.; Sheng, Y. Study on influencing factors of maternal self-efficacy in primiparous women. *Chin. J. Mod. Nurs.* **2010**, *16*, 2980–2982. (In Chinese)
30. Porter, C.H.; Hsu, H.C. First-time mothers 'perceptions of efficacy during the transition to motherhood: Links to infant temperament. *J. Fam. Psychol.* **2003**, *17*, 54–64. [CrossRef]
31. Gavin, N.I.; Gaynes, B.N.; Lohr, K.N.; Meltzer-Brody, S.; Gartlehner, G.; Swinson, T. Perinatal depression: A systematic review of prevalence and incidence. *Obstet. Gynecol.* **2005**, *106*, 1071–1083. [CrossRef]
32. Hewitt, C.; Gilbody, S.; Brealey, S.M.; Paulden, M.; Palmer, S.; Mann, R.; Green, J.; Morrell, J.; Barkham, M.; Light, K.; et al. Methods to identify postnatal depression in primary care: An integrated evidence synthesis and value of information analysis. *Health Technol. Assess.* **2009**, *13*, 1–145. [CrossRef]
33. Zhu, J.M.; Ebert, L.; Liu, X.Y.; Wei, D.; Chan, W.C. Mobile Breast Cancer e-Support Program for Chinese Women With Breast Cancer Undergoing Chemotherapy (Part 2): Multicenter Randomized Controlled Trial. *JMIR mHealth uHealth* **2018**, *6*, e104. [CrossRef]

International Journal of
Environmental Research and Public Health

MDPI

Article

Chinese Women's Acceptance and Uptake of Referral after Screening for Perinatal Depression

Wenjie Gong [1,2,3], Xin Jin [1], Kar Keung Cheng [2], Eric D. Caine [3], Richard Lehman [2] and Dong (Roman) Xu [4,*]

1 Xiangya School of Public Health, Central South University, 110 Xiangya Road, Changsha 410078, China; gongwenjie@csu.edu.cn (W.G.); jinx0423@csu.edu.cn (X.J.)
2 Institute and of Applied Health Research, University of Birmingham, Birmingham B15 2TT, UK; K.K.Cheng@bham.ac.uk (K.K.C.); R.Lehman@bham.ac.uk (R.L.)
3 Department of Psychiatry, University of Rochester, 300 Crittenden Blvd, Rochester, NY 14642, USA; eric_caine@urmc.rochester.edu
4 Global Health and Health System, ACACIA Labs and Department of Health Management, School of Health Management, Southern Medical University, 1023 South Shatai Road, Guangzhou 510515, China
* Correspondence: romanxu@i.smu.edu.cn

Received: 7 October 2020; Accepted: 18 November 2020; Published: 23 November 2020

check for updates

Abstract: China recently issued a national plan on perinatal depression (PND) screening. Previous studies elsewhere suggested that uptake of referral after screening for PND is suboptimal, but little is known in China. In this cohort study including 1126 women in Hunan, we identified women at a high risk of PND using the Edinburgh Postpartum Depression Scale (EPDS) over multiple time points. We texted them and offered free consultations with a psychiatrist/psychologist. Among 248 screen-positive women, only three expressed interest and one attended the appointment. We surveyed the women about their reasons for declining referrals and preferred means of care. Of the 161 respondents, 128 (79.5%) indicated that they could cope with the condition without professional assistance and 142 (88.2%) chose their families as the preferred source of help. Only 15 (9.3%) chose professionals as their first option. Implementing a referral policy for screen-positive women would mean approximately one-third of women who gave birth in China would be eligible. Our result argues against referring all screen-positive women for professional services at this time. Interventions should instead build upon the tradition of family support in a more engaged response. These considerations are relevant for the implementation of national screening for PND in China.

Keywords: perinatal depression; routine screening; referral; preferences for care; mental health

1. Introduction

On 11 September, 2020, the National Health Commission of China (NHC) issued a work plan to introduce screening for depression during pregnancy and childbirth to routine pregnancy tests and postpartum visits [1]. Depression during pregnancy and childbirth, also known as perinatal depression (PND), is a public health problem that encompasses clinically significant depressive conditions occurring during pregnancy or within the first 4–6 weeks after delivery. The reported prevalence of PND in low- and middle-income countries is 15.6% antenatally and 19.8% postnatally [2]. In mainland China, the prevalence was estimated to be 16.3% [3]. Negative consequences for the mother and, in turn, for her infant and family may include impaired mother–infant attachment with resulting impact on healthy child development, suicidal thinking, and, in the extreme, suicide [4–6]. Health agencies in the EU, the U.S., and other developed countries recommend regular screening of pregnant and post-partum women to detect symptoms suggestive of PND [7–12].

PND screening alone, although potentially increasing the identification of symptomatic women, is not sufficient for improving health outcomes if it does not lead to timely referrals and effective interventions. A previous systematic review found that only 22% (13.8–33.0%) of women who screened positive for PND received at least one mental health visit when referred to care. Higher acceptance rates followed additional interventions, including resource provision to women, perinatal care provider training, on-site assessment, and access to mental health consultation for perinatal care providers. All 17 studies included in this review were conducted in economically developed countries, with 13 from the United States [13]. We updated this review and found 41 studies related to the acceptance of referral after PND screening [14]. Only two were not conducted in high-income countries; they were from South Africa and Turkey. We could not find any study from mainland China.

In 2019, there were approximately 14.65 million births in China [15], with an estimated 5.06 million (34.53%) women who would have been screen-positive for PND if the Patient Health Questionnaire-9 (PHQ-9) was used as a screening instrument (which was recommended in the work plan) [16]. Whether the large number of women affected would accept the results of the screening, whether they would be referred, and whether they would accept help will directly determine the effectiveness of the previously mentioned work plan. A large majority of the women follow Chinese customary practices during the postpartum period, especially the tradition of "doing the month"—a socially prescribed period of rest and restraint when women are confined to their homes and strictly limited in their activities, while their mothers or mothers-in-law take charge of their wellbeing and that of the newborn [17,18]. This practice is deeply entrenched in Chinese culture and is different in many ways from Western cultures [17–19] and is likely to affect the attitudes and responses to referral for PND. In this study, we sought to assess whether women who screen positive for PND during or after pregnancy would accept an offer of a mental health consultation. We also explored their preferences for support from the health service and other sources.

2. Materials and Methods

2.1. Participants

This study was part of a cohort study that examined the incidence, detection, trajectory, and correlates of depression among women from the first trimester of pregnancy through 6 weeks postpartum, with a maximum of seven assessments [20]. The study received approval from the institutional review board of the Institute of Clinical Pharmacology of Central South University (No.CTXY-140002-2). During 6 consecutive months, we approached every pregnant woman, gestation ≤ 12 weeks, in two collaborating maternal and child hospitals in Hunan Province, PRC: the major provincial teaching hospital located in the capital, Changsha (a city of approximately 7.9 million), and a second county-level institution in Yiyang (population approximately 4.3 million). Both hospitals draw people from urban and surrounding rural areas. All participants provided informed consent. In total, 1126 women were recruited from September 2016 to February 2017.

2.2. Procedures and Outcome

Trained research staff collected basic socioeconomic and demographic information at the time of participant recruitment.

Identifying individuals reporting symptoms consistent with what we labeled as having "high risk" of perinatal depression was the primary objective of our study. We screened participants with the Edinburgh Postpartum Depression Scale (EPDS), which was administered prenatally at (approximately) weeks 12, 20, 24, 32, and 38; within one week after delivery; and at 42 days postpartum when women returned for a routine follow-up appointment (Figure 1). For this study, we set the following more stringent criteria for inclusion as high risk compared to the typical cut-off score of 10 or more: (1) women scoring 13 or more at least twice (consecutively or non-consecutively) or (2) a positive response to EPDS item 10 on any survey, indicating suicidal thoughts or (3) both.

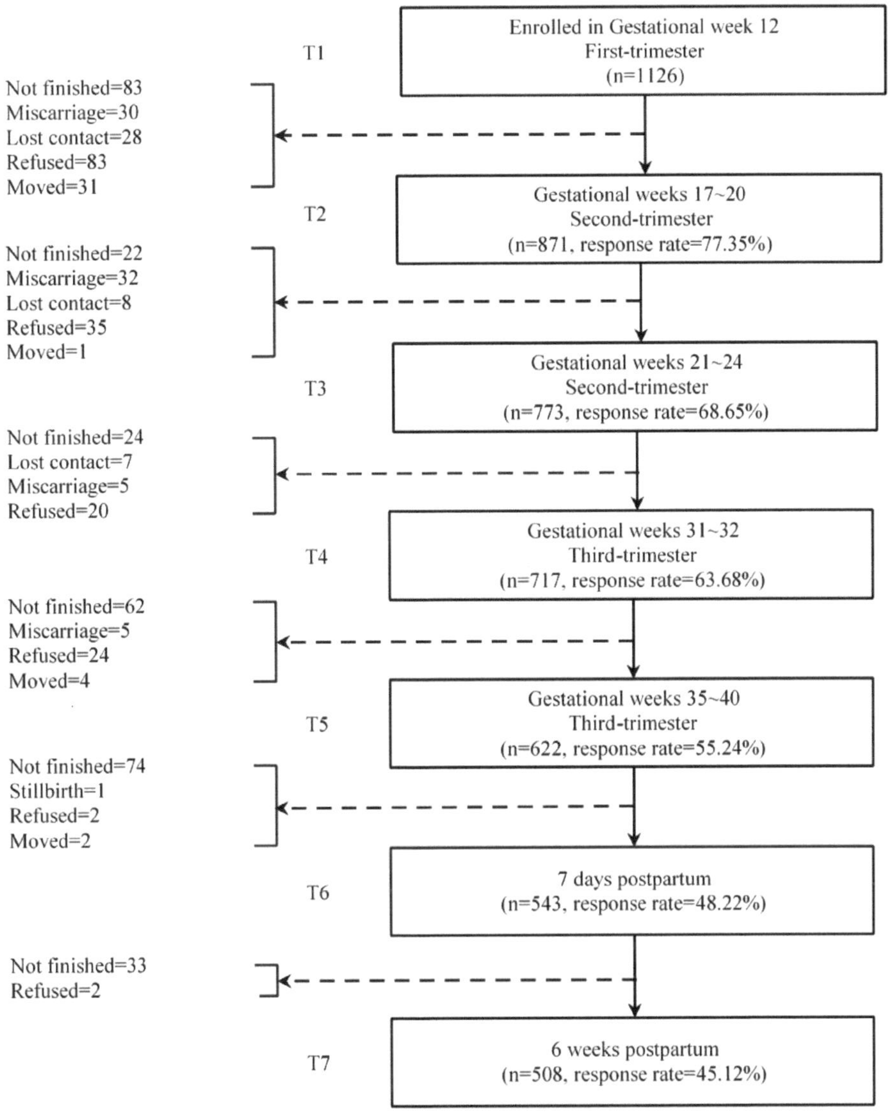

Figure 1. Flow chart of the cohort study.

We sent each screen-positive respondent an alert message by text (all participants consented to contact) to inform them of their results if the pregnant women met the criteria for high risk and offered a consultation with psychiatrists or psychologists. The alert message stated: "Thank you for participating in our screening project. We found that you have a high score for the screening, which indicates a heightened risk for depression. You do not need to panic as this high score may be due to changes in hormones and environment. Timely consultation with health specialists may help you obtain expert advice on improving your situation. If you need any assistance in a referral or more relevant information, please contact us at [phone number]." If individuals ignored our initial alert, we resent it a week later.

For those having no response after two alerts, we sent a text message connecting them to an anonymous online survey that we developed to understand their reasons for not seeking referrals. Questions included: (1) What did you feel when you received our message (i.e., surprised, suspicious, or accepting)? (2) What prevents you from asking for further information (i.e., stigma, cost, or medication side effect)? (3) Would you visit a psychiatrist/psychologist if we made an appointment for you? If not, why? (4) Would you like to use a smart-phone therapeutic application to treat depression? Why not? (5) What resource of help would you want to get to deal with the depression (i.e., family, specialist, or social worker)? In this survey, questions 2–5 asked respondents to rank their reasons/resources by placing options in order of preference. The average ranking score (a continuous variable starting from 0) was calculated for each option, with a higher score indicative of a stronger overall preference for a specific choice [21]. The last survey link was sent in August 2017.

2.3. Analysis

We conducted descriptive analyses of the data, which are presented as tables and figures. When necessary, appropriate statistical tests were performed. We asked people to sort reasons in order of importance for questions 2–5. We calculated a ranking score for those items—a higher score indicating the weighted higher frequency of selecting this item by the respondents (Σ frequency by weight)/number of subjects who responded with the weight determined by where the respondents order this item in terms of its importance [22].

3. Results

3.1. Profile of Women Having a High Risk of Depression

Of the 1126 subjects recruited, 508 (45.1%) were assessed with the EPDS the maximum of seven times and an additional 257 (765, 65.3%) participants completed at least five EPDS assessments [20].

From among the entry sample, 248 women (22.0%) were identified as high risk. Of these, 63 scored 13 or more on the EPDS at least twice, 111 responded to EPDS item 10 indicating thoughts of self-harm on at least a single survey, and 74 met both criteria. Twelve reported being diagnosed with major depression before the start of the study. Table 1 shows that high-risk women had a median age of 29 years; most lived with their families, were employed, and were highly educated. With few exceptions, demographic characteristics did not differentiate screen-positive women from their asymptomatic peers. However, fewer of the screen-positive respondents were satisfied with their spousal relationship, while a higher percentage of screen-positive respondents were somewhat satisfied. Although slightly fewer screen-positive women said that they would "do the month," the vast majority of both groups affirmed traditional Chinese postpartum family care. Among positive responders, there was a small though statistically significant tendency for families to favor boys over girls.

Table 1. Participant profile (n = 1126).

Variable	High Risk Women (n = 248)	Other Women in Cohort (n = 878)	p
Age (years)			0.905
<25	37 (15.04%)	120 (13.89%)	
25–30	139 (56.50%)	480 (55.56%)	
30–35	51 (20.73%)	188 (21.76%)	
>35	19 (7.72%)	76 (8.80%)	
Average	28.28	28.83	
Missing	2	14	
Parity			0.806
Primiparas	64 (25.91%)	229 (26.97%)	
Multiparas	183 (74.09%)	620 (73.03%)	
Missing	1	29	
Education			0.891
Middle school graduate or less	31 (12.60%)	96 (11.03%)	
High school	58 (23.58%)	200 (22.99%)	
College degree	136 (55.28%)	501 (57.59%)	
Graduate or professional degree	21 (8.54%)	73 (8.39%)	
Missing	2	8	
Jobs			0.900
Government workers	51 (21.07%)	185 (21.46%)	
Enterprise managers	43 (17.77%)	151 (17.52%)	
Private business owner	31 (12.81%)	136 (15.78%)	
Workers/Farmers	11 (4.55%)	39 (4.52%)	
Unemployed (due to disease or other reasons)	66 (27.27%)	214 (24.83%)	
Others	40 (16.53%)	137 (15.89%)	
Missing	6	16	
Income per month			0.471
0	69 (28.28%)	236 (27.73%)	
¥1–2000	12 (4.92%)	53 (6.23%)	
¥2001–5000	122 (50.00%)	389 (45.71%)	
Over ¥5001	41 (16.80%)	173 (20.33%)	
Missing	4	27	
Depression history			0.005 **
No	164 (93.18%)	609 (97.91%)	
Yes	12 (6.82%)	13 (2.09%)	
Missing	72	256	
Living Situation			0.233
Nuclear family	87 (35.80%)	375 (43.20%)	
Nuclear family and parents in law	91 (37.45%)	296 (34.10%)	
Nuclear family and parents	40 (16.46%)	107 (12.33%)	
Living alone	20 (8.23%)	71 (8.18%)	
Else	5 (2.06%)	19 (2.19%)	
Missing	5	10	
Relationship with spouse			<0.001 ***
Satisfied	174 (71.90%)	731 (84.12%)	
Somewhat satisfied	65 (26.86%)	136 (15.56%)	
Dissatisfied	2 (1.24%)	2 (0.23%)	
Missing	7	9	
Family's wishes about child's sex			0.041 *
Boy	44 (18.11%)	106 (12.24%)	
Girl	32 (13.17%)	103 (11.89%)	
Does not matter	167 (68.72%)	657 (75.87%)	
Missing	5	12	
Willingness to do the month			0.018 *
Yes	207 (85.19%)	786 (90.66%)	
No	36 (14.81%)	81 (9.34%)	
Missing	5	11	

* $p \leq 0.05$; ** $p \leq 0.01$; *** $p \leq 0.001$.

3.2. Responses to Referral

Among the 248 high-risk women to whom we sent the initial alert message, only 3 (3/248, 1.2%) contacted us for further information. Each attended the provincial hospital in Changsha. Although we helped arrange an appointment with psychiatrists to coincide with their routine maternal care visit and offered to cover their outpatient expenses, only one (0.4%, 1/248) went to the appointment.

Of the 245 women who did not respond to alerts, 161 (64.7%), divided nearly equally between the major provincial maternal-child hospital (n = 80) and the county hospital (n = 81), completed the online survey regarding their reasons for not accepting the referral. Among them, 71 (44.1%) agreed with the results about being depressed, while 44 (27.3%) contested the accuracy of the results. Among the latter, 32 (19.3% of the online responders) had never considered the possibility of developing some type of depressive condition (Figure 2a).

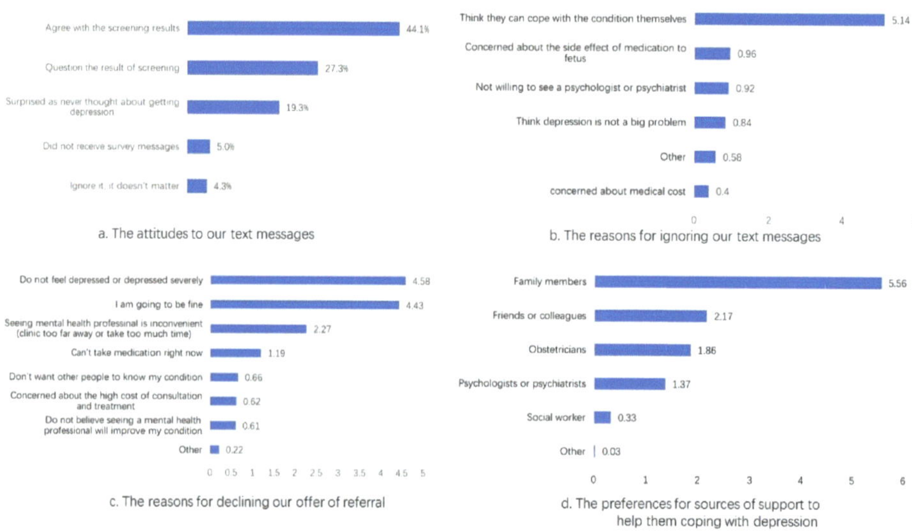

Figure 2. The responses of screen-positive women using ranking scores to indicate the importance of the items among our survey respondents.

3.3. Reasons for not Accepting Referrals

The majority (128/161; 79.5%) of the respondents affirmed that they did not ask for further information because "I can cope with the condition myself." Of the 128, 89 (84.0%) selected this option as their primary reason for not seeking help. After weighted sorting, the importance of each reason is shown in Figure 2b. Among the other reasons for not seeking assistance, 5 of 19 respondents listed, "I am fine/good," and three mentioned time conflict. Only one person explained that she had been treated in the psychology department already.

Of the 161 women, 106 (65.8%) said they would not accept our offer for arranging appointments with mental health specialists; 68 (64.2%) agreed with the statement, "I feel that I am not depressed or my depression is not severe." Another 63 (59.4%) indicated: "I am going to be fine." Only 13 (12.3%) expressed concerns about the cost of diagnosis and treatment, and only three ranked this choice as most important. All the reasons sorted by importance are shown in Figure 2c. It is notable, however, that 134 (83.2%) of the 161 respondents expressed interest in trying smartphone application (app)-based therapies. Of the 27 (16.77%) people who did not express an interest, most indicated that they believed that they were not depressed or they could care for themselves.

3.4. Preference for Care

When asked about which sources of help they might seek for their depression, 151 (93.8%) women indicated their families, and 142 listed their families as the most important source of support, followed by friends and colleagues (n = 77; 47.8%). Few preferred services from professionals (n = 15; obstetricians for nine and psychologists or psychiatrists for six), and none chose social workers. All the sources sorted by preference are shown in Figure 2d.

4. Discussion

We found that symptoms consistent with PND were common among the Chinese women who participated in this study. Using a generally conservative threshold for defining positive screening with EPDS, we found that 248 of 1126 women (22.0%) in our sample were screen-positive, reflecting either a repeated score ≥13 or a positive self-harm score. If we had used ≥10 as our screening cut-off, as recommended by the validity study of the Chinese version of the EPDS [23,24], nearly 40% of our participants would have screened positive at least once, similar to other PND studies in China [25,26]. Even with more stringent criteria, it was readily evident that participants had little interest in pursuing further medical evaluation or treatment of their conditions: only 3 out of 248 women (1.21%) who screened positive for depression in our study expressed interest in obtaining a mental health evaluation, and only 1 (0.40%) of 248 availed herself of this service.

If we were to implement a mental health referral policy for screen-positive women during the perinatal period using PHQ-9, approximately one-third of women who gave birth in China would have been eligible, as we calculated in the introduction [16]. However, the lack of services and clinical expertise precludes such a policy. Few obstetrician-gynecologists or primary care providers in China have dealt with PND in their practices [27]. With nearly all of China's psychiatrists (29,924 in 2017) based in large psychiatric hospitals with overcrowded outpatient clinics [28], the potential for symptomatic women to receive careful evaluations and appropriate treatment is extremely limited.

The results of our study demonstrated that the women responding to our survey did not regard their mental distress as a medical problem. Having resources available was a moot issue, given the lack of demand. In the systematic review of 17 studies from Western cultures, the highest referral acceptance rate was 33.0%, the lowest was 13.8% without any intervention [29,30]. Our finding was much lower than prior studies—only 0.4%.

After we uncovered this low uptake of referral, we published a systematic review on the issue of uptake of referral [14]. In that review, we found that the top reasons were lack of time and perception that mood had improved [31–37]. Other reasons included cost concerns, transportation problems, and the perception of the nature of PND [31,33,38]. Stigma associated with psychiatric treatments deterred the uptake of referral as well [38,39]. Furthermore, the perception that it is normal to have some depression in the puerperium prevented the need for further health care [40,41]. Women's preferences for the type of service offered also influenced the level of acceptance. The literature suggests that many women prefer home visitation to specialized services and that some women tended to use their own resources instead of professional care [32,33,42,43]. We are currently conducting qualitative research to explore in depth the causes behind this observation in China.

Cultural differences may partially explain the extraordinarily low uptake rate for referral for mental health services among Chinese women. Traditional Chinese culture emphasizes self-restraint and introspection, requiring people to rely on their own strength to solve internal conflicts [44]. Many studies have found that cultural barriers, consisting of credibility of treatment, recognition of need, and fear of loss of reputation are reasons for the low rate of seeking of mental health care among Chinese immigrants [45–48]. Similar to the stigmatization of mental disorders in many societies, this cultural attitude would reduce uptake of referral and would need to be addressed by health education in the long term. Cost was a less important factor influencing the low uptake rate. This is different from many studies in Western countries [33,38,49]. While the relatively low cost of psychiatric care in China may be one reason, it may also indicate that practical barriers are not really important until cultural barriers are overcome.

It is debatable whether the screening-based referral constitutes the most cost-effective approach for tackling this mental health challenge in China. In our related longitudinal study, we found that even without any medical treatment, many women may have recovered from their depression. Our web-based survey indicated a large proportion of the high-risk women's EPDS scores dropped below 12.5, and more than half of them were below 9.5 at 6 months and one year following the delivery (Appendix A). The 50% attrition rate of the cohort was relatively high, although no difference was shown between at-risk and other women. These findings taken one year postpartum suggest spontaneous resolution of symptoms for many women without professional interventions.

Women's reliance on their family members to the exclusion of health professionals suggests that families provide a socially supportive environment that can be the basis for therapeutic interventions when needed [50]. Most Chinese women still practice doing the month and a small case report found it may reduce women's risk for depression [51,52]. It suggests that perinatal depression, especially postnatal, could be usefully managed in traditional family settings, making use of the special nature of interactions afforded by the practice of doing the month.

Our findings point to the need and opportunity for the development of culturally attuned ways of addressing the needs of women with symptoms indicative of PND. First, we recommend building on women's preferences for family support and care and the emphasis in Chinese culture on family bonding and family responsibility for the care of pregnant and postpartum women. Second, we recommend educating women and their families about PND, especially emphasizing when it would be timely to seek professional help if their condition does not improve or deteriorates, considering the importance of the family structure in dealing with PND. Lastly, as 83% of our respondents expressed an interest in trying smartphone-app-based therapies, well-designed pragmatic trials may be useful to assess the effectiveness of those apps in real-world settings.

There are several limitations to the study. The cohort on which this study was based was a convenience sample. Although we approached every eligible woman during the 4-month recruitment period, we did not record their overall number or basic demographic features, and thus were unable to rule out undetected forms of sample bias. Only 64.9% of the high-risk participants completed the questionnaire (161 of 248). As this was an anonymous survey, we do not have information on who completed the questionnaire or whether individuals' likelihood to respond to the survey was associated with their conditions. Finally, it is possible that the EPDS is overly sensitive to the complaints among Chinese women such that their scores overstate what are generally mild complaints. If this were true, their reticence to seek follow-up consultation may have been a reflection of their relatively unimpaired conditions. However, we sought to set a high bar for positive screening, and we did not find an inordinate proportion of screen-positive respondents when comparing our results with prior reports.

5. Conclusions

Depressive symptoms are common among Chinese women during the perinatal period; however, the majority of symptom-positive women do not accept subsequent referral to mental health services. Our result argues against referring all screen-positive women for professional services at this time. Feasible options should build upon the tradition of family support for more engaged and educated response to PND.

Author Contributions: Conceptualization, W.G. and D.X.; methodology, W.G. and D.X.; formal analysis, X.J.; writing—original draft preparation, W.G., D.X., and E.D.C.; writing—review and editing, E.D.C., R.L., and K.K.C.; funding acquisition, W.G. All authors have read and agreed to the published version of the manuscript.

Funding: This work was financially supported by the National Natural Science Foundation of China (NNSFC, grant numbers 81973059, 81773446). The NNSFC played no roles in the study design, collection, analysis, and interpretation of data, writing of this article, or in the decision to submit it for publication.

Acknowledgments: We thank all the mothers involved in this project. We are also deeply grateful for Hua Liu and Fengyun Tian from Yiyang Ziyang District Maternal and Child Health Hospital for their kind assistance in recruiting our participants and tracking. Thanks to Wenqing Xue for assistance on references and providing information on her unpublished systematic review.

Conflicts of Interest: The authors declare no conflict of interest.

Appendix A

In the related longitudinal study, we found that even without any medical treatment, many women may be able to recover from their depression. Our web-based survey indicated a large proportion of the high-risk women's EPDS scores dropped below 12.5, and more than half of them scored below 9.5 at 6 months and one year following the delivery.

Table A1. Follow-up about depression of women in the cohort.

EPDS Scores	High-Risk Women (n = 248)	Other Women in Cohort (n = 878)
Half year after delivery		
>12.5	42 (34.43%)	19 (5.85%)
<12.5	80 (65.57%)	306 (94.15%)
missing	126 (50.80%)	553 (63.98%)
One year after delivery		
>12.5	26 (23.42%)	11 (3.48%)
<12.5	85 (76.58%)	305 (96.52%)
missing	137 (55.24%)	562 (64.00%)

References

1. General Office of the National Health Commission. Notice of the General Office of the National Health Commission on Exploring the Implementation of Special Services for the Prevention and Treatment of Depression and Senile Dementia. Available online: http://www.nhc.gov.cn/jkj/s7914/202009/a63d8f82eb53451f97217bef0962b98f.shtml (accessed on 3 October 2020).
2. Fisher, J.; Mello, M.C.D.; Patel, V.; Rahman, A.; Tran, T.; Holton, S.; Holmes, W. Prevalence and determinants of common perinatal mental disorders in women in low-and lower-middle-income countries: A systematic review. *Bull. World Health Organ.* **2012**, *90*, 139–149. [CrossRef] [PubMed]
3. Nisar, A.; Yin, J.; Waqas, A.; Bai, X.; Wang, D.; Rahman, A.; Li, X. Prevalence of perinatal depression and its determinants in Mainland China: A systematic review and meta-analysis. *J. Affect. Disord.* **2020**, *277*, 1022–1037. [CrossRef] [PubMed]
4. Plant, D.T.; Pariante, C.M.; Sharp, D.; Pawlby, S. Maternal depression during pregnancy and offspring depression in adulthood: Role of child maltreatment. *Br. J. Psychiatry* **2015**, *207*, 213–220. [CrossRef] [PubMed]
5. Corman, H.; Curtis, M.A.; Noonan, K.; Reichman, N.E. Maternal depression as a risk factor for children's inadequate housing conditions. *Soc. Sci. Med.* **2016**, *149*, 76–83. [CrossRef] [PubMed]
6. Davalos, D.B.; Yadon, C.A.; Tregellas, H.C. Untreated prenatal maternal depression and the potential risks to offspring: A review. *Arch. Women's Ment. Health* **2012**, *15*, 1–14. [CrossRef] [PubMed]
7. National Collaborating Centre for Mental Health. *Antenatal and Postnatal Mental Health: Clinical Management and Service Guidance: Updated Edition*; British Psychological Society: Leicester, UK, 2014.
8. American College of Obstetricians and Gynecologists. Screening for depression during and after pregnancy. Committee Opinion No. 453. *Obstet. Gynecol.* **2010**, *115*, 394–395. [CrossRef]
9. US Preventive Services Task Force. Screening for depression in adults: US Preventive Services Task Force recommendation statement. *JAMA-J. Am. Med Assoc.* **2016**, *315*, 380–387. [CrossRef]
10. Austin, M.-P.; Highet, N. Guidelines Expert Advisory Committee. Clinical practice guidelines for depression and related disorders—anxiety, bipolar disorder and puerperal psychosis—In the perinatal period. In *A Guideline for Primary Care Health Professionals*; Beyondblue: The National Depression Initiative: Melbourne, Australia, 2013.

11. Myers, E.; Aubuchon-Endsley, N.; Bastian, L.; Gierisch, J.; Kemper, A.; Swamy, G. *Efficacy and Safety of Screening for Postpartum Depression*; Comparative Effectiveness Review No. 106; Agency for Healthcare Research and Quality: Rockville, MD, USA, 2013.
12. Hickie, I. Beyondblue: The national depression initiative. *Australas. Psychiatry* **2001**, *9*, 147–150. [CrossRef]
13. Byatt, N.; Levin, L.L.; Ziedonis, D.; Simas, T.A.M.; Allison, J. Enhancing participation in depression care in outpatient perinatal care settings: A systematic review. *Obstet. Gynecol.* **2015**, *126*, 1048. [CrossRef]
14. Xue, W.Q.; Cheng, K.K.; Xu, D.; Jin, X.; Gong, W.J. Uptake of referrals for women with positive perinatal depression screening results and the effectiveness of interventions to increase uptake: A systematic review and meta-analysis. *Epidemiol. Psychiatr. Sci.* **2020**, *29*, e143. [CrossRef]
15. Zhang, Y. Population Growth Slowed and Urbanization Continued to Improve. Available online: http://www.stats.gov.cn/tjsj/zxfb/202001/t20200119_1723767.html (accessed on 3 October 2020).
16. Ming, G.; Zhihui, W.; Xiaohong, F. Application value of the 9-question depression scale from the patient health questionnaire in the screening of postpartum depression. *China Mod. Med.* **2019**, *26*, 104–106.
17. Wong, J.; Fisher, J. The role of traditional confinement practices in determining postpartum depression in women in Chinese cultures: A systematic review of the English language evidence. *J. Affect. Disord.* **2009**, *116*, 161–169. [CrossRef] [PubMed]
18. Holroyd, E.; Katie, F.K.L.; Chun, L.S.; Ha, S.W. "Doing the month": An exploration of postpartum practices in Chinese women. *Health Care Women Int.* **1997**, *18*, 301–313. [CrossRef] [PubMed]
19. XIE, R.H.; Yang, J.; Liao, S.; Xie, H.; Walker, M.; Wen, S.W. Prenatal family support, postnatal family support and postpartum depression. *Aust. N. Z. J. Obstet. Gynaecol.* **2010**, *50*, 340–345. [CrossRef]
20. Yu, M.; Li, H.; Xu, D.R.; Wu, Y.; Liu, H.; Gong, W. Trajectories of perinatal depressive symptoms from early pregnancy to six weeks postpartum and their risk factors-a longitudinal study. *J Affect Disord* **2020**, *275*, 149–156. [CrossRef]
21. Fabbris, L. Measurement scales for scoring or ranking sets of interrelated items. In *Survey Data Collection and Integration*; Springer: Berlin/Heidelberg, Germany, 2013; pp. 21–43.
22. Wenjuanxing. Rule of Points for Sorting Questions. Available online: https://www.wjx.cn/help/help.aspx?helpid=43 (accessed on 3 October 2020).
23. Guo, X.; Wang, Y.; Chen, J. Study on the efficacy of the Edinburgh postnatal depression scale in puerperas in Chengdu. *Chin. J. Pract. Nurs.* **2009**, *25*, 4–6.
24. Lee, D.T.; Yip, S.K.; Chiu, H.F.; Leung, T.Y.; Chan, K.P.; Chau, I.O.; Leung, H.C.; Chung, T.K. Detecting postnatal depression in Chinese women. Validation of the Chinese version of the Edinburgh Postnatal Depression Scale. *Br. J. Psychiatry* **1998**, *172*, 433–437. [CrossRef]
25. Zhang, H.-M.; Xu, Y.; Li, Y.-Y.; Wu, A.-Q. The Infuences Caused by Life Events, Social Support, Personality Agent and Antepartum Mental Stale on the Postpartum Depression. *Chin. J. Prev. Control Chronic Non-Commun. Dis.* **2007**, *15*, 321–325.
26. Zhang, L.; Li, Y.-H.; Bu, Y.-G.; Guan, H.; Liao, P.-P. Dynamic observation of female perinatal depression and study on the related factors. *Matern. Child Health Care China* **2015**, *30*, 2393–2397.
27. Zhong, B.-L.; Cui, J.; Chen, H.-H.; Zhang, J.-F.; Xu, H.-M.; Fan, Y.-P.; Wang, P.-H.; Zhou, L. Investigation of Postpartum Depression Among Medical Staff From 21 Maternal and Child Care Ceters in Wuhan: A Cross-Sectional Survey. *Chin. J. Obstet. Gynecol. Pediatr.* **2011**, *7*, 12–15.
28. National Health Commission of China. *Yearbook of China Health Statistics*; Peking Union Medical College Press: Beijing, China, 2019.
29. Goodman, J.H.; Tyer-Viola, L. Detection, treatment, and referral of perinatal depression and anxiety by obstetrical providers. *J. Womens Health* **2010**, *19*, 477–490. [CrossRef] [PubMed]
30. Marcus, S.M.; Flynn, H.A.; Blow, F.C.; Barry, K.L. Depressive symptoms among pregnant women screened in obstetrics settings. *J. Womens Health* **2003**, *12*, 373–380. [CrossRef] [PubMed]
31. Bauer, N.S.; Ofner, S.; Pottenger, A.; Carroll, A.E.; Downs, S.M. Follow-up of Mothers with Suspected Postpartum Depression from Pediatrics Clinics. *Front. Pediatr.* **2017**, *5*, 212. [CrossRef] [PubMed]
32. Honikman, S.; van Heyningen, T.; Field, S.; Baron, E.; Tomlinson, M. Stepped care for maternal mental health: A case study of the perinatal mental health project in South Africa. *PLoS Med.* **2012**, *9*, e1001222. [CrossRef]
33. Kim, J.J.; La Porte, L.M.; Corcoran, M.; Magasi, S.; Batza, J.; Silver, R.K. Barriers to mental health treatment among obstetric patients at risk for depression. *Am. J. Obstet. Gynecol.* **2010**, *202*, 312.e1–312.e5. [CrossRef]

34. Milgrom, J.; Holt, C.J.; Gemmill, A.W.; Ericksen, J.; Leigh, B.; Buist, A.; Schembri, C. Treating postnatal depressive symptoms in primary care: A randomised controlled trial of GP management, with and without adjunctive counselling. *BMC Psychiatry* **2011**, *11*, 95. [CrossRef]
35. Miller, L.S.; Boyd, B.J.; Chernov, A.J. Improving the identification and treatment of postpartum depression in a managed care organization. *J. Clin. Outcomes Manag.* **2004**, *11*, 157–161.
36. Miller, L.; Shade, M.; Vasireddy, V. Beyond screening: Assessment of perinatal depression in a perinatal care setting. *Arch. Womens Ment. Health* **2009**, *12*, 329–334. [CrossRef]
37. Trost, M.J.; Molas-Torreblanca, K.; Man, C.; Casillas, E.; Sapir, H.; Schrager, S.M. Screening for maternal postpartum depression during infant hospitalizations. *J. Hosp. Med.* **2016**, *11*, 840–846. [CrossRef]
38. Chen, H.; Wang, J.; Ch'ng, Y.C.; Mingoo, R.; Lee, T.; Ong, J. Identifying mothers with postpartum depression early: Integrating perinatal mental health care into the obstetric setting. *ISRN Obstet. Gynecol.* **2011**, *2011*, 309189. [CrossRef]
39. Robinson, S.; Young, J. Screening for depression and anxiety in the post-natal period: Acceptance or rejection of a subsequent treatment offer. *Aust. N. Z. J. Psychiatry* **1982**, *16*, 47–51. [CrossRef] [PubMed]
40. Harvey, S.T.; Pun, P.K.K. Analysis of positive Edinburgh depression scale referrals to a consultation liaison psychiatry service in a two-year period. *Int. J. Ment. Health Nurs.* **2007**, *16*, 161–167. [CrossRef] [PubMed]
41. Rowan, P.; Greisinger, A.; Brehm, B.; Smith, F.; McReynolds, E. Outcomes from implementing systematic antepartum depression screening in obstetrics. *Arch. Women's Ment. Health* **2012**, *15*, 115–120. [CrossRef] [PubMed]
42. Price, S.K.; Coles, D.C.; Wingold, T. Integrating Behavioral Health Risk Assessment into Centralized Intake for Maternal and Child Health Services. *Health Soc. Work* **2017**, *42*, 231–240. [CrossRef]
43. Reay, R.; Matthey, S.; Ellwood, D.; Scott, M. Long-term outcomes of participants in a perinatal depression early detection program. *J. Affect. Disord.* **2011**, *129*, 94–103. [CrossRef]
44. Lei, X.; Liu, L.; Li, D. The depression of chinese and the reflection related to their society and culture. *Chin. Gen. Pract.* **2004**, *7*, 315–317.
45. Chen, A.W.; Kazanjian, A.; Wong, H. Why do Chinese Canadians not consult mental health services: Health status, language or culture? *Transcult. Psychiatry* **2009**, *46*, 623–641. [CrossRef]
46. Kung, W.W. Cultural and practical barriers to seeking mental health treatment for Chinese Americans. *J. Community Psychol.* **2004**, *32*, 27–43. [CrossRef]
47. Tabora, B.L.; Flaskerud, J.H. Mental Health Beliefs, Practices, and Knowledge of Chinese American Immigrant Women. *Issues Ment. Health Nurs.* **1997**, *18*, 173–189. [CrossRef]
48. Ying, Y.-W.; Miller, L.S. Help-seeking behavior and attitude of Chinese Americans regarding psychological problems. *Am. J. Community Psychol.* **1992**, *20*, 549–556. [CrossRef]
49. Byatt, N.; Simas, T.A.; Lundquist, R.S.; Johnson, J.V.; Ziedonis, D.M. Strategies for improving perinatal depression treatment in North American outpatient obstetric settings. *J. Psychosom. Obstet. Gynaecol.* **2012**, *33*, 143–161. [CrossRef] [PubMed]
50. Abe-Kim, J.; Takeuchi, D.; Hwang, W.-C. Predictors of help seeking for emotional distress among Chinese Americans: Family matters. *J. Consult. Clin. Psychol.* **2002**, *70*, 1186. [CrossRef]
51. Liu, Y.Q.; Petrini, M.; Maloni, J.A. "Doing the month": Postpartum practices in Chinese women. *Nurs. Health Sci.* **2015**, *17*, 5–14. [CrossRef]
52. Ding, G.; Yu, J.; Vinturache, A.; Gu, H.; Lu, M. Therapeutic Effects of the Traditional "Doing the Month" Practices on Postpartum Depression in China. *Am. J. Psychiatry* **2018**, *175*, 1071–1072. [CrossRef]

International Journal of
Environmental Research and Public Health

MDPI

Review

Contemplating Help-Seeking in Perinatal Psychological Distress—A Meta-Ethnography

Minna Anneli Sorsa [1,2,*], Jari Kylmä [2,3,4] and Terese Elisabet Bondas [5]

1 Child Psychiatry, Tampere University Hospital, 33521 Tampere, Finland
2 Faculty of Social Sciences, Nursing Science, Tampere University, 33520 Tampere, Finland; jari.kylma@tuni.fi
3 Faculty of Medicine, Nursing Science, University of Oulu, 90014 Oulu, Finland
4 Faculty of Pharmacy, University of Helsinki, 00014 Helsinki, Finland
5 Faculty of Health Sciences, University of Stavanger, 4036 Stavanger, Norway; terese.e.bondas@uis.no
* Correspondence: minna.sorsa@tuni.fi

Abstract: Perinatal psychological distress (PPD) may cause delays in help-seeking in the perinatal period, which is crucial for families with small children. Help-seeking theories focus on rational processes of behavior wherein 'help-seeking' is viewed as a decision-making process, in which action is preceded by recognizing a problem. We identified the phase prior to actual help-seeking actions as a life situation and a phenomenon through which to gain a deeper understanding from women's own perspectives. The aim of this study was to integrate and synthesize knowledge of women's experiences of contemplating seeking help for PPD. We chose interpretative meta-ethnography by Noblit and Hare (1988) and implemented eMERGe guidelines in reporting. The search was performed systematically, and the 14 included studies were evaluated with Critical Appraisal Skills Programme checklist (CASP). We identified seven themes and a metaphor in a lines-of-argument synthesis, showing that contemplating help-seeking is a multidimensional phenomenon. We did not observe a straightforward and linear process (as previous research suggests) but instead a complex process of contemplating help-seeking. A clinical implication is that service providers should work with outreach and develop their tools to connect with mothers with PPD. Another suggestion is to improve training in mental health literacy prior to or during pregnancy.

Keywords: help-seeking behavior; meta-ethnography; meta-synthesis; perinatal mental health; perinatal depression/anxiety; prevention; treatment

Citation: Sorsa, M.A.; Kylmä, J.; Bondas, T.E. Contemplating Help-Seeking in Perinatal Psychological Distress—A Meta-Ethnography. *Int. J. Environ. Res. Public Health* **2021**, *18*, 5226. https://doi.org/10.3390/ijerph18105226

Academic Editors: M.Carmen Míguez Varela, Stuart Biddle and Sabrina Cipolletta

Received: 24 March 2021
Accepted: 8 May 2021
Published: 14 May 2021

1. Introduction

Experiences causing suffering for women during the perinatal period (pregnancy and the year following childbirth) are formed by culturally constructed encounters. Help-seeking is not solely related to diagnostic questions [1]. Therefore, we chose to focus on perinatal psychological distress (PPD), which has been identified as a holistic emotional state of discomfort that is experienced by an individual in response to specific stressors [2]. Psychological distress involves depression, stress, and anxiety [3]. PPD may be reflected in a person's behavior, such as adversely affecting interpersonal relationships. It is not well-defined, but it is closely linked to stress and coping [4]. Women may be unable to recognize their symptoms and name them as, e.g., depression [5]. PPD is associated with a number of poor outcomes for the mother, baby, and family, since PPD has an impact on parenting capacities, which is why also infants are at risk of adverse childhood experiences [6–8].

Psychological distress during the perinatal period is common, with rates at 21.2% prenatally and 26.7% postnatally [3]. Women are at higher risk for distress if they have low social support, are single, are less educated, are unemployed or experiencing financial instability, are older, use tobacco or alcohol, or have prior psychological problems [9]. In a French nationally representative cohort study, 12.6% of pregnant women reported prenatal psychological distress [10]. In a US national study, the prevalence of serious psychological distress in the previous month ranged from 3.9 to 6.4% during pregnancy and 4.6 to 6.9% postnatally [9]. The prevalence of perinatal depression is 11.4% in high-income countries [11]. Of those who screened positive for perinatal depression, 23% suffered from bipolar disorder [12].

The most widely used framework in help-seeking research is the theory of planned behavior [13,14]. Help-seeking viewed as a decision-making process emphasizes the assumption that persons are active and goal-directed and that they fulfill instrumental purposes by seeking help from somebody, such as for specific mental health concerns [13–15]. At an individual level, situational aspects and the person's background influence their help-seeking behavior and abilities by activating their beliefs about help-seeking; persons also weigh the benefits and utility in relation to the risks of their action [13]. When a person contemplates whether help-seeking is necessary, they decide whether change is necessary [16]. If a person decides that change is needed, she first tries to effect change through her own means, with self-help efforts, before making the decision to seek help from social and health care [16]. Help-seeking is a person-centered phenomenon incorporating the help-seeker's perspective, which differs from the supply side (defined in this context as access to care).

Saint Arnault [1] has explained that help-seeking is connected to social determinants and cultural humility, as people's perspectives, values, and preferences need to be taken into consideration in help-seeking encounters. Women's inability to disclose their feelings can be exacerbated by family members' and health professionals' reluctance to respond to mothers' emotional and practical needs [5]. Many women try and fail to live up to the idealized societal depiction of motherhood; however, each mother is unique, and thus the motherhood experience is different for all mothers [17].

It is important to study help-seeking in the context of perinatal mental health, since PPD often goes undetected and women do not use the resources available in the services. Women may not seek help, even though perinatal services have been developed and are available. Additionally, women may access helping resources but choose not to disclose their problems [5,8,18,19]. Research has shown that in the mental health context, persons seeking help might not exactly know what type of care is available and could help them, and they want to alleviate their psychological distress in whatever way they can [14]. Hadfield and Wittkowski [8] identified "an early stage of seeking help", when women seek informal support from friends, family, and the Internet; in this stage, women recognize that something is wrong, but they do not yet seek help. Accessing treatment for mental health issues is delayed in many cultures [16,20], and many choose to solve their problems themselves [16,20–22]. Women may lack knowledge around mental health and service use, or they may encounter negative attitudes toward mental illness. Help-seeking in PPD is important during the perinatal period, because the primary caregiver and infant ideally form an attachment relationship during this time. If the primary caregiver takes account of their own and others' mental states, an attachment relationship may evolve [19,23,24]. If women with PPD do not seek help, the infants will also suffer.

Existing reviews on help-seeking in perinatal mental health focus on overall help-seeking [25], on barriers to PPD help-seeking [5,8,18], depression [5,7,8,17], postnatal help-seeking [5,7,8,25], and peer support [17]. They primarily focus on help-seeking in services [4,5,7,8,18] or collect data in a specific country, such as the United Kingdom [4,18].

In existing reviews on help-seeking around perinatal mental health, mothers have revealed a range of emotions. Even negative experiences can be interpreted as normal symptoms related to pregnancy and motherhood [5,18,25], and mothers may choose to remain silent so as to not upset family members and to fulfill social expectations of good motherhood [4,5,8,17,18]. Family and friends are very important and influence women's choice to seek help or not [25]. When seeking help, women feel their vulnerability will have negative consequences, such as being judged by others [25–27], creating guilt and shame [8,17,18] and a fear that the baby could be taken away [5]. The individual-level barriers to seeking help include poor awareness and knowledge about PPD [4,5,8,18,25] and a lack of open discussion between family members and professionals [5,17,18]. The mothers may be unable to articulate how they feel [4,5], be hesitant to admit their symptoms [5], or feel isolated [6,17].

As women do not easily reveal PPD and seek help [5], an integration of current knowledge on the topic is needed. We recognize a gap in the existing knowledge, on an international level, at the stage of contemplation in the perinatal period concerning psychological distress. Understanding women's perspectives may guide the development of targeted support and interventions. Overall, help-seeking as a decision-making process versus as a multidimensional phenomenon draws our interest. What is needed is an integration of the body of knowledge related to women's experiences in their everyday life at a stage when they contemplate whether to seek help.

1.1. Theoretical Perspective

A person's life situation is central in making meaning of oneself. Relationships with others affect one's general being in the world as well as one's self-awareness [28]. This is an area that is very difficult to study and collect data on, since the complexity of the lifeworld and the lived reality is not necessarily recognized by the human herself. The existential context, the human history, and the society we live in shape our internal world of understanding, along with our feelings and thoughts [28]. Our study approach is informed by the philosopher Lauri Rauhala [29], who posited that experiences are labeled according to the meaning given to specific situations within the individual life situation. The unique life situation gives meaning to human existence [29]. However, the meaning may change as time passes [28]. We want to capture the perinatal period, which is considered a specific moment in time. Human experiences involve different levels of awareness or clarity, and the meanings individuals make are not always directly or clearly related to a specific phenomenon of interest [29]. Therefore, the idea of this study is to reach a description of the experiential level of women on psychological distress in perinatal help-seeking, including mental health issues such as depression, anxiety, mood disorders, and psychosis [2]. This experiential level may include emotions, sensations, experiences, description of everyday life events, and notions about life circumstances.

1.2. Aim and Research Question

The aim of this study is to integrate and synthesize knowledge of women's experiences around contemplating help-seeking for PPD. The specific research question is: "What are women's experiences of contemplating help-seeking for perinatal mental health distress?" The goal is to reach a new understanding and to develop practice by using a new innovative approach: to help women and their families, health care personnel (HCP) invite them to care services and discuss service options (psychiatric nurses in communities, public health nurses, midwives, etc.). The results can be used to develop a model of help-seeking in perinatal distress when mothers contemplate accessing mental health care. The focus is important from the perspective of families seeking help, as well as from the perspective of health and social care policymakers and professionals.

2. Materials and Methods

Meta-synthesis originating in meta-ethnography, as developed by Noblit and Hare [30], was chosen for this study; as a complex synthesizing process, it has the option of dealing with adverse data, is clearly structured, and can be used to gain understanding of meaning via interpretation [31]. Meta-synthesis also offers room for novel interpretation [32], openness, and creativity to gain new insights beyond the original research [31,33]. A meta-synthesis can facilitate gaining greater understanding in both depth and breadth than the findings of individual studies [34]. Noblit and Hare [30] suggested that rather than a predetermined framework, an inductive approach should be used to capture the uniqueness and meaning in a specific context.

We followed the eMERGe guidelines, which provide recommendations for conducting and reporting of meta-ethnography, developed by France et al. [31] (Table 1).

Table 1. The implemented eMERGe Reporting Guidance in this study [31].

Criteria Headings		Reporting Criteria	Page
Phase 1 Selecting meta-ethnography and starting	1. Rationale and context for the meta-ethnography	Describe the gap in research or knowledge to be filled by the meta-ethnography, and the wider context of the meta-ethnography	1–3
	2. Aim(s) of the meta-ethnography	Describe the meta-ethnography aim(s)	3–4
	3. Focus of the meta-ethnography	Describe the meta-ethnography review question(s) (or objectives)	3
	4. Rationale for using meta-ethnography	Explain why meta-ethnography was considered the most appropriate qualitative synthesis methodology	3-4
Phase 2 Deciding what is relevant	5. Search strategy	Describe the rationale for the literature search strategy	5–7
	6. Search processes	Describe how the literature searching was carried out and by whom	6-7
	7. Selecting primary studies	Describe the process of study screening and selection, and who was involved	6–7
	8. Outcome of study selection	Describe the results of study searches and screening	6
Phase 3 Reading included studies	9. Reading and data extraction approach	Describe the reading and data extraction method and processes	15
	10. Presenting characteristics of included studies	Describe characteristics of the included studies	8–14, 15-16
Phase 4 Determining how studies are related	11. Process for determining how studies are related	Describe the methods and processes for determining how the included studies are related: • Which aspects of studies were compared AND • How the studies were compared	15
	12. Outcome of relating studies	Describe how studies relate to each other	15
Phase 5 Translating studies into one another	13. Process of translating studies	Describe the methods of translation: • Describe steps taken to preserve the context and meaning of the relationships between concepts within and across studies • Describe how the reciprocal and refutational translations were conducted • Describe how potential alternative interpretations or explanations were considered in the translations	15
	14. Outcome of translation	Describe the interpretive findings of the translation	15–22
Phase 6 Synthesizing translations	15. Synthesis process	Describe the methods used to develop overarching concepts ("synthesized translations") Describe how potential alternative interpretations or explanations were considered in the synthesis	15–20
	16. Outcome of synthesis process	Describe the new theory, conceptual framework, model, configuration, or interpretation of data developed from the synthesis	21–22
Phase 7 Expressing the synthesis	17. Summary of findings	Summarize the main interpretive findings of the translation and synthesis and compare them to existing literature	22–23
	18. Strengths, and limitations	Reflect on and describe the strengths and limitations of the synthesis: • Methodological aspects: for example, describe how the synthesis findings were influenced by the nature of the included studies and how the meta-ethnography was conducted.	23–24
	19. Recommendations and conclusions	Describe the implications of the synthesis	22–24

2.1. Search Strategy and Criteria

We conducted an extensive search in December 2019 with the aid of a librarian, who assisted us with database selection and choice of terms for the search. We used the PRISMA flowchart [35] to describe the process of selecting relevant studies for the meta-ethnography (Figure 1).

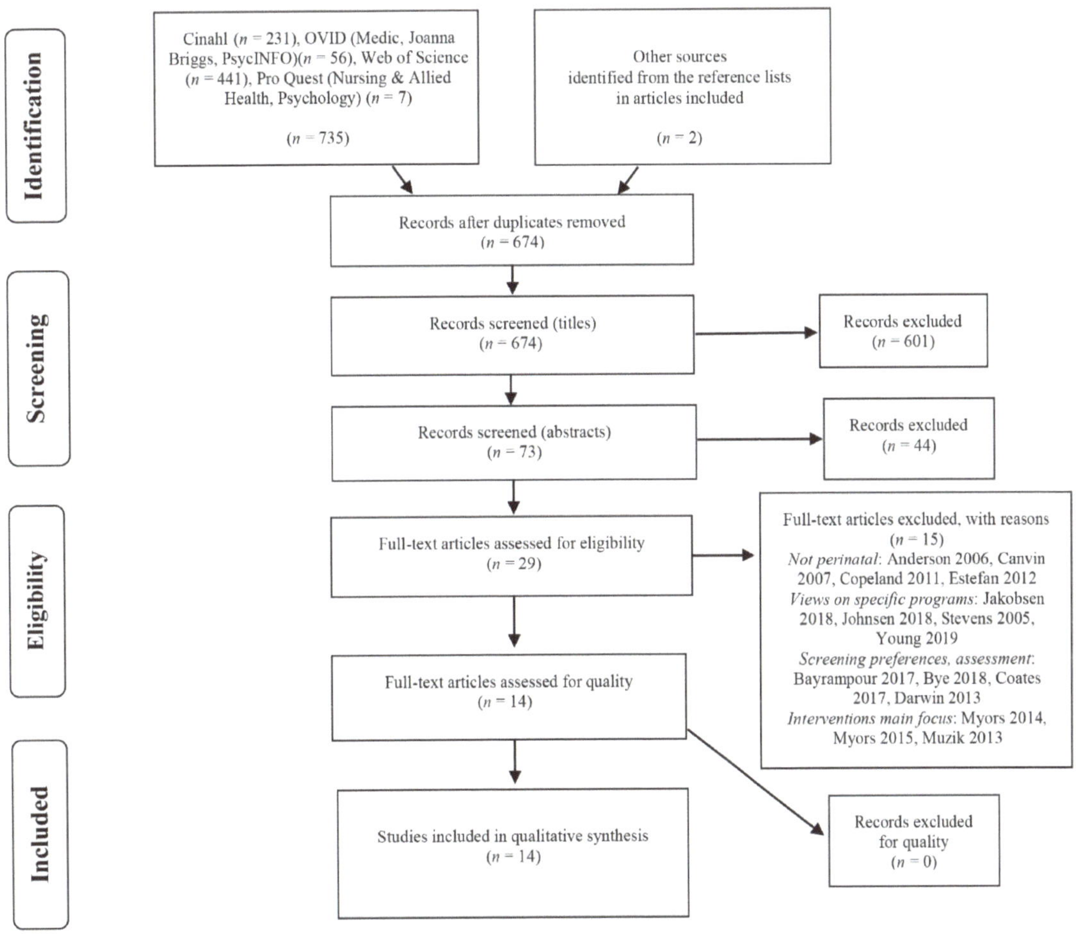

Figure 1. The PRISMA flow chart of the current study.

The search was completed through separate steps, which were combined at a later stage. The terms were searched in titles and additionally as MeSH terms were:

- mental disorders* OR help seeking behavior* AND mothers* OR maternal
- help-seeking behavior OR health care seeking behavior OR health behavior OR acceptability of health care OR patient acceptance of healthcare OR services utilization OR health care utilization OR health seeking OR health care seeking behavior OR perceived barriers OR barriers to OR facilitators to OR perceived access OR perceived barrier OR client participation OR client engagement OR client involvement

We intended to include all types of mental illness and disorders:

- mental disorders OR mental health disorder OR mental health or anxiety OR anxiety disorders OR depression OR depressive symptoms OR mental illness OR psychiatric and anxiety OR psychotic disorders

As the focus was on the perinatal period, we also included the terms:

- pregnancy OR infant OR baby OR child OR perinatal time. Finally, we wanted to focus on qualitative studies, so we combined the previous searches with AND qualitative studies OR qualitative research OR phenomenology. We did not include alternate spellings such as 'utilisation' in addition to 'utilization'.

The inclusion criteria: perinatal period from women's perspective, primiparous and multiparous, peer-reviewed publications, published in English, age of women over 18 years, and research from Western cultures.

The exclusion criteria: women and girls under 18 years, quantitative studies, reviews, RCTs, protocols, child-related problems during the perinatal period, focus on fathers, immigrants seeking help, focus on physical health, staff perspective on women's help-seeking.

We did not set a time limit in the original search: our idea had been to include wide ranges of mental health questions around PPD, including dual disorders and substance-related questions, yet we removed early entries from our search terms, and as such articles were scarce. By the stage of reading the full texts, we identified studies outside the perinatal period and excluded studies that described single interventions, feasibility studies, screening tools, or perinatal services (programs). As cultural context impacts help-seeking and experiential stigma of mental illness [1,4,5,18,25], we focused solely on Western societies, and we acknowledged the differences, such as those in the healthcare systems in specific countries. EndNote online software (Clarivate Analytics, Philadelphia, PA, USA) was used to facilitate the process of choosing relevant references. The search and inclusion strategy are presented in Figure 1.

The first author screened the titles first, and then the abstracts. All authors were involved in developing the data screening strategy and in screening the full texts. Disagreements among the reviewers about inclusions and exclusions were resolved by discussion and finding consensus. The inclusion and exclusion criteria required refinement throughout the steps (see Figure 1).

2.2. *Qualitative Appraisal of the Studies*

We used the Critical Appraisal Skills Programme Qualitative checklist (CASP) [36] to ensure quality assessment of the studies. Two researchers read the articles independently, then evaluated and scored the studies (yes = 2, to some degree = 1, and no = 0). The CASP evaluations were discussed together in the study group, and the average sum was used as the basis of scoring. The maximum CASP score was 20, and the included articles were rated in the range of 13–20: no articles were excluded. Most scores were lowered by the CASP question "Has the relationship between researcher and participants been adequately considered?": only 4/14 articles received full grading. The CASP scores can be seen in Table 2.

Table 2. Characteristics and CASP scores of included studies.

Author(s), Year, Country	Aim/Objective	Participants	Psychological Distress and Inclusion	Setting	Data Collection, Method	Results	CASP Qualitative Evaluation
Bell, Feeley, Hayon, Zelkowitz, Tait et al. (2016) Canada	To explore perceived barriers and facilitators to the use of mental health services experienced by women and their partners.	30 women, 32.5 years (average)	Postnatal depression, inclusion EPDS * 12	Two hospitals providing tertiary care and mental health services	Interviews with couples Content analysis	Five principal barriers and facilitators: accessibility and proximity, appropriateness and fit, stigma, encouraged to seek help, and personal characteristics.	20
Bilszta, Ericksen, Buist and Milgrom (2010) Australia	To explore barriers to care by asking women who are experiencing postnatal depression (PND) and who have accessed treatment and support services; how they recognized and acknowledged their depression; how being depressed affected their ability to actively seek help; what sort of help they wanted and why and how the attitudes of health professionals, friends and family, and the general community influenced the type of treatment sought.	37 women, 34 years (mean)	Postnatal depression, EPDS * 14 median, most participated in structured treatment program	Hospital outpatient postnatal depression programs, community based mutual support programs	Focus groups Interpretative phenomenology (Smith)	Findings suggest the lived experience of PND and associated attitudes and beliefs result in significant barriers to accessing help. Eight theme clusters were identified: expectations of motherhood; not coping and fear of failure; stigma and denial; poor mental health awareness and access; interpersonal support; baby management; help-seeking and treatment experiences and relationship with health professionals.	13
Byatt, Cox, Moore, Simas, Kini et al. (2018) United States	To elucidate in a sample: (1) the challenges associated with under-recognition of bipolar disorder in obstetric settings; (2) what barriers they face when trying to access psychiatric care; and (3) their perspectives regarding how obstetric practices can facilitate the identification of bipolar disorder in this population and connect women with mental health care.	25 women, age 18–55 years	Bipolar disorder, inclusion EDPS * 10 and DSM-IV criteria for bipolar disorder I, II	Five obstetrics practices, tertiary care center	Mixed. Qualitative study interviews Qualitative study modified grounded theory with phenomenological emphasis	Participants want their obstetric practices to proactively screen for, discuss, and help them obtain mental health treatment. Most were unaware of their diagnosis. Self-blame, stigma, fear, and lack of support prevent women from seeking help.	15

Table 2. *Cont.*

Author(s), Year, Country	Aim/Objective	Participants	Psychological Distress and Inclusion	Setting	Data Collection, Method	Results	CASP Qualitative Evaluation
Foulkes (2011) Canada	To explore the barriers and enablers identified by women experiencing a postpartum mood disorder (PPMD) that preclude and facilitate their help-seeking behaviors.	10 women, age 32.5 (mean)	PPMD, inclusion with no preexisting psychiatric illness and a diagnosis of postpartum mood disorder	Well-baby clinics and a parent resource center	Interviews Grounded theory (Strauss and Corbin)	The core category of "having postpartum" captured the essence of women's experiences in seeking help for a PPMD. Women identified four main stressors that contributed to their development of a PPMD, two barrier categories, and an enabler category that influenced their help-seeking behaviors. Through navigation of formal and informal help, women were able to begin to reclaim the mothering instincts they had lost to mental illness.	19
Guy, Sterling, Walker and Harrison (2014) United States	To use Jorm's (2000) framework to understand mental health literacy in one sample of lower income women to share participants' knowledge and beliefs about recognizing postpartum depressive symptoms and seeking help for these symptoms.	25 women, 24.3 years (mean)	Postnatal depression, inclusion CES-D ** over 16	Prenatal care through Medicaid	Focus groups Deductive analysis based on mental health literacy conceptual categories (Jorm), qualitative thematic analysis	Women recognized behavioral changes indicating mental distress, but fears prevented them from seeking help, and some resorted to risky behaviors.	18
Holopainen (2002) Australia	To explore women's experiences of support and treatment for postnatal depression.	7 women, age 24–43 years	Postnatal depression, inclusion current or recent perinatal depression	Postnatal support group in community health services, sexual assault center	Interviews Phenomenology (Creswell)	Women did not know where to seek help and were unaware of perinatal depression. Women were ambivalent of the use of medication. Women had ambivalent personal beliefs of being weak. Women wanted to be understood. Programs did not involve the family.	20
Jarrett (2015) United Kingdom	To explore women's perspective of care from GPs and midwives, when they experience symptoms of depression during pregnancy.	22 women, age not known	Prenatal depression, inclusion self-reported symptoms of depression	Internet discussion group for mental health during pregnancy	Online questions in two discussion forums Qualitative descriptive design (Neergaard), thematic analysis (Braun and Clarke)	Themes were identified from the data including women's disclosure of symptoms to GP's and midwives; lack of knowledge of perinatal mental health among health providers; attitudes of staff and systemic issues as barriers to good care; anti-depressant therapy and care that women found helpful.	19

Table 2. *Cont.*

Author(s), Year, Country	Aim/Objective	Participants	Psychological Distress and Inclusion	Setting	Data Collection, Method	Results	CASP Qualitative Evaluation
Jesse, Dolbier, and Blanchard (2008) United States	To identify: (1) potential barriers to sharing depressive symptoms with health care providers, (2) suggestions about how health care providers can best help women with depressive symptoms overcome barriers to seeking care, and (3) feedback regarding prenatal interventions that might be helpful for low-income women with depressive symptoms or depression in pregnancy.	21 women, all over 18 years	Prenatal depressive disorders, inclusion if assessed with high psychosocial risk in pregnancy	Prenatal clinic	Focus groups and two individual interviews Content analysis	Participants identified themes regarding barriers to seeking help. These were: (1) lack of trust, (2) judgment/stigma, (3) dissatisfaction with the health care system, and (4) not wanting help. Themes identified regarding overcoming barriers were: (1) facilitating trust and (2) offering support and help.	17
Letourneau, Duffett-Leger, Stewart, Hegadoren, Dennis et al. (2007) Canada	To assess the support needs, support resources, barriers to support, and preferences for support intervention for women with postpartum depression.	52 women, 31.3 years (mean)	Postnatal depression, inclusion depressive symptoms within past 2 years, 12 weeks of delivery, for longer than 2 weeks	Settings within integrated mental health services and postpartum follow-up	Interviews, group interviews Thematic content analysis	For most mothers, one-on-one support was preferred when postpartum depression is recognized. Group support should be available once the mothers start to feel better and are able to comfortably interact with other mothers in a group format.	15
McCarthy and McMahon (2008) New Zealand	To investigate the acceptance and experience of treatment for postnatal depression.	15 women, age 27–41 years	Postnatal depression, inclusion diagnosis of postnatal depression and in treatment since 3–12 months, with antidepressant medication	Community mental health setting	Interviews Grounded theory, "analytic induction method" (Glaser and Strauss)	The majority of women interviewed had reached "crisis point" before they sought and received treatment. The stigma attached to an inability to cope and being a "bad mother" emerged as the main barrier to seeking help earlier. In addition, women were unable to differentiate between "normal" levels of postpartum distress and depressive symptoms that might require intervention. Talking about their distress and experiences, both with health professionals and other mothers, was regarded as of primary importance in the recovery process.	16

Table 2. *Cont.*

Author(s), Year, Country	Aim/Objective	Participants	Psychological Distress and Inclusion	Setting	Data Collection, Method	Results	CASP Qualitative Evaluation
Raymond, Pratt, Godecker, Harrisin, Kim et al. (2014) United States	To explore the following research objectives: What perceived needs do women describe they have in relation to their mental health through the perinatal period? What help do women describe current seeking in relation to addressing mental health concerns during the perinatal period? What support do women describe wanting for addressing mental health concerns during the perinatal period?	37 women, 27.5 years (average)	Perinatal mental health needs, inclusion if receiving prenatal or postnatal care	Three healthcare clinics in disadvantaged parts of urban areas	Focus groups Thematic analysis, social constructivist version of grounded theory (Charmaz)	Thirteen themes emerged which were described in relation to mental health needs, help currently accessed and the type of support wanted. The themes included the various mental health needs including dealing with changing moods, depression, feelings of isolation, worrying and a sense of being burdened. Women described using a limited range of supports and help. Participants expressed a preference for mental health support that was empowerment focused in its orientation, including peer support. Women also described the compounding effect that social and economic stresses had on their mental health.	19
Sword, Busser, Ganann, McMillan and Swinton (2008) Canada	To explore care seeking among women after public health nurse referral for probable postpartum depression, including responses to being referred, specific factors that hindered or facilitated care seeking, experiences seeking care, and responses to interventions offered.	18 women, 29.4 years (mean)	Postnatal depression, inclusion EPDS * 12	Public health setting with early prevention	Interviews Socioecological framework of health services, conventional content analysis (Hsieh)	Women's normalizing of symptoms, limited understanding of postpartum depression, waiting for symptom improvement, discomfort discussing mental health concerns, and fears deterred care seeking; symptom awareness and not feeling like oneself were facilitating influences. Family and friends sometimes hindered care seeking because they, too, normalized symptoms or had limited understanding of postpartum depression. Care seeking was facilitated when women encouraged a health professional visit or expressed worry and concern.	18

Table 2. *Cont.*

Author(s), Year, Country	Aim/Objective	Participants	Psychological Distress and Inclusion	Setting	Data Collection, Method	Results	CASP Qualitative Evaluation
Thomas, Scharp and Paxman (2014) United States	What IM ***-derived constructs permeate mothers' talk about the postpartum depression experience?	30 women, age not known	Postnatal depression, inclusion if writing represents a woman's 1st person account of her experiences	Online discussion group on postpartum depression	Anonymous online stories IM ***, inductive open coding; closed-coding procedure (Strauss and Corbin)	Five constructs (i.e., social norms; severity; barriers to help-seeking; facilitators to, and cues to action for, help-seeking; and self-efficacy) were prevalent.	18
Viveiros and Darling (2018) Canada	To explore access to PMH care services from a midwifery perspective: What do recipients of midwifery care perceive to be the factors that prevent or facilitate access to mental health care for women who experience depression, anxiety, and other mental health concerns in the perinatal period?	16 women, all over 18 years	Perinatal mental health, inclusion if self-identification of mental health concerns	Midwifery care	Interviews, focus groups Deductive thematic analysis (Braun and Clarke) based on Levesque's et al. framework on access to health care	Five salient themes emerged from the data: cultural values, knowledge, relationships, flexibility, and system gaps. Barriers and facilitators to accessing perinatal mental health services are grouped under each theme. Stigma and fear, broken referral pathways, distant service location, lack of number/capacity of specialized services, baby-centeredness, discharge from midwifery care at six weeks postpartum, and cost were barriers to accessing care. Information and midwives' knowledge/experience were context-specific factors that could hinder or facilitate access. Continuity, community, and advocacy were facilitators to accessing care.	19

* EPDS: Edinburgh Postnatal Depression Scale. ** CES-D: Center for Epidemiologic Study-Depression Scale. *** IM: Integrative Model of Behavioral Prediction (Fishbein).

2.3. The Interpretation and Synthesis Process

The eMERGe steps for the data comparison [31] began with determining how the studies are related, which required several readings. We made an initial assumption about the relationship between the included studies being analogous [30]. We performed data extraction using first- and second-order concepts, independently in pairs by listing the findings using line-by-line coding [31]. The meaning units were discussed in the research group and thematized (see Supplementary File, Table S1 for all themes extracted). The first author maintained an overall view by participating in both pairs. Translating the studies into one another was meant to compare the findings from one study with those from another. This step was also done in pairs, and discussions led to consensus. The themes were clustered and reflected on (see Supplementary File, Figure S1 for preliminary clusters). The relationships among the clusters were reflected on and discussed in the study group. We went back to the original studies for confirmation and understanding. QSR NVivo software (QSR International, London, UK) was used to facilitate the process. Synthesizing translations meant that we analyzed the translations, thus going beyond the findings of the individual studies to a second level of synthesis [30,31,33]. All authors were involved in the process of searching for refutational findings. A lines-of-argument synthesis based on the metaphorical themes (Figure 2) was created through an in-depth, back-and-forth, iterative analysis process between the translations and the articles.

Figure 2. The inner experiences of women with perinatal psychological distress contemplating help-seeking.

3. Results

All study characteristics of the 14 studies included in the meta-ethnography are presented in Table 2, with information about the author, year, country, aim/objective, participants, type of psychological distress and inclusion criteria, setting, data collection method, results, and CASP evaluation. Over a third (36%) of the studies were from either the United States or Canada, two (14%) were from Australia, and one (7%) was from New Zealand and the United Kingdom. The publications dated from 2002–2018.

The total number of participants in the included studies was 345 mothers (range 18–52 years, 25 years on average). The age of the women was over 18 in all studies, although the age was not known in two studies. Most studies described women suffering from depression (71%); one study (7%) included women with bipolar disorder, one (7%)

with postpartum mood disorders, and two (14%) women with more general mental health problems. A majority of the studies (57%) focused on postnatal depression or on prenatal depression (14%). Usually, screening was used to determine participants' inclusion in the studies, with the most common assessment being the Edinburgh Postnatal Depression Scale (EPDS). The settings and contexts for data collection varied: mental health settings were used in three studies (21%), and obstetrics settings, midwifery care, public health settings, well-baby clinics, or parent resource centers in the majority of studies (50%). Two studies (14%) collected data through a combination of tertiary care and mental health services. Two studies (14%) collected data in internet discussion groups for mental health concerns.

The data collection tools used were interviews (43%), focus groups (29%), a combination of interviews and focus groups (14%), and open-ended questions in an online forum (14%). The analysis methods varied as well, including content analysis (29%), grounded theory (29%), thematic analysis (21%), and phenomenology (14%). One study (7%) was a mixed-methods study, with the qualitative analysis facilitated by grounded theory with a phenomenological emphasis.

Women's experiences of contemplating help-seeking for PPD involve a time period of existential turmoil without a solution. Unresolved PPD consists of aspects that may exist separately or simultaneously, and no linear process could be detected. These aspects were: 'Falling into pieces', 'Trying so hard', 'Having no energy to act', 'Lacking shared experiences', 'Not understanding one has an illness', 'Emerging awareness', and 'Placing hope in oneself' (Figure 2). We did not observe a straightforward and linear process, as previous research had suggested, but rather a multidimensional and ambiguous life-situation wherein women try to solve their situation.

3.1. Falling into Pieces

Contemplating help-seeking in PPD was a time of extreme experiences, with one aspect being 'Falling into pieces'. Being very tired all the time might lead to others claiming it is a normal state with a new baby, even though the women were at an extreme [37]. They felt overwhelmed by emotions, lack of functioning [37], and mood changes [38]. They might have experienced joy for a few days, but changed into losing control of their lives, a comparison to life prior to the baby was born, and struggling with the "loss of life as it used to be" [39]. Women felt they had entered a downward spiral, where experiences added on to one another [39–41]. Women went through a range of emotions [38]: feeling helpless [37,42], feeling hopeless [42], being more negative [39,41], dwelling in anxiety [37], being irritated, frustrated, and angry [38], or presuming they must be lazy [42]. Losing control appeared with a fear of 'going crazy' and 'panicking' [42].

> "Problems quickly generalised to all aspects of infant care: 'once you failed at one thing, for example you thought you'd failed at your breastfeeding, you then decided you were going to fail at everything. So it kind of just circles off'." [39]

Experiencing sadness felt contradictory, such as when the home or baby were beautiful and life should have been enjoyable [39] or when one should be grateful for pregnancy [27]. Women with previous mental illness were able to analyze their condition and make decisions about when help-seeking was ultimately required [41,43].

The emotions related to their infants were manifold, with anxiety about being alone with the baby [40], feelings of not loving the baby [37], and even thoughts of hurting the baby [42]. The irrational thoughts they experienced also impacted other children in the family:

> "I was afraid to show my new baby any affection in front of my toddler for fear that she would think I didn't love her anymore." [42]

Women felt they were unable to care for their baby [37,42]. Some women expressed that they spent their days doing nothing but crying [42,44], and they experienced a sense of failure at parenting [39]. If they noticed their actions in relation to their infants were out of control and contrasted with their ideals [42], the anxiety with the baby and the experience of falling into pieces might lead to help-seeking. However, the experience of shame and guilt might inhibit them seeking help [40–42,45] until their condition was no longer manageable [41]. When they could not take it anymore, they sought help after months of suffering [42].

Women were "their own enemy and barrier for support" [40]. The worst situations were dramatic events, where even police and emergency health care were involved, and the women were forced to go to the hospital [46]. Ultimate crisis points included suicide risks [27,37,38,40,42–44].

3.2. Trying so Hard

The theme 'Trying so hard' describes women trying to adjust to external norms while also trying to solve the situation, surrounded by the opinions of their loved ones, and pondering whether a change was needed. The confusion was ongoing and related to social expectations of what was required at the time of being a new mother: it seemed that external expectations/norms suggested that denial of one's own feelings was favorable. Women may struggle to admit there are problems [47], and they can blame themselves for being "dramatic" [45] or "weak and stupid" [42]. The women had high expectations of themselves: they were proud, and they felt like they were failing in parenting. They did not want "to be seen as a failure", and they blamed themselves when they were not able to live up to their own expectations or those of others [39,45]. In the eyes of others, the women should keep up appearances [39]. The need to be viewed as the "perfect mother" motivated many women to mask or deny their condition [40]. Women said their family members' obliviousness of the fact that things were not right made the women lie to family members [39]. According to cultural and social norms, motherhood should be a joyful and happy time in life [42,48], yet the women did not seem to be able to perceive their life situation in the same way as the cultural expectations around motherhood suggested [48].

> "I'd be told it was normal, that it was fine, that everybody felt that way, that it shouldn't matter because I should just be happy that I have a healthy baby." [48]

Women reported that HCPs or peer groups had "normalized" or minimized their condition [27,37,38,40,44,48]. Their conditions were dismissed by HCPs as normal for pregnancy or due to "pregnancy hormones" [27], with a view of "pregnancy as a time of mental health challenges" [38] or the situation was labeled as "having postpartum" [41], "adjustment to motherhood", or the "baby blues" [44]. Their condition and symptoms were not severe enough and might have been explained by other circumstances [37]. Thus, women believed their explanations were not taken seriously, and they themselves also tried to normalize their experiences [44]. "Women should not need emotional support during pregnancy or the postpartum period" [45]: expressing their concerns to loved ones may result in invalidation. Women were left feeling shaken and forced to manage their condition on their own [41]. For others, however, "normalizing" meant making the difficult questions easier to discuss [41]. Some women just needed to talk about the different feelings and to accept them [49]. Talking about something that was considered normal for the life situation was considered safer than the risk of mental illness, which had a scary feeling [41]. Women struggled with the distinction between "normal" feelings of distress and exhaustion versus the distinction of an overwhelming condition that might justify seeking help [37].

> "I even went in at 3 months and I talked to a health nurse, and I just lied through my teeth because I thought, "What are they going to do if they find out I can't be a good mom?" [40]

External expectations have an impact on creating or enforcing direction. Social norms, with beliefs and attitudes on both intensive mothering and mental illness, created situations where seeking help was not an option [39,42]. In contrast, some women said that normalizing lowered the threshold for seeking and receiving help [41]. Given the impact of cultural and social factors, the women may not have been able to perceive personal needs or make choices based on their own perceived wishes [48]. The negative experience of other peoples' viewpoints was called stigma, and women feared being stigmatized by others [40,41,45,47–49]. Stigma included the labels of "being a bad mother" [39], "being disorganized and unmotivated" [37], "being lazy" [42], and showing that "women could not cope" [40,41,43].

PPD led to labels related to diagnoses [41,45]: women feared that a statement in the records would follow with a label of a psychiatric patient [47]. Women also expressed a fear of medications [43]. In general, PPD could be denied with an expectation that "it can't happen to me" [39], or PPD made the mother feel like a "second class citizen" [27]. They did not want others to know that their family was imperfect, and thus self-blame ensued [45]. The idea of experiencing mental illness caused feelings of guilt and shame [39–43,47,49].

Women said they tried or even "tried hard" to obtain help from HCPs [27]. Authors explained that some mothers had the ability to seek help [42,46,48]. Women had to strive in midst of their sense of self-agency and cultural pressure.

3.3. Having no Energy to Act

Women reported feeling overwhelmed by their emotions: "everything just got too much for me, and I couldn't go anywhere to get any help". Consequently, motivation, along with the strength to make decisions, were lacking [39]. The women said that one reason for not seeking help was an experience of exhaustion: they had no energy to seek help [37,38,40,42,48]. Women spent the whole day at home dressed in nightclothes [42], experiencing fatigue, anxiety, and stress around leaving the house and keeping appointment times [48].

> "When I was experiencing mental health issues, it was harder for me to get out, sort of on a schedule and be punctual." [48]

Leaving the home was difficult with a small child [47], because it required so much effort [40]. Difficulties were faced, as services are run on a fixed schedule, which requires mothers to travel with their newborn to these locations outside their home [48]. Women reserved appointment times and yet canceled appointments [42]. As women did not have sufficient information about available services, seeking care also required having the energy to identify what resources existed [48]. With their exhaustion and fatigue, the women simply did not have the energy to act.

3.4. Lacking Shared Experiences

Many women reported loneliness [40,42,43,47]. Some women saw themselves as weak if they were not managing alone at home [45]. They felt isolated [38,40,42,47], felt alone [40], felt worthless [40], and withdrew from contacts [40]. The isolation was related to a view of oneself being a private person, who kept a lot inside and only opened up to a handful of people [42]. Others imposed isolation from friends and other mothers on themselves [37]. A lack of support prevented women from seeking help [45], while others expressed that they felt unworthy of support [40] and lacked trust [49].

> "I still felt so alone as nobody in my close knit group of friends and family had ever had gone thought this and could not truly relate." [42]

Thus, many women described a lack of shared experiences [42]. They felt they could not speak to anyone [37], and many women did not have supportive relationships to rely on [38]: they described limited or absent friend and family networks, which was worsened by having unsupportive or absent close relationships lacking sufficient communication or responsiveness [38,40]. Childless friends did not understand, and friends with children were too busy [40].

> "I ask my husband for help, and he tries for maybe two days, then it's right back to being unhelpful and uncaring." [42]

Others wanted more help and support from their partners [27,37,40,45,47]. Women appreciated caring partners [38,42,43,48] and instrumental support from friends [40]. They wanted proactivity, such as friends or partners intervening when they saw that help was needed rather than waiting for the mother to ask for help [40]. A lack of support from their spouse or partner contributed to making it even more difficult to seek help [45], as their partner often discouraged them from seeking help because they "just need to calm down and stop crying" [45]. The changed situation—with a newborn baby and mental illness—put a strain on their relationship, which was at times difficult to emotionally and physically sustain [39]. Some women with unsupportive partners ended the relationship within weeks or months of the baby's birth [43]. Conflict with a partner may have existed prior to childbirth, or it may have worsened due to the mother's mental health struggles [43]. Some women blamed their partner for hindering help-seeking [38,40,42].

As women lacked shared experiences, their actions as they tried to seek help may have seemed chaotic: women struggled to decide whether to seek help [47], and those who sought help expressed that it was difficult to find [39]. Women did not know where to seek help [43] or from whom to seek it [41]. A gap in knowledge seemed to exist, since women were unaware of what services were available and for what [45], and they did not understand how hospitals could help or what they could expect from medications offered to them [43,45].

"I don't think I sought outside help because I didn't know." [43]

Some women sought for information and emotional support help online, via Internet searches and new-mothers websites [40]. One source of knowledge about treatment options was media [39,46].

> "The participant developed negative beliefs about the side effects of medications. Whether or not the information gained by participants through experience with family members or the media is accurate, it influenced their beliefs about postpartum depressive symptoms and possible treatments." [46]

A lack of shared experiences resulted in less reflection on one's own life situation and condition. Disclosing their thoughts or reaching out was an issue for many mothers [47], since they believed they could not talk, felt uncomfortable talking [37,42,48], or felt that discussing mental illness was troublesome [44].

> "There's the fear of really telling the truth and I felt safer telling the midwife than I did telling my doctor the depth of how I was feeling because I was really scared and I was having pretty awful thoughts and even though I was seeing them both at the same time and they were both referring me, I didn't really open up to my doctor and tell her the truth if you know what I mean?" [48]

Even though mothers shared that talking with HCPs and others about their distress and experiences was perceived highly significant in the recovery process [37], they did not disclose their thoughts to HCPs if they risked being criticized, so they waited for a suitable time to talk [27]. Women wanted compassion and care, but they were not always successful. Women said their experience of depression was a low priority for health professionals [27]. If a woman had hope for communication with an HCP and noticed that the HCP did not understand, she may have experienced the communication as insensitive and may not have felt cared for [47]. Women seemed to avoid conflict and chose to believe that time would heal [44,47]. Lacking shared experiences made help-seeking intentions challenging, because of how they interpreted care encounters with HCPs.

3.5. Not Understanding One Has an Illness

At a certain stage, women noticed that something in their everyday life experiences had altered, yet they did not have a resolution at hand. The situation, emotions, or behavior might have become difficult to explain, and even if describing it was possible, they could not name the experience [37,40]. Women noticed they were not themselves, thinking clearly and logically was challenging, and a lack of motivation emerged [39]. Without knowledge and understanding, the identification of an illness was not possible [37,44,48], and they were confused as to whether depression should be regarded as normal or not normal [37]. Losing interest in everyday life activities (such as showering) felt confusing [42].

"I just didn't know what I wanted at the time and I didn't know what I wanted to get out of it. I didn't know what was going on." [47]

The life situation might have been experienced as unclear: some reasoned that it was due to being tired and that the lack of clarity might be related to major sleep deprivation [37].

Some women discussed with their friends, and even though close relations suggested whether the strange feelings could be depression, the women might be reluctant to take the advice [37]; additionally, the expressed worry and concern was not always taken as a sign of illness or the need of HCP involvement [44]. Others reacted when their partner, friend, or close relative said "You're not yourself" [40].

Mothers did not recognize that they were depressed until they could not take it anymore [42] or their mental illness was later identified by a health professional [37]. PPD can be an unclear condition from the perspective of the new mother.

3.6. Emerging Awareness

The women described awareness of their own life situation as though it was emerging via several steps, observations, and perceptions, as well as living through the situation. At the start, women may not have known that the changed life situation was such that they could seek help to solve the situation [48]. Emerging awareness was described in several studies [27,40–42,44–48]. It included recognition of behavioral changes, which indicated mental distress [46], and awareness of their own condition [44].

The recognition of the changes may have arisen via a close personal relationship [46] —e.g., a partner or relative labeling their experience as mental distress. The woman could then note that the suggestion of a relative prompted her to consider whether she was suffering from postpartum depression [46]. Another point of recognition was when women recognized and became aware of "irrational thoughts and crippling guilt" [42]. Women may not be aware of the varying degrees or different symptoms, which do not fit everyone, and therefore delay their help-seeking [48].

"It's as though you have to figure it out for yourself first before you actually get the resources you need." [48]

Other family members were unaware of what was happening [43] and of the magnitude of women's problems [40] until hospitalization occurred. If family members were not aware of mental illness or did not note that some action in relation to help-seeking might be needed, the mother was not supported [40,42,47]. Without knowledge of PPD, family members may minimize the situation by attributing the condition to other factors, such as lack of sleep [40,42], which may deeply contradict the women's own experiences. As women may want to hide or not disclose their situation, family members do not always have the opportunity to be supportive [43]. Some family members helped mothers extensively, such as a mother's mother moving in for a month or the partner waking up at night to feed the baby [42].

Speaking and reflection may be a way to raise awareness [42,47]. Reading and obtaining more information [47] can be experienced as empowering if the mother learns more about illness, the importance of treatment, and the availability of helpful resources [45]. However, other women did not seek information [46].

"The knowledge of mental health. I think it is probably the biggest thing, knowing, recognizing the signs and symptoms. Just knowing that I needed to seek help before it got worse." [45]

A partner's engagement in discussion and learning about perinatal mental health was highly appreciated and might have impacted women [38]. Recognition of stigma around mental health issues may have opened the women's eyes to seeing their lack of understanding and awareness of depression during their pregnancy [27]. In the situation of PPD, the continued discomfort creates a need for change and a search for solutions, which may or may not include informal or formal help-seeking. Women try to solve the inner conflict by various means.

3.7. Placing Hope in Oneself

The mothers made choices themselves and relied on themselves [38,40,42,44,47,48]. Relying on the self was seen as important in identifying how to address one's mental health needs [38], as women needed to place hope in themselves.

When some women relied on themselves, they did not rely on others to take care of their babies:

> "I had to do it all on my own, because nobody could do it well enough. I had a lot of anxiety. I didn't want anybody holding him, I didn't want anybody touching him. I didn't want anybody in my house, because if I turned around and left him alone for a second, somebody would hurt my baby." [40]

The mothers tried to handle their situation through positive self-talk, adhering to daily routines [40,48] or journaling [38,48]. Guy et al. [46] shared actions related to self-help: leaving the house; taking time for oneself; letting emotions out through activities like crying, using substances, and eating comfort foods. Women used actions related to making changes in family functioning by asking family members for help or implementing a schedule for the children. They also pursued change by seeking employment or attending religious events. Some of the listed self-help options, such as using substances, were actually self-destructive in the long run [46].

The mothers sometimes decided to wait for the situation to improve by itself [44]. In group discussions, women shared that they "just did not like to be supported" [43]. Relying on partners, friends, and service providers was the next best option [40].

3.8. The Metaphor of a Seed

Contemplating help-seeking for PPD may be understood as a life situation in turmoil, as mothers make meaning in a specific life situation or context where several levels of experiences coexist, and the women contemplate whether to seek help. We have interpreted this as the metaphor of a seed describing symbolically the perinatal mental health time period with psychological distress as a multidimensional concurrent life situation: 'Falling into pieces', 'Trying so hard, 'Having no energy to act', 'Lacking shared experiences', and 'Not understanding one has an illness' may result in 'Emerging awareness' and 'Placing hope in oneself' (Figure 2).

The metaphor of a seed represents an interpretation of the phase prior to seeking help. As seeds need to have suitable conditions for growth, help-seeking for PPD involves the inner unresolved individual experiences. Individual experiences manifest as a symbolic seed, at risk of being cracked into pieces by the surrounding circumstances and inner experiences. In describing the situation of women experiencing PPD, the metaphor of a symbolic seed also describes women's own resources and possibilities. The solution lies within the women themselves, as emerging awareness and hope may co-exist or evolve. Each of the identified themes involves ambiguity and emotional turmoil—an unresolved life situation. Women try to solve the inner conflict through different means. They experience experiential turmoil as a metaphor of falling into pieces, and they may not have the words to express their needs. Since women may experience inner isolation and they do not have the strength or knowledge to seek help, they may not be able to seek help. Their solution may be to continue to solve the situation themselves, but they may not have the opportunities or strength to resolve the uncomfortable situation. This is why family and other loved ones play a crucial role along with HCPs.

4. Discussion

We have identified a gap in the existing help-seeking literature of the step prior to seeking help. We call this contemplating help-seeking, and we approached the phenomenon with a perspective inspired by the philosopher Lauri Rauhala [29] and the nursing researcher Karin Dahlberg [28]. We chose to focus on women's lived experiences, the experiential level—including emotions, sensations, and perceptions—which may involve experiences of different levels of awareness and clarity, and the meanings can be ambiguous. In a meta-ethnography, new interpretations can be revealed in the qualitative evidence synthesis through the identification of new approaches and viewpoints [30,31].

Studying help-seeking for PPD is important, because previous research has shown that help-seeking is faced with delays [20,21]. Even though women participate in and access health or social services and programs, they may not disclose their problems [5,8,18,19]. Contemplating help-seeking in the perinatal period is important to a health policy perspective, because PPD may impact parenthood, be reflected in a person's everyday life, and have an impact on an attachment relationship being formed between the parent and the infant [19,23,24]. In the phase of contemplating help-seeking for PPD, a focus on only the mother needs to be replaced with a focus on mother–baby relationships and family aspects.

In existing help-seeking theories, a cognitive level is the primary focus, and help-seeking research is based on perceived needs, viewing persons as rational decision-makers and action-takers when they decide to seek help [1,13–15]. We did not find such a phenomenon; instead, we identified a layered and multidimensional life situation. Pregnancy, birth, and becoming a mother may collectively represent a critical period of physical and emotional upheaval in a woman's life [41]. An intentional human being performs goal-directed tasks, but with mental health-related issues, such as PPD, the intentions may be out of the person's reach. According to Viveiros and Darling [48], the ability to perceive the need for care is determined by health literacy, knowledge about health, and beliefs related to health and sickness. Previous reviews on perinatal mental health showed poor awareness of and insufficient knowledge on PPD [4,5,8,18,25]. Women may be unable to recognize or express their emotions [4,5]. Through our theoretical perspective, we see that humans create meaning in the context of their individual life situation, where the present and the past impact current meaning-making, and we can assume that humans grow in relation to each other [28,29]. Our results showed that women wanted to be sensitive toward their family members: this might lead to a lack of open discussion in the family or women not wanting to upset family members [4,5,8,17,18]. Given that women seem to want to protect their loved ones and are sensitive to critique, societal stigma around mental illness may be especially harmful. Therefore, it is essential to develop information and provide education for society around mental health-related questions and make such information available for women by pregnancy at the latest.

Women as individuals experiencing situations of seeking help around mental health issues try to solve burdens their own way. Isolation was identified in our meta-ethnography, as it was found in previous research [6,17]. We identified a lack of recognition and support, and lacking shared experiences, why it is especially important for family members to acknowledge the mothers need for support, also in a proactive way. Many mothers are unwilling to disclose their situation, due to emotions of shame and guilt [8,17,18] or being judged by others [25–27], as the expectations of them seemed to involve being "supermoms". Our findings add to this by synthesizing the complexity of PPD and by identifying a time period of existential turmoil without a solution. The non-linear themes involving unresolved questions during PPD consist of aspects that may exist separately or simultaneously: 'Falling into pieces', 'Trying so hard, 'Having no energy to act', 'Lacking shared experiences', 'Not understanding one has an illness', 'Emerging awareness', and 'Placing hope in oneself' (Figure 2). In describing the situation of women during the perinatal period, we established the metaphor of a seed. Individual experiences manifest as the seed, at risk of being cracked into pieces by the surrounding circumstances and inner experiences. In describing the situation of women experiencing PPD, the metaphor of a seed also describes women's own resources and possibilities. Each theme involves ambiguity and emotional turmoil—an unresolved life situation. Help-seeking actions are possible in all these phases, possibly resulting in change. Women try to solve the inner conflict through different means and endure a lot before a solution starts to emerge. During this time period, they are especially vulnerable and susceptible to the viewpoints and advice of their loved ones.

4.1. Implications for Practice

If the HCPs recognize the phase of contemplating help-seeking, HCPs can address women's concerns seriously prior to clients accessing services. Women with PPD during the perinatal period may not recognize an illness, perceive a need, name a disorder, or search for suitable care providers. Women may not view their life situation as a barrier to care from HCPs but rather try to manage their life situation in the best possible way. As the perinatal period is a unique time during women's and infants' lives, our results question how women are approached by health and social care services and programs. It has been indicated that HCPs should develop their skills at an attitudinal level, as well as from the perspective of how to approach women with mental illness during the perinatal period. Mothers with PPD lacking shared experiences need an especially sensitive and appreciative manner of encouraging and enhancing reflection, possibly supporting the close relatives. Understanding mothers' contemplating help-seeking for PPD in more detail would enable the engagement of whole families with services. Understanding more might also counteract women dropping out of treatment before even starting to use the services.

As women's inner possibilities and awareness have a crucial impact on their decision to seek help, finding solutions that enhance their inner capacities and experiences of hope in the current life situation is important. Contemplating help-seeking for PPD may be connected with empowerment and growth in the role of mothering, as maternal well-being is a prerequisite for the health of the children. HCPs might use reflexive tools to assist in co-creating awareness and to implement a positive approach. We suggest that existing strategies and recommendations on perinatal mental health issues would benefit from the micro perspective, as women can only be helped by services if they themselves are willing to participate and share their lifeworld with those helping them in the services. In our study we focused on mothers, yet the study of contemplating help-seeking from the fathers' perspective would be important as well.

4.2. Strengths and Limitations

The chosen search strategy was useful, as we reached a sufficient amount of data and excerpts to support a robust analysis [31]. The studies included were versatile in many aspects, which is a strength of meta-ethnography. We used the CASP qualitative appraisal tool [36] for quality assessment of the studies.

As our focus was on PPD, most of the studies included in the meta-ethnography focused on depression [27,37–40,42–47,49]. Only a few studies described other types of psychological distress, such as post-partum mood disorders [41] or bipolar disorders [45]. Viveiros and Darling [48] discussed perinatal mental health, which included depression, anxiety, and other mental health concerns; Raymond et al. [38] discussed "a range of emotional and mood challenges". We did not identify any studies on women with psychosis seeking help during the perinatal period. The area of PPD is so wide that we can see that our data were restricted; on the other hand, the current focus on PPD enhanced our interpretations, and our sample was versatile in many ways (Table 2), which is preferred for meta-ethnographies [31].

Research in studies related to mental illness has its restrictions, since researchers often choose a problem and illness paradigm, such as in the purpose of delineating the study purpose. In our search terms, we used diagnostic labels. This is a limitation, since the search terms and aim of the study did not focus on aspects such as positive mental health [50]. In our data, 'Placing hope in oneself' included both the active stance of oneself as well as women trying to solve issues through self-help means and by identifying positive aspects as self-care. Even in the most difficult life situation, with mental illness and strain, the positive approach of mental health can also co-exist [29,50]. The philosopher Lauri Rauhala explained that experiences like unpleasant life events are labeled, and the unique life situation gives meaning to human existence [29]. The positive aspects may be relevant in the meaning-making of the everyday life situation. From a lifeworld perspective, the lived reality is not necessarily recognized by the human herself, which is why researchers must be aware of how their approach impacts the study results. Using the lifeworld perspective in this meta-ethnography proved to be productive. Using a metaphor with a picture to visualize the interpretation of the inner experiences can open understanding, and may however, also be considered a novel way of scientific description of phenomena [28,29]. The interpretation is connected with the Results section as a whole and will need to be read in connection with the multidimensional themes.

5. Conclusions

The meta-ethnography in this study provides a thorough picture of contemplating help-seeking as the phase prior to seeking help in perinatal psychological distress. We did not observe a straightforward and linear process (as previous research suggested) but rather a multidimensional and ambiguous life situation, where women try to solve their situation and lack skills that promote help-seeking. Women with perinatal psychological distress try to solve their situation first by themselves; their life situation is such that help-seeking may not be an option, even though helping resources are available. A clinical implication to improve practice, policy, and service user outcomes in health and other fields is that service providers should work with outreach and develop tools to connect with these mothers. HCP's need an especially sensitive and appreciative manner of encouraging and enhancing reflection, possibly supporting the close relatives, since mothers contemplating help-seeking for PPD may lack shared experiences or have the skills for reflection. Another suggestion is to improve training in mental health literacy prior to or during pregnancy.

Supplementary Materials: The following are available online at https://www.mdpi.com/article/10.3390/ijerph18105226/s1, Table S1. All themes extracted, and Figure S1. Preliminary Clusters: (a) Cluster own feelings; (b) Cluster system; (c) Cluster taking action.

Author Contributions: Conceptualization, M.A.S. and T.E.B.; methodology, M.A.S. and T.E.B.; software, M.A.S.; validation, M.A.S., T.E.B. and J.K.; formal analysis, M.A.S., T.E.B. and J.K.; investigation, M.A.S., T.E.B. and J.K.; data curation, M.A.S.; writing—original draft preparation, M.A.S.; writing—review and editing, M.A.S., T.E.B. and J.K.; visualization, M.A.S.; supervision, T.E.B.; project administration, M.A.S.; funding acquisition, M.A.S. All authors have read and agreed to the published version of the manuscript.

Funding: This study was partly supported by the Competitive State Research Financing of the Expert Responsibility area of Tampere University Hospital, grant number 9AB073 and Finnish Nursing Education Foundation (M.A.S.).

Institutional Review Board Statement: Review study. Included articles checked for ethical issues using the CASP instrument.

Informed Consent Statement: Not applicable for a meta-ethnography. Written informed consent has been obtained in the original studies from the patient(s).

Data Availability Statement: We have published the themes and preliminary clusters of the analysis of the meta-ethnography as Supplementary Table S1 and Figure S1. Please contact the authors for additional information.

Acknowledgments: This study was financially partly supported by the Competitive State Research Financing of the Expert Responsibility area of Tampere University Hospital and Finnish Nursing Education Foundation.

Conflicts of Interest: The authors declare no conflict of interest. The funders had no role in the design of the study; in the collection, analyses, or interpretation of data; in the writing of the manuscript, or in the decision to publish the results.

References

1. Saint Arnault, D. Defining and Theorizing About Culture. The evolution of the Cultural Determinants of Help-Seeking, Revised. *Nurs. Res.* **2018**, *16*, 161–168. [CrossRef] [PubMed]
2. Ridner, S.H. Psychological distress: Concept analysis. *J. Adv. Nurs.* **2004**, *45*, 536–545. [CrossRef]

3. Obrochta, C.A.; Chambers, C.; Bandoli, G. Psychological distress in pregnancy and postpartum. *Women Birth* **2020**, *33*, 583–591. [CrossRef] [PubMed]
4. Button, S.; Thornton, A.; Lee, S.; Shakespeare, J.; Ayers, S. Seeking help for perinatal psychological distress: A meta-synthesis of women's experiences. *Br. J. Gen. Pract.* **2017**, *67*, E692–E699. [CrossRef] [PubMed]
5. Dennis, C.L.; Chung-Lee, L. Postpartum depression help-seeking barriers and maternal treatment preferences: A qualitative systematic review. *Birth-Issues Perinat. Care* **2006**, *33*, 323–331. [CrossRef] [PubMed]
6. Myors, K.A.; Schmied, V.; Johnson, M.; Cleary, M. 'My special time': Australian women's experiences of accessing a specialist perinatal and infant mental health service. *Health Soc. Care Community* **2014**, *22*, 268–277. [CrossRef] [PubMed]
7. Liberto, T.L. Screening for Depression and Help-Seeking in Postpartum Women During Well-Baby Pediatric Visits: An Integrated Review. *J. Pediatric Health Care* **2012**, *26*, 109–117. [CrossRef] [PubMed]
8. Hadfield, H.; Wittkowski, A. Women's Experiences of Seeking and Receiving Psychological and Psychosocial Interventions for Postpartum Depression: A Systematic Review and Thematic Synthesis of the Qualitative Literature. *J. Midwifery Womens Health* **2017**, *62*, 723–736. [CrossRef] [PubMed]
9. Glasheen, C.; Colpe, L.; Hoffman, V.; Warren, L.K. Prevalence of Serious Psychological Distress and Mental Health Treatment in a National Sample of Pregnant and Postpartum Women. *Matern. Child Health J.* **2015**, *19*, 204–216. [CrossRef]
10. Bales, M.; Pambrun, E.; Melchior, M.; Glangeaud-Freudenthal, N.M.C.; Charles, M.A.; Verdoux, H.; Sutter-Dallay, A.-L. Prenatal psychological distress and access to mental health care in the ELFE cohort. *Eur. Psychiatry* **2015**, *30*. [CrossRef]
11. Woody, C.A.; Ferrari, A.J.; Siskind, D.J.; Whiteford, H.A.; Harris, M.G. A systematic review and meta-regression of the prevalence and incidence of perinatal depression. *J. Affect. Disord.* **2017**, *219*, 86–92. [CrossRef] [PubMed]
12. Wisner, K.L.; Sit, D.K.Y.; McShea, M.C.; Rizzo, D.M.; Zoretich, R.A.; Hughes, C.L.; Eng, H.F.; Luther, J.F.; Wisniewski, S.R.; Costantino, M.L.; et al. Onset Timing, Thoughts of Self-harm, and Diagnoses in Postpartum Women with Screen-Positive Depression Findings. *JAMA Psychiatry* **2013**, *70*, 490–498. [CrossRef] [PubMed]
13. Chan, M.E. Antecedents of Instrumental Interpersonal Help-Seeking: An Integrative Review. *Appl. Psychol. Int. Rev. Psychol. Appl. Rev. Int.* **2013**, *62*, 571–596. [CrossRef]
14. Rickwood, D.; Thomas, K. Conceptual measurement framework for help-seeking for mental health problems. *Psychol. Res. Behav. Manag.* **2012**, *5*, 173–183. [CrossRef]
15. Cornally, N.; McCarthy, G. Help-seeking behaviour: A concept analysis. *Int. J. Nurs. Pract.* **2011**, *17*, 280–288. [CrossRef]
16. Saunders, S.; Bowersox, N. The Process of Seeking Treatment for Mental Health Problems. *Ment. Health Learn. Disabil. Res. Pract.* **2007**, *4*, 99–123. [CrossRef]
17. Jones, C.C.G.; Jomeen, J.; Hayter, M. The impact of peer support in the context of perinatal mental illness: A meta-ethnography. *Midwifery* **2014**, *30*, 491–498. [CrossRef]
18. Smith, M.S.; Lawrence, V.; Sadler, E.; Easter, A. Barriers to accessing mental health services for women with perinatal mental illness: Systematic review and meta-synthesis of qualitative studies in the UK. *BMJ Open* **2019**, *9*, 1–9. [CrossRef]
19. Sperlich, M.; Seng, J.S.; Li, Y.; Taylor, J.; Bradbury-Jones, C. Integrating Trauma-Informed Care Into Maternity Care Practice: Conceptual and Practical Issues. *J. Midwifery Womens Health* **2017**, *62*, 661–672. [CrossRef]
20. Wang, P.S.; Angermeyer, M.; Borges, G.; Bruffaerts, R.; Chiu, W.T.; de Girolamo, G.; Fayyad, J.; Gureje, O.; Haro, J.M.; Huang, Y.; et al. Delay and failure in treatment seeking after first onset of mental disorders in the World Health Organization's World Mental Health Survey Initiative. *World Psychiatry* **2007**, *6*, 177–185.
21. Sareen, J.; Jagdeo, A.; Cox, B.J.; Clara, I.; ten Have, M.; Belik, S.L.; de Graaf, R.; Stein, M.B. Perceived barriers to mental health service utilization in the United States, Ontario, and the Netherlands. *Psychiatr. Serv.* **2007**, *58*, 357–364. [CrossRef]
22. van Beljouw, I.; Verhaak, P.; Prins, M.; Cuijpers, P.; Penninx, B.; Bensing, J. Reasons and Determinants for Not Receiving Treatment for Common Mental Disorders. *Psychiatr. Serv.* **2010**, *61*, 250–257. [CrossRef]
23. Fonagy, P.; Steele, M.; Steele, H.; Moran, G.S.; Higgitt, A.C. The Capacity for Understanding Mental States—The Reflective Self in Parent and Child and its Significance for Security of Attachment. *Infant Ment. Health J.* **1991**, *12*, 201–218. [CrossRef]
24. Berthelot, N.; Ensink, K.; Bernazzani, O.; Normandin, L.; Luyten, P.; Fonagy, P. Intergenerational Transmission of Attachment in Abused and Neglected Mothers: The Role of Trauma-Specific Reflective Functionin. *Infant Ment. Health J.* **2015**, *36*, 200–212. [CrossRef] [PubMed]
25. Rouhi, M.; Stirling, C.; Ayton, J.; Crisp, E.P. Women's help-seeking behaviours within the first twelve months after childbirth: A systematic qualitative meta-aggregation review. *Midwifery* **2019**, *72*, 39–49. [CrossRef]
26. Bayrampour, H.; McNeil, D.A.; Benzies, K.; Salmon, C.; Gelb, K.; Tough, S. A qualitative inquiry on pregnant women's preferences for mental health screening. *BMC Pregnancy Childbirth* **2017**, *17*, 11. [CrossRef] [PubMed]
27. Jarrett, P.M. Pregnant women's experience of depression care. *J. Ment. Health Train.* **2016**, *11*, 33–47. [CrossRef]
28. Dahlberg, K.; Dahlberg, H.; Nyström, M. *Reflective Lifeworld Research*, 2nd ed.; Studentlitteratur: Malmö, Sweden, 2008.
29. Rauhala, L. *Ihmiskäsitys ihmistyössä*; Gaudeamus: Jyväskylä, Finland, 1983.
30. Noblit, G.; Hare, R. *Meta-Ethnography*; Sage Publications Inc.: London, UK, 1988.
31. France, E.F.; Cunningham, M.; Ring, N.; Uny, I.; Duncan, E.A.S.; Jepson, R.G.; Maxwell, M.; Roberts, R.J.; Turley, R.L.; Booth, A.; et al. Improving reporting of meta-ethnography: The eMERGe reporting guidance. *Bmc Med Res. Methodol.* **2019**, *19*. [CrossRef] [PubMed]

32. Sandelowski, M.; Barroso, J. *Handbook for Synthesizing Qualitative Research*; Springer Publishing Company: New York, NY, USA, 2007.
33. Bondas, T.; Hall, E. Challenges in approaching metasynthesis research. *Qual. Health Res.* **2007**, *17*, 113–121. [CrossRef] [PubMed]
34. Bondas, T.; Hall, E. A decade of metasynthesis research in health sciences: A meta-method study. *Int. J. Qual. Stud. Health Wellbeing* **2007**, *2*, 101–113. [CrossRef]
35. Moher, D.; Shamseer, L.; Clarke, M.; Ghersi, D.; Liberati, A.; Petticrew, M.; Shekelle, P.; Stewart, L.A. Preferred reporting items for systematic review and meta-analysis protocols (PRISMA-P) 2015 statement. *Syst. Rev.* **2015**, 4. [CrossRef]
36. Critical Appraisal Skills Programme. CASP (Qualitative) Checklist 2018. Available online: https://casp-uk.net/casp-tools-checklists/ (accessed on 20 January 2020).
37. McCarthy, M.; McMahon, C. Acceptance and experience of treatment for postnatal depression in a community mental health setting. *Health Care Women Int.* **2008**, *29*, 618–637. [CrossRef] [PubMed]
38. Raymond, N.C.; Pratt, R.J.; Godecker, A.; Harrison, P.A.; Kim, H.; Kuendig, J.; O'Brien, J.M. Addressing perinatal depression in a group of underserved urban women: A focus group study. *BMC Pregnancy Childbirth* **2014**, *14*, 7. [CrossRef] [PubMed]
39. Bilszta, J.; Ericksen, J.; Buist, A.; Milgrom, J. Women's experience of postnatal depression—Beliefs and attitudes as barriers to care. *Aust. J. Adv. Nurs.* **2010**, *27*, 44–54.
40. Letourneau, N.; Duffett-Leger, L.; Stewart, M.; Hegadoren, K.; Dennis, C.-L.; Rinaldi, C.M.; Stoppard, J. Canadian Mothers ' Perceived Support Needs During Postpartum Depression. *Jognn-J. Obstet. Gynecol. Neonatal Nurs.* **2007**, *36*, 441–449. [CrossRef]
41. Foulkes, M. Enablers and Barriers to Seeking Help for a Postpartum Mood Disorder. *Jognn-J. Obstet. Gynecol. Neonatal Nurs.* **2011**, *40*, 450–457. [CrossRef]
42. Thomas, L.J.; Scharp, K.M.; Paxman, C.G. Stories of Postpartum Depression: Exploring Health Constructs and Help-Seeking in Mothers' Talk. *Women Health* **2014**, *53*, 373–387. [CrossRef]
43. Holopainen, D. The Experience of Seeking Help for Postnatal Depression. *Aust. J. Adv. Nurs.* **2002**, *19*, 39–44.
44. Sword, W.; Busser, D.; Ganann, R.; McMillan, T.; Swinton, M. Women's care-seeking experiences after referral for postpartum depression. *Qual. Health Res.* **2008**, *18*, 1161–1173. [CrossRef]
45. Byatt, N.; Cox, L.; Moore Simas, T.A.; Kini, N.; Biebel, K.; Sankaran, P.; Swartz, H.A.; Weinreb, L. How Obstetric Settings Can Help Address Gaps in Psychiatric Care for Pregnant and Postpartum Women with Bipolar Disorder. *Arch. Women's Ment. Health* **2018**, *21*, 543–551. [CrossRef]
46. Guy, S.; Sterling, B.S.; Walker, L.O.; Harrison, T.C. Mental Health Literacy and Postpartum Depression: A Qualitative Description of Views of Lower Income Women. *Arch. Psychiatr. Nurs.* **2014**, *28*, 256–262. [CrossRef] [PubMed]
47. Bell, L.; Feeley, N.; Hayton, B.; Zelkowitz, P.; Tait, M.; Desindes, S. Barriers and Facilitators to the Use of Mental Health Services by Women With Elevated Symptoms of Depression and Their Partners. *Issues Ment. Health Nurs.* **2016**, *37*, 651–659. [CrossRef] [PubMed]
48. Viveiros, C.J.; Darling, E.K. Barriers and facilitators of accessing perinatal mental health services: The perspectives of women receiving continuity of care midwifery. *Midwifery* **2018**, *65*, 8–15. [CrossRef] [PubMed]
49. Jesse, D.; Dolbier, C.; Blanchard, A. Barriers to seeking help and treatment suggestions for prenatal depressive symptoms: Focus groups with rural low-income women. *Issues Ment. Health Nurs.* **2008**, *29*, 3–19. [CrossRef] [PubMed]
50. Vaillant, G.E. Positive mental health: Is there a cross-cultural definition? *World Psychiatry* **2012**, *11*, 93–99. [CrossRef] [PubMed]

www.ingramcontent.com/pod-product-compliance
Lightning Source LLC
Chambersburg PA
CBHW041400210926
51850CB00013B/3142
* 9 7 8 3 0 3 6 5 2 1 3 2 9 *

MDPI
St. Alban-Anlage 66
4052 Basel
Switzerland
Tel. +41 61 683 77 34
Fax +41 61 302 89 18
www.mdpi.com

International Journal of Environmental Research and Public Health Editorial Office
E-mail: ijerph@mdpi.com
www.mdpi.com/journal/ijerph